Social Work 701

TABLE OF CONTENTS
& ACKNOWLEDGEMENTS

PAGE

CALEDON

INSTITUTE OF
SOCIAL POLICY

The federal role in poverty reduction

presentation to the Standing Committee on Human Resources, Skills and Social Development and the Status of Persons with Disabilities

by

Ken Battle and Sherri Torjman

March 10, 2009

ISBN 1-55382-361-3

Published by:

Caledon Institute of Social Policy
1390 Prince of Wales Drive, Suite 401
Ottawa, ON K2C 3N6
CANADA
Phone: (613) 729-3340
Fax: (613) 729-3896
E-mail: caledon@caledoninst.org
Website: *www.caledoninst.org*

Table of Contents

Introduction

Social advocates often cite the 1989 all-party Resolution of the House of Commons to 'abolish' child poverty by 2000 as proof of the abject failure of the federal government. In 1989, a substantial 11.7 percent of children lived in low-income families, but it was even worse by 2000 – 13.8 percent. At last count, in 2006, 11.3 percent of children lived in low-income families, only fractionally less than the 11.7 percent figure for 1989 – and a long way off the supposed 0 percent target for 2000.

But the picture is more complicated than it may seem. For one thing, the famous 1989 Resolution has been mythologized somewhat; in fact, the actual wording of the Resolution is that Canada "should seek to achieve the goal of eliminating poverty among Canadian children by the year 2000." There is a world of difference between seeking and achieving. We interpret the careful phrasing of the Resolution as recognition that reducing child poverty all the way to 0 would be a difficult if not quixotic quest, doomed to failure. However, contrary to the government's critics, there has been some seeking to achieve that goal, notably the federal-provincial National Child Benefit reform that started in 1998, though it never pretended to attempt to abolish child poverty outright.

The 1989 Resolution against poverty could not have been worse timed from the point of view of the federal government. A key determinant of the poverty rate is the state of the economy. When the Resolution was passed in 1989, child poverty (11.7 percent that year) had been declining since its peak of 16.0 percent in 1984 following the early 1980s recession. After 1989,

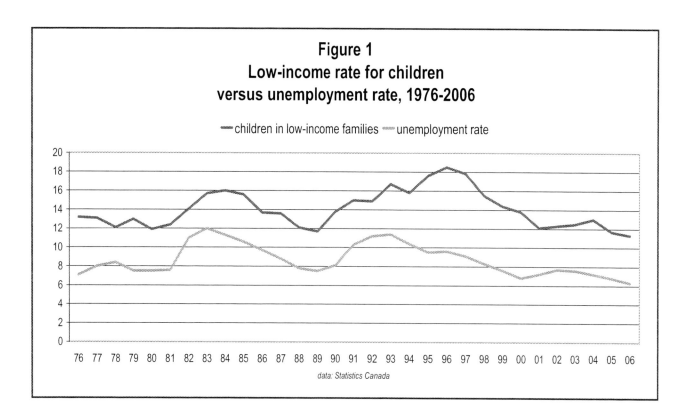

Figure 1
Low-income rate for children
versus unemployment rate, 1976-2006

── children in low-income families ⸺ unemployment rate

data: Statistics Canada

the early 1990s recession drove the child poverty rate back up to 18.5 percent by 1996, and then it fell again to 13.8 percent in 2000 and 11.3 percent by 2006. So even if Ottawa had announced an anti-poverty initiative in immediate response to the 1989 Resolution, it would have been swimming upstream against the flood of rising poverty caused by the recession.

Figure 1 shows the close correspondence between the trends in the low-income rate for children and the unemployment rate, the latter a key indicator of the health of the economy. Canada's jobless rate rose sharply from 7.5 percent in 1989 to 11.4 percent in 1993, then declined to 6.3 percent in 2006. The low-income rate for children shows the same up-and-down pattern, climbing from 11.7 percent in 1989 to a peak of 18.5 percent in 1996 and then declining to 11.3 percent by 2006.

The lesson here is that it is especially hard to reduce poverty when the economy is in bad shape: Economic reality trumps social policy. The significant multi-year increase in federal child benefits that started in 1989 may have played some small role in the improvement in the child poverty rate after 1996, but it was falling unemployment and growth in the economy that drove the trend down so significantly. Thanks largely to increasing employment and somewhat to improvements in child benefits, the poverty rate for female-led single-parent families was almost cut in half from 52.7 percent in 1996 to 28.2 percent in 2006.

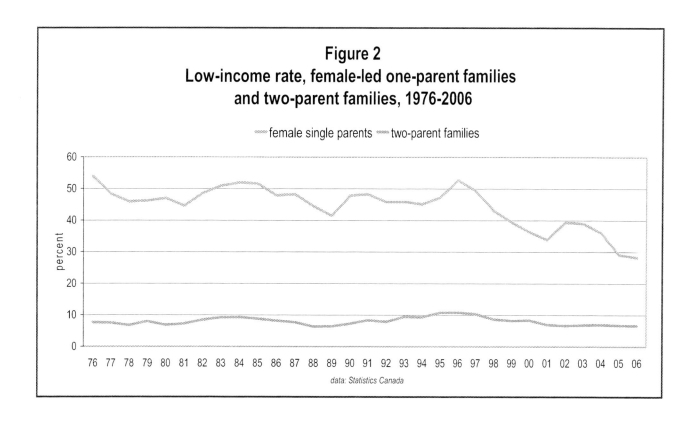

Figure 2
Low-income rate, female-led one-parent families
and two-parent families, 1976-2006

female single parents ▪▪▪ two-parent families

data: Statistics Canada

Female-led single-parent families face a much higher risk of low income than do two-parent families, as demonstrated in Figure 2. However, the gap between them has narrowed somewhat since the mid-1990s due to the larger proportionate decline in poverty for single-parent mothers than two-parent families. In 1996, the low-income rate for female-led lone parent families was a very high 52.7 percent – almost 4.9 times the 10.8 percent rate for two-parent families. By 2006, the low-income rate for female-led lone parent families had decreased to 28.2 percent as opposed to 6.6 percent for two-parent families – 4.3 times greater.

Another lesson is that, to fairly measure the impact of social programs on poverty, we must also calculate the low-income rate based on market income (i.e., income from employment, savings, private pensions and other private sources) and compare it to the low-income rate after income taxes and income programs. Otherwise during recessions, even if governments boost social spending, they could be unfairly criticized as failing to address poverty, when in fact income programs at least slow the increase in the poverty numbers.

However, the powerful force of market-driven poverty does not mean that government is powerless to do anything about the problem. In fact, governments have made more progress against poverty and income inequality than many people realize – even though there is still a long way to go and the challenge is daunting.

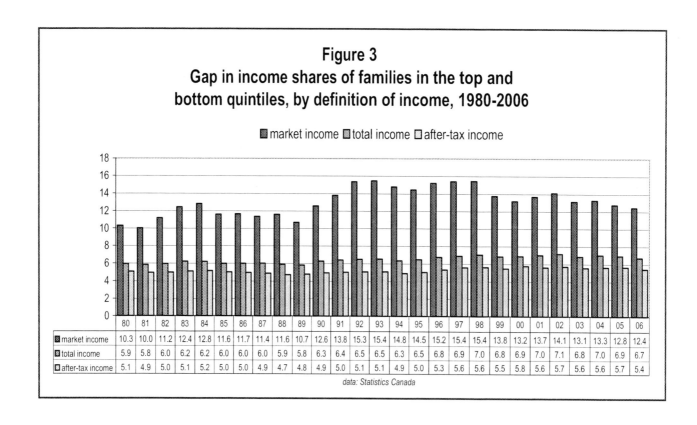

Figure 3
Gap in income shares of families in the top and bottom quintiles, by definition of income, 1980-2006

■ market income   ▨ total income   ☐ after-tax income

	80	81	82	83	84	85	86	87	88	89	90	91	92	93	94	95	96	97	98	99	00	01	02	03	04	05	06
■ market income	10.3	10.0	11.2	12.4	12.8	11.6	11.7	11.4	11.6	10.7	12.6	13.8	15.3	15.4	14.8	14.5	15.2	15.4	15.4	13.8	13.2	13.7	14.1	13.1	13.3	12.8	12.4
▨ total income	5.9	5.8	6.0	6.2	6.2	6.0	6.0	6.0	5.9	5.8	6.3	6.4	6.5	6.5	6.3	6.5	6.8	6.9	7.0	6.8	6.9	7.0	7.1	6.8	7.0	6.9	6.7
☐ after-tax income	5.1	4.9	5.0	5.1	5.2	5.0	5.0	4.9	4.7	4.8	4.9	5.0	5.1	5.1	4.9	5.0	5.3	5.6	5.6	5.5	5.8	5.6	5.7	5.6	5.6	5.7	5.4

data: Statistics Canada

Figure 3 shows the gap between families in the top and bottom income quintiles (i.e., fifths) using three definitions of income – market income (from earnings, investments, private pensions, rent and other non-governmental sources), total income (market income plus income from government programs such as old age pensions, the Canada and Quebec Pension Plans, Employment Insurance, child benefits and welfare) and after-tax income (total income less federal and provincial/territorial income taxes).

High-income families received almost half (46.0 percent) of market income at last count, 2006, which is 12.4 times the small 3.7 percent share for families in the lowest group. But when we shift from market to total income, upper-income families' share of total income falls to 42.3 percent whereas the share of families in the lowest group increases to 6.3 percent – narrowing the gap considerably to 6.7 times. Families in the highest quintile got 39.6 percent of after-tax income as opposed to 7.3 percent for those in the bottom group, further reducing the gap to 5.4 times.

The blue bars indicate the gap in shares of market income between families in the highest and lowest quintiles. Inequality in market income as measured by the gap between the well-off and the poor is large and has varied considerably over the years, ranging from a low of 10.0 times in 1981 to a high of 15.4 times in 1993, 1997 and 1998.

The gap in total income, shown by the red bars, is smaller – from a low of 5.8 times in 1981 and 1989 to a high of 7.1 in 2002 – though has crept up a bit since the mid-1990s.

The after-tax income gap has remained much the same over the years even when market income inequality has increased, as illustrated in Figure 3.

Income inequality is wide no matter what definition of income we use. However, government intervention in the marketplace in the form of income programs and income taxes lessens the income gap significantly.

Poverty is a complex, diverse and tough issue that requires a range of interventions by a number of actors – all three orders of government, employers, unions, educational and health institutions, voluntary organizations and communities. Close cooperation between the federal and provincial/territorial governments is particularly important.

We believe that the federal government has the dominant role to play in tackling reduction. It can reduce poverty, it does reduce poverty and it should reduce poverty a lot more.

Ottawa has not followed the example of other governments at home and abroad – including Newfoundland, Quebec and Ontario, as well as the UK and Ireland – which have launched formal poverty reduction strategies replete with analysis, evaluation, reform initiatives and targets. But the federal government does have at its disposal some potentially powerful instruments to help reduce poverty, which can serve as key elements of a full-blown poverty reduction strategy.

This morning, we will briefly discuss some examples of federal programs that can help reduce poverty, and offer some suggestions for improving their poverty reduction capacity. We distinguish between incremental improvements to existing programs and deeper changes to the architecture of social policy.

Although the federal role in poverty reduction takes mainly the form of income security programs, it also has roles to play in financially supporting services provided by provinces and territories. The federal government also can help create an enabling environment that supports community interventions to reduce poverty.

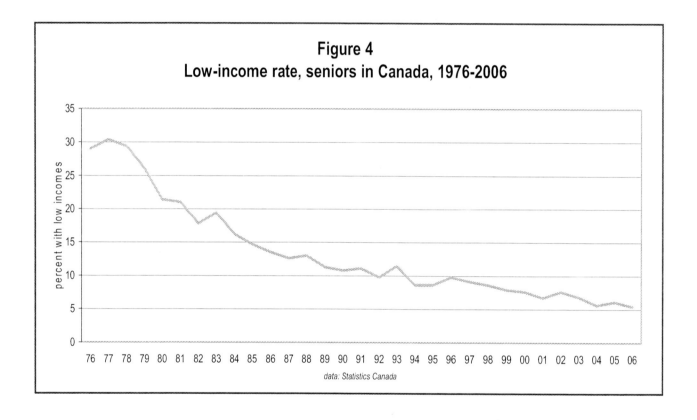

Figure 4
Low-income rate, seniors in Canada, 1976-2006

data: Statistics Canada

seniors' benefits

Canada has made substantial strides in reducing poverty among the elderly, the rate plummeting from 29.0 percent in 1976 to 5.4 percent in 2006 as illustrated in Figure 4. Canada ranks third lowest among 23 industrialized nations, bested only by Finland (5.2 percent) and Sweden (2.7 percent).

This huge reduction in poverty is due largely to improvements in public pension programs (Old Age Security, the Guaranteed Income Supplement and the Canada and Quebec Pension Plans) and the historic rise in the labour force participation of women, who thereby become eligible for pensions in their own right from the Canada and Quebec Pension Plans and employer-sponsored plans (though of women belong only to the latter).

However, the work is not finished: Some seniors remain in poverty – 16.1 percent of single elderly women and 14.0 percent of single elderly men – and many more live just above the poverty line.

The Guaranteed Income Supplement for low-income seniors received small increases in 2005, the first real improvements in 22 years (for single seniors, by $216 in 1995 and by $43 in 1996, and for senior couples by $348 in 1995 and $696 in 1996). Even a small improvement in the GIS will move enough seniors above the poverty line to make a (similarly modest) dent in the low income statistics.

Further improvements to the GIS are an obvious incremental way to improve the incomes of the elderly poor. Another change, which would be architectural because it involves the structure of social policy, is to convert the existing age credit – which is nonrefundable and so does not help the poorest of the elderly poor who owe no income tax – to a refundable credit that would reach the poorest seniors who are below the taxpaying threshold.

child benefits

Ottawa has significantly boosted the Canada Child Tax Benefit, a major social program that also served as its contribution to the federal-provincial/territorial National Child Benefit reform of the architecture of child benefits in Canada that began in 1997. Maximum payments for the first child rose from $1,520 in July 1996 to $3,416 in July 2009. Caledon and other groups have set a maximum $5,000 CCTB as the target for a mature child benefit that reduces poverty and helps parents with their childrearing expenses. This is an incremental reform that can be easily achieved in coming years.

Child benefits take a hefty whack out of the poverty statistics. If there were no federal child benefits, the low-income rate for families with children would be 15.0 percent. Under the current system of federal child benefits, the low-income rate for families with children is 9.3 percent. Caledon's proposal for a $5,000 maximum CCTB would reduce that figure to 8.3 percent.

Without federal child benefits, there would be an estimated 566,600 low-income families with children. That number is 352,800 under present child benefits and would fall to 312,800 under our proposed $5,000 Canada Child Tax Benefit.

The average depth of poverty, $10,159 in the absence of federal child benefits, is $7,546 under the current system and would be $7,153 under our option.

Substantial increases in federal child benefits in recent years have enabled them to contribute a growing share of income over the years for poor families. For a single parent in Ontario with one child under 6 and earned income of $15,000, federal child benefits rose from 15.0 percent of income in 1993 to 15.8 percent in 1988, 22.1 percent in 2005 and 29.8 percent in

2007. Under our proposed $5,000 Canada Child Tax Benefit, the 2007 rate would reach 33.3 percent – one-third of earnings.

The National Child Benefit reform involves more than just an increase in cash benefits. It aims at eliminating that part of the welfare wall that was caused by the irrational system of welfare-embedded child benefits. Early exploratory evaluation evidence suggests that the National Child Benefit reform has helped reduced welfare caseloads by assisting some families to get over the welfare wall.

help for the working poor

In 2007 the federal government filled a big hole in Canada's architecture of income security by creating the Working Income Tax Benefit, a program that supplements the earnings of the working poor. WITB has two major objectives – to reduce disincentives to work for Canadians recipients stuck behind the welfare wall, and to enhance incentives to work among the working poor. So it does more than just provide a cash benefit: It also is intended to provide an incentive to work.

An important feature of WITB is that the federal government allows provinces and territories to configure the program to fit with their income security systems and priorities. So far Quebec, BC and Nunavut have done so.

In its first two years WITB was very lean, providing a small benefit and only to those working poor employed part-time or part-year. The 2009 Budget substantially boosted the Working Income Tax Benefit, from a maximum $510 for single recipients in 2008 to $925 in 2009 – a hefty real (i.e., inflation-adjusted) increase of 77.2 percent. The net income level where eligibility for WITB ends will increase from $13,081 in 2008 to $16,667 in 2009.

For single parents and couples, the maximum WITB payment will rise from $1,044 in 2008 to $1,680 in 2009, for a substantial real increase of 60.9 percent. The net family income level above which eligibility for WITB ends will rise from $21,576 in 2008 to $25,700 in 2009.

But even with these improvements, the Working Income Tax Benefit will not reach all working poor Canadians. Take the case of a worker living in Toronto whose earnings equal the after-tax low income cut-off, an estimated $18,670 in 2009. That amount is $2,012 above the $16,667 level where eligibility for WITB ends. To receive the maximum benefit of $925 from WITB in 2009, the most a worker can make is $10,500 – far ($8,170) below the $18,670 level for someone earning at the poverty line. (see comment in my e-mail about this)

Ottawa should continue to grow WITB through incremental improvements over time – so that it extends higher up the income ladder and becomes a substantial income support for Canadians who work but remain poor.

Employment Insurance

Unemployment insurance should act as an automatic economic stabilizer in a modern economy such as Canada's. It must fulfill a dual role during an economic downturn. It should provide income support by replacing lost wages for the growing ranks of the unemployed, including those with low incomes. And, by injecting money into the economy, it should help sustain businesses that rely upon consumer spending.

But Employment Insurance – the name change from Unemployment Insurance that accompanied Ottawa's draconian cuts in 1996 – is a troubled program that has broken the social insurance contract between Ottawa and employed Canadians. Virtually all employees pay Employment Insurance premiums, but only some can draw upon the program's income benefits and employment services when they become unemployed. The flawed social insurance contract effectively discriminates against low-wage workers, most of them in nonstandard jobs. Women fare worse than men.

Employment Insurance tends to exclude the long-term unemployed, recent immigrants, the underemployed, new workers, part-time workers (including persons with disabilities and Canadians working part time due to family care responsibilities) and workers in precarious jobs. Most low-wage workers are excluded from Employment Insurance. The program does not cover the self-employed or those who are self-employed as 'independent' contractors.

Coverage of the unemployed has fallen from 83 percent in 1990 to 43 percent in 2008, which is the lowest ever. There is a gender gap – only 39.1 percent of unemployed women received regular Employment Insurance benefits in 2008 as opposed to 45.5 percent of jobless men. This gap has widened in recent years from 2.0 percentage points in 1996 to 6.4 percentage points in 2008.

Benefits are by no means generous. The maximum weekly regular benefit is $447 in 2009 or a maximum $22,350 taking into account the 2009 Budget's increase of up to five weeks for a maximum of 50 weeks; in 1995, it was $595 in inflation-adjusted terms ($448 in current dollars). Today's maximum weekly benefit is just three-quarters of what it was in 1995.

In 2007, maximum average benefits for women ($298) amounted to $13,410 – $4,544 below the after-tax LICO for a metropolitan area of 500,000 or more residents ($17,954). In 2007, maximum average benefits for men ($360) amounted to $16,200 – $1,754 below the after-tax LICO for a metro area ($17,954).

The 2009 Budget chose only to temporarily improve matters for the minority of the unemployed who qualify for benefits because they meet existing work requirements. Current Employment Insurance beneficiaries, and those who lose their jobs over the next two years and meet the eligibility requirements, will draw benefits for an extra five weeks, up to a maximum of 50 weeks.

Progressive groups have called for changes to Employment Insurance to address the low coverage and benefit problems, as well as the inequities caused by the variable entrance requirement whereby weeks worked to qualify for benefits and the duration of benefits depends on the regional unemployment rate (58 of them).

There is growing consensus among Canadians that EI must be restored, and no dearth of suggestions for how to do it. For example, the Canadian Labour Congress has recommended:

1. uniform entrance requirement of 360 hours to replace both variable entrance requirements and the 600 hours required for special benefits (e.g., maternity and parental)

2. earnings replacement rate raised from current 55 percent to 60 percent of insurable earnings, and on the best 12 weeks of earnings (not the current 26 weeks of actual earnings)

3. extend maximum duration of benefits up to 50 weeks (which Ottawa did, but only temporarily)

4. eliminate the 2-week waiting period.

The Caledon Institute concurs in terms of immediate changes to Employment Insurance to strengthen its capacity to help fight the recession. We recommended levelling the playing field on qualifying rules and duration of benefits and boosting the program's earnings-replacement level to 70 or 75 percent.

But these changes, while welcome, are not enough to solve the deep-rooted weaknesses of Employment Insurance. Caledon has been working on a new architecture for adult benefits in which reform of Employment Insurance would play a key role along with a radically reformed welfare system.

We do not have the time today to sketch out our ideas, except to say that we envisage a three-tier core adult benefits system made up by two federal unemployment programs, an employment preparation system operated by the provinces and territories that would replace much of welfare, and a federal basic income program for persons with severe disabilities and others who cannot be expected to work. The three tiers would fit into the context of an overall system architecture including allied services and benefits.

The first tier, unemployment assistance, would be a modernized system of time-limited income support for the temporarily unemployed, with a non-contributory income tested component (Temporary Income Program) and a contributory income replacement component (Employment Insurance) working together, analogous to OAS/GIS and C/QPP.

Temporary Income (TI)
- time-limited (e.g., six months) income-tested component that is non-contributory serving temporarily unemployed who do not qualify for EI
- time limits could be adjusted to be regionally sensitive
- could also deliver paid parental leave and other social benefits
- could be delivered as tax credit with retrospective income testing or through a current income reporting system

Employment Insurance (EI)
- contributory social insurance component provides enhanced income replacement (70-75 percent of insurable earnings)
- simplified structure with no regionalization (which is instead shifted into income-tested component if deemed politically necessary)

disability income

An estimated half million Canadians with disabilities rely on provincial and territorial welfare programs for their income, due largely to the fact that persons with disabilities have significantly lower and more sporadic participation in the labour force.

Among the working age population (15-64), 36.5 percent of men with disabilities did not work in 2000 – almost three times the 12.8 percent figure for men without disabilities. Close to half (46.7 percent) of women with disabilities did not work – double the 22.5 percent figure for women without disabilities.

Only 34.9 percent of men with disabilities had full-time, all-year employment compared with 53.2 percent of men without disabilities. The comparable figures for women are 23.2 percent for those with disabilities and 37.4 percent of those without disabilities.

As a result of wide-ranging employment barriers, persons with disabilities often have no choice but to depend on various income security programs for most or all of their income. Most must rely on social assistance (welfare) because they are not able to qualify for income programs whose eligibility involves significant attachment to the labour market. Persons with disabilities comprise, on average, close to half (45.5 percent) of the social assistance caseload throughout the country.

Welfare benefits fall below poverty levels, virtually ensuring a life of low income for recipients with disabilities. Their low income is compounded by the fact that most persons with severe disabilities incur additional costs related to their disability. These may be direct expenses in the form of aids or equipment and household or vehicle modification. There may also be indirect costs such as wear and tear on clothing, travel to accessible shopping or additional babysitting costs for a child with a severe disability.

Strict asset rules within social assistance prevent persons with disabilities from receiving additional cash or gifts to make their lives even slightly more bearable. (On a positive note, most jurisdictions have fully or partly exempted the value of the newly introduced federal Registered Disability Savings Plan whose purpose is to ensure a good life, or at least a slightly better life, for persons with disabilities.)

Social assistance was never intended to provide lifetime income. Its original and continuing purpose is to serve as a benefit of last resort in the absence of other sources of income and until the gap can be filled in some other way – typically through employment.

One possible alternative that Caledon has been exploring as part of architectural reform for persons with disabilities is an income-tested basic program that would provide adequate long-term financial support with no time limits for persons with severe disabilities. The proposed new measure would be financed and operated by the federal government and modelled on its Guaranteed Income Supplement.

Benefit levels could equal the combined Old Age Security (OAS) and Guaranteed Income Supplement (GIS) payments, which are widely regarded as having eliminated the deepest poverty among the elderly. In 2008, seniors with no other income receive an annual maximum $13,731 from OAS and GIS. The proposed new disability income program would pay the same maximum amount. As with OAS and GIS, benefits would be adjusted quarterly in line with the Consumer Price Index.

Eligibility for the new benefit would be on the basis of a modified test currently used for two other federal measures – the disability tax credit and Canada Pension Plan disability benefit.

Because most social assistance recipients with severe disabilities would move off provincial/territorial welfare and onto the proposed new federal program, the provinces and territories would reap substantial savings. Under the terms of a negotiated accord, provinces and territories could use these savings to invest in a comprehensive system of disability supports, including assistance for independent living, employment and community participation.

The first and immediate step that the federal government could take in moving toward this type of comprehensive reform would be to make refundable the current nonrefundable disability tax credit that helps offset the additional (sometimes referred to as 'hidden') costs of disability. Currently (2008 tax year), the disability tax credit provides federal tax savings of a maximum $1,053. This change would provide assistance to the thousands of persons with disabilities with incomes too low to benefit from the current nonrefundable disability tax credit.

early learning and child care

High-quality early learning and child care services are not just sound social policy: They equally are crucial elements of economic policy because they invest in the critical first years of human capital development and allow parents to work or study.

From an economic perspective, high-quality affordable child care enables labour market participation, education and training. It is a vital component of an anti-poverty strategy in that it can make the difference between a below- and above-poverty line income for many single parents and couples.

Canada lags embarrassingly behind other advanced nations when it comes to early learning and child care. The demand for quality, affordable services far outstrips the available supply. Among 25 OECD countries surveyed recently, Canada ranked last along with Ireland on a set of internationally applicable benchmarks for early childhood care and education.

The federal government has a pivotal role to play in contributing to a secure financial base for this crucial investment. Ottawa should make a significant commitment to support this infrastructure as it did in the federal-provincial/territorial Early Childhood Development Agreement in signed in 2000 and the Agreement on Early Learning and Child Care in 2003.

Federal investment in this sector would recognize high-quality child care not only as an essential support to tackling poverty, but also as an economic stimulus strategy. Canadians need good-quality, affordable child care in order to participate in the labour market. Moreover the child care system itself creates jobs for early childhood educators – primarily for women, many of whom feel that they have been left out of the employment creation picture through all the funds announced for shovel-ready infrastructure.

social housing

The availability of high-quality, affordable housing is another core component of any poverty reduction strategy. It is also an important form of infrastructure spending that will help create jobs, if spent expeditiously.

We were pleased to see that as part of its economic stimulus package, Ottawa announced a one-time $1 billion injection over the next two years for renovation and energy retrofits to improve the quality and energy efficiency of up to 200,000 social housing units throughout the country. This federal spending is to be matched 50-50 by the provinces and territories.

The 2009 federal Budget also allocated targeted funds over two years for First Nations reserves ($400 million), seniors ($400 million), the North ($200 million) and persons with disabilities ($75 million).

Over the longer term, the new $1 billion federal investment will build on the $1.9 billion over five years that the federal government announced in September 2008 to extend housing and homelessness programs for low-income Canadians. These programs include the Affordable Housing Initiative, Homelessness Partnering Strategy and housing renovation programs, such as the Residential Rehabilitation Assistance Program.

In a recent media interview, however, the Minister of Human Resources and Skills Development reinforced the one-time nature of the government investment in social housing. She stated that the money was intended for economic stimulus purpose and did not represent a policy shift to a larger federal role in social housing. Why not?

As a vital component of a serious anti-poverty strategy, Canada needs a comprehensive strategic and long-term plan for affordable housing that involves all players including Ottawa, the provincial and territorial governments, municipalities and the voluntary sector. The federal government can play a crucial leadership role in addition to its financial investment.

social infrastructure

An essential component of a robust poverty reduction strategy is a focus on place – not just the four walls and roof where families live, but the broader community that includes the amenities which contribute to a good-quality life.

Our understanding of the importance of these amenities derives from research into resilience that has documented the role of non-income resources in helping families cope with the stress of life below the poverty line and protecting children from its risks. Studies on population health have also found links between community design and amenities, and health and social well-being.

Strong neighbourhoods are created through safe community spaces and activities that encourage positive participation. These safe spaces comprise essential social infrastructure, which is as important as traditional physical infrastructure – i.e., local hardware in the form of roads, sewers, water systems and other elements that form its physical plant.

Schools are a leading example of community spaces that serve important social needs – in addition, of course, to their primary educational role. They can provide a locale for before- and after-school child care and early learning services. They can be convenient centres for organizing continuing education, cultural and recreational activities. They can act as places for residents to meet and discuss common concerns, such as community health or safety, or for parents to learn language skills or improve their literacy proficiency.

The 2009 Budget established a two-year $4 billion Infrastructure Stimulus Fund to enable provinces/territories and municipalities to repair, renew and upgrade infrastructure. A sum of $1 billion over five years was allocated to the Green Infrastructure Fund to support projects related to sustainable energy. A maximum $2 billion has been set aside for the repair, retrofit and expansion of postsecondary educational facilities.

The Budget also announced up to $500 million over the next two years for infrastructure in smaller communities whose resource-dependent economies are being hit hard by the recession.

16

Two new agencies – for northern economic development and for southern Ontario – are being created to bolster economic activity in these regions.

In addition to providing the physical spaces that can be used for social purposes, social infrastructure includes programs that contribute to positive well-being. There are strong links between participation in recreation and cultural activities, and good physical health, mental health and social well-being.

We were pleased to see the allocation of $500 million over two years to build and renew community recreation facilities across Canada. Caledon had called for this type of investment over a previous budgetary measure that took the form of what we termed a 'designer' tax break for participation in fitness programs, which benefits primarily middle- and higher-income Canadians – and for so few dollars in tax savings ($75) that it makes no real difference. Nor can such minor tax cuts for individual taxpayers possibly substitute for the significant investments required to upgrade, repair and renew community spaces, such as recreation facilities.

The problem with infrastructure investment is that political and regulatory barriers invariably get in the way of expeditious spending. The latter is crucial given the explicit purpose of infrastructure measures – to counter rising unemployment through the immediate creation of jobs. Nearly $8 billion in previously announced infrastructure funding has gone unspent and accumulated on the federal books. Delays in implementation mean that the monies could go into the economy at a time when it will already be growing again.

enabling environment

Many communities throughout the country are engaged in long-term comprehensive efforts to find local solutions to reduce poverty. The federal government can support these initiatives by providing direct assistance or indirect aid in the form of data collection and interpretation, and cross-community learning.

It is difficult to find financial backing for long-term comprehensive work. All orders of government, community funders and private funders prefer to support specific, narrowly defined projects where they can see the immediate results of their investment. A related problem is that funding tends to be directed toward short-term interventions, while comprehensive initiatives that tackle complex and stubborn problems – such as poverty – often involve a long-term time frame.

The collection and analysis of poverty data are crucial for developing strategic community approaches. But relevant statistical data that aid in this type of neighbourhood-based targeting are often difficult to obtain at the local level.

National data generally are not easily disaggregated, making it difficult for communities to paint their own profile. Statistics Canada currently charges a substantial sum for unpublished data, which makes this information inaccessible to most community organizations. Governments can help by providing the required figures or the technical assistance to enable communities to interpret the data.

Learning is another area that usually does not emerge spontaneously in communities. It is a process that must be carefully developed and strategically pursued. Governments can play an important role in supporting cross-community learning to enable the application of effective local approaches.

COMMUNITY DEVELOPMENT: Journal of the Community Development Society, Vol. 38, No. 1, Spring 2007

Theories of Poverty and Anti-Poverty Programs in Community Development

Ted K. Bradshaw

In this paper I explore how five competing theories of poverty shape anti-poverty strategies. Since most rural community development efforts aim to relieve causes or symptoms of poverty, it makes a difference which theory of poverty is believed to be responsible for the problem being addressed. In this paper five theories of poverty are distilled from the literature. It will be shown that these theories of poverty place its origin from (1) individual deficiencies, (2) cultural belief systems that support subcultures in poverty, (3) political-economic distortions, (4) geographical disparities, or (5) cumulative and circumstantial origins. Then, I show how each theory of poverty finds expression in common policy discussion and community development programs aimed to address the causes of poverty. Building a full understanding of each of these competing theories of poverty shows how they shape different community development approaches. Although no one theory explains all instances of poverty, this paper aims to show how community development practices that address the complex and overlapping sources of poverty more effectively reduce poverty compared to programs that address a single theory.

Key-words: *anti-poverty strategies, theories of poverty, origins or causes of poverty, structural inequality, social inequality, social capital*

> Which view of poverty we ultimately embrace will have a
> direct bearing on the public policies we pursue.
> —Schiller 1989, p. 4

Community development has a variety of strategies available to meet the needs of those persons and groups who are less advantaged, usually in poverty. Community developers help all communities, but their passion lies disproportionately with people who do not have adequate personal resources to meet their needs or with communities with large populations of people who need assistance. These people and communities receiving attention from community developers are extensively varied in most respects other than being poor—the poor are both rural and urban, they are ethnically minority

Ted K. Bradshaw (October 28, 1942—August 5, 2006) was professor, chair, and research sociologist in the Human and Community Development Department at the University of California, Davis. Since 2002, he was Editor of *COMMUNITY DEVELOPMENT: Journal of the Community Development.* In 1974, he received his Ph.D. in Sociology at the University of California, Berkeley. With co-author Woodrow W. Clark II, Bradshaw published *Agile Energy Systems: Global Lessons from the California Energy Crisis* in 2004. Ted Bradshaw died suddenly while running near his home in Oakland, California. This article represents a revision of papers presented at the meetings of the Community Development Society (2001) and the Rural Sociology Society (2003). Research assistance from students, Vlade Stasuc and Christine McReynolds, is greatly appreciated.

or not, they live in places with weak and strong economies, and they have been helped for decades or neglected for as long. In short, fixing poverty is a dominant theme within community development, but we have infrequently examined the theories that underlie the dominant practices addressing poverty.

The thesis of this paper is that community anti-poverty programs are designed, selected, and implemented in response to different theories about the cause of poverty that "justify" the community development interventions. The definition of poverty and theories that explain it are deeply rooted in strongly held research traditions and political values, reinforced by encompassing social, political, and economic institutions that have a stake in the issue. Thus, a purely objective explanation of poverty is displaced by a proliferation of socially defined issues and concerns from both liberal and conservative perspectives. Moreover, no one theory of poverty has emerged that either subsumes or invalidates the others (Blank, 1997). Explaining poverty remains a lucrative field for academics, policy makers, book publishers, and ideologues, and as a consequence the range of explanations has proliferated.

A sampling of community-based poverty programs shows how varied community level anti-poverty efforts can be.

1. A county directed its schools to identify children not attending school more than ten days per school-year without medical excuses, and then if the family received Temporary Assistance for Needy Families (TANF) benefits, the child's portion of the family welfare payments were withheld to enforce school attendance and assure that welfare kids not get left behind for another generation.

2. Pre-school programs are advocated in order to help poor kids gain skills and internalize the value of learning that will help them succeed in school, and after-school programs are designed to keep children away from negative influences of unsupervised street cultures.

3. Public programs (such as equal opportunity) help remove social and economic barriers to housing, good jobs, health care, and political processes, based on the premise that otherwise qualified people are commonly excluded from poverty reducing opportunities by race, class, gender, or other factors not relevant to ability to perform.

4. Communities utilize a range of local economic development tools such as redevelopment, business attraction, or enterprise zones to stimulate development of poor and disadvantaged areas hurt by regional isolation, economic backwardness, blight, and disinvestment.

5. Non-profits and community development corporations (CDCs) develop comprehensive approaches to poverty based on a multifaceted approach including employment development, education, housing, access to health care and social services, as well as personal networks and participation in community programs that increase social capital.

The first example is based on theories that poverty is perpetuated by individual or family irresponsibility, which should be stopped by stiff penalties; the second example addresses subcultures of poverty and tries to acculturate poor children into mainstream values; the third sees poverty not as an individual problem but a social one that needs to be addressed politically and structurally; the fourth addresses regional or geographic concentrations of poverty through spatially targeted benefits; and the final addresses poverty in a comprehensive and cumulative way. Each example reflects a different theory of what causes poverty and how to address it.

I consider a theory an explanation that links several concepts; in this case theories explain poverty (as defined below) by linking different factors thought to cause or perpetuate poverty through distinctive social processes. Interventions that reduce a cause of poverty should reduce poverty as a consequence. The emphasis here is on poverty in developed countries such as the USA. The purpose of this paper is to expand our understanding of five different theories of poverty that underlie the common toolbox of programs, which community developers apply to address the problem of poverty in their community. In contrast to the typical focus that limits theoretical review to only two or three contrasting perspectives (Ropers, 1991; Egendorf, 1999; Epstein, 1997), this paper suggests that there are five major theoretical explanations for poverty.[1] Poverty, it is argued, is a very complex social problem with many variants and different roots, all of which have validity depending on the situation (Blank, 2003; Shaw, 1996, p. 28).

Definitions of Poverty

Poverty in its most general sense is the lack of necessities. Basic food, shelter, medical care, and safety are generally thought necessary based on shared values of human dignity. However, what is a necessity to one person is not uniformly a necessity to others. Needs may be relative to what is possible and are based on social definition and past experience (Sen, 1999). Valentine (1968) says that "the essence of poverty is inequality. In slightly different words, the basic meaning of poverty is relative deprivation." A social (relative) definition of poverty allows community flexibility in addressing pressing local concerns, although objective definitions allow tracking progress and comparing one area to another.

The most common "objective" definition of poverty is the statistical measure established by the federal government as the annual income needed for a family to survive. The "poverty line" was initially created in 1963 by Mollie Orshansky at the U.S. Department of Agriculture based on three times her estimate of what a family would have to spend for an adequate but far from lavish diet. According to Michael Darby (1996, p. 4), the very definition of poverty was political, aimed to benchmark the progress of poverty programs for the War on Poverty. Adjusted for inflation, the poverty line for a family of four was $17,050 income in 2000 according to the U.S. Census. Most poverty scholars identify many problems with this definition related to concepts of family, cash income, treatment of taxes, special work-related expenses, or regional differences in the cost of living (Blank, 1997, p. 10; Quigley, 2003).

Regardless of how we look at the "science" of poverty, or what O'Connor calls the "knowledge of poverty," it is essential to retain focus on the fact that the definition of poverty and the policies addressing it are all shaped by political biases and values.

> It is this disparity of status and interest that make poverty research an inescapably political act: it is an exercise of power, in this case of an educated elite to categorize, stigmatize, but above all to neutralize the poor and disadvantaged through analysis that obscures the political nature of social and economic inequality (O'Connor, 2001, p. 12).

In this sense, political agenda are the overriding factors in poverty that not only influence the choice of theory of poverty but also the very definition of poverty to be explained by each theory. Powerful interests manage how poverty is discussed and what is being done about it; unfortunately this paper can only identify the politicization of theories of poverty rather than separate them out for analysis.

9

Sources and Approach

The approach in this paper is to review strategically selected programs and approaches used by communities to address poverty in the United States. The approach starts by examining some of the most significant recent books and articles (and several classics) that discuss poverty in America,[2] and then it distills from them the theoretical perspectives most central to their analysis. The task here is not to do a complete review of all the literature on poverty, as that includes thousands of items and is beyond the scope of this paper. Nor is the task to distill all the recent abundance of information on poverty, especially the empirical evidence of who the poor are and what their condition is.

I approach poverty programs from the community development perspective, addressing the range of programs available to a typical community. Since this portfolio of programs changes rapidly over time and from community to community, I attempt to generalize and build grounded theory that captures the range, even if it blurs some details. I was guided in this task by the recent books on poverty policy such as Sar Levitan's colleagues whose inventory of "Programs in Aid of the Poor" (Levitan et al., 2003) catalogued many federal programs available to local areas. In addition, I base my analysis on those programs I have known over years of community-based work. Simply put, the task of this paper is to look in the literature for theoretical explanations of poverty that link up with the practices at the core of community development.

For each of the five theories that make up the bulk of the poverty literature, I identify the set of variables most significantly associated with causing poverty according to that theory, the mechanisms by these variables cause poverty, the potential strategies that can be addressed in response to poverty, and finally community-based examples of how anti-poverty programs based on that particular theory are implemented. These five theories are summarized in Figure 1.

Figure 1. Five Theories of Poverty and Community Anti-Poverty Programs

Theory	What causes Poverty?	How does it work?	Potential Community Development responses	Community examples to reduce poverty
1. Individual	Individual laziness, bad choice, incompetence, inherent disabilities	Competition rewards winners and punishes those who do not work hard and make bad choices	Avoid and counter efforts to individualize poverty, provide assistance and safety net	Drug rehabilitation, second chance programs, making safety net easier to access, use training and counseling to help poor individuals overcome problems
2. Cultural	Subculture adopts values that are non-productive and are contrary to norms of success	Use community to the advantage of the poor; value diverse cultures, acculturation, and community building; alternative socialization through forming new peer groups	Head Start, after school, leadership development within subcultures, asset-based community development	Head Start, after-school leadership development within subcultures, asset-based community development

10

Figure 1. Cont'd.

Theory	What causes Poverty?	How does it work?	Potential Community Development responses	Community examples to reduce poverty
3. Political-economic structure	Systematic barriers prevent poor from access and accomplishment in key social institutions including jobs, education, housing, health care, safety, political representation, etc.	Selection criteria directly or indirectly exclude some groups of persons based on inappropriate criteria	Community organizing and advocacy to gain political and economic power to achieve change; create alternative organizations	Policies to force inclusion and enforcement
4. Geographic	Social advantages and disadvantages concentrate in separate areas	Agglomeration, distance, economies of scale, and resource distributions reinforce differences	National redistributions, concentration of development on local assets	Redevelopment areas, downtowns, rural networking, urban revitalization
5. Cumulative and cyclical	Spirals of poverty, problems for individuals (earnings, housing, health, education, self confidence) are interdependent and strongly linked to community deficiencies (loss of business and jobs, inadequate schools, inability to provide social services), etc.	Factors interact in complex ways. Community level crises lead to Individual crises and vice versa, and each cumulate to cause spirals of poverty	Breaking the spiral of poverty with a spiral of success through a comprehensive program that addresses both individual and community issues	Comprehensive CDC programs that build self-sufficiency in a community reinforced environment, programs that link individuals and community organizations, asset-based approaches

FIVE THEORIES OF POVERTY IN CONTEMPORARY LITERATURE

Recent literature on poverty uniformly acknowledges different theories of poverty, but the literature has classified these theories in multiple ways (e.g., compare Blank, 2003; Goldsmith & Blakely, 1992; Jennings & Kushnick, 1999; Rodgers, 2000; Schiller, 1989; Shaw, 1996). Virtually all authors distinguish between theories that root the cause of poverty in individual deficiencies (conservative) and theories that lay the cause on broader social phenomena (liberal or progressive). Ryan (1976) addresses this dichotomy in terms of "blaming the victim." Goldsmith and Blakely, for example, distinguish "poverty as pathology" from "poverty as incident or accident" and "poverty as structure." Schiller (1989, pp. 2-3) explains it in terms of "flawed characters, restricted opportunity, and Big Brother." Jennings

11

(1999) reviews variants on these individual vs. society conceptions, giving emphasis to racial and political dynamics. Rank is very clear: "The focus on individual attributes as the cause of poverty is misplaced and misdirected." Structural failings of the economic, political, and social system are causes instead (Rank, 2004, p. 50). The various theories are divergent, and each results in a different type of community development intervention strategy.

1. Poverty Caused by Individual Deficiencies

This first theory of poverty consists of a large and multifaceted set of explanations that focus on the individual as responsible for his or her poverty situation. Typically, politically conservative theoreticians blame individuals in poverty for creating their own problems and argue that with harder work and better choices, the poor could have avoided (and now can remedy) their problems. Other variations of the individual theory of poverty ascribe poverty to lack of genetic qualities such as intelligence that are not so easily reversed.

The belief that poverty stems from individual deficiencies is old. Religious doctrine that equated wealth with the favor of God was central to the Protestant reformation (Weber, 2001) and blind, crippled, or deformed people were believed to be punished by God for either their or their parents' sins. With the emergence of the concept of inherited intelligence in the nineteenth century, the eugenics movement went so far as to rationalize poverty and even sterilization for those who appeared to have limited abilities. Books like Herrnstein and Murray's *The Bell Curve* (1994) are modern uses of this explanation. Rainwater (1970, p. 16) critically discusses individualistic theories of poverty as a "moralizing perspective" and notes that the poor are "afflicted with the mark of Cain. They are meant to suffer, indeed must suffer, because of their moral failings. They live in a deserved hell on earth." Rainwater goes on to say that it is difficult to overestimate the extent to which this perspective (incorrectly) under-girds our visions of poverty, including the perspective of the disinherited themselves.

Ironically, neoclassical economics reinforces individualistic sources of poverty. The core premise of this dominant paradigm for the study of the conditions leading to poverty is that individuals seek to maximize their own well being by making choices and investments, and that (assuming that they have perfect information) they seek to maximize their well being. When some people choose short-term and low pay-off returns, economic theory holds the individual largely responsible for their individual choices—for example to forego college education or other training that will lead to better paying jobs in the future.

The economic theory that the poor lack incentives for improving their own conditions is a recurrent theme in articles that blame the welfare system's generosity on the perpetuation of poverty. In a *Cato Journal* article, economists Gwartney and McCaleb argue that the years of the war on poverty actually increased poverty (adjusted for non-cash transfers) among working age adults in spite of unprecedented increases in welfare expenditures. They conclude that "the application of simple economic theory" suggests that the problem lies in the war on poverty programs:

> They [welfare programs] have introduced a perverse incentive structure, one that penalizes self-improvement and protects individuals against the consequences of their own bad choices. (1985, p. 7)

This and similar arguments that cast the poor as a "moral hazard" also hold that "the problem of poverty continues to fester not because we are failing to do enough, but because we are doing too much that is counterproductive" (Gwartney & McCaleb, 1985, p. 15). Their economic model would solve poverty by assuring that the penalty of poverty was great enough that none would choose it (and welfare would be restricted to the truly disabled or otherwise unable to work).

12

A less widely critiqued version of the individualistic theory of poverty comes from American values of individualism—the Horatio Alger myth that any individual can succeed by skills and hard work, and that motivation and persistence are all that are required to achieve success (see Asen, 2002, pp. 29-34). Self-help literature reinforces the belief that individuals fail because they do not try hard enough. Frank Bettger (1977, pp. 187-188), in the Dale Carnegie tradition, tells how he got a list of self-improvement goals on which to focus and became one of the most successful and highly paid salesmen in America. He goes on to say that anyone can succeed by an easy formula—focused goals and hard work. This is the message of hundreds of self-help books, articles, and sermons. By extension, this literature implies that those who do not succeed must face the fact that they themselves are responsible for their failure.

Although scientifically it is routine to dismiss the individual deficiency theory as an apology for social inequality (Fischer, et al., 1996), it is easy to see how it is embraced in anti-poverty policy that suggests that penalties and incentives can change behavior.

Anti-Poverty Programs from the Perspective of an Individual Theory of Poverty

Community development practice, embedded in decades of welfare and social policy, frequently deals with programs aiming to remedy poverty based on individual deficiency theories. Explicitly or implicitly, individual deficiencies represent an easy policy approach not always carefully explored as it gets implemented. The key initiatives today are to push the poor into work as a primary goal, what Maskovsky calls the "workist consensus." Indeed this move is accompanied by an increasing emphasis on "self help" strategies for the poor to pull themselves from poverty, strategies encouraged by the elimination of other forms of assistance (Maskovsky, 2001, pp. 472-473). Earned income tax credits are one aspect of the strategy to assure that the poor work even at below living-wage jobs.

However, from a community development perspective, addressing poverty by focusing on individual characteristics and bad choices raise fundamental conflicts in philosophy and in what is known to succeed. The compassion of community development shies away from blaming the individual, and individual level programs are usually embedded in community efforts by the very nature of community development. Thus, anti-poverty programs in community development tend to oppose strategies that punish or try to change individuals as a solution to poverty, though working with individual needs and abilities is a constant objective. This tension runs through all anti-poverty programs.

However, many contemporary anti-poverty programs are not designed with compassion in mind; they use punishment and the threat of punishment in order to change behavior and get people off public assistance (see O'Connor, 2001; Quigley, 2003). The best example of this response to poverty is to limit the number of years people can be on family assistance and to require participation in work activities after two years on welfare (see Levitan et al., 2003, pp. 59-72), a core part of the politically conservative (and ironically named) Personal Responsibility and Work Opportunity Reconciliation Act (PRWORA). The threat of a cut-off in assistance is believed to change behavior since a person will loose assistance after five years. Another program I have been studying (MERCAP) reduces assistance payments to families if their children fail to attend school; it is hoped that children will eventually graduate from high school and will not become another generation of welfare recipients. This study found that the punishment did little to change behavior, although attention from teachers and school administrators helped identify more complex reasons for poor school attendance (Campbell & Wright, 2005). The punitive approach of individual theories of poverty justifies policies that

13

restrict public assistance to services and goods instead of cash because there is a lack of trust in the discretion of poor people. Providing food for children at school and offering homeless people shelters rather than offering cash to pay for housing are examples.

Individual level anti-poverty efforts have a social component, however. First a reliable safety-net that can help people who are otherwise unable to help themselves is really a civic responsibility. The disabled, elderly, children, and even the unlucky are part of every community, and without blame, their individual needs can be met by collective action. A safety net, without pejorative connotations, is a key to civility. Making the safety net work and available is broadly accepted.

In sum, to the extent that policy makers or program leaders hold the individual theory of poverty, it is increasingly unlikely that they will pursue a community development approach to solving poverty. Thus, despite the widespread societal view that individuals are responsible for their own poverty, community developers look to other theories of poverty for more positive approaches.

2. Poverty Caused by Cultural Belief Systems that Support Subcultures of Poverty

The second theory of poverty roots its cause in the "Culture of Poverty." This theory is sometimes linked with the individual theory of poverty or other theories to be introduced below, but recently it has become so widely discussed that its special features should not be minimized. This theory suggests that poverty is created by the transmission over generations of a set of beliefs, values, and skills that are socially generated but individually held. Individuals are not necessarily to blame because they are victims of their dysfunctional subculture or culture.

American sociology has long been fascinated by subcultures of immigrants and ghetto residents as well as the wealthy and powerful. Culture is socially generated and perpetuated, reflecting the interaction of individual and community. This social interaction makes the "culture of poverty" theory different from the "individual" theories that link poverty explicitly to individual abilities and motivation. Technically, the culture of poverty is a subculture of poor people in ghettos, poor regions, or social contexts in which they develop a shared set of beliefs, values, and norms for behavior that is separate from but embedded in the culture of the main society.

Oscar Lewis was one of the main writers to define the culture of poverty as a set of beliefs and values passed from generation to generation. He writes,

> Once the culture of poverty has come into existence it tends to perpetuate itself. By the time slum children are six or seven they have usually absorbed the basic attitudes and values of their subculture. Thereafter they are psychologically unready to take full advantage of changing conditions or improving opportunities that may develop in their lifetime. (*Scientific American*, October 1966, quoted in Ryan, 1976, p. 120).

Cultures are socialized and learned, and one of the tenants of learning theory is that rewards follow to those who learn what is intended. The culture of poverty theory explains how government anti-poverty programs reward people who manipulate the policy to stay on welfare. The underlying argument of conservatives such as Charles Murray in *Losing Ground* (1984) is that government welfare perpetuated poverty by permitting a cycle of "welfare dependency" in which poor families develop and pass on to others the skills needed to work the system rather than to gain paying employment. The net result of this theory of poverty is summed by Asen's (2002, p. 48) perceptive phrase, "from the war on poverty to the war on welfare."

This theory of poverty based on perpetuation of cultural values is fraught with controversy. No one disputes that poor people have subcultures or that the subcultures of the poor are

14

distinctive and perhaps detrimental. The concern is over what causes and constitutes the subculture of poverty. Daniel Patrick Moynihan found the concept particularly applicable to his study of Black poverty in the early 1960s and linked Black poverty to the largely "dysfunctional" African American family found in central cities. Valentine (1968, p. 20) criticizes E. Franklin Frazier, who with Daniel Patrick Moynihan (1965) portrayed the culture of the Negro poor as an "immoral chaos brought about by the disintegration of the black folk culture under the impact of urbanization."

In other subcultural situations the cultural portrayal of the poor is more sympathetic. For example, many liberal scholars understand the cultural problems that Native Americans face trying to assimilate middle class value systems. Ironically, after a number of generations we recall the "heroic" efforts of Irish or Italian immigrant groups and their willingness to accept hard work and to suffer for long-term socioeconomic gains; we forget the cultural discrimination they faced for not fitting in during the first generations after they arrived. Today, the subcultural values for higher education and entrepreneurship among Asian and Indian immigrant groups are prized as an example of how subcultures can work in the favor of groups trying to escape poverty.

Anti-Poverty Programs from a Culture of Poverty Perspective

From a community development perspective, if the theoretical reason for poverty lies in values and beliefs, transmitted and reinforced in subcultures of disadvantaged persons, then local anti-poverty efforts need to intervene to help change the culture. This is socialization as policy, which may work in three ways based on Valentine's (1968) suggestion of different models of cultural theories of poverty.

1. If one thinks of the culture of the poor as a dysfunctional system of beliefs and knowledge, the approach will be to replace that culture with a more functional culture that supports rather than undermines productive work, investment, and social responsibility. Innovative prisoner release programs, for example, may try to relocate prisoners from the environment where they got in trouble and assure that they adopt new values appropriate for work. Some experiments were tried with mixed results, relocating the poor from ghetto housing projects to suburbs with the hope that the new culture will help the family emerge from poverty (Goetz, 2003; Goering, Feins, & Richardson, 2003).

2. On the other hand, if one thinks of the culture of poverty as an opportunistic and non-productive subculture that is perpetuated over generations, then the focus will shift to youth to stop the re-creation of the detrimental culture. Head Start and many educational programs according to Zigler and Styfco (1996) are successful at providing an alternative socialization for the next generation to reduce poverty, though the programs need more coherence and quality. Similarly, community developers are often involved in helping establish after-school programs for teens where their peer culture is monitored and positive social values are established, while keeping youth away from gangs and detrimental behavior. These programs are a policy favorite (Levitan et al., 2003) because they are believed to change the culture of youth while their values and norms are still malleable.

3. A third approach to the culture of poverty is to try to work within the culture to redefine culturally-appropriate strategies to improve the group's well being. For example, community developers can enhance and build upon cultural values with the subcultures of the poor that can become assets for economic development. Local crafts cooperatives are examples, as are programs that tap the traditions of small business and entrepreneurship found in subcultures as different as urban gangs and middle class single mothers. Institutions by which ethnic groups or clans assist each other in creating and financing businesses are well documented in the literature. Although programs

15

promising micro-enterprise as a path from poverty are often oversold (Goldstein, 2001), the mystique of Grameen Bank-type programs as a road out of poverty offers culturally compatible strategies that build on a group's strengths.

3. Poverty Caused by Economic, Political, and Social Distortions or Discrimination

Whereas the first "individualistic" theory of poverty is advocated by conservative thinkers and the second is a culturally liberal approach, the third to which we now turn is a progressive social theory. Theorists in this tradition look not to the individual as a source of poverty but to the economic, political, and social system that causes people to have limited opportunities and resources with which to achieve income and well-being. Research and theories in this tradition attempt to redress the problem noted by Rank, Yoon, and Hirschl: "Poverty researchers have in effect focused on who loses out at the economic game, rather than addressing the fact that the game produces losers in the first place" (2003, p. 5).

The nineteenth century social intellectuals developed a full attack on the individual theory of poverty by exploring how social and economic systems overrode and created individual poverty situations. For example, Marx showed how the economic system of capitalism created the "reserve army of the unemployed" as a conscious strategy to keep wages low. Later Durkheim showed that even the most personal of actions (suicide) was in fact mediated by social systems. Discrimination was separated from skill in one after another area, defining opportunity as socially mediated. Taken to an extreme, radical thinkers argued that the system was flawed and should be radically transformed.

Much of the literature on poverty now suggests that the economic system is structured in such as way that poor people fall behind regardless of how competent they may be. Partly the problem is the fact that minimum wages do not allow single mothers or their families to be economically self sufficient (Jencks, 1996, p. 72). The problem of the working poor is increasingly seen as a wage problem linked to structural barriers preventing poor families from getting better jobs, complicated by limited numbers of jobs near workers and lack of growth in sectors supporting lower skilled jobs (Tobin, 1994). Interestingly research is showing that the availability of jobs to low income people is about the same as it has been, but wages that workers can expect from these jobs have fallen. In addition, fringe benefits including health care and promotions became scarce for low-skilled workers. These and related economic changes documented by Blank (1997) and Quigley (2003) show the way the system creates increasingly difficult problems for those who want to work.

Elimination of structural barriers to better jobs through education and training was the focus of extensive manpower training and other programs, generating substantial successes but also perceived failures. However, despite perceived importance of education, funding per student in less advantaged areas lags behind that which is spent on richer students, teachers are less adequately trained, books are often out of date or in limited supply, amenities are few, and the culture of learning is under siege. This systemic failure of the schools is thus thought to be the reason poor people have low achievement, poor rates of graduation, and few who pursue higher education (Chubb & Moe, 1996).

A parallel barrier exists with the political system in which the interests and participation of the poor is either impossible or is deceptive. Recent research confirms the linkage between wealth and power, and shows how poor people are less involved in political discussions, their interests are more vulnerable in the political process, and they are excluded at many levels. Coupled with racial discrimination, poor people lack influence in the political system that they might use to mobilize economic benefits and justice.

A final broad category of system flaws associated with poverty relates to groups of people being given a social stigma because of race, gender, disability, religion, or other groupings,

16

leading them to have limited opportunities regardless of personal capabilities. No treatment of poverty can be complete without acknowledging that groups against which discrimination is practiced have limited opportunities regardless of legal protections. The process of gaining stronger rights for minorities in poverty is an ongoing one, for which legal initiatives and public policy reform must work with efforts to change public attitudes.

Anti-Poverty Programs from a Structure of Poverty Perspective

If the problem of poverty is in the system rather than in the poor themselves, a community development response must be to change the system. This is easy to say but hard to do, which may explain why so many policy programs revert to trying to change individual behavior. How can one get more jobs, improve schooling for the poor, equalize income distributions, remove discrimination bias from housing, banking, education, and employment, and assure equal political participation by poor persons? None of these tasks are easy and all require interventions into the systems that create the barriers that block poor persons from gaining the benefits of society.

Changing the system can take place at three levels. From a grassroots level, *social movements* can exert pressures on vulnerable parts of the system to force desired change. Although most studies show a decline in support for poor people's social action, Rank (2004, pp. 189-191) argues that change could be mobilized to support better jobs for the poor and a more effective system since as the subtitle of his book states, "American poverty affects us all." For example, public pressure including unionization can increase wages and gain employment for persons systematically excluded. Civil rights movements have had a strong impact on breaking down formal barriers, as has the woman's movement. Community organizing in the Alinsky (1945) tradition has helped reduce poverty across the country (Rank, 2004, p. 233).

A second strategy within community development for changing the system involves creating and developing alternative institutions that have access, openness, innovation, and a willingness to help the poor gain well being. This strategy is at the cornerstone of most community development corporations that aim to provide alternative businesses, housing, schooling, and programs. In addition, business strategies such as employee ownership or networks of minority or women's businesses function admirably. Community owned businesses such as community banks provide alternative structures.

Finally, change can occur through the policy process (Page & Simmons, 2000). The range of federal and social policies that can be adjusted to accomplish poverty reduction include providing jobs, raising wages, expanding the safety net, assuring effective access to medical care, and coordinating social insurance programs. In order to protect these programs in an era of governmental retrenchment, it is increasingly clear that the poor and their advocates need to be more politically mobilized. Legal changes to enforce civil rights of the poor and to protect minority groups are needed. For example, the Americans with Disabilities Act (ADA) established many gains for otherwise able persons who happen to be blind, deaf, or with limited mobility. One of the boldest policy moves is suggested by Quigley (2003) and others who advocate a constitutional amendment to guarantee a job to anyone who wants one and to guarantee that anyone working full time would be able to earn a living wage.

4. Poverty Caused by Geographical Disparities

Rural poverty, ghetto poverty, urban disinvestment, Southern poverty, third-world poverty, and other framings of the problem represent a spatial characterization of poverty that exists separate from other theories. Although this geographically-based theory of poverty builds on the other theories, this regional theory calls attention to the fact that people, institutions, and cultures in certain geographic areas lack the objective resources needed to generate well-being and income, and that they lack the power to claim redistribution. As Shaw (1996, p. 29) points out, "Space is not a backdrop for capitalism, but rather is restructured by it and contributes to the system's survival. The geography of poverty is a spatial expression of the capitalist system."

That poverty is most intense in certain areas is an old observation, and explanations abound in the development literature about why particular regions lack the economic base to compete. Recent explanations include disinvestment, proximity to natural resources, density, diffusion of innovation, and other factors (see Morrill & Wohlenberg, 1971, pp. 57-64). In a thorough review of the literature on rural poverty, Weber and Jensen (2004) note that most literature finds a "rural differential" in poverty, but the spatial effect is not as clearly isolated from individual effects as needed for confidence. Goldsmith and Blakely offer a comprehensive perspective on the link between development and poverty in urban contexts. In their book, *Separate Societies*, they argue that the joint processes of movement of households and jobs away from poor areas in central cities and rural regions creates a "separation of work, residence, and economic, social and political life" (1992, pp. 125). These processes, which we already discussed, are multiplied by racism and political indifference of the localities in which they flourish.

One theoretical perspective on spatial concentrations of poverty comes from economic agglomeration theory. Usually used to explain the emergence of strong industrial clusters (Bradshaw, King, & Wahlstrom, 1999) agglomeration shows how propinquity of similar firms attracts supportive services and markets, which further attracts more firms. In reverse, the propinquity of poverty and the conditions leading to poverty or the consequences of poverty (crime and inadequate social services) generate more poverty, while competitive areas attract business clusters, drawing away from impoverished communities. Low housing prices in such locations may attract more poor persons, for example, leading to housing disinvestment by building owners. In a world in which the criteria for investment is "location, location, location," it is not unreasonable to track investment going to neighborhoods, communities, and regions in which there is already substantial investment, while leaving less attractive areas.

A second theoretical insight is from central place theory and related "human ecology" examinations of urban growth that traces the flows of knowledge and capital (*Rural Sociological Society*, 1990, pp. 71-74). As Niles Hansen (1970) points out, rural areas are often the last stop of technologies, and low wages and competitive pricing dominate production. Infrastructure allows the development of human resources, but if it is lacking, economic activity is stifled that might use these resources. Places left behind (Lyson & Falk, 1992) experience the largest competition in restructuring of the economy because the jobs in these categories are most likely to move to less developed countries. An increasing body of literature holds that advantaged areas stand to grow more than disadvantaged areas even in periods of general economic growth and that there will be some "trickle-down" but not as equalizing as classical economists would have us believe (*Rural Sociological Society*, 1990, pp. 114-119).

A third perspective involves selective out-migration. One part of Wilson's book, *The Truly Disadvantaged* (1987), holds that the people with the highest levels of education, the greatest skills, widest world-view, and most extensive opportunities are those who migrate out from ghetto areas of central city locations to other places. In addition, he argues, these departing people are the community's best role models and are often civic leaders. Rural poverty is similarly attributable to selective out-migration. Population density (both low rural density and the negative impact of high density) is another part of a growing body of theory on spatial variables in social science using the tools of GIS to track spatial dynamics of opportunity and poverty (Bradshaw & Muller, 2003).

18

Anti-Poverty Programs from a Geography of Poverty Perspective

A geographical theory of poverty implies that responses need to be directed to solving the key dynamics that lead to decline in depressed areas while other areas are growing. Instead of focusing on individuals, businesses, governments, welfare systems, or cultural processes, the geographical theory directs community developers to look at places and the processes by which they can become self-sustaining. Interestingly, a few disadvantaged communities around the world are finding their way out of poverty and as such show that it can be done. However, as Morrill and Wohlenberg (1971, pp. 119-120) point out, it is hard.

Some who view regional poverty analyses made proposals in the 1970s to encourage out-migration under the premises that it would reduce poverty to have people in a place where there was a growing economy. Instead, the rural poor people moving to the city became urban poor, with much the same hopeless situation. It is said that much of urban poverty is actually displaced rural poverty.

No matter how badly buffeted by geographical forces, community development programs attempt to help communities identify their assets and address their condition. Many government and foundation programs assist in this effort, and progress can be demonstrated. Several approaches were taken to build stronger geographical areas; the following represent examples rather than an exhaustive list.

- Improved local industry competitiveness through cluster development (Blakely & Bradshaw, 2002) or development of creative communities (Florida, 2002)
- Enterprise zones, redevelopment, and other tax-based incentive programs to promote economic development and channel private investments
- Inclusionary zoning, affordable housing, and similar programs that place conditions on development
- Downtown revitalization and civic improvements that increase amenities and make areas more attractive to stimulate employment and tax revenues
- Investment in infrastructure, including interstate highways, parks, water, waste disposal, schools and other public facilities
- Community organizing
- National and regional reinvestment that shifts funds from one area to another, such as a commitment that helped the Southern United States grow after WW II

The community development approach through community visioning, planning, and especially community investment is central to efforts to turn around distressed areas and places where poverty is rampant. Because community developers understand community, their efforts often leverage community assets, integrate economic development in an area with housing and other spatially allocated factors, and hope that the changes will increase opportunities for residents.

5. Poverty Caused by Cumulative and Cyclical Interdependencies

The previous four theories demonstrate the complexity of the sources of poverty and the variety of strategies to address it. The final theory of poverty I will discuss is by far the most complex and to some degree builds on components of each of the other theories in that it looks at the individual and their community as caught in a spiral of opportunity and problems, and that once problems dominate they close other opportunities and create a cumulative set of problems that make any effective response nearly impossible (Bradshaw, 2000). The cyclical explanation explicitly looks at individual situations and community resources as mutually dependent, with a faltering economy, for example, creating individuals

19

who lack resources to participate in the economy, which makes economic survival even harder for the community since people pay fewer taxes.

This theory has its origins in economics in the work of Myrdal (1957, p. 23) who developed a theory of "interlocking, circular, interdependence within a process of cumulative causation" that helps explain economic underdevelopment and development. Myrdal notes that personal and community well being are closely linked in a cascade of negative consequences, and that closure of a factory or other crisis can lead to a cascade of personal and community problems including migration of people from a community. Thus the interdependence of factors creating poverty actually accelerates once a cycle of decline is started.

One place where the cycle of poverty is clearly defined is in a book on rural education by Jonathan Sher (1977) in which a focus is on the cycle by which education and employment at the community and individual level interact to create a spiral of disinvestment and decline, while in advancing communities the same factors contribute to growth and well being. For example, at the community level, a lack of employment opportunities leads to out-migration, closing retail stores, and declining local tax revenues, which leads to deterioration of the schools, which leads to poorly trained workers, leading firms not to be able to utilize cutting edge technology and to the inability to recruit new firms to the area, which leads back to a greater lack of employment.

This cycle repeats itself at the individual level. The lack of employment leads to lack of consumption and spending because of inadequate incomes, and to inadequate savings, which means that individuals cannot invest in training, and individuals lack the ability to invest in businesses or to start their own businesses, which leads to lack of expansion, erosion of markets, and disinvestment, all of which contribute again to inadequate community opportunities. Health problems and the inability to afford preventive medicine, a good diet, and a healthy living environments become reasons the poor fall further behind. In addition, the cycle of poverty means that people who lack ample income fail to invest in their children's education. Their children do not learn as well in poor quality schools, they fall further behind when they seek employment, and they are vulnerable to illness and poor medical care.

A third level of the cycle of poverty is the perspective that individual lack of jobs and income leads to deteriorating self-confidence, weak motivation, and depression. The psychological problems of individuals are reinforced by association with other individuals, leading to a culture of despair, perhaps a culture of poverty under some circumstances. In rural communities this culture of despair affects leaders as well, generating a sense of hopelessness and fatalism among community leaders.

This brief description of the cycle of poverty incorporates many of the previous theories. It shows how people become disadvantaged in their social context, which then affects psychological abilities at the individual level. The various structural and political factors in the cyclical theory reinforce each other, with economic factors linked to community and to political and social variables. Perhaps its greatest value is that it more explicitly links economic factors at the individual level with structural factors that operate at a geographical level. As a theory of poverty, the cyclical theory shows how multiple problems cumulate, and it allows speculation that if one of the linkages in the spiral were broken, the cycle would not continue. The problem is that the linkages are hard to break because each is reinforced by other parts of the spiraling system.

Anti-Poverty Programs from a Cycle of Poverty Perspective

The complexity of the cycle of poverty means that solutions must be equally complex. Poverty has many aspects but our anti-poverty efforts seem to focus on only part of the solution. Community developers are specialists in appreciating the interdependence of different parts of the community, and their solution is to try to address issues like poverty from a multifaceted approach. Steps taken to break the cycle of poverty are necessarily complex. However, multi-pronged initiatives offer a better solution to poverty than most single approaches. Broad-based community development initiatives are embedded in some of the most successful anti-poverty programs such as community development corporations, local neighborhood revitalization projects, and other efforts linking grass roots problem-solving with diversified organizational management. The limitations to the first four theories of poverty lead us to want to look closely at the cyclical theory. On the whole, the cycle of poverty is rarely mentioned by poverty scholars, but its success in programs such as the Family Independence Initiative (FII) in Oakland gives hope. I highlight this program just as an example of the cycle-breaking efforts of many innovative community-based development organizations.

Helping poor people achieve "self-sufficiency" is an increasingly significant phase in poverty reduction. Although called by various names, the emphasis is on providing both "deep and wide" supports and services for people. A full step from poverty requires six interdependent elements of self-sufficiency that can be identified and tracked (Miller et al., 2004):

1. Income and economic assets,
2. Education and skills,
3. Housing and surroundings (safe, attractive),
4. Access to health care and other needed social services,
5. Close personal ties, as well as networks to others, and
6. Personal resourcefulness and leadership abilities.

An essential piece of this comprehensive approach towards helping individuals from poverty is that there is no way the public can do all of this for every person without first increasing social capital among communities or subcultures of the poor. Miller has a strong belief that strong interpersonal ties as in villages or organized groups can provide shared assistance that professionals can not. The key is helping groups of poor people build supportive communities with shared trust and mutuality. This program consciously seeks the benefits of building social capital (following Putnam, 2000) based on "affinity groups" in which people share common interests from their ethnicity, religion, family history, living area, or other sources of friendship. Building personal ties and leadership linking individual families to their community is perhaps the most challenging part of the FII model. Thus, this model is vital to see the interrelation between financial and material resources and ties to the community.

In facing the overwhelming task of helping both poor people and their poverty neighborhoods, there is no easy answer in breaking the cycle of poverty. Asset-mapping (Kretzmann & McKnight, 1993) offers a way to identify whatever strengths the community has and to use them to solve problems in the most effective way, rather than to spend time identifying problems for which there may be no adequate answers. Moreover, previously existing organizations with roots in the community are generally more effective in bridging the range of problems in a community facing poverty cycles than new single-purpose organizations.

Community development programs structure their efforts around three focal points for breaking the cycle of poverty. These program structures, like the cyclical theory itself, combine strategies and tools from response to the other theories of poverty.

1. Comprehensive Program. The first strategy in breaking the cycle of poverty is to develop comprehensive programs. Comprehensive programs are those that include a variety of services that try to bridge the individual and community needs.

21

2. Collaboration. The key to managing extensive programs without their becoming too uncontrolled is to collaborate among different organizations to provide complementary services that by the combination of efforts, the output is greater than what could be done by any alone. Collaboration involves networks among participants, though the coordination can vary from formal to informal.
3. Community Organizing. Finally, community organizing is a tool by which local people can participate to understand how their personal lives and the community well-being are intertwined. Breaking the cycle of poverty must include individuals to participate as a community in the reversal, just like individuals create the spiral downward when they and their community interact in a cycle of failure. For the poor, empowerment is central to this issue.

It is interesting that this approach to poverty is the least commonly described in the poverty literature, but community-based examples are brought out whenever successes are discussed. There are no comprehensive community-based self-sufficiency programs from the federal government or most states. The bulk of efforts remain experimental and rooted in programs from foundations. In our review of what works to build community and improve the lives of poor people, we recall examples such as the Dudley Street Neighborhood Initiative of Roxbury, Massachusetts (Medoth & Sklar, 1994)—quite the contrast to a welfare office scenario. The key to these successes is as Fung (2004) suggests, empowered participation.

IMPLICATIONS

This essay started with the premise that the theory or explanation of poverty that is held shapes the type of anti-poverty efforts that community developers pursue. The fact that poverty theory addresses individuals, their culture, the social system in which they are embedded, the place in which they live, and the interconnection among the different factors suggests that different theories of poverty look at community needs from quite different perspectives. The diversity and complexity of causes of poverty allow for these multiple points of view. Although none are "wrong" from a community development perspective, it is consequential which theories are applied to particular anti-poverty efforts. How one frames the question of community development determines who receives various types of services and who gets left out.

However, this essay also argues that the first four theories do not fully explore the relation between individuals and their community in the process of placing people in poverty, keeping them there, and potentially getting them out. The growing realization is that individuals are shaped by their community, and communities are as a consequence shaped by their individual members. The strength of the growing interest in social capital by social scientists following Putnam (2000) points to this interdependence in which individuals through association memberships create communities characterized by more trust and reciprocity; and in these communities with more social capital, thousands of small activities are possible that contribute to reversing the spiral of decent into poverty. It is no wonder that communities with strong social capital (or similarly entrepreneurial communities described by Flora and Flora) are shown to be more resilient to adversity—and thus they protect their residents from the spiral into poverty that less civic communities experience when facing similar challenges.

Similarly, community economic and political systems and institutions reflect community values and respond to the social capital that underlies these values. Although reforming social institutions is a policy response to poverty essential in

22

34

poverty communities, Duncan (1999) concludes her book on rural poverty with the observation: communities that value equality and have narrow gaps of opportunity also have institutions reflecting these values and to a greater degree try to not leave anyone behind too far. She thinks that education is the most important local institution capable of reversing this dynamic in poor communities. In their book, *Separate Societies* (1992), Goldsmith and Blakely make the same type of argument. Policies that build community institutions help to close the gap between impoverished and rich communities; many policies that obstruct community institutions help to widen the gap.

Increasing the effectiveness of anti-poverty programs requires that those designing and implementing programs need not only to develop adequate theories of poverty to guide programs, but also to ensure that community development approaches are as comprehensive as possible.

NOTES

1 Several authors distinguish similar lists or theories. Blank (2003) covers six theories that are variations on my first and third theory. Morrill and Wohlenberg (1971) also offer a selection of six theories, though they differ slightly from the ones used here.

2 The perspective developed here is paralleled by discussions in Europe. See for example Alcock (1993).

REFERENCES

Alcock, P. (1993). *Understanding Poverty*. London: Macmillan.

Alinsky, S. D. (1945). *Reveille for Radicals*. Chicago: University of Chicago Press.

Asen, R. (2002). *Visions of Poverty: Welfare Policy and Political Imagination*. East Lansing: Michigan State University Press.

Bettinger, F. (1977). *How I Raised Myself from Failure to Success in Selling*. New York: Simon & Schuster.

Blakely, E. J., & Bradshaw, T. K. (2002). *Planning Local Economic Development*. Thousand Oaks: Sage.

Blank, R. M. (1997). *It Takes a Nation: A New Agenda for Fighting Poverty*. Princeton NJ: Princeton University Press.

Blank, R. M. (2003). Selecting Among Anti-Poverty Policies: Can an Economics Be both Critical and Caring? *Review of Social Economy*, 61(4), 447-471.

Bradshaw, T., & Muller, B. (2003). Shaping policy decisions with spatial analysis. In M. F. Goodchild & D. G. Janelle (Eds.), *Spatially integrated social science: Examples in best practice* (Chapter 17). New York: Oxford University Press.

Bradshaw, T. K. (2000). Complex Community Development Projects: Collaboration, Comprehensive Programs and Community Coalitions in Complex Society. *Community Development Journal*, 35(2), 133-145.

Bradshaw, T. K., King, J. R., & Wahlstrom, S. (1999). Catching on to Clusters. *Planning*, 65(6), 18-21.

Campbell, D., & Wright, J. (2005). Rethinking Welfare School Attendance Policies. *Social Service Review*, 79(1), 2-28.

Chubb, J. E., & Moe, T. M. (1996). Politics, markets, and equality in schools. In M. R. Darby (Ed.), *Reducing Poverty in America: Views and Approaches* (pp. 121-153). Thousand Oaks: Sage.

Darby, M. R. (1996). Facing and Reducing Poverty. In M. R. Darby (Ed.), *Reducing Poverty in America: Views and Approaches* (pp. 3-12). Thousand Oaks, California: Sage.

Duncan, C. M. (1999). *Worlds Apart: Why Poverty Persists in Rural America*. New Haven: Yale University Press.

Egendorf, L. K. Ed. (1999). *Poverty: Opposing Viewpoints*. San Diego: Greenhaven Press.

Epstein, W. M. (1997). *Welfare in America: How Social Science Fails the Poor*. Madison: University of Wisconsin Press.

Fischer, C. S., Hout, M., Jankowski, M. S., Lucas, S. R., Swidler, A., & Voss, K. (1996). *Inequality by Design: Cracking the Bell Curve Myth*. Princeton: Princeton University Press.

Florida, R. (2002). *The Rise of the Creative Class*. New York: Basic books.

23

Fung, A. (2004). *Empowered Participation: Reinventing Urban Democracy*. Princeton: Princeton University Press.

Goering, J., Jeins, J. D., & Richardson, T. M. (2003). What have we learned about housing mobility and poverty deconcentration. In J. Goering, & J. D. Feins (Eds.), *Choosing a Better Life? Evaluating the Moving to Opportunity Social Experiment* (pp. 3-36). Washington D.C.: Urban Institute Press.

Goetz, E. G. (2003). *Clearing the Way: Deconcentrating the Poor*. Washington, D.C.: Urban Institute Press.

Goldsmith, W. W., & Blakely, E. J. (1992). Separate Societies: Poverty and Inequality in American Cities. Philadelphia: Temple University Press.

Goldstein, D. M. (2001). Microenterprise training programs, neo-liberal common sense, and the discourses of self-esteem. In J. Goode, & J. Maskovsky (Eds.), *The New Poverty Studies* (pp. 236-272). New York: New York University Press.

Gwartney, J., & McCaleb, T. S. (1985). Have Anti-poverty Programs Increased Poverty. *Cato Journal*, 5(5), 1-16.

Handler, J. F., & Hasenfeld, Y. (1997). *We the Poor People*. New Haven: Yale University Press.

Hansen, N. (1970). *Poverty and the Urban Crisis*. Bloomington: Indiana State University.

Herrnstein, R. J., & Murray, C. (1994). *The Bell Curve*. New York: Free Press.

Jencks, C. (1996). Can we replace welfare with work? In M. R. Darby (Ed.), *Reducing Poverty in America* (pp. 69-81). Thousand Oaks: Sage.

Jennings, J. (1999). Persistent Poverty in the United States: Review of Theories and Explanations. In L. Kushnick, & J. Jennings (Eds.), *A New Introduction to Poverty: The Role of Race, Power, and Politics*. New York: New York University Press.

Jennings, J., & Kushnick, L. (1999). Introduction: Poverty as Race, Power, and Wealth. In L. Kushnick & J. Jennings (Eds.), *A New Introduction to Poverty: The Role of Race, Power, and Politics* (pp. 1-12). New York: New York University Press.

Kretzmann, J. P., & McKnight, J. L. (1993). *Building Communities from the Inside Out*. Chicago: ACTA Publications.

Landau, M. (1988). *Race, Poverty and the Cities*. Berkeley: Institute of Governmental Studies.

Levitan, S. A., Mangum, G. L., Mangum, S. L., & Sum, A. M. (2003). *Programs in Aid of the Poor*. Baltimore: Johns Hopkins University Press.

Lyson, T. A., & Falk, W. W. (1992). *Forgotten Places: Uneven Development and Underclass in Rural America*. Lawrence: University of Kansas Press.

Maskovsky, J. (2001). Afterword: Beyond the privatist consensus. In J. Goode, & J. Maskovsky (Eds.), *The New Poverty Studies*. New York: New York University Press.

Medoff, P., & Sklar, H. (1994). *Streets of Hope: The Fall and Rise of an Urban Neighborhood*. Cambridge: South End Press

Miller, M. L., Mastuera, M., Chao, M., & Sadowski, K. (2004). *Pathways Out of Poverty: Early Lessons of the Family Independence Initiative*. Oakland: Family Independence Initiative.

Morrill, R. L., & Wohlenberg, E. H. (1971). *The Geography of Poverty*. New York: McGraw Hill.

Moynihan, D. (1965). *The Negro Family*. Washington, D.C.: U.S. Department of Labor, Office of Policy Planning and Research.

Murray, C. (1984). *Losing Ground*. New York: Basic.

Myrdal, G. (1957). *Economic Theory and Underdeveloped Regions*. London: Gerald Duckworth and Co.

O'Connor, A. (2001). *Poverty Knowledge*. Princeton: Princeton University Press.

Page, B. I., & Simmons, J. R. (2000). *What Government Can Do: Dealing With Poverty and Inequality*. Chicago: University of Chicago Press.

Parisi, D., McLaughlin, D. K., Grice, S. M., Taquino, M., & Gill, D. A. (2003). TANF Participation Rates: Do Community Conditions Matter? Rural Sociology, 68(4), 491-512.

Putnam, R. D. (2000). *Bowling Alone*. New York: Simon Schuster.

Quigley, W. P. (2003). *Ending Poverty As We Know It*. Philadelphia: Temple University Press.

Rainwater, L. (1970). Neutralizing the Disinherited: Some Psychological Aspects of Understanding the Poor. In V. L. Allen (Ed.), *Psychological Factors in Poverty* (pp. 9-28). Chicago: Markham.

Rank, M. R. (2004). *One Nation, Underprivileged*. Oxford and New York: Oxford University Press.

24

Rank, M. R., Yoon, H.-S., & Hirschl, T. A. (2003). American Poverty as a Structural Failing: Evidence and Arguments. *Journal of Sociology & Social Welfare*, 30(4), 5.

Riessman, F. (1969). *Strategies against Poverty*. New York: Random House.

Rodgers, H. R., Jr. (2000). *American Poverty in a New Era of Reform*. Armonk, New York: M. E. Sharp.

Ropers, R. H. (1991). *Persistent Poverty: The American Dream Turned Nightmare*. New York: Plenum.

Rural Sociological Society Task Force on Persistent Poverty. (1990). *Persistent Poverty in Rural America*. Boulder: Westview Press.

Ryan, W. (1976). *Blaming the Victim*. New York: Vintage.

Schiller, B. R. (1989). *The Economics of Poverty and Discrimination*. Englewood Cliffs, NJ: Prentice Hall.

Sen, A. (1999). *Development as Freedom*. New York: Anchor.

Shaw, W. (1996). *The Geography of United States Poverty*. New York: Garland Publishing.

Sher, J. P. (1977). School Based Community Development Corporations: A New Strategy for Education and Development in Rural America. In J. P. Sher (Ed.), *Education in Rural America* (pp. 291-346). Boulder: Westview.

Tobin, J. (1994). Poverty in Relation to Macroeconomic Trends, Cycles, Policies. In S. H. Danzinder, G. D. Sandefur, & D. H. Weinberg (Eds.), *Confronting Poverty: Prescriptions for Change*. Cambridge: Harvard University Press.

Valentine, C. A. (1968). *Culture and Poverty*. Chicago: University of Chicago Press.

Weber, B., & Jensen, L. (2004). *Poverty and Place: A Critical Review of Rural Poverty Literature*. Oregon State University: Rural Poverty Research Center, Working Paper 2004-2003.

Weber, M. (2001). *Protestant Ethic and the Spirit of Capitalism*. New York: Routledge.

Wilson, W. J. (1987). *The Truly Disadvantaged: The Inner City, the Underclass and Public Policy*. Chicago: University of Chicago Press.

Zigler, E., & Styfco, S. J. (1996). Reshaping early childhood intervention to be a more effective weapon against poverty. In M. R. Darby (Ed.), *Reducing Poverty in America* (pp. 310-333). Thousand Oaks, CA: Sage.

25

Universal Health Care: Normative Legacies Adrift

Mike Burke and Susan Silver

Introduction

Canada's national health care system, known as medicare, is a source of immense collective achievement. Unlike other facets of Canadian social policy, it sets out a vision of distributive justice based on the principle of "equity." Equity as a distributive principle requires that "need," not ability to pay, be the sole determinant of access and distribution of health services. Equity based on need alone means that no one has a prior entitlement based on status, wealth, race, or other social differences (Churchill, 1987, p. 94). Medicare escaped the "residual trap" (Taylor, 1978), characteristic of other social policy measures, by adopting a universal, one-tier, publicly financed model of insurance covering hospital services and physician services for all Canadians, rich and poor alike. Though aggressively contested, the founding principle of "equity of access" has endured as a normative legacy in relation to "medically necessary" hospital services and doctor's services. Medicare has remained an egalitarian institution in an otherwise inegalitarian society.[1]

While escaping this residual trap, we have not succeeded in quelling privatization pressures that are inevitable in a nation that allows the private market, with its inherent inequities, to prevail as the dominant mechanism for allocating income and other scarce resources. These privatization pressures, while a mainstay of capitalist society, have been increasingly fuelled by the current neo-liberal political climate. Neo-liberalism, as a political ideology, calls for a profound reconfiguration of social welfare responsibilities among the public sector, the private sector, the family, and the non-profit sector (Burke, Mooers, & Shields, 2000). It seeks to minimize the social role of the state by recommodifying public services and, consequently, to expand the space available for the market provision of such services. It justifies this reconfiguration by an appeal to a narrow and distorted discourse of "efficiency" that equates efficiency with cutting public expenditures on social services.[2] In the case of health care, neo-liberalism identifies efficiency as the predominant if not sole criterion of health policy evaluation, asserts that publicly funded

rallying call to progressive social work activists to add their voices and values to the social policy debate, clearly articulating the normative possibilities of collective action.

Normative Policy Framework

A normative analysis attempts to expose and clarify the values that influence policy debates and policy outcomes (Titmuss, 1974). Values are conceptions of the desirable within every individual and society and serve as standards or normative criteria to guide action, attitudes, and judgments. A primary objective of a normative analysis is to clarify and understand the values that represent a nation's policy choices (Silver, 1993). Public policies, thus, constitute choices among alternative normative intentions, among competing perceptions of the common good (Kronick, 1982). Normative choices are fundamentally distributive, defining what constitutes a "social" as opposed to a "private" good, and setting out the conditions of allocation.

Titmuss distinguished between residual/selective and institutional/universalist modes of distribution (1968). Services delivered on a residual/selective basis almost always involve means tests that foster "both the sense of personal failure and the stigma of a public burden" (Titmuss, 1968, p. 134). With residually delivered services or programs, state responsibility begins only when the private realms of the family and the market fail. In contrast, universalist services are distributed as a social right, accessible to all citizens in a manner that does not involve any "humiliating loss of status, dignity or self respect" (Titmuss, 1968, p. 129). There is no assumption of personal blame or failure. The service or program in question is considered an appropriate institutional, and not residual, function of the state. Mediating this universalist discourse of institutional function, Ife (1997) has introduced a relativist understanding of need. Responding to the postmodern critique of universalism, Ife has offered a humanist vision in which social justice is both an expression of universal understandings of human rights, and an endorsement of contextualized and culturally appropriate definitions of need (Ife, 1997, p. 126).

Esping-Andersen (1989) maintains that the essence of a welfare state is its capacity to grant "social rights," rights that are embedded in citizenship and distributed outside of the market. The concept of decommodification is used to refer to the degree to which a service or basic good is detached from the market as the distributive mechanism. Social rights cease being commodities, emancipating individuals from their market dependence (Esping-Andersen, 1989, p. 21). Commodification in health care refers generally to an increasing reliance on the market for either the financing or delivery of health care services (Esping-Anderson, 1989; Offe, 1984).

With this framework, we will now explore the normative foundations of medicare, specifically examining the set of social rights and allocative principles that were established.

systems of health care are inefficient by definition, and concludes that the state's role in health care must be severely curtailed in order to contain public costs. This definition of efficiency threatens to undermine the *quality* of our medicare system, disrupt considerations of equity, and exacerbate disparities in the health of Canadians.

These issues are critical, and the stakes are high for Canadians in general and for vulnerable populations such as Aboriginal peoples and racialized immigrant groups specifically. However, with total health care expenditures exceeding $130 billion in 2004 alone (Canadian Institute for Health Information [CIHI], 2004), proponents of privatization stand to achieve huge financial rewards. As expressed by an American health care firm, medicare is "one of the largest unopened oysters in the Canadian economy" (quoted in Canadian Centre for Policy Alternatives [CCPA], 2000, p. 4).

These are the fundamental choices facing policy-makers. Do we reaffirm and strengthen the public system and thereby the equity principle, or seek to further accelerate the neo-liberal program of privatization and the inevitable erosion of accessibility and quality? The health care debate is, however, not explicitly framed in terms of choices, but as a fiscal imperative obligating privatization.

This chapter begins with the assumption, borrowed from Richard Titmuss, that values are central to policy debates. Titmuss contends that "policy is all about values" (1974, p. 132), and he defines policy as the "principles that govern action directed towards given ends" (p. 23). Titmuss further argues that the goal of policy analysis is to "expose more clearly the value choices confronting society" (p. 136). Using this framework for policy analysis, this chapter initially examines the normative foundations or dominant values that framed the original intentions of medicare. The chapter then briefly reviews the early successes and the political shift from a concern with equity to a concern with cost control. Recent federal and provincial commissions and health policy initiatives are reviewed in relation to their contribution to the debate over the future of medicare. Three challenges to the normative foundations are then examined. These challenges, central to the neo-liberal project, are (1) the retrenchment of the federal role in relation to national standards; (2) the privatization thrust, and with it the increasing commodification of health care services; and (3) the relegation of responsibility from the public sector to the family and the community. These challenges threaten to erode the normative foundations of medicare and widen the gap between the "promise of citizenship and the reality of exclusion" (Galabuzi, 2004, p. 246) experienced by members of vulnerable populations such as racialized groups and immigrants.

Medicare's accomplishments extend far beyond the field of health care. Medicare is a beacon, a constant reminder of the possibilities of equality and inclusiveness within Canadian society. The ties that bind Canadians together are the shared and common experiences that result from a consistent interpretation of our fundamental national values. The chapter concludes with a

Normative Foundations of Medicare

Medicare originated with two pieces of legislation: the Hospital Insurance and Diagnostic Services Act of 1957, insuring hospital services; and the Medical Care Act of 1966, insuring doctor's services. Four federal–provincial cost-sharing conditions were imposed:

1. Universal coverage: every provincial resident must be covered under uniform terms and conditions

2. Portability: requires that all Canadians can receive health care services across Canada

3. Comprehensiveness: all medically necessary hospital services and physician services are to be covered

4. Public administration: each provincial plan must be publicly administered on a non-profit basis without the involvement of the private sector.[3]

By the end of 1971, every province had taken advantage of the federal cost-sharing incentive and approximately 100% coverage was attained in Canada.[4] The national plan was achieved through interlocking ten provincial plans, all of which shared certain common features. Canadians are free to choose their own physician and hospital. There is no limit on the benefits payable as long as medical need is determined. There are no limits on the number of days of hospital care or the number of visits to physicians. With respect to the scope of coverage, benefits are intended to be virtually complete. There is no distinction between basic and non-basic services. Instead, all medically necessary physician and hospital services are covered by all provincial plans.

From the onset, physician and acute-care hospital services have been the defining national aspects of our health care system. Specifically excluded from coverage were psychiatric hospitals, tuberculosis sanatoria, and institutions providing custodial care, such as nursing homes. These categories were excluded on the grounds that care in such hospitals was already being provided by the provinces, virtually without cost to provincial residents (LeClair, 1975). Other services not covered under the cost-shared agreement were home care services, ambulances services, drugs administered outside hospitals, dentists, and any health care services not provided by physicians. These omissions have resulted in an over-emphasis on doctors and hospitals, resulting in the lack of comparable national standards across these other health care services.[5]

With medicare, a right to "medically necessary" health care services was established and medical services were "de-commodified." Access to these services was determined solely on the basis of medical need and not on one's ability to pay. The doctor's office and the acute care hospital ward became "public" spaces where all Canadians shared common experiences of citizenship. Consequently, the principle of equal access became the normative foundation of medicare. The principle of equal access was further embedded by the stipulations that over 90% of residents must be covered by provincial plans and that each provincial plan was to operate on a non-profit basis and

be administered by a public agency. These two conditions essentially eliminated any incentives for private insurers and, with it, a private tier of coverage. Our one-tier system has successfully precluded an "exit option" for Canadians wishing to "jump the queue." The lack of an exit option requires that the system meet the expectations of all Canadians, a necessary prerequisite for high-quality public services.

Medicare further established a dynamic, and often tense, federal–provincial relationship that has remained a mainstay of the continuous health policy debates. Canadian constitutional practice has evolved to make the provision of health care services primarily a provincial responsibility. The Constitution further generated a fiscal imbalance in which the pre-eminent ability to raise money resides with the federal government while the significant obligations to spend money for health, education, and other social services reside with the provincial governments (Van Loon & Whittington, 1971). Many provinces initially resisted or otherwise disagreed with trading their jurisdictional powers for federal funds. Through the federal conditional grant and the cost-shared program, the federal government gained access to areas of health and social assistance. However, the degree of "shared" responsibility in medicare was unparalleled in Canadian social policy at the time.[6]

Much to the dismay of reluctant provincial governments and medical associations, the four program conditions for cost sharing resulted in a substantive set of national standards that were uniformly implemented across all provincial plans. The federal government's pivotal role as the guardian of national standards was indelibly etched in the foundations of medicare.

Early Success

By the end of 1971, every province had been in medicare for at least one full year, and 100% coverage was achieved in virtually every province. Canada experienced marked changes in many vital statistics. Prior to the introduction of the Hospital Insurance Program, Canada's infant mortality rate was approximately 40% higher than Australia's, 30% higher than that of England, and 5% higher than that of the United States. By the end of 1971, Canada's infant mortality rate was almost identical to Australia's and England's and 10% lower than that of the United States. Maternal mortality rates also dropped by a third towards the end of 1971, and studies indicated that pregnant women were seeking medical attention a few months earlier than they had been (LeClair, 1975, p. 43)

With respect to utilization rates, hospital admission rates increased from 143.4 per 1,000 in the mid-fifties to 165.9 per 1,000 in 1970 (Taylor, 1987, p. 417). By enacting the hospital insurance program ten years before the physicians' services insurance program, Canadians became accustomed to using hospitals wherever possible. During the mid-1970s Canada had the highest hospital admission rate in the world and spent 60% of all health care expenditures on institutional care (Van Loon, 1978, p. 457). Physician utilization patterns also reflected an initial spurt of about a 4% increase within the first year of medicare (LeClair, 1975, p. 47). By 1975, it was also recognized that adding a new physician to the system costs an additional $200,000 to $250,000 per year in health services utilization (Van Loon, 1978, p. 457).

By 1974, medicare had successfully replaced income-based access with needs-based access, with consumption patterns more closely aligned with health care risks (Manga, 1987). The association between income and health care utilization was inversed, with the lowest income groups consuming more than double the health care services of the higher groups (National Council of Welfare, 1982, p. 23). Total government spending on health services by 1976 accounted for 7.2% ($7.1 billion, or 10.8 billion in current dollars as derived by CIHI) of the GNP in Canada. At that time the United States was spending at 8.6% of GNP on health care, while England was spending 5.4% of GNP (Van Loon, 1978, p. 456).

With these early successes, the politics of medicare quickly moved from a concern with equal access to issues of cost containment. More recently, a social rights analysis has been eclipsed by a preoccupation with controlling, and significantly reducing, the public role in the financing and delivery of health care to Canadians. We will now more closely examine the current debate and the related challenges to medicare's normative legacies.

Current Challenges

Canadians are reminded, on an almost daily basis, of the fragility of the health care system and warned of the pressure points that are destined to destroy it. Newspaper headlines are replete with stories of insured services being delisted; increasing numbers of private, for-profit clinics and hospitals; ever-growing waiting lists for medical treatment and diagnostic services; overcrowded emergency departments; escalating conflicts between health care providers and governments; shortages of nurses and physicians; shorter hospital stays coupled with decreasing home care budgets; an increasing expectation that families and friends assume responsibility for care in the home; and the repeated posturing of federal and provincial governments, each accusing the other of funding shortfalls.

Recently, there has been an intensification of the debate on the future of health care in Canada, exemplified by the explosion of intergovernmental negotiations on health and the proliferation of federal and provincial health reports. This debate centres on two related issues: (1) securing and allocating sufficient resources to ensure the sustainability of the health care system and the respective roles of the public and private sectors in the funding and delivery of health care; and (2) constructing adequate and transparent mechanisms of public accountability, and the relative weight of federal and provincial priorities in those mechanisms. The continuous intergovernmental acrimony and deal making over the past decade can be understood in this light. The provinces have been struggling to recover the health funds lost in the initial cuts in the mid-1990s, and some of the difficulty that delayed full

intergovernmental agreement on health care was related to substantial differences over both the level of federal funding for health and extent of federal control of accountability mechanisms.

The questions of sustainability and accountability also figure prominently in major federal and provincial reports on health care. In his interim report in February 2002, Roy Romanow noted that Canadians' concerns with the fiscal sustainability of health care were undermining public confidence in the system (Commission on the Future of Health Care in Canada, 2002a; 2002b). He framed his final report in November in an expanded conceptualization of sustainability and remarked that "The changes I am proposing are intended to strengthen and modernize medicare, and place it on a more sustainable footing for the future" (Commission on the Future of Health Care in Canada, 2002c, p. 3). The final report calls for a strong federal role in a national, transparent, and accountable health care system. It recommends that a new "Canadian Health Covenant" be established, in part to clarify the responsibilities of governments in the funding and delivery of health care; that accountability be added as a sixth principle of the Canada Health Act; and that a new institutional means—the Health Council of Canada—be created to implement accountability (Commission on the Future of Health Care in Canada, 2002d).

Within the context set by sustainability and federal-provincial dispute, the Canadian health care debate is insistently fuelled by parallel forms of neo-liberal welfare state dismantling, three of which will be examined here: the decentralization of the federal system of government, the commodification of health care, and the relegation of health care. Taken together, these forms of dismantling constitute an unmistakable shift from collective to individual responsibility and from universal to residual modes of distribution, as health care increasingly becomes a private commodity.

Decentralization

The debate about the decentralization of the Canadian federation is intimately linked to the debate about national standards in social policy. Arguments for and against decentralization are often arguments about which level of government should take the primary fiscal and legislative responsibility for social policy. Although the provinces have primary constitutional jurisdiction for the general area of health care policy, the historical use of federal spending power has given Ottawa a large role in determining the resources available for health and in setting the broad conditions of health care provision.

Subsequent to the establishment of medicare in the 1960s, the use of the federal spending power in relation to national standards reached a pinnacle with the Canada Health Act (CHA), passed in 1984. The purpose of the CHA was to consolidate the Hospital Insurance and Diagnostic Services Act of 1957 and the Medical Care Act of 1966, and to define more precisely the terms and conditions upon which federal payments would continue to be made. The Act reaffirmed the four program conditions that had been previously included in the Medical Care Act of 1966 and added a fifth: reasonable access. The most controversial aspect of the Act pertained to Section 12(1), in which the conditions relating to the criterion of accessibility were specifically operationalized. The Act stated that provincial plans "must provide for insured health services on uniform terms and conditions and on a basis that does not impede or preclude, either directly or indirectly whether by charges made to insured persons or otherwise the reasonable access to those services by insured persons." For every dollar of extra-billing or hospital user fees, the federal government would withhold one dollar from its cash contribution. With the CHA, the "equity of access" was affirmed as a national standard, and with the elimination of user fees, the CHA did succeed in harnessing efforts at privatizing physician and hospital services.

A decade later, the trend towards decentralization of power or "provincialism" is unmistakable and is supported by both Ottawa and the provinces. The passage of the Canada Health and Social Transfer (CHST) in 1996 clearly signalled this trend. The CHST consolidated funding into a single block transfer for health, post-secondary education, social assistance, and social services. According to Ottawa, one purpose of the fundamental restructuring of social policy arrangements embodied in the CHST was to decentralize power by providing provinces with "greater flexibility in determining priorities and in designing programs to meet local needs" (Canada, 1996, p. 10). Battle and Torjman regard the CHST as "a watershed in the history of Canadian social policy" that consolidates "a withdrawal of both federal *dollars* and federal *presence* from the provincially run welfare, social services, post-secondary education and health programs that constitute a significant part of Canada's social security system" (Battle and Torjman, 1995, p. 1). They also point out that it represents a declining federal commitment to maintaining national standards in social policy.[7] Others have likewise suggested that strengthening the federal presence is the only way to prevent the erosion of national standards in health care and other areas of social policy (Barlow, 2002; Begin, 1999; Osberg, 1996; Silver, 1996).

The creation of the CHST, with the announcement that Ottawa *was* decreasing federal transfer payments to the provinces by $7 billion over two years, underlined a key dimension of the decentralization debate: What is the appropriate federal–provincial balance between the level of responsibility for health care and the level of control over the fiscal resources necessary to fund health care?[8] From the moment the federal government announced the CHST cuts, provincial governments have been lobbying Ottawa to reverse them. As a result of this intense private bargaining and heated public disputation, Ottawa has regularly increased health funds to the provinces since 1996.

The Social Union Framework Agreement (SUFA) of February 1999 between the federal government, all provincial governments except Quebec, and the territories was in no small part about health care funding. SUFA was accom-

panied by a side agreement on health care that saw Ottawa increase CHST funding by $11.5 billion over five years (Canada, 1999a; Canada, 1999b, Canada, 1999c, chap. 4). SUFA is also a prime example of the linkages between decentralized federalism and declining federal interest in maintaining national standards. In the Agreement, Ottawa reconfirmed its policy not to introduce any new national initiatives in health care, post-secondary education, and social assistance without the agreement of a majority of provincial governments; recognized the provincial role in identifying the national priorities and objectives of such initiatives; and acknowledged the authority of the provinces and territories to determine the details of program design and mix.

SUFA evoked much negative comment from social policy advocates and other observers. Recalling the opposition to the CHST, critics noted that the Social Union discussions indicated a weakening of federal support for enforceable national standards in health care and social assistance. They also noted that the requirement of gaining majority provincial support for new initiatives would probably prove to be an insurmountable obstacle to the creation of new programs in pharmacare, home care, and child care (Council of Canadians, 1999; PovNet, 1999; Walkom, 1999).

The three intergovernmental health agreements reached since 1999 committed Ottawa to increase health funding by a total of $23.4 billion over five years (2000), $34.8 billion over five years (2003), and $41.3 billion over ten years (2004) (Canadian Intergovernmental Conference Secretariat, 2000; Canada, 2003a; Canada, 2004b).[9] The 2003 accord also resulted in the creation of two new transfers, formed from the partition of the CHST: the Canada Health Transfer (CHT) for health and the Canada Social Transfer (CST) for post-secondary education, social assistance, and social services, including early childhood development (Canada, 2003b, p. 83). Establishing the CHT was consistent with the Romanow Commission's call for the creation of a separate transfer dedicated to health (Commission on the Future of Health Care in Canada, 2002d, p. 65).

In his final report on Canadian health care in November 2002, Romanow stated that the "medicare bargain" committed the federal government to provide a cash contribution equal to 25% of provincial–territorial expenditures on publicly insured health services. He found that, in fiscal year 2001–02, the federal cash share was only 18.7% of relevant provincial–territorial expenditures. To meet its commitment of paying a 25% share, Ottawa would be required to spend an additional $15 billion between 2003 and 2006 (Commission on the Future of Health Care in Canada, 2002d, p. 64; 2002c). The Romanow Gap became the popular term used to describe this shortfall in federal funding of provincial–territorial health expenditures. A major part of provincial dissatisfaction with the 2003 health accord was that it did not provide sufficient federal funds to eliminate the Gap (Laghi & McCarthy, 2003).

The 2004 Health Agreement closed the Gap by providing additional federal funds, more money in fact than the Romanow Commission had recommended. Part of that funding included an annual 6% CHT escalator, of the kind Romanow had proposed, to ensure predictable growth in the federal share of provincial–territorial expenditures under the Canada Health Act; but if the funding gap disappeared, another Romanow Gap emerged in the accord's vague provisions on conditionality, accountability, and enforcement.

In an article published on the eve of the intergovernmental accord, Romanow warned of the need to address "unresolved obstacles to a truly renewed health care system" by developing clear accountability structures that ensure additional monies are spent on effecting positive change in the system and by expanding coverage under the Canada Health Act (Romanow, 2004). It was in precisely these areas that the provisions of the 2004 health accord fell significantly short of the recommendations of the Romanow Commission.

On the question of accountability, the Romanow Commission envisioned a strong and vibrant Health Council playing a crucial role in (1) sustaining effective federal involvement in health care to ensure similar levels of quality and service around the country; and (2) developing a new approach to national leadership founded on the cooperation of federal, provincial, and territorial governments (Commission on the Future of Health Care in Canada, 2002d, chap. 2). The Health Council described in the 2003 and 2004 accords may prove to be that kind of institution, but the early prognosis is not promising. The Klein government in Alberta, for instance, has refused to cooperate with the Health Council and has not yet named a councillor to sit on it.

The 2004 agreement's provisions on wait times are another instructive example of the governments' ambivalent position on accountability and enforcement. The issue of wait times is crucial. The first ministers themselves agree in the accord "that access to timely care across Canada is our biggest concern and a national priority" (Canada, 2004b, n.p.). It is the issue on which the Supreme Court of Canada rendered its highly controversial and potentially far-reaching judgment in the Chaoulli case (Chaoulli v. Quebec, 2005). The accord's section on reducing wait times contains some of the strongest governmental commitments on accountability. It talks of the need for developing indicators, establishing targets, and reducing wait times. It sets numerous deadlines by which these tasks should be accomplished. Importantly, however, it fails to specify any consequences for missing deadlines. There was much speculation that at least three provincial governments would fail to meet the deadline of December 31, 2005, for formulating evidence-based benchmarks for medically appropriate wait times for selected medical and diagnostic services (Bueckert, 2005a). It now appears that the deadlines may be met, but in a restricted way that offers limited help to patients (Galloway, 2005). The failure to establish extensive benchmarks by the agreed date puts other wait-time deadlines in jeopardy.

The accord's separate and specific arrangements for Quebec, in which the Quebec government states that it will follow its own health plans and

objectives in accordance with its fiscal capacity, may simply be an example of Ottawa's formal recognition of the need for "asymmetrical federalism" (Canada, 2004a); but, given the tenor of the accord's accountability provisions, such arrangements may also be an indication of the federal government's abiding lack of interest in enforcing national standards in health care.

If the 2004 accord fails to heed Romanow's warning on the need to develop meaningful structures of accountability and enforcement, it likewise fails to respond to his call for expanding health care coverage under the Canada Health Act. The final report of the Romanow Commission foresees that home care, prescription drugs and diagnostic services will be included in the Act. The 2004 accord does not bring these health care sectors into medicare nor does it attempt to modernize or expand the Canada Health Act in any way, with the result that the accord's provisions are not enforceable under the Act and stand entirely outside its criteria and conditions.

The 2004 intergovernmental agreement on health is an example of "decentralizing federalism": the absence of meaningful structures and processes of accountability, the lack of conditionality and the failure to strengthen the Canada Health Act point to ineffective federal engagement and declining national standards. As Boismenu and Jenson suggest, though, this debate goes beyond the question of decentralizing power from Ottawa to the provinces:

despite often being presented in the language of "decentralizing federalism," and sometimes vaunted as a solution to the constitutional tangle of Quebec–Canada relations, the social union concept is more than that. It is *not a shift within federalism* of decision-making power going from one level of government to the other, however. Rather, the power that is being decentralized is going from states to markets, and from public to private. The private sector, communities, families, and individuals are being exhorted to take more responsibility, as governments scale back their roles. At the same time … the nine provinces acting together assert themselves as *co-managers* of the social union, seeking to establish institutional guarantees that they will be consulted and involved in Ottawa's actions in their areas of constitutional jurisdiction. (Boismenu & Jenson, 1998, pp. 60–61)

Commodification

This shift from states to markets and from public to private brings us to the second challenge to medicare, that of intensified commodification. In the process of commodification, health care service itself becomes a commodity, that is, it becomes a "unit of output" that is produced and packaged for sale in the sphere of capital accumulation (Leys, 2001, p. 84). The intricate and ever-changing mix of public and private principles in Canadian health insurance obscures some of the trends towards commodification (Deber, 2000;

Deber et al., 1998; Naylor, 1986), but there are identifiable trends whose recognition is made easier by explicit comparisons that policy-makers draw between the proper roles and responsibilities of the public and private sectors.

First, the discourse of health care reform is becoming increasingly characterized by the language, meanings, values, and assumptions of the market. Deber et al. (1998) capture the generality of, and tensions between, the old and new paradigms in health:

> In general, every industrialized country, with the exception of the United States, espouses the principle of universal health coverage for its people as a right of citizenship, rather than as a commodity to be bought and sold in the open market. Historically, principles of universality and equity of access have been the driving force behind decisions about financing health. These principles have recently been challenged as the general social and economic climate has turned to questions of efficiency and cost-effectiveness. (Deber et al., 1998, p. 504)

In the neo-liberal conception of efficiency, to decrease waste and increase sustainability, public expenditures on social policy must be curtailed by expanding the role of the market and diminishing the role of the state.

The tensions between the binaries of public–private and state-market are well illustrated by the different positions taken by the final reports of the Romanow Commission and the Senate Committee on Social Affairs, Science and Technology, chaired by Michael Kirby. While both reports recommend the continuation of government as the single payer for publicly insured hospital and doctor services, they diverge sharply on the question of the private delivery of health care.[10] The Romanow Commission is not only strongly opposed to the expansion of private provision but suggests that current levels be curtailed: "Rather than subsidize private facilities with public dollars, governments should choose to ensure that the public system has sufficient capacity and is universally accessible" (Commission on the Future of Health Care in Canada, 2002d, p. 9). The Kirby report, in contrast, is much more favourable to the commodification of health care. It recommends that government be neutral or indifferent on the question of public versus private delivery, and proposes the development of internal competitive markets among service providers that would, in all likelihood, see a steady expansion of private delivery (Canadian Health Coalition, 2002; Courchene, 2003; Kirby, 2002; Kirby & Keon, 2004; Senate, 2002).

Another example of commodification is the process of "privatization by default" or "passive privatisation" in which the private share of health care spending has been slowly creeping up over time, until very recently (Tholl, 1994, p. 61). In virtually each year from 1984 to 1997, private health spending increased faster than did public expenditure. In this period, the private share of health expenditures rose from under 24% to almost 30%. The discrepancy in public and private annual growth rates was particularly wide from 1992 to 1996, years in which governmental restraint measures held the average annual

rate of growth of public health spending to only 0.6%, the lowest in twenty years. In the late 1990s, the situation was reversed, with public growth higher than private growth, reflecting particularly heavy governmental spending on capital projects and drugs. By 2002, private sector growth had recovered and the private share of spending stood at 30.3% (CIHI, 2001, 2004).

The commodification of health care is, however, a much more vigorous, explicit, and purposeful process than is suggested by the term "passive privatisation." To be sure, the passive privatization of health care that characterized most of this period was partly the result of technological change. Increasingly, health care was moving out of sectors dominated by public insurance, like hospital and medical services, and into sectors in which private financing played a much larger role, like home care and drug therapy outside hospitals. This kind of privatization was not simply passive, however. It was also the result of proactive governmental decisions that constrained the growth of public health expenditures, removed health services from coverage under the public insurance plan, encouraged a kind of asymmetrical competition that marginalized not-for-profit health care providers and privileged for-profit providers, and failed to reinvest in community care the resources that were saved by closing and restructuring hospitals (Baranek, 2000; Browne, 2000; Epps & Flood, 2001; Fuller, 1998; Tuohy, Flood, & Stabile, 2001).

Pat Armstrong uses the phrase "cascading privatization" to describe the process in which decisions made by different health care players interact to reinforce the privatization of the heath care system: the federal government adopts the neo-liberal project and slashes social spending; neo-liberal provincial governments justify their own project of cutting costs, downloading services, and closing hospitals by pointing to federal cutbacks; the community health care sector, which remains seriously under-resourced, is overwhelmed by the spiralling demands for its services; these engineered problems in the publicly funded system are used as evidence that medicare is not working and become a rationale for further privatization; the principle of universality is eroded as the wealthy pay for private health services; and the publicly funded system becomes increasingly vulnerable to additional privatization (Browne, 2000; CCPA, 2000).

The recent Supreme Court decision in the Chaoulli case gives new impetus to the already vibrant dynamic of privatization. In a 4–3 ruling on June 9, 2005, the Court invalidated those sections of Quebec's laws that disallow private health insurance for medically necessary services delivered under the publicly funded plan. The ruling affects only Quebec's laws, and the Court suspended the effect of its judgement for one year, but the implications of the case are potentially far reaching.[11] In a scathing critique of the questionable legal, political, and evidentiary bases of the majority opinion, the three dissenting justices point out the likely devastating consequences of the ruling: (1) it is the policy of the Canada Health Act and its provincial offspring "to provide health care based on need rather than on wealth or status"; (2) "it cannot be contested that as a matter of principle, access to private health care

reluctant to become the champion of the 1997 recommendation of the National Forum on Health that home care be considered "an integral part of publicly funded health services" (National Forum on Health, 1997, p. 21).[14]

Overcoming the Challenges

Paradoxically, the pressure for privatization continues to grow in the face of overwhelming and incontrovertible evidence that undermines virtually all the assumptions and conclusions of privatized health care. Recent examinations of the Canadian health care system show that the sustainability of the system is not in question (Friends of Medicare, 2002; Murnighan, 2001) and that there is no fiscal crisis in health, although public opinion polls show that there is a popular perception of crisis (Deber et al., 1998; Evans, Barer, Lewis, Rachlis, & Stoddart, 2000; Rachlis, Evans, Lewis, & Barer, 2001). Increasing the role of the private sector in health will expand, not contain, costs and jeopardize equity of access, the quality of care, and the comprehensiveness of coverage (Deber et al., 1998; Evans et al., 2000; Tuohy, Flood, & Stabile, 2002). Downloading responsibilities and offloading costs to the family and non-profit sector will place a disproportionate burden on women because of their social role as primary caregiver. This will threaten the quality of care, as informal caregivers are increasingly asked to provide sophisticated kinds of care requiring skills that they do not have. It will further increase total costs to the system in the form of increased stress on caregivers and inadequate care of patients, and lead to a debilitating transformation of the non-profit sector as it loses government support and competes with for-profit providers (Browne, 1996; CCPA, 2000; Hall & Reed, 1998).

Direct comparisons of the relative benefits of publicly and privately financed health care systems end with the endorsement of the public system. One such review suggests "the evidence generally points away from increased private financing as a means to achieve effective health care reform," and it concludes that "in order to achieve the goals of a publicly funded health care sector (to allocate care on the basis of need and not ability to pay) requires that the *funding* of the system remain concentrated within the realm of the public and quasi-public (social insurance systems)" (Flood, Stabile, & Tuohy, 2001, p. 42).

Government failure to expand public coverage under the Canada Health Act and to attach meaningful conditions to the infusion of federal funds has put the entire system of medicare at risk by affording enhanced legitimacy to proposals that privilege private over public health care. This marginalization of arguments supporting medicare occurs partly because the health care debate is, in its essentials, a political matter. Just as the so-called fiscal crisis in health is less an economic trend than a political construction, so the case for privatization is based more on political myth than reasoned argument.

Further, mounting evidence of the disparities in health, disproportionately experienced by vulnerable and racialized populations (see Beiser & Stewart,

based on wealth rather than need contradicts one of the key social policy objectives expressed in the Canada Health Act"; (3) "it is Quebeckers who have the money to afford private medical insurance and can qualify for it who will be the beneficiaries" of the Court's decision; and (4) "the proposed constitutional right to a two-tier health system for those who can afford private medical insurance would precipitate a seismic shift in health policy for Quebec" that could frustrate the realization of the objectives of the Canada Health Act (*Chaoulli v. Quebec*, 2005).

In an article written the day after the ruling, Roy Romanow concluded that the Chaoulli decision "certainly creates the appearance that the slide to privatization has increased in the province of Quebec" (Romanow, 2005). Two weeks later, he had stiffened his opposition to the ruling and warned that it could undermine medicare (Bueckert, 2005b). Certainly, the Court's decision helped prepare the ideological and policy ground for the Klein government's enthusiasm for increasing the weight of private health insurance in Alberta and the Canadian Medical Association's recent policy resolutions in favour of the privatization of health care (Friends of Medicare, 2005; Picard, 2005).

Relegation

Relegating health care is a third challenge to medicare. Relegation refers to the direct or indirect transfer of responsibility for health care to the family and the non-profit sector.[12] It involves shifting the provision and costs of care to family and friends, volunteer labour, and organizations that rely disproportionately on volunteer labour or are otherwise in the non-profit sector. There is an observable trend towards relegating health care, with more and more patients receiving informal care at home from friends and relatives or in the community from volunteers and voluntary organizations (Armstrong & Armstrong, 1996). Governments certainly see relegation as an attractive policy option. For some years, both the federal and provincial levels of government have been calling for increased voluntarism and developing initiatives to encourage donations and enhance the resources available to charitable organizations (Canada, 1997; Ontario, 1995).

Governments often use the progressive language of health promotion, community development, social empowerment, and mutual support to justify this shift in the responsibility for health care; but the predominant concerns of the neo-liberal agenda in health care demand that relegation be used to contain or externalize costs. This view of the economic rationale for relegating health care is consistent with the conclusion of a recent study of home care in Ontario: it is likely that the "real driving force of the shift to home care has been governments' desire to reduce costs" (Browne, 2000, p. 82).[13] The transfer of funds to the family and community sector usually lags behind the transfer of responsibility. Governments are not generally willing to make a substantial financial commitment to home care and, consequently, have been

2005; Galabuzi, 2004; Raphael, 2004) signify the human casualties of an eroding health care system combined with the neo-liberal social policy agenda. As examined by Galabuzi, "other determinants such as income, gender, race, immigrant status and geography increasingly define the translation of universality as unequally differentiated" (2004, p. 246). Groups particularly vulnerable to low health status include Aboriginal peoples, immigrants, refugees, the disabled, the poor, the homeless, and other groups in precarious life circumstances. For example, Aboriginal babies in Canada are three times more likely to die in their first year of life than non-Aboriginal babies (Beiser & Stewart, 2005, p. S4). While immigrants make up 18% of Canada's population, they account for almost 60% of all cases of tuberculosis (Beiser, 2005, p. S32).

Meeting these challenges to medicare and to growing health disparities requires that health care analysts and social work activists do things differently. They need to do a better job at popular education by engaging and mobilizing social constituencies in support of progressive political change. The battle for medicare and for the health of all Canadians will not be won in academic journals, although it may be lost there. It will be won by constructing a political coalition to oppose the disproportionate and debilitating political influence wielded by neo-liberalism.

Notes

1. This conception of "equity" was formulated in Silver (1993).
2. This argument is based on the analysis in Burke (2000).
3. Reasonable access subsequently became the fifth independent program condition in the 1984 Canada Health Act.
4. When the program began on July 1, 1968, only Saskatchewan and British Columbia were operating schemes that were eligible for cost-sharing.
5. The earlier proposals contained in the Heagerty report on Health Insurance in 1945 had included the full range of benefits such as dental, pharmaceutical, and nursing services, but were then omitted, to be implemented in the next series of health care reforms which, due to costs, never did materialize (Guest, 1985).
6. In contrast, with the Canada Assistance Plan, also passed in 1966, the federal government neither specified the precise eligibility conditions nor the level of benefits. Consequently, very little in the way of national standards of assistance have emerged. The amount of provincial discretion permitted by the legislation has resulted in a social assistance system that is extremely complex, treats similar cases of need differently, relies on an intrusive and stigmatizing determination of need, and sets assistance rates well below the most conservative poverty lines (National Council of Welfare, 1987, p. 7).
7. In recent budgets, Ottawa has increased the cash component of the CHST, but the money restored to health does not equal the money taken from health.
8. In the 1995 federal budget that announced the restructuring of social transfer payments, the CHST was originally called the Canada Social Transfer (CST).
9. CHST funding increases support not only for health but also for post-secondary education, social assistance, and social services.
10. Earlier Kirby reports seemed to contemplate a much larger role for private insurance than did the final report (Canadian Labour Congress, 2002; Senate, 2001a; Senate, 2001b).
11. See the useful caveats in CUPE's analysis of the Chaoulli decision (CUPE, 2005).

12. This definition is similar to but broader than what Brodie calls refamilialization: "the growing consensus among policy-makers that families (whatever their form) should look after their own and that it is up to the neo-liberal state to make sure that they do" (Brodie, 1996, 22–23).
13. The quoted phrase is emphasized in the original.
14. As Health minister, Allan Rock showed a rhetorical commitment to home care and pharmacare but did not transform the rhetoric into public policy (Canada, 1998).

References

Armstrong, P., & Armstrong, H. (1996). *Wasting away: The undermining of Canadian health care.* Toronto: Oxford University Press.

Baranek, P.M. (2000). *Long term care reform in Ontario: The influence of ideas, institutions and interests on the public/private mix.* PhD dissertation, Department of Health Administration, Faculty of Medicine, University of Toronto.

Barlow, M. (2002, February). *Profit is not the cure.* Ottawa: Council of Canadians.

Battle, K., & Torjman, S. (1995). *How finance re-formed social policy.* Ottawa: Caledon Institute of Social Policy.

Begin, M. (1999, September). *The future of medicare: Recovering the Canada Health Act.* Ottawa: Canadian Centre for Policy Alternatives.

Beiser, M. (2005, March/April). The health of immigrants and refugees in Canada. *Canadian Journal of Public Health: Reducing Health Disparities in Canada.* 96, S30–S44.

Beiser, M., & Stewart, M. (2005, March/April). Reducing health disparities. *Canadian Journal of Public Health:Reducing Health Disparities in Canada.* 96, S4–S5.

Boismenu, G., & Jenson, J. (1998). A social union or a federal state? Competing visions of intergovernmental relations in the new Liberal era. In L.A. Pal (Ed.), *How Ottawa spends, 1998–99: Balancing act: The post-deficit mandate* (pp. 57–79). Toronto: Oxford University Press.

Brodie, J. (1996). Canadian women, changing state forms, and public policy. In J. Brodie (Ed.), *Women and Canadian public policy* (pp. 1–28). Toronto: Harcourt Brace Canada.

Browne, P.L. (1996). *Love in a cold world? The voluntary sector in an age of cuts.* Ottawa: Canadian Centre for Policy Alternatives.

Browne, P.L. (2000). *Unsafe practices: Restructuring and privatization in Ontario health care.* Ottawa: Canadian Centre for Policy Alternatives.

Bueckert, D. (2005a, October 13). Health accord promise will be broken, provincial officials say. *Globe and Mail,* p. A9.

Bueckert, D. (2005b, June 17). Romanow says Supreme Court ruling may kill Canada Health Act. Canadian Press.

Burke, M. (2000). Efficiency and the erosion of health care in Canada. In M. Burke, C. Mooers, & J. Shields (Eds.), *Restructuring and resistance: Canadian public policy in an age of global capitalism* (pp. 178–193). Halifax: Fernwood.

Burke, M., Mooers, C., & Shields, J. (2000). Critical perspectives on Canadian public policy. In M. Burke. C. Mooers, & I. Shields (Eds.), *Restructuring and resistance: Canadian public policy in an age of global capitalism* (pp. 11–23). Halifax: Fernwood.

Canada. (1996). *Renewing the Canadian federation: A progress report.* Background document for the First Ministers' meeting, June 20–21, 1996.

References

Canada. (1997). *Budget plan*. Department of Finance. Ottawa: Public Works and Government Services Canada.

Canada. (1998, February 4). *Minister marks first anniversary of National Forum on Health report*. Health Canada news release. Online at <www.hc-sc.gc.ca/english/media/releases/1998/98_07e.htm>.

Canada. (1999a, February 4). *The federal-provincial-territorial health care agreement*. Prime Minister's Office. News release.

Canada. (1999b, February 4.) *A framework to improve the social union for Canadians*. Online at <www.socialunion.ca/news/020499_e.html>.

Canada. (1999c, February 16). *Budget plan 1999*. Ottawa: Department of Finance.

Canada. (2003a). *2003 First Ministers' accord on health care renewal*. Ottawa: Health Canada.

Canada. (2003b). *Budget plan 2003*. Ottawa: Department of Finance.

Canada. (2004b, September 16). *10-year plan to strengthen health care*. Ottawa: Health Canada.

Canada. (2004a, September 15). *Asymmetrical [sic] federalism that respects Quebec's jurisdiction*.

Canada Health Act, R.S. 1985, c. C-6.

Canadian Centre for Policy Alternatives (CCPA). (2000, November). *Health care, limited: The privatization of medicare*. Synthesis report prepared by the CCPA for the Council of Canadians. With guidance from CCPA research associates P. Armstrong, H. Armstrong, and C. Fuller, and in collaboration with the Canadian Health Coalition.

Canadian Health Coalition. (2002, October 25). *A recipe for commercialization and privatization*. News Release. Online at <www.healthcoalition.ca/kirby-release.html>.

Canadian Institute for Health Information (CIHI). (2001) *National health expenditure trends, 1975–2001: Report; Executive Summary*. Online at <www. secure. cihi.ca>.

Canadian Institute for Health Information (CIHI). (2004) *National health expenditure trends, 1975–2004*. Online at <www. secure. cihi.ca>.

Canadian Intergovernmental Conference Secretariat. (2000, September 11). News Release. First Ministers' Meeting; Communiqué on Health.

Canadian Labour Congress. (2002, October 29) *CLC analysis of the Standing Senate Committee on Social Affairs, Science and Technology report; Vol. 6: The health of Canadians—the federal role*.

Chaoulli v. Quebec (Attorney General), S.C.C. 35. (2005).

Churchill, L.R. (1987). *Rationing health care in America: Perceptions and principles of justice*. Notre Dame: University of Notre Dame Press.

Commission on the Future of Health Care in Canada. (2002a, February 6). Statement by Roy J. Romanow, QC, Commissioner, on the release of the interim report of the Commission on the Future of Health Care in Canada at the National Press Theatre, Ottawa.

Commission on the Future of Health Care in Canada. (2002b). *Shape the future of health care: Interim report* (Romanow report). Saskatoon: Author.

Commission on the Future of Health Care in Canada. (2002c, November 28). Statement by Roy J. Romanow, QC, Commissioner, on the release of the final report of the Commission on the Future of Health Care in Canada at the National Press Theatre, Ottawa.

Commission on the Future of Health Care in Canada. (2002d, November 28). *Building on values. Final report* (Romanow report). Saskatoon: Author.

Council of Canadians. (1999, January). Power game: Five problems with the current social union talks. Online at <www.canadians.org>.

Courchene, T.J. (2003). Medicare as a moral enterprise: The Romanow and Kirby perspectives. *Policy Matters, 4*(1), 1–20.

CUPE. (2005, September 1). *Inside the Chaoulli ruling: A CUPE backgrounder*. Online at <www.cupe.ca/www/insidechaoulli>.

Deber, R. (2000). *Getting what we pay for: Myths and realities about financing Canada's health care system*. Background paper prepared for the Dialogue on Health Reform: Sustaining confidence in Canada's health care system.

Deber, R., Narine, L., Baranek, P., Sharpe, N., Duvalko, K.M., Zlotnik-Shaul, R., Coyte, P., Pink, G., & Williams, A.P. (1998). The public-private mix in health care. In National Forum on Health (Ed.), *Canada health action: Building on the legacy; Papers commissioned by the National Forum on Health*, vol. 4 (pp. 423–545). Sainte-Foy: Editions MultiMondes.

Epps, T., & Flood, C. (2001). *The implications of the NAFTA for Canada's health care system: Have we traded away the opportunity for innovative health care reform?* Working draft.

Esping-Andersen, G. (1989). The three political economies of the welfare state. *Canadian Review of Sociology and Anthropology, 26*(1), 10–35.

Evans, R.G., Barer, M.L., Lewis, S., Rachlis, M., & Stoddart, G.L. (2000). *Private highway, one-way street: The deklein and fall of Canadian medicare?* Centre for Health Services and Policy Research, University of British Columbia. Online at <www.chspr.ubc.ca>.

Flood, C., Stabile, M., & Tuohy, C.H. (2001, September). The borders of solidarity: How countries determine the public/private mix in spending and the impact on health care. *Health Matrix, 12*(2), 277–356.

Friends of Medicare. (2002, January 9). Real reform or road to ruin: Friends of Medicare analysis of the Premier's Health Advisory Council report. Online at <www.hsaa.ca/news_and_media/reports_submission/fom.pdf>.

Friends of Medicare. (2005, July 26). *Premier's third way evolves into a two-tier health care monster*. News Release. Online at <www.keepmedicarepublic.ca/medicare/news.shtml>.

Fuller, C. (1998). *Caring for profit: How corporations are taking over Canada's health care system*. Vancouver: New Star.

Galabuzi, G.E. (2004). Social exclusion. In D. Raphael, (Ed.), *Social determinants of health: Canadian perspectives* (pp. 235–250). Toronto: Canadian Scholars' Press.

Galloway, G. (2005, October 24). Deal set on waiting times. *Globe and Mail*. Online at <www.theglobeandmail.com/servlet/story/RTGAM.20051024.wxhealth24/BNStory/National/>.

Guest, Dennis. (1985). *The emergence of social security in Canada*. Vancouver: University of British Columbia Press.

Hall, M.H., & Reed, P.B. (1998. Spring). Shifting the burden: How much can government download to the non-profit sector? *Canadian Public Administration, 41*, 1–20.

Hospital Insurance and Diagnostic Services Act, S.C. 1957, c. 28.

Ife, J. (1997). *Rethinking social work*. Australia: Longman.

References

Kirby, M. (Chair of the Senate Standing Committee on Social Affairs, Science and Technology). (2002, December). Response to the Romanow Report.

Kirby, M.J.L., & Keon, W. (2004, September). Why competition is essential in the delivery of publicly funded health care services. *Policy Matters, 58,* 1–32.

Kronick, J. (1982). Public interest group participation in congressional hearings on nuclear power development. *Journal of Voluntary Action Research, 11,* 45–59.

Laghi, B., & McCarthy, S. (2003, February 6). Premiers grumble, but PM gets deal on health. *Globe and Mail,* p. A1.

LeClair, M. (1975). The Canadian health care system. In A. Spyros (Ed.), *National health insurance: Can we learn from Canada?* (pp. 11–88). Malabar: Krieger.

Leys, C. (2001). *Market-driven politics: Neo-liberal democracy and the public interest.* New York: Verso.

Manga, P. (1984). Preserving medicare: The Canada Health Act. *Perception, 70,* 12–15.

Medical Care Act, S.C. 1966, c. 64.

Murnighan, B. (2001, April). *Selling Ontario's health care: The real story on government spending and public relations; Ontario Alternative Budget* (Technical Paper no. 11). Canadian Centre for Policy Alternatives.

National Council of Welfare. (1982). *Medicare: The public good and private practice.* Ottawa: Supply and Services Canada.

National Council of Welfare. (1987). *Welfare in Canada: The tangled safety net.* Ottawa: Supply and Services Canada.

National Forum on Health. (1997). *Canada health action: Building on the legacy. Vol. 1: The final report of the National Forum on Health.* Ottawa: Minister of Public Works and Government Services.

Naylor, D.C. (1986). *Private practice, public payment: Canadian medicine and the politics of health insurance, 1911–1966.* Montreal: McGill-Queen's University Press.

Offe, C. (1984). *Contradictions of the welfare state.* (John Keane, Ed. and Introd.). Cambridge: MIT Press.

Ontario. (1995). *1995 fiscal and economic statement.* Toronto: Queen's Printer for Ontario.

Osberg, L. (1996, January). *The equity, efficiency and symbolism of national standards in an era of provincialism.* Ottawa: Caledon Institute of Social Policy.

Picard, A. (2005, August 18). Private health care should be available to all, doctors say. *Globe and Mail,* p. A4.

PovNet. (1999, February 4). *Social union framework heartless say social justice groups.* PovNet social union press release and backgrounder. Online at <www.povnet.web.net/socialunion.html>.

Rachlis, M., Evans, R.G., Lewis, P., & Barer, M.L. (2001, January). *Revitalizing medicare: Shared problems, public solutions.* A study prepared for the Tommy Douglas Research Institute. Online at <www.tommydouglas.ca>.

Raphael, D. (2004). Introduction to the social determinants of health. In D. Raphael (Ed.), *Social determinants of health: Canadian perspectives* (pp. 1–18). Toronto: Canadian Scholars' Press.

Romanow, R. (2004, September 13). Scrutiny is the best medicine. *Globe and Mail,* p. A15.

Romanow, R. (2005, June 10). Now is the time to stand up for medicare. *Globe and Mail,* p. A17.

Senate. Standing Committee on Social Affairs, Science and Technology. (2001a, September). *The health of Canadians: The federal role. Vol. 1: The story so far.* Interim report on the state of the health care system in Canada (Kirby report). Ottawa: Government of Canada.

Senate. Standing Committee on Social Affairs, Science and Technology. (2001b, September). *The health of Canadians: The federal role. Vol. 4: Issues and options* (Kirby report). Ottawa: Government of Canada.

Senate. Standing Committee on Social Affairs, Science and Technology. (2002, October). *The health of Canadians: The federal role. Vol. 6: Recommendations for reform; Final report* (Kirby report). Ottawa: Government of Canada.

Silver, S. (1993). *Universal health care: The Canadian definition.* PhD dissertation, Bryn Mawr College, Philadelphia.

Silver, S. (1996). The struggle for national standards: Lessons from the federal role in health care. In J. Pulkingham & G. Ternowetsky (Eds.), *Remaking Canadian social policy: Social security in the late 1990s* (pp. 67–80). Halifax: Fernwood.

Taylor, M. (1987). *Health insurance and Canadian public policy: The seven decisions that created the Canadian health insurance system.* Montreal: McGill-Queen's University Press.

Tholl, W.G. (1994). Health care spending in Canada: Skating faster on thinner ice. In J. Blomqvist & D.M. Brown (Eds.), *Limits to care: Reforming Canada's health system in an age of restraint* (pp. 53–89). Toronto: C.D. Howe Institute.

Titmuss, R. (1968). *Commitment to welfare.* London: George Allen and Unwin.

Titmuss, R. (1974). *Social policy.* London: George Allen and Unwin.

Tuohy, C.H., Flood, C.M., & Stabile, M. (2001, June). *How does private finance affect public health care systems? Marshalling evidence from OECD nations.* Working paper.

Van Loon, R.J. (1978). From shared cost to block funding and beyond: The politics of health insurance in Canada. *Journal of Health Politics, Policy and Law, 2* (Winter), 454–478.

Van Loon, R., & Wittington, M. (1971). *The Canadian political system.* Toronto: McGraw-Hill.

Walkom, T. (1999, February 9). Social union deal a step backward for Canadians. *Toronto Star,* p. A2.

Additional Resources

Badgely, R., & Wolfe, S. (1967). *Doctor's strike.* Toronto: Macmillan of Canada.

Begin, M. (1988). *Medicare: Canada's right to health.* Ottawa: Optimum.

Canadian Association for Community Care. Online at <www.cacc-acssc.com/page2.html>.

Canadian Centre for Policy Alternatives. Online at <www.policyalternatives.ca/>.

Canadian Council on Social Development. Online at <www.ccsd.ca/>.

Canadian Health Coalition. Online at <www.healthcoalition.ca/>.

Canadian Home Care Association. Online at <www.cdnhomecare.on.ca/e-index.htm>.

Canadian Institute for Health Information. Online at <secure.cihi.ca/cihiweb/dispPage.jsp?cw_page=home_e>.

Canadian Public Health Association. Online at <www.cpha.ca/english/index.htm>.

396

References

Centre for the Study of Living Standards. Online at <www.csls.ca/>.

Evans, R., & Stoddart, G. (Eds.). (1986). *Medicare at maturity*. Calgary: University of Calgary Press.

Hall, E.M. (1980). *Canada's national-provincial Health Insurance Program for the 1980s: A commitment for renewal*. Ottawa: Department of National Health and Welfare.

Health Action Lobby (HEAL). Online at <www.cna-nurses.ca/heal/healframe.htm>.

Health Canada. Online at <www.hc-sc.gc.ca/>.

Lalonde, M. (1974). *A new perspective on the health of Canadians*. Ottawa: Supplies and Services.

National Council of Welfare. Online at <www.ncwcnbes.net/>.

National Council of Welfare. (1990). *Health, health care and medicare*. Ottawa: Supply and Services.

Tommy Douglas Research Institute. Online at <www.tommydouglas.ca/>.

World Health Organization. Online at <www.who.int/home-page/>.

Social Worker Participation in Policy Practice and Political Activity

SUZANNE DUDZIAK AND JOHN COATES
DEPARTMENT OF SOCIAL WORK, ST. THOMAS UNIVERSITY

This article presents the results of a study on the participation of social workers in politics and policy-making in the Maritime provinces. It examines the political involvement of social workers in terms of what they do in practice. Building on the work of Domanski (1998) and Gray (1996) this exploratory study reveals the types of political activities engaged in, as well as the nature of social workers' direct involvement in policy-making activities. The results from 720 respondents reveal that while social workers pay a high degree of attention to social issues, their involvement in action is more work related; they engage in more passive (talking, voting) than active (campaigning, lobbying) forms of political activity; and they seek to influence policy-making in a variety of ways. Areas for further study are identified.

Cet article présente les conclusions d'une étude portant sur la participation des travailleurs sociaux des provinces Maritimes aux politiques et à leur élaboration. Il étudie l'implication politique de ces derniers dans leurs pratiques. Développant les travaux de Domanski (1998) et de Gray (1996), cette étude exploratoire décrit les types d'activités politiques dans lesquels ils s'engagent, tout comme la nature de leur participation directe dans les activités d'élaboration de politiques. Les résultats obtenus à partir de 720 répondants révèlent que tandis que les travailleurs sociaux sont profondément concernés par les enjeux sociaux, leur participation à l'action est principalement reliée à leur travail. Ces derniers sont engagés dans les diverses activités politiques de manière plus passive (conversations, votes) qu'active (campagnes, lobbying) et cherchent à influencer l'élaboration des politiques de plusieurs façons. Des domaines d'études à développer davantage sont aussi identifiés.

51

Introduction

This article presents the results of a study on the participation of social workers in politics and policy-making in the Maritime provinces (New Brunswick, Nova Scotia, and Prince Edward Island). Despite the emphasis in social work education on the importance of policy and advocacy as areas for practice, this is a significant new study as it is the first time, to our knowledge, that such a study has been undertaken in Canada.

The study examines the political involvement of social workers in terms of what they do in practice. The political activities of social workers are defined in terms of their involvement in implementing policy, influencing policy and decision-making processes, and working to change policy (Gray, 1996). While Gray's levels of involvement are general, more detailed activities are assessed using the work of Domanski (1998). Domanski theorizes that social workers engage in political processes by adopting various political roles such as advocating, lobbying, persuading, collaborating, voting, campaigning, etc. The study utilized her typology to assess the nature of social worker involvement in policy-making processes.

Results indicate that contrary to conventional wisdom about the laid-back nature of Maritime political culture and about social workers' political interests generally, there is a high degree of attention paid to social issues, and social workers seek to influence policy-making in a variety of ways. As an exploratory study, this research lays a foundation for further examination of the depth of political involvement, its meaning for social workers, and the overall impact that social workers have in terms of bringing about social change through political activity and policy practice.

Purpose of the Study

Gray (1996), Mazibuko (1996a & b), and Ntusi (1998) have all drawn attention to the need for social workers to play a proactive role in the political realm. Gray states, "Social workers cannot avoid political involvement if they accept that their primary function is to create and maximise opportunities for social development" (1996, p. 34). Many Canadian and American social work writers (Carniol, 1990; Jacobson, 2001; Mullaly, 1997; Wharf & McKenzie, 1998) argue for the importance of social workers becoming engaged in policy-making processes at national, regional, and local levels. "Social policy is permeated by politics ... all important policies will be assessed through the lens of votes" (Wharf & McKenzie, 1998, p. 38).

Despite the attention placed on policy in social work educational programs, social workers are generally very inactive politically and shy away from policy: "Many social workers consider the area of policy and actions to change policy to be the concern of others — administrators, academics, government — but not

themselves" (Coates, 2003, p. 138). Jacobson reports that "the contribution of the profession, and its leadership role in innovative systems reform and social change work, has virtually disappeared" (2001, p. 51). Perhaps social workers are immersed in the immediate needs of their clients, or fear reprisals from superiors, or feel overwhelmed by the demands of their work, or think their actions are futile. However, references to non-involvement (see for example, Jacobson, 2001) run counter to the expressed need for social worker involvement (Moreau & Leonard, 1989; Mullaly, 2002; Wharf & McKenzie, 1996).

Despite these conclusions, no Canadian studies have taken place that attempt to assess the nature of the involvement of social workers in political processes. The ultimate purpose of the study is to enhance social workers' understanding of the political dimensions of social work practice and to identify ways that social workers engage in political processes.

In the context of a major assault on Canada's social programs in the 1990s, the issue of political involvement by social workers in the Maritime provinces is particularly pertinent. Traditionally considered "have not" provinces, New Brunswick, Prince Edward Island, and Nova Scotia have suffered proportionally greater consequences as a result of the elimination of the Canada Assistance Program and the further cutbacks and restructuring of federal funding to the provinces in the form of the Canada Health and Social Transfer, implemented in 1995. In this context, the importance of political involvement would appear more compelling.

Dimensions of Political Participation and Policy-Making

Politics and engagement in political activity can be understood in a myriad of ways, from broad philosophical understandings of the *polis*, where all institutions and related activity by individuals or groups constitute and impact the public realm, to more narrow interpretations which focus on the formal and informal dynamics of electoral politics. For this research, a functionalist approach has been adopted to the study of political participation. The focus is on the actual activities and behaviours of social workers in formal and informal political processes, both during elections and in the course of their everyday interactions with social institutions. Regarding the latter, policy-making is further examined as a way to understand specific political practices in which social workers engage.

Policy-Making

In order to provide a consistent analytical framework for comparison with other countries participating in the study, the analysis of the political activities of social workers has focussed primarily on the policy realm. Based on her analysis of the practices of Australian social workers, Gray (1996) describes social work involvement in policy-making along the dimensions of implementation, influence, and change:

1. Policy implementation: In their daily practice, most social workers were implementing policy and, in doing so, were ensuring that clients obtained all the benefits to which they were entitled by making them aware of the protection the legislation afforded them and the services that were available to them.

2. Policy influence: Social workers influenced policy-makers by participating in decision-making processes.

3. Policy change: Social workers contributed to policy change when they: analyzed, commented on, and responded to pending legislation; served on policy-making structures; formed pressure groups for or against legislative proposals; and lobbied for the support of influential politicians, government officials, and prominent individuals and organizations in the community.

Political Participation

In studying political behaviour, involvement in political activities can be characterized in terms of political roles. In her study of political participation among social workers in the U.S., Domanski (1998) conceptualized a broad range of political activities under ten roles that social workers play in relation to policy-making. Her typology of political participation (Figure 1) was adapted for use in this study.

Design and Limitations of the Study

The questionnaire administered in this research project is part of an international study that compares, for the first time, data on political participation of social workers in Canada, the United Kingdom, South Africa, and Australia.[1]

The methodology involved a questionnaire mailed to all English-speaking registered social workers in the Maritime provinces of New Brunswick, Nova Scotia, and Prince Edward Island. The questionnaire was designed in three sections: a profile of participants (age, gender, years of practice, field of practice, education, ideological orientation, and level of workplace responsibility); a multi-part section (37 items) designed to elicit responses in relation to involvement in political activities; and a section to describe involvement in policy-making processes. The majority of questions used a forced choice (yes/no) format. These were complimented by some self-report items which asked social workers to identify policy issues and policy documents read and/or responded to. The data analysis largely involved summarizing the responses to the various questions.

Figure 1: Social Workers' Political Participation Activities

1. Lobbyist
- Contacted government officials by telephone, letter, fax on a national government policy problem.
- Contacted government officials by telephone, letter, or fax on a local government policy problem.
- Responded to the American Hospital Association Action Alert.
- Lobbied individual policymakers or legislators.

2. Voter
- Voted in the 1994 state elections.
- Voted in the 1994 national congressional elections.
- Voted in 1994 city or county elections.
- Voted in the 1994 primary elections.

3. Campaigner
- Actively worked for a political party during 1994.
- Actively worked for a specific candidate during 1994.
- Attended a political meeting or rally held by a candidate for office.
- Participated in the activities of a political party or a political organization.
- Attended a town meeting held by a legislator currently in office.

4. Collaborator
- Organized a professional or community group to work on a government policy problem.
- Organized a professional or community group to work on an agency or organizational problem.
- Organized or maintained a social action coalition.
- Participated in the lobbying activities of a professional public interest association or organization.
- Worked with others on resolution of a government policy problem.

5. Advocate
- Provided services to a community agency or group involved in social action or policy reform.
- Advocated for change within my organization to improve services.
- Made efforts in a professional capacity to influence opinion among coworkers about an agency policy problem.
- Worked to influence media coverage of an issue.
- Advocated with a government agency on behalf of a client.

6. Individualist
- Contacted government officials by telephone, letter, or fax on a local government problem of personal concern.
- Contacted government officials by telephone, letter, or fax on a national government problem of personal concern.
- Contacted government officials by attending or testifying at a public hearing on a local government problem of personal concern.

7. Witness
- Contacted government officials by attending or testifying at a public hearing on a local government problem of personal concern.

53

Figure 1: Social Workers' Political Participation Activities Continued

• Contacted government officials by attending or testifying at a public hearing on a national government issue of personal concern.

8. **Activist**
• Participated in an organized demonstration supporting a government policy.
• Participated in an organized demonstration protesting a government policy.

9. **Persuader**
• Attempted to persuade others how to vote.
• Made efforts in a professional capacity to influence opinion among the general public about a government policy problem.

10. **Communicator**
• Keep informed about political and social policy issues.
• Engaged in electoral or political discussions with family, friends, and colleagues.

Adapted from Domanski (1998)

Table 1: Sample

Questionnaires Distributed:		
	Nova Scotia	1,425
	New Brunswick	600
	Prince Edward Island	160
	Total	2,185
Questionnaires Returned:		720
Response Rate:		33%

Of the 2,185 questionnaires sent out in the late spring of 2002, 720 usable responses were tabulated. This represents a 33% response rate which is fairly high for this type of study, especially when the potentially sensitive nature of the issue of political involvement is considered.

As this study was part of a larger international study, the design of the survey and nature of the questions had to be consistent with those used elsewhere. While the phrasing of questions was altered to reflect existing political structures and local terminology, the focus could not shift. Further, as this was not a probability sample, and because the response rate was thought too low to be considered representative (less than 50%), the results were not generalizable to the total population of English-speaking, registered social workers in the Maritimes. Additionally, as the respondents are likely to be those for whom political activity is a greater concern, the sample can safely be considered to reflect the activities of those social workers who are more involved, interested, or attracted to political involvement.

It should be noted that the questionnaire only provides for descriptive statistics, an approach which is useful for the purpose of an initial exploratory study. However, this means that the data do not hold explanatory power and thus the results do not provide us with any indication of depth of involvement or reasons for involvement or lack of involvement. Lastly, for the substantive issues explored here the data has been left in aggregate form for the Maritime provinces in order to ensure anonymity.

Findings

The findings will be discussed in three sections: the profile of the social workers participating in the study, their political engagement, and the nature of their actual involvement in policy practices.

Profile of Participants
Table 2: Demographic Summary

Gender:		77% female
Age Range:		22-89 years
Average Age:	(in practice)	45 years
	(not in practice)	54 years
Education:	BSW	43%
	MSW	46%
	Other	9%
Average Number of Years in Practice: Currently in Practice:	11-13 years	89%

Demographic information summarized in Table 2 reveals that the majority of respondents (77%) were female, typically reflecting the profession in Canada. The average age was 45 years and 89% of respondents were currently in practice. The vast majority of respondents were experienced social workers; the median years of practice for the sample was 11-13 years. Of the 11% not in practice, the average age was 54 years. Additionally, of those currently in practice, 21% of respondents held supervisory or managerial positions (see Table 3). Given years of practice, age, and workplace responsibility, one could reasonably expect that the respondents had been involved in policy-making processes and thus could provide some insight into social workers' political participation. At the same time, when field of service is examined, it is likely that a large number of the respondents either trained or practised in a "clinical" approach and, as a result, were less familiar in their daily practice with some of the prototypes such as "activist."

54

involvement as a campaigner in the 2000 federal election could indicate a lack of interest in the formal politics of political parties as a means to bring about social change. However, over 50% of respondents indicated contact with officials at local or provincial levels on issues of personal concern. Involvement in provincial and local politics can have significant direct impact on social services and policy in the region. Given the smaller urban and more rural context of social work practice in the Maritimes generally, and the devolution of responsibility for the social agenda from the federal to provincial governments over the last fifteen years, involvement in formal politics at these levels should be explored further.

Table 4: Social Worker's Political Participation (In Rank Order)

1. Communicator:

Attempted to keep informed on issues with personal impact	93%
Attempted to keep informed on issues with professional impact	96%
Engaged in electoral discussions with family	93%
Engaged in electoral discussions with friends	95%
Engaged in electoral discussions with colleagues	91%

2. Voter:

Voted in the 2000 federal election	94%
Voted in the most recent provincial elections in your province	92%
Voted in the most recent municipal elections in your area	75%
Intend to vote in the next election	97%

3. Advocate:

Have you ever advocated for change within your organization to improve services	93%
... made efforts in a professional capacity to influence opinion among co-workers	87%
... worked to influence media coverage of an issue	42%
... advocated with a government agency for your client	94%

4. Individualist:

... contacted government officials in any manner about a local government issue of personal concern	55%
... contacted government officials in any manner on a provincial government issue of personal concern	53%
... contacted government officials in any manner on a federal government issue of personal concern	36%

5. Collaborator:

Have you ever organized a professional or community group to work on a government policy problem	34%

Table 3: Practice Profile

Field of Service			Workplace Responsibility			Urban/Rural		
Child Welfare	31%	213	Social Worker	58%	404	Urban	50%	346
Mental Health	17%	116	Management	13%	93	Rural	34%	235
Hospital	8%	57	Supervisor	8%	56	Urban/Rural	10%	69
Addictions	6%	44	Private Practice	5%	36	Other	6%	43
Adult/Senior Services	6%	40	Education	3%	18	no response		27
Counselling	5%	36	other SW	11%	73			
Community	4%	30	non-SW	2%	16			
other	23%	146	no response		24			
no response		38						

N = 720

Table 3 indicates that a significant percentage of respondents worked predominantly in rural areas (34%) or in both urban and rural (10%). It is also important to note that in the Maritime context, "urban" means primarily cities of less than 100,000 population. This profile differs generally from the notion of social work as a profession that is based in large urban centres. In terms of political activity, involvement in smaller communities could suggest a different approach to politics and policy-making than those assumed in a centralized urban political environment.

Political Engagement

Using Domanski's (1998) prototypes, Table 4 indicates the level of political participation of respondents, in rank order. Table 4 indicates that the most dominant form of political activity engaged in by social workers is that of "communicator" (93.6%), followed by that of "voter" (89.5%), while the least active political roles are those of "campaigner" (18%) and "activist" (30%). When assessed as a continuum, these results suggest that the greatest involvement occurs in more passive forms of political activity and that social workers are least involved in the most active political roles. However, the high response to both "communicator" and "voter" roles indicates that these social workers take seriously the importance of keeping informed about political and social issues and of their responsibility as citizens to be active voters. The fact that 96% of the sample "attempted to keep informed on issues with professional impact," the highest score for any single activity, indicates a very high level of awareness that could impact on the nature of services offered by social workers. Additionally, the fact that 95% of respondents "engaged in electoral discussion with friends" suggests that their interest in issues goes beyond a professional necessity to be informed.

At the other end of spectrum, the relatively low response rate (18%) for active

Table 4: Social Worker's Political Participation (In Rank Order) Continued

... organized a professional or community group to work on an agency or organizational problem	53%
... organized or maintained (in your personal capacity) a social action group or coalition	32%
... participated in the lobbying activities of a professional public interest association or organization	53%
... worked with others on resolution of a government policy problem	56%

6. Lobbyist:

Contacted government officials by telephone, letter, fax, e-mail or in person on a national government policy problem	41%
Contacted government officials by telephone, letter, ... a provincial government policy problem	62%
Contacted government officials by telephone, letter, ... a municipal government policy problem	35%
Lobbied individual policy makers or legislators	43%

7. Persuader:

Attempted to persuade others how to vote	34%

8. Witness:

... attended a public hearing or commission of enquiry on local or other level of government	48%
... testified at a public hearing or commission of enquiry on a government issues of personal concern	19%

9. Activist:

Participated in an organized demonstration supporting a government policy	9%
Participated in an organized demonstration protesting a government policy	50%

10. Campaigner:

Actively worked for a political party as part of the 2000 federal election campaign	9%
Actively worked for a political party prior to the 2000 federal campaign	22%
Are you actively working for a political party at present	3%
Do you intend to working for any political party as part of the next election campaign	13%
Attended a political rally or meeting prior to the 2000 federal election campaign	41%

When the outlying categories of "voter" and "campaigner" are excluded, the results suggest some recognition of the importance of political involvement as social workers and an active engagement in terms of civil society. This is evident

in the responses to political activities such as advocacy (79%), contacting government officials personally (48%), collaborating with the wider community on issues (46%), and lobbying government officials (45%). Social workers in this sample are not adverse to making their concerns known professionally and personally, and they appear to take active steps to engage their agencies, the broader community, and elected officials on issues.

Given both a reported interest in social issues and some familiarity with political roles such as advocacy and lobbying, one would expect that the role of "activist" would also elicit a high response rate. Defined by participation in organized demonstrations, this category was split between those demonstrating for and against a government policy. Half the sample (50%) reported participating in protesting against a government policy while 9% participated in a demonstration supporting a government policy. Although 50% of participants have expressed their opposition to many of the negative social policy changes that have occurred in recent years, the data suggests that "activism", in general, is a less preferred mode of political involvement.

Overall, the results of social workers' participation in political activities in this Maritime study indicate a moderate degree of political interest and involvement across a range of political roles. Keeping in mind this general perspective on political activity, we turn now to a more specific analysis of the nature of social workers' involvement in policy practice.

Policy Practice

Respondents were asked to report on their direct involvement in policy-making activities from 1994-2001, the period in which a major assault on Canada's social programs took place. Involvement in policy-making was explored according to three categories: awareness/attention to particular policies, involvement in influencing policy direction, and direct engagement in policy-making processes. Table 5 lists the different levels of involvement in policy practice and points out that social workers were very attentive to (92%) and informed about (81%) policy issues, but that only a minority (27% and 30%) were involved actively in policy-making processes.

Table 5: Involvement in Policy Practice

	N	Overall %	% Who Identified Policies	Average # Identified per Respondent	Range
Attention to Policy Issues	671	92%	92%	3	1-14
Read Policy Documents	584	81%	74%	3	1-9
Responded to Policies Read	191	27%	24%	2	1-6
Participated in Policy Process	214	30%	16%	1	1-4

56

Policy Awareness

In terms of awareness of policy issues, the vast majority of respondents (92%) reported a wide variety of issues that gained their attention in this period of major changes to Canada's social policies. On average, these respondents identified three policy issues of social import with the number of issues identified ranging from 1-14. The issues identified were clustered into 40 policy categories. The policy categories mentioned over 50 times are listed in rank order in Table 6.

Table 6: Attention to Policy Issues

Policy Issue Identified	Frequency	
Healthcare	414	57.5%
Addictions	169	23.4%
Homelessness	152	21.1%
Child welfare	140	19.4%
Income support	130	18.0%
Poverty	110	15.3%
Employment/labour	91	12.6%
Education	87	12.1%
Private practice/ethics	69	9.6%
Mental health	57	7.9%
Environment	51	7.1%

If conceptualized as policy priorities, the issues identified by these social workers constitute a mix of traditional social work concerns such as addictions, child welfare, income support, and mental health, with issues of broad social concern such as healthcare, homelessness, poverty, unemployment, education, and the environment. The latter could reflect issues that have received significant coverage in the Canadian media in recent years and/or issues of particular relevance to the Maritimes (i.e., high rates of poverty and unemployment).

Influencing policy

With respect to influencing current policy directions, respondents were asked to identify the policy documents they had read, and a separate question asked social workers to identify which policy documents they had responded to since 1994. 81% of the respondents indicated having read policy documents in this period. 74% listed the documents they had read, with the average number being two documents per respondent (range 1-9). The policy categories of documents read are listed in rank order in Table 7. Items identified less than ten times are not included.

Table 7: Attention to Policy Issues

Policy Issue Identified	Frequency	
child welfare	338	46.9%
health care	218	30.3%
early childhood devlp.	118	16.4%
income support	49	6.8%
adult/senior services	36	5.0%
child and family	32	4.4%
women/elder abuse	24	3.3%
mental health	21	2.9%
employment	18	2.5%
family violence	18	2.5%
poverty	17	2.4%
disabilities	17	2.4%
young offenders	15	2.1%
fiscal policy	15	2.1%
foster care	13	1.8%
adoption	10	1.4%

While social workers were interested in a broad range of policy issues (see Table 6), Table 7 points out that policy work in relation to actual policy documents read clustered around traditional social work concerns such as child welfare and health, areas in which most social workers are employed in the Maritimes (see Table 3). The relatively high involvement with policy documents concerning early childhood development, which ranked low in terms of the policy interests of social workers, likely reflects new legislation directed at early intervention in child welfare as well as funding launched for such initiatives by the federal government in this period.

In terms of action involving response to policy documents by means of written submissions or comments to policy-makers, the number of respondents declined from 81% to 27%. 24% of respondents went on to identify the policy issues and documents about which they had commented. The documents responded to are identified in rank order in Table 8. Items identified less than ten times are not included.

Table 8: Policy Issue Read

Policy Issue Identified	Frequency	
child welfare	49	6.8%
health care	47	6.5%
income support	25	3.5%
child/family services	15	2.0%
corrections	12	1.7%

The policy issues that social workers identified in Table 8 are consistent with areas identified as traditional fields of social work employment, namely child welfare and health care. The pattern of commenting on issues defined in and by the work environment noted in Table 7, is repeated here.

Involvement in Policy-Making Processes

Regarding direct involvement in policy-making processes, 30% of respondents indicated they had been involved, on average twice, since 1994. This represents a slight increase of 3% from the 27% of respondents who reported responding to policy documents. 16% of respondents went on to comment on the nature of their participation in policy-making processes. From their responses, several types of policy involvement were identified. The nature of their participation in policy-making is profiled in Table 9.

Table 9: Nature of Participation in Policy-Making

Policy Issue Identified	Frequency	
Committee member	63	8.7%
Task/focus group	60	8.3%
Advisory committee	55	7.6%
Comment solicited	8	1.1%
Wrote briefs	7	1.0%
Research assistant	7	1.0%
Consultant	6	.8%
Manager	5	.7%
Board of Directors	2	.3%
Did not say	47	6.5%

While this data is derived from only a small portion of the respondents, it does identify a range of capacities and means that some social workers use to engage directly in policy-making processes. These social workers engage primarily with others as members of groups (e.g. committees, boards) and, to a much lesser degree, participate as individuals on the basis of their expertise (e.g. consultant, research assistant) or their position (e.g. manager) vis-a-vis policy structures. Several respondents (N=47) identified the policy rather than their role.

Discussion

The overall results are informative for further study. It is evident that among this group of social workers in the Maritimes there is a high awareness of social issues and that they are widely read in terms of social policy documents. However,

also notable is a discrepancy between the broad range of issues of concern to these social workers and the range of issues in which they are actively involved. Larger structural issues are identified as areas for concern among social workers yet their reading and response to actual policy documents focuses primarily on traditional social work issues. Their reading and response to policy documents appears to be largely determined by the environment in which social workers are employed. Lundy and Gauthier (1989) in Canada and Thompson (1994) in the U.S. have written about the real and perceived restrictions governing political activity by social workers as employees of the state. Further study is required to determine what impact these forms of regulation have on the profession's ability to advocate for structural change.

This study also reveals that as the policy-making process comes to demand a more politically active response, social worker participation appears to decrease, as evidenced in the decline from 81% of participants engaged who read documents to 27% who responded to documents. Again, this may reflect various constraints of the workplace or, alternatively, a lack of interest or belief in the efficacy of political engagement.

A potential parallel trend is evident in terms of political participation: most social workers engage in the more passive forms of political practice such as informal communication and voting and they are least involved in the most active forms of engagement such as political campaigns or organized demonstrations.

Perhaps where political participation and involvement in policy practice most converge is in terms of advocacy, which 79% of participants identified as a significant political activity in which they engage. As an activity sanctioned by the social work profession, this category legitimizes political involvement within the work environment and on behalf of clients. Jansson discusses the connection between policy advocacy and policy practice from a social work perspective:

By policy *advocacy*, we mean policy practice that aims to help relatively powerless groups, such as women, children, poor people, African Americans, Asian Americans, Latinos, gay men and lesbians, and people with disabilities, improve their resources and opportunities ... Because social workers usually work with people who *are* relatively powerless, their policy practice usually *is* policy advocacy (1999, p. 10).

The data also reveal a potential for further political engagement in policy-making beyond current activities in the workplace regarding traditional social work issues. The fact that 92% of respondents reported on a wide variety of social issues that drew their attention and that they identified, on average, at least three social issues of importance indicates a high degree of interest for potential action. Furthermore, the finding that half the participants sampled contacted government officials on social issues of personal concern, participated in collective work on

Suzanne Dudziak and John Coates

issues, and lobbied government on policy issues, indicates a willingness to be more active in terms of influencing policy through accepted democratic practices. Given this expressed interest and willingness to act, the question arises as to why social workers are not more politically active and involved in policy-making activities outside of the workplace.

Beyond this discussion of the immediate issues raised by this exploratory survey, several other lines of inquiry should be considered for interpreting future data. These concern the potential difference in engaging in political activity in rural and small urban contexts, the impacts on political involvement of the economic structure and political culture of the Maritimes as a unique region in Canada, participation rates of social workers compared with the general population or other professions, and the overall state of social work in Canada with regard to political and policy engagement for social transformation.

Conclusions

From the above discussion, it is evident that more study (qualitative and quantitative) is called for in terms of the extent and depth of political involvement, the types of policy-making practices in which social workers engage, and the potential interplay of historical, cultural, economic, and region-specific factors that impact political involvement and practices.

In conditions of sustained inequality, as experienced in the Maritimes, a different kind of politics for social change may be required by social workers. Several social work academics maintain that social work must go beyond advocacy to more direct forms of political involvement. Leonard argues for new forms of "organized solidarity" in the interests of oppressed groups aimed "at winning of state power through the electoral process" (1997, p. 176). While offering critiques of left-wing governments in power during the 1980s and early 1990s in the Western world, Mullaly (2002) maintains that involvement in electoral politics continues to be one relevant strategy for re-legitimating and revitalizing the state on the grounds that

Despite its relative weakening in the face of global capitalism, no other institution has the capacity or the resources necessary to rebuild our neglected social and public infrastructure. The promised benefits of a global economy have not been delivered. "Without a legitimate public sector there are not public citizens, only private consumers" (Fisher & Karger, 1997, p. 177).

— Mullaly, 2002, p. 202.

As a point of critical self-reflection, this knowledge leads us to question what we are doing as social workers toward revitalizing the public sector in Canada in

the wake of the destruction caused by the implementation of a neoliberal agenda by corporate and political elites? This study, as a first exploratory step, indicates that a substantial number of social workers in the Maritimes are very interested and concerned about these issues and that they are willing to take action. However, as one reviewer noted, most social workers remain passive policy-takers rather than being active, engaged policy-makers. Hopefully, future study can help us to understand what hinders social workers from being more involved politically both in the workplace and in the public sphere, and what strategies can be employed to those ends.

Suzanne Dudziak, MSW, PhD, is an associate professor in the Department of Social Work at St. Thomas University. Suzanne was a community activist and policy advocate for many years prior to teaching. Her current research interests include political activism, impacts of globalization and social movements, and social development approaches to social work.

John Coates, MSW, PhD, is a professor and former Chair of the Department of Social Work at St. Thomas University where he has taught for many years. John has held leadership roles in many community organizations, and his current research activities include spirituality, the political activity of social workers, ecology, and youth homelessness.

Notes

1   Copies of the research questionnaire can be obtained from the authors. Contact John Coates at jcoates@stu.ca.

References

Carniol, Ben. (1990). *Case Critical: Challenging Social Work in Canada.* Second Edition. Toronto: Between the Lines Press.

Coates, John. (2003). *Ecology and Social Work: Toward a New Paradigm.* Halifax, NS: Fernwood Press.

Domanski, Margaret Dietz. (1998). "Prototypes of Social Work Political Participation: An Empirical Model." *Social Work,* 43(2), 156–167.

Fisher, Robert and Howard J. Karger. (1997). *Social Work and Community in a Private World: Getting Out in Public.* White Plains, NY: Longman.

Gray, Mel. (1996). "Social Work and Politics." *Social Work/Maatskaplike Werk,* 32(1),1–8.

Jacobson, Wendy. (2001). "Beyond Therapy: Bringing Social Work Back to Human Services Reform." *Social Work,* 46(1), 51–61.

Jansson, Bruce. (1999). *Becoming an Effective Policy Advocate: From Policy Practice to Social Justice.* Third Edition. Pacific Grove, CA: Brooks/Cole Publishing.

Lundy, Colleen and Larry Gauthier. (1989). "Social Work Practice and the Master-Servant Relationship." *The Social Worker/Le Travailleur Social,* 57(4), 190–194.

Leonard, Peter. (1997). *Postmodern Welfare: Reconstructing an Emancipatory Project.* London: Sage.

Mazibuko, F. N. M. (1996a). "Social Workers and Social Policy: Related Functions and Skill in Practice." *Social Work/Maatskaplike Werk,* 32(2), 148–161.

Mazibuko, F. N. M. (1996b). "Policy Analysis as a Strategy of Welfare Policy Development: The White Paper Process." *Social Work/Maatskaplike Werk,* 32(3), 234–241.

Moreau, M. and Leonard, L. (1989). *Empowerment Through a Structural Approach to Social Work: A Report from Practice.* Ottawa: Carleton University School of Social Work.

Mullaly, Bob. (1997). *Structural Social Work: Ideology, Theory and Practice.* Second Edition. Toronto: Oxford University Press.

Mullaly, Bob. (2002). *Challenging Oppression: A Critical Social Work Approach.* Toronto: Oxford University Press.

Ntusi, T. M. (1998). "Professional Challenges for South African Social Workers: Responses to Recent Political Changes." *Social Work/Maatskaplike Werk,* 34(4), 380–388.

Thompson, Joanne J. (1994). "Social Workers and Politics: Beyond the Hatch Act." *Social Work,* 39(4), 457–465.

Wharf, Brian and Brad McKenzie. (1998). *Connecting Policy to Practice in the Human Services.* Toronto: Oxford University Press.

CHAPTER 8

The Medicare Debate, 1945–80

The government sponsors the TB testing of cattle, pays for loss and has blood testing every year free of charge. What about humans? Let's take our hats off to Russia as far as health is concerned." This was the conclusion of a group of farmers in Seaforth, Ontario, meeting in late 1943 to discuss the idea of a national universal medical care program. Sponsored by *Farm Radio Forum*, a CBC radio series, groups of farmers across the country responded to the proposals that were being mooted for state medical insurance. But the proposals being discussed were more radical than Canada's current medicare system. Medical care was to be removed from the private marketplace completely, and the costs of hospital care, doctors' visits, pharmaceutical costs, dental care, and eyecare were to be covered by a state-funded regime.

The farmers' groups revealed that conditions of health care in Canada, particularly in rural areas, were often grim. For example, a farmer in Elderbank, Nova Scotia, stated "Our doctor has 275 miles of highway to travel. Many do not consult him because of cost of services. Immediate federal action is needed." In Leader, Saskatchewan, another reported: "Our school is never visited by either doctor or nurse. This fall one family had a child with contagious disease....fi nally the school was closed up, as teacher and all pupils were sick. Mothers here, who never have a doctor at the birth of a child, least of all pre-natal care, most of them are wrecks and old long before their time."[2] Polls suggested that a national medicare scheme was the most popular reform discussed during the Second World War and its aftermath. In both 1944 and 1948, 80 per cent of Canadians expressed support, with the Québécois sharing this sentiment despite the claims of their provincial government and the Catholic Church that national medicare posed a threat to Quebec's traditions of individualism and Church control of social services.[3]

The dismal state of health services across the country fuelled the demand for state action. Canadians had reason to believe that they did not enjoy the full benefits of the medical knowledge of their time. While Sweden and New Zealand, both with universal state medical programs, had the world's lowest infant death rates in 1942—29 per 1,000 live births—Canada's rate was 54. In all provinces, the infant mortality rate in rural areas was higher than the urban rate, usually quite significantly, for example 79 to 51 in Nova Scotia, 76 to 43 in Manitoba, and 63 to 30 in British Columbia. Significantly, Saskatchewan, where pressure from women's groups in the interwar period had led to the hiring of municipal doctors and the creation of "union" hospitals (hospitals operated by several municipalities uniting to pay for their construction and operation), had the country's lowest rural death rate for infants. In that province, 52 children per 1,000 died in their first year of life compared with 43 in the province's cities.[4]

Still, the State Hospital and Medical League of Saskatchewan estimated that 34 per cent of all deaths were premature and that half of all provincial residents suffering disabling illnesses could have been free of disease if preventive care had been applied. As Tommy Douglas, soon-to-be premier of that province and generally regarded as the "father of Canadian medicare," noted in a broadcast in 1943, "If the average person were checked over by a clinic at stated intervals, and treatment were available before the illness had reached a critical stage, not only would we live longer but the cost of health services in the aggregate would be less than it is now."[6] The National Committee for Mental Hygiene reported in 1939 that only 10 per cent of Canadians could comfortably pay for their medical services in a free-market system while 25 per cent were completely dependent on charity; the remaining 65 per cent could pay for normal services but were forced into debt or rejection of treatment if an operation or long-term care was required.[7]

Yet, despite popular support for medicare, it was not implemented in the early postwar period and, over the next two decades, pro- and anti-medicare

forces were locked in constant battle. Advocates of medicare seemingly won, but the program that emerged disappointed them both in the limitations of its coverage and the structure of medical care that it embraced. This chapter explores the structures of political decision making, formal and informal, that resulted in the creation of a particular type of medicare in 1968.

FROM THE GREEN BOOK TO HOSPITAL INSURANCE

Though the federal government balked at the potential costs of national health insurance in 1945, it recognized that Canadians expected governments at all levels to invest in health care.[8] In 1948, it announced a program of conditional health grants to provinces to build and operate hospitals, train medical personnel, and carry out health research. The wealthier provinces, in turn, also provided funding to expand their network of hospitals and to increase the number of graduates from medical schools. From 1948 to 1953 alone, forty-six thousand hospital beds were added across Canada.[9]

Saskatchewan had elected a CCF government led by T.C. Douglas in 1944, and it had pledged to take steps towards the creation of a universal medicare scheme. Despite the unavailability of matching federal funds after the collapse of the Green Book process, Saskatchewan forged ahead with plans to create universal hospital insurance in the province and end the distinction in hospitals between paying clients and charity cases. It immediately undertook a hospital construction project to ensure that most residents lived close enough to a hospital to receive care close to home. Then it legislated tax-funded hospitalization insurance in 1947, becoming the first jurisdiction in North America to implement such a program. The province's general revenues as well as a prepaid monthly premium levied on families and singles would pay the costs of insuring that need, and not financial means, determined who used Saskatchewan hospitals. Saskatchewan physicians largely supported this measure, while hospital administrators who opposed the legislation kept quiet after the premier threatened that the province could take control of the hospitals if the existing administrators no longer wished to run them.[10]

British Columbia's Coalition government of Liberals and Conservatives faced serious competition from that province's CCF and also decided to implement a universal hospital insurance program, financed by premiums and a 3 per cent sales tax. Claiming that it wanted to blend the concepts of private and public responsibility, it included "co-insurance" (user fees) within its hospital insurance program, despite protests from the CCF and the labour movement.

Alberta presented yet a third model for paying hospital and other medical bills. Decrying both compulsory participation and centralization, the government established a series of health districts in 1946. District boards, which included both physician and consumer representatives, negotiated a health insurance scheme with municipalities, including the services to be covered for a maximum payment of $10 per adult. While most costs were borne by the voluntary subscriber to the insurance scheme, hospital fees were set at $1 per day, with the municipality and the province splitting the remaining operating costs. Manitoba and Newfoundland also had voluntary programs, which had been established before Newfoundland joined Canada, enrolling about half the province's population.[11]

Louis St. Laurent, like Mackenzie King, was less than enthusiastic about the federal government creating a national health insurance scheme. But he was under tremendous pressure from the five provinces that were heavily subsidizing patients' costs to implement a national program and lift at least half the burden of costs from the provinces.[12] Ontario weighed in on the provinces' side in 1955. About 70 per cent of Ontario residents enjoyed some form of hospital insurance coverage, but Premier Leslie Frost faced public pressure for the federal government to fund hospital insurance. This included pressure from hospital authorities. The community elites that ran the hospitals had been dealt a body blow by the Depression, as the number of paying customers dwindled while charity cases climbed. In the postwar period, they came to believe that their institutions needed the economic stability that public insurance alone could provide.[13]

Frost responded by insisting that federal involvement was required, a viewpoint he stressed at a federal-provincial conference in October 1955. St. Laurent reluctantly agreed to federal-provincial discussions on hospital insurance. These discussions led to the Hospital Insurance and Diagnostic Services Act of April 1957, which established a formula for federal grants to provinces that implemented a provincial hospital insurance scheme. About half of all hospital costs would be borne by the federal government. The provinces chose the method of financing for their plans, but there were penalties for provinces that levied user fees. Passage of the legislation was eased by the lack of opposition from the Canadian Medical Association (CMA), which, since 1949, had supported user-pay hospitals.[14] Their change of heart was dictated by the need to assuage public anger regarding high costs for hospital stays and to avoid more radical medicare programs that included costs of doctors' visits. The private insurance companies were the big losers in the debate, but were determined

to fight to maintain the rest of their health insurance business by denouncing further state intervention in medical care.

TOWARDS MEDICARE

The CMA's rejection of public hospital insurance in 1949 was part of a broader rejection of health insurance by Canadian doctors after the war. With average incomes rising quickly, physician groups expanded or launched health insurance plans that proved successful beyond the doctors' expectations. The plans tabulated total annual medical bills for given populations and set insurance rates that would yield the income expected by physicians plus administrative costs needed to run the plan. For physicians, it meant that they collectively set the rates for various types of treatment. Private insurance companies, which covered over 1.5 million Canadians in 1962,[15] were required to accept the physician-dictated rates as the price for having a place in the health insurance industry.

By contrast, if governments were to get involved in medical insurance, it was likely that they would require physicians to accept lower rates for various procedures as a means of reducing overall medical costs. In the United States, the growth of the private health insurance industry, also dominated by physicians, gave the American Medical Association (AMA) an incentive to spend lavishly to lobby politicians and propagandize Americans regarding the evils of a public health insurance program. Their efforts forestalled President Harry Truman's plans in the late 1940s to introduce a national universal medical insurance scheme despite widespread popular support for such a policy. In the context of the Cold War, the AMA painted state medicine as an exemplar of the programs that unfree Communist states imposed upon their hapless citizens, an image that was ironic in light of the introduction of state medicine in Britain and other European democracies. Supported by big business organizations, the AMA developed an impregnable opposition to state medicine in Congress that united northern Republicans with southern Democrats, the latter often wealthy conservatives elected from pro-medicare constituencies but able to avoid the issue by making the preservation of racial segregation the key to their election strategies.[16]

At the federal-provincial conference in 1955, St. Laurent indicated that the federal government would only consider a national health insurance program when a majority of provinces representing a majority of citizens were prepared to institute provincial programs. The three Atlantic premiers responded that they could only consider a program if the federal government promised in advance to provide most of the funding. The premiers of Alberta and Manitoba wanted more unconditional grant money from the federal government in preference to universal medicare, and wanted any universal scheme to incorporate the private insurance schemes already in operation rather than replace them with a public plan. Ontario was only willing to commit to a national study of the possible scope and costs of a federal health scheme while Premier Duplessis of Quebec opposed a federal program.[17]

As with hospital insurance, it was the provinces that stepped up to the plate first to offer universal programs and then put the federal government on the hot seat for failure to make such provision a national responsibility. Once again, it was Saskatchewan's CCF government that led the way. Tommy Douglas, running for re-election in 1960, announced that with the federal government now paying half of Saskatchewan's hospital bills, his government could afford to implement universal medicare. Both the urban and rural poor, including most farmers, were unable to buy medical coverage, and the Saskatchewan government, like other provincial governments, was picking up the tab for medical bills for a growing section of the poor. It argued that this was unfair, first because it stigmatized those required to rely on state aid and discouraged them from seeing doctors, and second because it placed heavy financial burdens on the state that a universal plan would offset with the tax or premium contributions of the better-off, which the private insurers claimed for themselves. But Saskatchewan faced a huge fight in implementing its program.

Saskatchewan had played a pioneering role in the provision of medical services in Canada. Its municipal doctor schemes and union hospitals of the interwar period, the result of the work of the farm women's movement, and particularly Violet McNaughton, challenged the notion of health as a commodity to be purchased by those with the wherewithal to do so. Nonetheless, such programs relied on voluntary participation by doctors rather than state coercion. The CCF's experiments with full-state operation of medical services before the 1960s were limited to a few areas of the province in which the government was able to enlist the support of progressive-minded physicians. However, after the government announced its intentions to have a province-wide medical insurance scheme, a community clinic movement sprang up, a natural outgrowth of the populism that had produced both the major farm movements in Saskatchewan and the CCF itself. Health clinics with a holistic model of health, in which nurses, social workers, nutritionists, and dentists worked alongside

doctors, enrolled about fifty thousand people in thirty-five regional associations in a province of less than 1 million people.[18]

Most physicians had no intention of becoming salaried professionals working in state-run clinics whose policies were determined by elected boards of non-physicians. In line with the CMA, which aided them in carrying out an extensive propaganda campaign against the government's plan, Saskatchewan doctors insisted that individuals and families should pay their medical bills via private insurance. If the province insisted that all citizens should be insured, it should direct them to buy insurance from a private plan. Only the poor should have their bills paid by the state, with the state paying physician-dictated rates for services that private plans paid. In July 1962, when the government proved adamant that it would proceed with its plans, the Saskatchewan branch of the CMA organized a withdrawal of physician services.[19]

Upper- and middle-class supporters of the physicians formed "Keep Our Doctors" committees that accused the government of imposing an unworkable policy for socialist ideological reasons. The corporate-owned daily papers, always hostile to the CCF government, terrified people by suggesting that the province might lose most of its doctors. With both the CMA and national business organizations spending extravagantly to reinforce this message through television and radio advertising, as well as by using the appearances of "expert" witnesses on news shows, Saskatchewan residents were subjected to non-stop propaganda against state medicare. This was offset by the support for medicare from the Saskatchewan Federation of Labour and the major farm organizations, though these groups had limited access to the media.

The doctors' strike ended after twenty-two days as a result of government negotiations with the Saskatchewan branch of the CMA, in which the doctors conceded a universal state program and the government conceded many of the demands of the doctors. There would be no salaries for doctors or payments by the number of patients that they served. Instead, fee for service, the principle that governed private insurance plans, would remain sacrosanct. Doctors would continue to operate from their own private offices, and not only would doctors not be forced to participate in a community clinic, but those who chose to practise in a clinic would receive direct funding from the state rather than have to deal with the community clinic board. Finally, doctors would have the choice of participating directly in the state plan either by requiring patients to pay bills and then bill the plan or by staying out of the plan altogether and billing patients with whatever fees they deemed appropriate. This was simply a face-saving measure since both sides understood that most patients would choose to patronize doctors who were in the prepaid medicare scheme.

THE HALL COMMISSION

Saskatchewan's decision to launch a compulsory, state-run medicare scheme placed pressure on the national political parties to respond to demands from Canadians in all provinces for universal medical insurance. The NDP made implementation of a national medicare scheme a central plank in its platform. Out of office, the Liberals as well recommitted themselves to the national medicare program that they had promised in the 1945 election but had never delivered. Business stalwarts among former ministers, including C.D. Howe, Charles Dunning, and Brooke Claxton, opposed medicare. But the reformers who had taken over the party machinery in the late 1950s convinced delegates at the 1961 national convention to recommit the party to a national medicare program.[20]

While John Diefenbaker faced fewer demands within his party for state medicare, and considerable business pressures against such a measure, he was leery of simply dismissing any solution that might appease public demands for guaranteed access to medical care. He turned in 1961 to Justice Emmett Hall, a fellow Saskatchewan Conservative, to head a commission to study options for improving the health care available to Canadians. Commentators assumed that the commission, largely composed of hand-picked Tory supporters, would opt for a non-compulsory scheme.

While the commission deliberated, the Social Credit governments of Alberta and British Columbia attempted to counter the "socialist" Saskatchewan scheme with state programs that avoided "coercion" of doctors or "conscription" of citizens into a state plan. First, Alberta in 1963, and then British Columbia in 1964, announced voluntary plans that directed most residents into existing doctor-controlled and insurance-company plans, but provided state subsidies for the poor so that they could also receive coverage. The Alberta plan was endorsed by the provincial College of Physicians and Surgeons, which the government consulted as it set the premium and determined what services were covered. Such plans left many families who were just above the low-income cut-offs in the position of having to decide whether they could afford the high costs of private insurance or should risk going without coverage. Even in wealthy Alberta, the province calculated that only 60 per cent of provincial residents were covered by the voluntary medical-care scheme.[21]

The commission heard ample testimony from organized groups as well as individuals who favoured the Alberta and British Columbia approach over the Saskatchewan plan. While 40 per cent of Canadians had no medical insurance and many more had coverage only for catastrophes, elite groups that opposed a universal state program, led by the CMA and the Canadian Chamber of Commerce, insisted that only 15 per cent of Canadians were unable to afford medical coverage.[22] This figure seemed suspicious in light of a Statistics Canada study in 1961 that placed 27 per cent of Canadians below the poverty line and another 14 per cent on or just over that line.[23] However, to admit that private medical insurance was a hardship for almost half of the population would weaken the argument against state medicine.

MEDICARE'S OPPONENTS

Supporters of continued privatization and voluntary participation in medical insurance included the Canadian Medical Association, the Canadian Dental Association, the Canadian Chamber of Commerce, the entire private insurance industry, the pharmaceutical industry, and representatives of most other industries. The premiers of British Columbia, Alberta, Manitoba, and Ontario opposed medicare while Quebec's Premier Lesage was opposed to federal legislation in a sphere of provincial competence. The Atlantic premiers generally supported medicare but wanted the federal government to pay the lion's share of the costs and to give them time to phase in any universal program because they faced shortages of medical personnel. Only Woodrow Lloyd in Saskatchewan was an unequivocal supporter of a fully state-operated scheme.[24]

The advocates of private insurance used a variety of arguments before the commission. For example, the British Columbia Medical Association, following the lead of the CMA,[25] argued that the monies that medicare would absorb could be better spent on "scholarships for medical students, to add rehabilitative and chronic care kids to our hospitals, to extend our mental health programme, and for many other important services." Directing taxes instead towards paying medical insurance was "foolhardy" because it meant "providing a service to those who are already providing it for themselves, as most British Columbians are doing through our system of voluntary health insurance."[26]

The CMA's brief added that the hospital insurance program, which the physicians regarded favourably, had expanded demand for hospital beds. The federal and provincial governments, it suggested, having created this demand by making hospitalization a free good, now had to cough up the money for more state funding of necessary services for destitute Canadians. If governments were going to provide state dental service programs, they should restrict their programs to children.[29]

Not one recognized organization of health professionals in Canada placed itself on record as supporting medicare, with the exception of the nurses' association in Saskatchewan where medicare already was an established program.[30] The rest of the nursing profession in Canada, which later would become a militant supporter of public medicine, restricted itself to calling for greater public support for nursing education and better salaries for nurses.[31]

Both pharmacists and the pharmaceutical industry strongly opposed inclusion of prescription drugs in a state medical insurance plan, since it carried the implicit threat of state regulation of drug prices. The Canadian Pharmaceutical Manufacturers' Association (CPMA) reported soothingly that competition was lively at the manufacturing and retail levels of the industry: "The competitive aspect of research and development, combined with behaviour of prices and promotional activities, indicates that a satisfactory level of competition exists in the industry. Furthermore, this competition is directed in a manner which is socially desirable. Growth, product development and the general level of prices have been favourable rather than unfavourable to the consumer."[32] The pharmaceutical manufacturers assured the commissioners that after-tax profits of the industry were modest and the industry's expenditures on promotion were fairly restrained and served the purpose of informing physicians and others about useful pharmaceuticals.

In fact, the industry's profits, measured as a percentage of invested capital, were double the average for Canadian industries as a whole from 1953 to 1958. A study prepared in 1961 for the federal Department of Justice by the director of Investigation and Research, Combines Investigation Act, noted that apart from making large profits, the industry was absolutely profligate in its promotion expenditures, as it worked tirelessly to press physicians to use various new drugs. Patent laws protected drug companies that developed a new pharmaceutical product, and it was the knowledge that they had a monopoly for many years over a particular drug that caused pharmaceutical companies to spend millions trying to convince physicians to prescribe their product.

But, while monopolistic practices affected only "certain drugs" at the manufacturing level, the retail level was a dead loss to market forces despite being wholly private. Wrote the justice investigator: "The practices of retail druggists...have resulted in the virtual elimination of price competition at the retail level."[33] Such monopolistic practices did not lead to calls for either a public

beds. Implicit, however, in this argument was that prior to the existence of a public program, the real health needs of the population, in the area of hospitalization, had been underserved despite the availability of private hospitalization insurance.[27] Nor did the physicians try to claim that private health insurance was meeting everyone's needs. They conceded that to achieve universal medical insurance coverage, about 3 million Canadians would have to have their bills paid by taxes collected from the rest of Canadians, who, in turn, would also have to pay for their own private insurance.

The CMA, while avoiding the Cold War rhetoric of its American counterpart in its opposition to state medicine, emphasized that doctors as a group would be hostile to state medical insurance and even more hostile to any efforts by the government to move them away from individual practice into group settings that might also include other types of medical practitioners. "Physicians by nature and by training are strongly individualistic and it is not given to all doctors to function happily and efficiently as a member of a group." It could lead, in any case, to "assembly-line medicine."[28]

The Canadian Dental Association (CDA) also claimed that state moneys could be better directed at other goals than a national insurance program. Admitting that most Canadians had little or no access to dentists, they pointed out that there was a dismal ratio of dentists to population—1 to 3,000, compared with 1 to 1,900 in the United States, with regional gaps that were best demonstrated by Newfoundland and Labrador's ratio of 1 dentist per 11,000 residents. If all Canadians suddenly had access to dental services, there would simply be too few dentists to accommodate them. Steps to increase the number of dentists would have to precede the implementation of any government plan, and, in any case, any such plan had to be placed under the control of dentists. The dentists called for greater state funding for dental programs and lower fees for dental students.

The dentists admitted that "education and income separately and together are strongly associated with going to the dentist." Yet the dentists largely ignored their own insight that money kept many Canadians from properly caring for their teeth, focusing instead on "people's lack of interest in preventative measures" as the way to improve dental health. They recommended that provinces make fluoridation of water supplies mandatory for municipalities, that Canadians consume less sugar, and that more government funds go to dental research. While cool to state involvement in dentistry, outside of dental education and research, the CDA did recognize some need for governments to fund potential consumers of dentists' services. Like the physicians, they supported takeover of the manufacture and distribution of pharmaceuticals in Canada or for new public regulations over the industry from any segment of the health care industry. Health care providers, such as doctors, dentists, and pharmacy owners, had a common interest in establishing a high price for their services, and happily confounded private provision with competition and efficient pricing.

Ultimately, the two arguments that were heard most frequently to discredit a compulsory public medical system were that it would deprive health practitioners of the freedoms that all business people ought legitimately to have in a democratic society, and that it would be so costly as to provoke crushing levels of taxation that would destroy Canada's industrial competitiveness. The CMA stated starkly: "We consider government intervention into the field of prepaid medical care to the point of becoming a monopolistic purchaser of medical services, to be a measure of civil conscription. We would urge this Royal Commission to support our view that, exclusive of states of emergency, civil conscription of any segment of the Canadian population is contrary to our democratic philosophy."[14] Premier Leslie Frost of Ontario was prominent among anti-medicare politicians to invoke the industrial competitiveness argument. The country, he averred, "has already become a high cost economy. And that is affecting our trading and developmental position."[15]

MEDICARE'S SUPPORTERS

Medicare's supporters suggested that Canadians had collective rights to the best medical treatments that were available regardless of income, and that the right of individuals to receive affordable medical service outweighed the alleged rights of medical practitioners to price their services as they deemed best. Despite the crushing majority support for medicare evident in opinion polls, few Canadians were willing to come forward as individuals and suggest that they had received second-rate medical treatment because they were poor. A careful scouring of the thousands of briefs before the Hall Commission reveals only one case where an individual Canadian denounced her doctors for providing her family mediocre care because of their inability to pay. Her physician's scathing personal attack upon her in response demonstrated why few Canadians had the temerity to reveal personal cases of receiving poor treatment or being driven to bankruptcy to obtain necessary medical attention.[16] Instead, the horror stories that the commissioners heard as well as the main arguments countering the claims of private medicine came from organizations. Trade unions, social worker and welfare organizations, farmers' federations, and the United

Church of Canada convinced the commissioners that they should adopt an ambitious national program.

The Canadian Association of Social Workers placed the case before the Hall Commission that programs that limited free state care to the destitute, which were in operation in many Canadian provinces, did not work. Many were deterred from seeking medical assistance at clinics because several hours might be required for them to fill out forms at the accounting department. Meanwhile, many people of middle means who did not qualify for the state care available to the indigent avoided seeking needed medical care because "it is going to come out of the food budget, or come out of the youngsters' clothing budget or something like this." The social workers observed that the stigma of receiving a charitable service discouraged usage of the service. It also created problems regarding the proper cut-off income for recipients. Better to have medicare available to all Canadians so that no one had to see it as either a special right or a special shame.

The social workers unsurprisingly made a strong pitch for closely co-ordinating health and welfare services so as to improve the physical and mental health of the population. Many of their clients suffered poor health because of poor housing and the stresses that resulted from limited incomes. They also called for the definition of medical services under medicare to include convalescent hospitals, home care and replacement homemakers for convalescing mothers, and the provision of prosthetic appliances.[17]

The Canadian Federation of Agriculture (CFA) and several other major farm groups appeared before the commission and indicated that the majority of farmers could not afford private health insurance.[18] The United Church of Canada, whose General Council had called for a contributory national health plan since 1952, confirmed the CFA's impressions. The United Church brief added that urban immigrants, particularly unskilled workers from southern Italy, were perhaps even more vulnerable. These people were underpaid, ill-housed, insecure about their income, and prone as a result to both physical and mental illness. Yet they were too impoverished to be able to set aside the money for private health insurance.[19]

But the trade union movement probably proved the most effective in demolishing the arguments of industry and physicians that Canadians were gradually meeting their medical needs privately. In the postwar period, the trade union movement, which enrolled about a third of Canadian workers thanks to wartime and early postwar organizing successes, had succeeded in winning a variety of "fringe benefits" for their members in addition to wage increases and improvements in working conditions. A medical benefits package had become a common gain for trade unionists, and such prepaid medical insurance swelled the numbers of families whom the private insurance companies could claim as they pooh-poohed the need for a public program.

Unions' characterizations of the limitations of private coverage undermined such insurance industry boasting. National, provincial, and labour federations complained to the Hall Commission that the profit-driven insurance schemes that enrolled their members tended to severely restrict or deny coverage altogether in such areas as preventive health services, rehabilitation, mental health, dental services, and social services. Prescription drugs, nursing aid, appliances, eyeglasses, and hearing aids were rarely covered. Yet most of these plans had "costly deductible and co-insurance charges." As the Canadian Labour Congress (CLC) concluded. "It is too much to expect that a complete range of services can be made available on a universal basis to the Canadian people within the near future through the mere extension of the private pre-payment schemes. It is not physically, financially nor administratively possible."[40]

The CLC led the way in labour's deliberations before the commission, answering point-by-point the claims made to the commission by the CMA. It noted that, even using the CMA's definition of poverty, 4.5 million Canadians would require that their medical bills be paid for by the state. Apart from the layouts for these people, the state would have to spend millions in carrying out the means tests necessary for determining who was eligible, in the process stigmatizing them.[41]

Trade union federations in poorer provinces emphasized the disparities in medical services among Canada's regions that resulted from a market-driven allocation of resources. In Newfoundland, for example, the number of doctors per capita was less than half the Canadian average, while many rural areas had no physicians at all. The imbalance in the availability of nurses with the rest of Canada was similar. There were few dentists outside the two major cities, and St. John's institution for the aged and infirm was "a blot on the decency of the Canadian nation." Not only was a national medicare plan needed, according to the Newfoundland Federation of Labour, but such a plan had to provide for regional hospitals and clinics to be built and staffed in deprived provinces.[42]

THE HALL REPORT AND THE IMPLEMENTATION OF MEDICARE

Emmett Hall and the majority of his fellow commissioners were won over, in large part, by the values and arguments of the supporters of a universal medi-

care program. Their 1964 report made some obeisance in the direction of business and physicians by recognizing that no doctor should be forced to join a national medicare program, and that doctors should remain in private practice even if they joined medicare rather than becoming civil servants working in government offices. Even more of a victory for the physicians was the commission's rejection of the National Health Service model of salaried physicians, which the labour movement had endorsed. Instead, the commissioners supported continuation of the fee-for-service model which was a hallmark of private insurance.[43]

However, the overall direction of the report reflected the persuasiveness of the opponents of the argument made by businesses and physicians. Wrote the commissioners: "The achievement of the highest possible health standards for all our people must become a primary objective of national policy and a cohesive factor contributing to national unity, involving individual and community responsibilities and actions. This objective can best be achieved through a comprehensive, universal Health Services Programme for the Canadian people."

"Comprehensive," in Hall's view, included "all health services, preventive, diagnostic, curative and rehabilitative, that modern medical and other services can provide."[44] This meant that governments should not only provide universal coverage for physicians' services and for hospitalization but should also cover prescription drug payments for all Canadians, home care and prosthetic services as required, dental services for children, expectant mothers, and public assistance recipients, and eyecare for children and the poor. Most of these programs would exclude user fees, though each prescription would bear a dollar user fee and adults would be expected to pay one-third the cost of eyeglasses, which would however be free for children.[45] Taxation would pay for all Canadians to be covered by the national health program. In short, Hall had rejected the voluntary medical insurance schemes that Ontario, Alberta, and British Columbia had proposed as alternatives to the Saskatchewan plan because only the latter appeared to guarantee the potential of full coverage to all Canadians for all necessary medical services.

Hall recommended that the federal government pay half the costs for any provincial medicare scheme that provided universal coverage. The provinces could determine their priorities in terms of the various components of the medicare scheme and the timing of their introduction. Federal government grants would help to establish the training programs required to produce the additional personnel needed once medical services were universally available, as well as the facilities required to build the medical and dental clinics to house

CHAPTER 8 THE MEDICARE DEBATE, 1945–80

185

The government had a built-in excuse for delay because of the need to convince the provinces to implement medicare programs. There were meetings in April and May of 1965 in which federal officials representing the cabinet and the Departments of National Health and Public Welfare along with the Department of Finance heard the views of ministers of health and their officials from the provinces. Two federal–provincial conferences that year also provided the provinces with a forum for their disparate views, but provided little detail from Pearson regarding the federal government's plans. Pearson did, however, insist that the federal government, following Hall, would insist that federal funds would only go to provincial programs that met four criteria: comprehensive coverage of physicians' services, universality of coverage, public administration, and portability of services so that citizens were covered when they lived outside of their home province.[49]

In Quebec, an exhaustive provincial review of social programs, headed by Claude Castonguay, had recently begun and tentatively looked favourably upon a program of universal medicare. Federal dollars to help fund such a program were desirable, but federal input into the design of the program was unacceptable. Alberta's Premier Manning continued to fulminate against any program that was universal and that did not involve co-insurance. His government was furious that Ottawa had penalized the province financially for its insistence on user fees in the hospitalization plan. Ontario, Manitoba, and British Columbia also insisted that provinces have more scope for the design of medicare than Pearson's four principles might allow. Other provinces accepted the principles of the Hall Report but wanted sufficient federal funding to make it affordable for them to establish a program. Only Newfoundland was anxious for a federal plan to be legislated immediately, though New Brunswick was committed to establishing a plan and Saskatchewan wanted a federal contribution to its program.[50]

The Liberals called a federal election in late 1965 but narrowly failed again to form a majority government. Their commitment to a modified version of the Hall recommendations during the election left them little alternative afterwards but to legislate a medicare bill. In 1966, the government introduced legislation to provide an average of 50 per cent of the costs of provincial schemes that met the four medicare principles (a formula was used that would provide a larger portion of federal funds per capita in poorer provinces),[51] but the legislation lacked a date for implementation. Initially, Pearson aimed for 1 July 1967, the one hundredth birthday of the country. However, continued provincial reluctance to accept the federal principles argued against such speed, as did the change in the balance of forces in the Liberal cabinet after the election.

these services. The federal government would, for example, share with the provinces the costs of building mental health wings in regular hospitals so that most inmates of mental health institutions could receive care in their community. It would also aid the provinces in providing funds that allowed parents to raise mildly intellectually disabled children at home.[46]

The Hall Report put pressure on Lester Pearson's Liberal government, which had been elected in 1963, albeit without a parliamentary majority, to live up to its medicare promises. The Liberals had promised a national medicare program that would provide comprehensive services free of charge to children till they left school and to Canadians over sixty-five years of age. Everyone else would have services by general practitioners, specialists, and surgeons, along with diagnostic services, covered, except for the first $25. Even the left-wingers in the government were taken aback by the scope of services that Hall wanted a national program to cover. For a year the government waffled, and even in the throne speech of 1965, the government committed itself to medicare in only the vaguest terms. The NDP, which had endorsed the Hall Report in toto, demanded that the government implement its full set of recommendations immediately.[47]

An exhaustive review of the Hall recommendations by the Department of National Health and Welfare demonstrated the substantial bureaucratic support for the tenor of the reforms proposed by the commissioners. Department officials endorsed Hall's views that "deterrent fees," that is user fees, could not be allowed for basic services because they contradicted the principle of universal availability of medical services. Federal funding of medical services along the lines of the existing federal formula for hospitals was "fundamental in making the most effective use of the nation's health resources to achieve the highest possible health standards for residents of Canada." The bureaucrats also endorsed the children's dental program and subsidizing of prescription costs, but with Finance and Privy Council officials serving as observers to the committee's deliberations, they couched such support with indications that both of these sets of services should be phased in over an unspecified period. Potential costs also caused the officials to reluctantly oppose Hall's embrace of government financing of home care.[48]

The eventual compromise reached within the government called for medicare to be introduced in phases. The first phase would add physician and diagnostic services to the existing hospitalization coverage, while other components of the Hall vision would be introduced as fiscal means became available. In practise, though few Canadians could know it at the time, there would be no second phase for medicare, at least during the twentieth century.

cidents were not addressed. The commissioners gave no consideration to the community-care model, which had already been piloted in Saskatchewan, accepting unquestioningly a hierarchical model of medical care in which physicians dictated the roles of other medical practitioners and patients had no input into either the character or payment structures of services.[57]

NATIVE PEOPLES AND MEDICAL CARE

Nothing illustrated better the argument that physician care alone could not guarantee a healthy population than the continued oppression and suffering of indigenous Canadians. In 1977, when the average age of death for Canadians was 66, the comparative figure for Natives was 42.4 years. They were four times as likely to die violent deaths in their twenties or thirties as other Canadians. Babies on reserves died in large numbers of gastroenteritis and pneumonia, diseases of poverty. Waters upon which Natives depended for their fish were often poisoned with waste mercury from chemical plants. On poor, isolated reserves with shabby housing and few facilities, Native children sniffed gas while their parents abused alcohol. Though the residential schooling system, which snatched children from their parents and placed them in environments where physical and sexual abuse were often rife, was being phased out, its scars on the Native psyche were reflected in substance abuse and poor parenting skills.

These woes were compounded by a lack of health workers, including doctors and nurses, on many reserves. There were only ten physicians and 221 nurses of Native descent in Canada in the mid-1970s and there was no national program to change this situation.[58] The federal government had over time taken a degree of responsibility for Native health care, always claiming, however, that constitutionally it was not compelled to do so. Until 1945, Indian Affairs had authority over Native health. After 1945, the Department of National Health and Welfare (DNHW) was given charge of this responsibility, and in 1962, a branch of DNHW called Medical Services was formed with a variety of programs under its control, including the former Indian Health Services.[59]

Community control initiatives at the grassroots attempted to compensate for government indifference and to pressure the federal government to provide Native communities with the wherewithal to deal with both their social and medical health needs. Reserves began to organize their own community medical schemes to hire doctors and nurses, to make up for the lethargy of Medical Services and to establish the right of Native communities to govern themselves

Walter Gordon, the progressive finance minister, took responsibility for having advised Pearson to hold an early election, and resigned from cabinet. His replacement, Mitchell Sharp, held views similar to those of organized business and appeared in no hurry to implement medicare, which he claimed could have an undue impact on the federal treasury. Robert Stanfield, the new leader of the Conservative party, denounced "a vast new spending program."[52] But Sharp and his supporters were only able to delay medicare's implementation by one year.[53] On 1 July 1968, funds would be available to provinces with a medicare scheme that met the four principles of medicare. Still, the division within the Pearson cabinet encouraged provinces that opposed universality and public administration to move slowly. Only Saskatchewan and British Columbia presented plans in the month after the medicare deadline and began to receive federal funding in July.

By then, the dithering Pearson had been replaced as head of the government by the more decisive Pierre Elliott Trudeau. Trudeau scotched any further attempts from within the cabinet or the provinces to allow for either delays or modification of the medicare legislation. Within a year all provinces but Quebec had announced plans that met the criteria of the Medical Services Act of 1968. Quebec entered the plan in 1972.[54]

MEDICARE, HEALTH, AND HIERARCHY

The Hall Report was less about health overall than about how to ensure that access to physicians was generally available and that physicians were adequately paid.

Hall did not challenge the medical profession's monopoly over medical care. The commissioners heard a variety of briefs from physicians from non-allopathic healers, but they largely accepted the equation of physicians with healing. Even the officials of the Department of National Health and Welfare who reviewed the report's recommendations observed the narrowness of Hall's focus: "Attention in the Recommendations was actually focused on personal health services provided mainly by physicians and others in private practice to the exclusion of public health services."[55]

In addition, the commissioners paid little attention to environmental pollution, which a few trade union briefs suggested was a factor in the health of individuals.[56] They had little to say about the roles of fitness, stress, nutrition, and poverty, outside of its impact on ability to pay medical bills. Industrial ac-

clusions. In practice, the desire to keep costs down resulted in a watering down of Hall's proposals that saw medicare's "first phase" limited to coverage of visits to hospitals and physicians, and diagnostic services. Further phases were not legislated. The late 1960s represented the high point of social reform rather than a first installment on social reforms that would fundamentally redistribute wealth in Canada. The next three chapters examine areas in which the postwar welfare state largely failed to meet the needs of Canadians—daycare, housing, and poverty.

NOTES

1 Health Study Bureau, *Review of Canada's Health Needs and Insurance Proposals* (Toronto, ON: Health Study Bureau, 1946), 41.
2 Ibid., 40–3.
3 Malcolm G. Taylor, *Health Insurance and Canadian Public Policy: The Seven Decisions that Created the Canadian Health Insurance System* (Montreal, QC: McGill-Queen's University Press, 1978), 166.
4 Health Study Bureau, *Review of Canada's Health Needs*, 3–4.
5 Historian Georgina Taylor nuances the notion of medicare having been single parented by a male, recalling that farm women, led by Violet McNaughton, had created the prototypes of medicare at a municipal level in the province. See Georgina M. Taylor, "Ground for Common Action: Violet McNaughton's Agrarian Feminism and the Origins of the Farm Women's Movement in Canada" (PhD thesis, Carleton University, 1997). See also Georgina M. Taylor, "Let Us Co operate': Violet McNaughton and the Co-operative Ideal," In *Co operatives in the Year 2000: Memory, Mutual Aid, and the Millennium*, ed. Brett Fairbairn and Ian Macpherson (Saskatoon, SK: Centre for the Study of Co-operatives, University of Saskatchewan, 2000), 57–78.
6 "CCF Broadcast by T.C. Douglas, MP," William Lyon Mackenzie King Papers, MG 26, J1, Vol. 346, p. 297811, *Library and Archives of Canada*, (LAC).
7 Ibid., p. 297809.
8 Many organizations expressed disappointment that the promised national health insurance program did not materialize. For example, the National Council of Women of Canada voted at their 1947 convention to "commend the Dominion Government on the Health Insurance Plan already prepared and urge its implementation as soon as possible." Resolutions, Annual Meeting, held in Regina June 6–11, 1947," National Council of Women of Canada (NCWC) Papers, MG 28 I 25, Vol. 90, File 1, LAC.
9 Malcolm G. Taylor, "The Canadian Health Care System: After Medicare," in *Health and Canadian Society: Sociological Perspectives*, 2nd ed., ed. David Coburn, Carl D'Arcy, George M. Torrance, and Peter New (Toronto, ON: Fitzhenry and Whiteside, 1987), 74.
10 Duane Mombourquette, "An Inalienable Right: The CCF and Rapid Health Care Reform, 1944–1948," in *Social Welfare Policy in Canada: Historical Readings*, ed. Raymond B. Blake and Jeff Keshen (Toronto, ON: Copp Clark, 1995), 298–302.
11 Taylor, "The Canadian Health-Care System," 74–84; Margaret A. Ormsby, *British Columbia: A History* (Vancouver, BC: Macmillan, 1958), 487; Alvin Finkel, *The Social Credit Phenomenon in Alberta* (Toronto, ON: University of Toronto Press, 1989), 123.
12 Eugene Vayda and Raisa B. Deber, "The Canadian Health Care System: A Developmental Overview," in *Social Welfare Policy*, ed. Blake and Keshen, 315.

in all areas, including health services. Native nurses formed an organization to promote nursing as an occupation for Native girls. Shamanistic healing practices, long suppressed by the colonial authorities on reserves, but never completely eradicated, made a comeback. The colonialism experienced by Native peoples and the health of the Aboriginal population seemed inextricably linked, and campaigns for community control over health services formed part of the struggle to shed the legacy of paternalistic, remote control by Ottawa over Native lives.[60]

The creation of a national network of provincial medicare programs, all subscribing to the principles of comprehensiveness, universality, portability, and public administration, represented a major victory for progressive forces in Canada, backed by overwhelming public opinion. The combination of public campaigning by important social movements, including labour, farmers, and social workers, with support from key elements of the Liberal Party and the civil service, resulted in a Tory-appointed royal commission failing to suggest some sort of public-private mix that largely subordinated health service provision to profit-seeking health insurance companies and physicians. In turn, this led the Liberal government, divided for two decades on whether to implement its promises originally made in 1919 for a national public program, to finally deliver.

The success of reformist forces in Canada in the area of medicare was a contrast with the United States where the politics of race, the lack of a social-democratic party, the bias of public expenditures towards military spending, and the immense power of organized medicine continued to prevent the introduction of a universal medicare program. As Canada legislated universal medicare, American President Lyndon Johnson, spending billions of dollars on an unpopular war in Indochina, felt only able to support medicare for the elderly and a Medicaid program for the destitute that held down costs for medical services for the poor by sending them to special medical clinics, which were generally understaffed and involved long waits for service.[61]

By contrast, Canada's "first phase" of medicare provided far less comprehensive coverage for illness prevention and treatment than the National Health Service in Britain and similar programs in Scandinavia and Holland. The Soviet Union and its Cold War satellites in eastern Europe all provided sweeping free comprehensive medical care programs. The Hall Commission had looked to western European models rather than the United States in framing its recommendations, and the government rhetorically accepted the commission's con-

13 David Gagan and Rosemary Gagan, *For Patients of Moderate Means: A Social History of the Voluntary Public General Hospital in Canada, 1890–1950* (Montreal, QC: McGill-Queen's University Press, 2002).

14 Brief of Canadian Medical Association, April 1962, Canada, Royal Commission on Health Services, RG 33, Series 78, Vol. 19, File 278, LAC.

15 "Brief from Great West Life and Metropolitan Life Insurance Company," n.d., Royal Commission on Health Services, Vol. 15, Exhibit 200.

16 Monte M. Poen, *Harry S. Truman Versus the Medical Lobby: The Genesis of Medicare* (Columbia, MS: University of Missouri Press, 1979); Lawrence R. Jacobs, *The Health of Nations: Public Opinion and the Making of American and British Health Policy* (Ithaca, NY: Cornell University Press, 1993).

17 "Reports of 1955 Federal-Provincial Conference," Department of National Health and Welfare Papers, RG 29, Vol. 918, LAC.

18 Joan Feather, "From Concept to Reality: Formation of the Swift Current Health Region," *Prairie Forum* 16, 1 (Spring 1991): 59–80; Joan Feather, "Impact of the Swift Current Health Region: Experiment or Model," *Prairie Forum* 16, 2 (Fall 1991): 225–48; Stan Rands, "Recollections: The CCF in Saskatchewan," in *Western Canadian Politics: The Radical Tradition*, ed. Donald C. Kerr (Edmonton, AB: NeWest, 1981), 58–64.

19 On the doctors' strike, see Robin F. Badgley and Samuel Wolfe, *Doctors' Strike: Medical Care and Conflict in Saskatchewan* (Toronto, ON: Macmillan, 1967).

20 P.E. Bryden, *Planners and Politicians: Liberal Politics and Social Policy, 1957–1968* (Montreal, QC: McGill-Queen's University Press, 1997), chap. 2 and 3.

21 Finkel, *The Social Credit Phenomenon*, 144; "Discussions with Provinces on Health Services Matters," Meeting with Alberta Officials, 22 April 1965, Department of National Health and Welfare Papers, RG 33, Vol. 45.

22 Evidence of Canadian Medical Association, April 1962, Canada, Royal Commission on Health Services, Vol. 19, File 278; Evidence of Canadian Chamber of Commerce, March 1962, Vol. 14, File 188.

23 Canada, Economic Council of Canada, *The Challenge of Growth and Change*, Fifth Annual Review (Ottawa, ON: Queen's Printer, 1968), 104–105.

24 "Discussions with Provinces on Health Services Matters," Department of National Health and Welfare Papers, Vol. 45.

25 Evidence of Canadian Medical Association, April 1962, Royal Commission on Health Services.

26 Evidence of British Columbia Medical Association, February 1962, Royal Commission on Health Services, Vol. 12, File 150.

27 Evidence of Canadian Medical Association, April 1962, Royal Commission on Health Services.

28 Ibid.

29 Evidence of Canadian Dental Association, March 1962, Royal Commission on Health, Vol. 14, Exhibit 192, 1962.

30 Evidence of Saskatchewan Registered Nurses Association, January 1962, Royal Commission on Health Services, Vol. 9, File 84.

31 See, for example, Evidence of New Brunswick Association of Registered Nurses, 9 November 1961, Vol. 8, File 44; Evidence of Manitoba Association of Registered Nurses, January 1962, Vol. 9, File 65; and Evidence of Association des Infirmières de la Province de Québec, April 1962, Vol. 15, File 219, Royal Commission on Health Services.

32 Evidence of Canadian Pharmaceutical Manufacturers Association, May 1962, Royal Commission on Health Services, Vol. 20, File 291.

33 Canada, Director of Investigation and Research, Combines Investigation Act, "Material Collected for Submission to the Restrictive Trade Practices Commission in the Course of an Inquiry under Section 42 of the Combines Investigation Act Relating to the Manufacture, Distribution and Sale of Drugs" (Ottawa, ON: Department of Justice, 1961), 258.

34 Evidence of Canadian Medical Association, 16 October 1962, Royal Commission on Health Services, Vol. 6, File 67.

35 Canadian Press Report of Leslie Frost Interview, 29 March 1961, Royal Commission on Health Services, Vol. 8.

36 Evidence of Mrs. Marguerite Miles, Toronto, n.d. File 355; Evidence of Dr. C. Collins-Williams, Toronto, n.d., File 375, Vol. 22, Royal Commission on Health Services.

37 Evidence of Canadian Association of Social Workers, 28 May 1962, Royal Commission on Health Services, Vol. 6, File 61.

38 Evidence of Canadian Federation of Agriculture, 27 March, 1962, Royal Commission on Health Services, Vol. 14, File 190.

39 Evidence of United Church of Canada, April 1962, Royal Commission on Health Services, Vol. 22, File 352.

40 Evidence of Canadian Labour Congress, 17 October, 1962, Royal Commission on Health Services, Vol. 6, File 68.

41 Ibid.

42 Evidence of Newfoundland Federation of Labour, October 1961, Royal Commission on Health Services, Vol. 7, File 25.

43 Royal Commission on Health Services, *Report*, vol. 1 (Ottawa, ON: Queen's Printer, 1964), 29.

44 Ibid., 11.

45 Ibid., 19.

46 Ibid., 19, 24–25, 36, 41.

47 "Election 1963 Pamphlets," National Liberal Federation Papers, MG 28, IV-3, Vol. 1024, LAC; Bryden, *Planners and Politicians*, 136.

48 "Departmental Review of the Report of the Royal Commission on Health Services: Departmental Appraisal and Proposals and Recommendations," March 1965, 24, 25, 28, 59, 62, 77, 87–92. Quote is from 28. Department of National Health and Welfare Papers, Vol. 45.

49 Ibid., 142.

50 Bryden, *Planners and Politicians*, 159; "Discussions with Provinces on Health Services Matters," Meeting with Quebec Delegation, 12 and 13 April 1965, Department of National Health and Welfare Papers, Vol. 45; Finkel, *The Social Credit Phenomenon in Alberta*, 150-51.

51 Eugene Vayda and Raisa B. Deber, "The Canadian Health Care System: A Developmental Overview," in *Social Welfare Policy*, ed. Blake and Keshen, 316. In 1973–74, the federal grant to Newfoundland covered 81.5 per cent of the province's medical bills and 57.6 per cent of its hospital costs while the grant to Ontario paid 44.8 per cent of medical care and 49.4 per cent of hospital costs. "For medical insurance, each province received 50 per cent of the average national per capita medical care expenditure multiplied by its population."

52 The continued opposition of the premiers was clear in File 618.4, "Correspondence with Premiers," Lester B. Pearson Papers, MG 26, N-4, Vol. 199, LAC. Other than Saskatchewan and British Columbia, no provinces were clearly prepared to join the medicare program in February 1968. Nova Scotia and Newfoundland were believed by the federal government to be only prepared to join it if Ontario did. But Ontario, New Brunswick, and Alberta were unprepared to join the program. Manitoba planned to defer participation for at least a year beyond July 1 in the hopes of convincing the federal government to concede support for a plan more in tune with Manitoba's free-enterprise views.

53 Ibid., 152–63.

54 Ibid., 164–67.

55 Department of National Health and Welfare, "Departmental Review," 2.

56 Evidence of United Electrical, Radio and Machine Workers of America, May 1962, Royal Commission on Health Services, Vol. 21.

57 Donald Swartz, "The Politics of Reform: Conflict and Accommodation in Canadian Health Policy," in *The Canadian State: Political Economy and Political Power*, ed. Leo Panitch (Toronto, ON: University of Toronto Press, 1977), 311–43; and Vivienne Walters, "State, Capital and Labour: The Introduction of Federal-Provincial Insurance for Physician Care in Canada," *Canadian Journal of Sociology and Anthropology* 19, 2 (1982): 157–72.

58 Paul Grescoe, "A Nation's Disgrace," in *Health and Canadian Society*, ed. Coburn, D'Arcy, Torrance, and New, 127–40.

59 James S. Frideres and René R. Gadacz, *Aboriginal Peoples in Canada: Contemporary Conflicts*, 6th ed. (Toronto, ON: Prentice Hall, 2001), 68–69.

60 Maureen K. Lux, *Medicine that Walks: Disease, Medicine, and Canadian Plains Native People, 1880–1940* (Toronto, ON: University of Toronto Press, 2001); T. Kue Young, *Health Care and Cultural Change: The Indian Experience in the Central Subarctic* (Toronto, ON: University of Toronto Press, 1988).

61 Poen, *Harry S. Truman Versus the Medical Lobby*; Paul Starr, *The Social Transformation of American Medicine* (New York, NY: Basic Books, 1982).

192

CHAPTER 12

The Welfare State since 1980

X.Y. was an Edmonton mother who was in great economic difficulty in the summer of 2003. A single working mom of three school-aged children, she had benefited a few years earlier from a non-profit agency program that bought and repaired older homes and then sold them, without financial markup, to lower income families. Though she earned barely more than the minimum wage at her clerical job, she could just afford the mortgage payments on the house. But, in the winter of 2003, the combination of colder than usual weather and government deregulation of utility rates doubled and then tripled her heating and electricity bills. Though she made use of food banks and worked extra hours, she could not pay these bills in addition to her mortgage, school fees, and the usual costs associated with raising children and running a household.

X.Y. invited social workers with the provincial Department of Social Services to help her with her financial dilemmas. While they were initially sympathetic, their focus shifted when the utility companies cut off her heat and electricity. They felt it was their duty to question whether her children could remain with her in conditions that were unsafe. Other children had been seized from parents who had become homeless or lived in unheated homes, even though there was no question of their parenting skills or devotion to their children. X.Y. was unwilling to part with her children. She could sell her old home at a loss. But she would then have to rent a substandard home in a crack-infested "welfare" district where she could never feel comfortable about her children's safety. Instead, she decided to face the uncertainty of life in another province where some regulation of utility costs remained and social assistance provisions were slightly better.

Few Canadians would have believed in 1970 that three decades later their fellow citizens might face X.Y.'s choices. Freshly minted reports from government commissions and task forces recommended guaranteed annual incomes, a fairer tax system, guaranteed spots for children in a national daycare network, and an extension of social housing. By the early 2000s, these reports were yellowed with age, their recommendations having been ignored by successive governments. Almost one Canadian in ten relied on social assistance for all or part of household income in 1999 (only tightened eligibility rules kept many more from collecting). 2 million in a population of 30 million relied on food banks for at least some of their food that year, and 200,000 Canadians were homeless.

Was the political will to enhance social equality in Canada ever really there? The 1965 annual convention of the Canadian Chamber of Commerce had listened somberly to the results of an extensive survey which concluded that the Chamber's efforts to influence Canadians' attitudes to social programs had backfired. Respondents had discounted the organization's research and public stances as the self-interested propaganda of the greedy rich.' Gradually, corporate leaders sought other ways to turn public thinking against social equality, particularly through funding of superficially independent research institutes that could become the main spokespersons for the corporate viewpoint. The Fraser Institute in British Columbia, the C.D. Howe Institute in Ontario, and the Atlantic Institute for Market Studies presented themselves as disinterested organizations of academics. The findings of their well-financed studies were regularly distributed to the corporate-controlled media and reported on as if they were news rather than editorials. Judging by public opinion polls that showed Canadians in the early 1990s to be more right wing than their counterparts in the late 1960s, the steady stream of alleged research results from the institutes influenced Canadian attitudes towards the proper balance between social spending and taxation. Left-wing institutes such as the Canadian Centre for Policy Alternatives were established as a counter-response to the

corporate-financed institutes. These institutes were funded by labour, social work, women's, and environmental groups, sponsors which lacked the financial means and media contacts to get their message across as effectively as the corporations did.

To a degree, neo-liberal ideas took hold in all of Canada's major political parties by the 1980s. They became especially entrenched in the national arena though the Reform Party, formed in 1986, and its successor, the Canadian Alliance (CA), formed in 2000, as well as the Progressive Conservative (PC) Party. The reconstructed Conservative Party of Canada, formed in 2004, which merged the CAs and PCs, made neo-liberal economics the cornerstone of its policy. Even the Liberal federal government, first elected in 1993, while rhetorically centrist, had been captured by neo-liberal forces, particularly in the person of Paul Martin Jr., finance minister from 1993 to 2002, and prime minister as of December 2003.

Most provincial regimes elected after 1980 subscribed to some version of neo-liberal ideology: the Progressive Conservatives in Alberta swung sharply to the right in 1993; Ontario's Progressive Conservative government elected in 1995 followed suit, as did the British Columbia Liberals elected in 2002 and the Quebec Liberals elected in 2003; and both old-line parties in the Atlantic provinces toed the neo-liberal line. The New Democratic regimes elected at various times in Ontario, Saskatchewan, Manitoba, and British Columbia, along with the Parti Québécois regimes, represented only partial exceptions to the neo-liberal thrust.[2] In Quebec, the vision of the Castonguay-Nepveu Report of the early 1970s, which promised to make a huge dent on poverty in the province, was quietly abandoned in 1984. The PQ had spent its early years in office raising the minimum wage and increasing social assistance payments, only to allow both to be eaten up by inflation in subsequent years. In its 1984 budget the PQ cut provincial taxes and spending despite the recession.'

Family allowances, CAP, and federal financial support for social housing had all disappeared by the 1990s. Two-tiered medical care, in which the better off could purchase services outside the public sector, had made some gains. The percentage of unemployed Canadians eligible to collect unemployment insurance had been eroded to levels unseen since the early 1950s. Yet the movements that had fought for the creation of social programs as citizen entitlements before the 1980s did not stand idly by as governments tried to rewrite the social contract. This chapter traces the evolution of both neo-liberal forces and popular forces in the struggle to control social policies after 1980.

in 1980. However, faced with declining revenues, he was unwilling to embrace the Carter Commission's recommendations for radical changes in the taxation system or to follow Keynesian monetary policies. Instead, he cut social spending so as to contain the rapidly growing deficits incurred by his government from 1975 onwards. Though he remained a supporter of social entitlements in theory, he lost interest in the guaranteed annual income that his government had earlier extolled.

Trudeau was also alarmed by the above-inflation increases in publicly financed health spending in the mid-1970s. Provincial health programs had responded in the early years of medicare to growing demands from patients and doctors for services. In 1977, Trudeau ended the guarantee of federal matching funds for provincial expenditures on health care and post-secondary education. Instead, the federal government would provide an annual Established Programs Funding (EPF) grant to provinces, based on past spending that was indexed to inflation. By handing over unconditional tax points to the provinces equal to about half of the monies they were already receiving annually from Ottawa for health care and post-secondary education, Trudeau softened criticisms from some premiers that the federal government was beginning a process that would lead to a federal withdrawal of funds to the provinces in these areas.[6]

The provinces responded to declining revenues from the federal government by trying to reduce the rate of growth in their health care and post-secondary education expenditures. Allowing universities to hike tuition fees by large amounts was the usual solution to the latter problem, along with reduced expenditures on the upkeep of buildings and eventually on programs. In health care, physicians' fees were curbed somewhat, but in some provinces, the doctors were allowed to recoup their losses by extra-billing patients. Federal National Health and Welfare Minister Monique Bégin denounced extra-billing as a violation of medicare's promise of accessibility to medical services, and in 1984, the federal government introduced the Canada Health Act, which imposed penalties on provinces that allowed extra-billing. Their annual EPF grants would be reduced by an amount equal to the number of dollars that physicians had been allowed to extra-bill patients. The premiers, recognizing that their voters were more opposed to extra-billing than to federal intervention in areas of provincial jurisdiction, beat a retreat.[7]

The Trudeau government also raised the Guaranteed Income Supplement in the early 1980s. The increase reduced the poverty rate for seniors, as measured by Statistics Canada, from 27 per cent in 1980 to 19 per cent in 1985,

---

PRELUDE TO NEO-LIBERALISM

The origins of the neo-liberal assault lie in the economic stagnation of the 1970s. As both inflation and unemployment rose in tandem throughout the decade, conservatives questioned the efficacy of the Keynesian approach to economic policy that supposedly had been utilized by governments since the war to keep both inflation and unemployment in check. They argued that government attempts to reduce unemployment were causing inflation without affecting joblessness. The funds required for stimulative expenditures were being financed by government deficits, which, in turn, were financed by loans from financial institutions both at home and abroad. The loans by these institutions to government allegedly "crowded out" loans to the private sector, forcing interest rates up to record levels. In turn, this fuelled inflation. With companies unable to make loans, jobs in the private sector were disappearing at a faster rate than those that could be created in the public sector. Such viewpoints were joined to the more traditional conservative ones that argued the provision of state aid to those without incomes encouraged them to refuse the jobs that were on offer.[4]

A minority of economists disputed the neo-liberal version of economic events as both ahistorical and lacking in rigour. The links between inflation and government deficits that neo-liberals claimed as fact were unsupported by historical evidence and, government surpluses in the early 1950s had not prevented double-digit inflation from occurring in later years. In any case, they argued, federal financial policy in the 1970s did not follow Keynesian prescriptions. While fiscal policy, which focused on unemployment, was mildly expansionary, monetary policy, which focused on inflation, was restrictionist. The two seemed to cancel each other out. Neo-liberal perspectives were firmly entrenched in the Bank of Canada, and after 1975, the Trudeau government, co-operating with the Bank, regarded tight money policies as a key ingredient in its efforts to stem inflation rates that had reached double digits annually. Opponents of this approach pointed out that Canada's unemployment rate, which had doubled from 4 per cent in 1970 to 8 per cent in 1978–79, would remain high until interest rates fell.[5]

Trudeau's embrace of contradictory economic policies was also evident when he campaigned against wage and price controls during the federal election of August 1974, only to turn around in October 1975 and impose controls for a three-year period in order to contain inflation. Trudeau did not embrace the full-blown neo-liberalism espoused by Margaret Thatcher, who was elected British prime minister in 1979, and Ronald Reagan, elected American president

the corporate elite's view that well-financed social programs pushed up taxation rates unnecessarily, Mulroney hoped to cut social spending early in his regime so that Canadians would forgive him by the time of the next election. But his first effort in that direction backfired. In 1985 he announced that old age pension payments, which rose annually by the rate of inflation, would only be partially indexed to inflation. Seniors, said the new prime minister cheerfully, recognized that all Canadians needed to make a contribution in the fight against inflation and ballooning government deficits. Seniors proved him wrong. The "grey power" movement of seniors' organizations had grown apace in the 1970s and 1980s as their numbers in the country grew. Demonstrations by old people embarrassed the government, particularly in one instance when Solange Denis, an Ottawa senior, confronted the prime minister and told him, with the network television news crews recording the moment, that if he did not rescind his change to the pension it would be "goodbye Charlie Brown" come the next election.

Mulroney's pension plans, along with earlier indications from Finance Minister Michael Wilson in November 1984 that the government planned to stiffen the UI program, sparked the creation of Solidarité Populaire Québec, which brought together seventy-five organizations, including the three competing trade union federations as well as women's, welfare advocacy, and seniors' groups.[11] Mulroney beat a strategic retreat, and turned his attention to the less politically charged area of EPF grants to the provinces. He announced in 1986 that his government would cut these grants by 2 per cent per year, a decrease that amounted to 6 per cent a year in real dollars when inflation was taken into account. Though his government held hearings regarding a national daycare program, no program was announced.

In part, because of Mulroney's apparent betrayal of the "sacred trust," though also because of scandals in the government and internal bickering within the Liberal Party, the NDP began a rise to the top of the polls. Canadians, who were somewhat ambivalent about neo-liberalism, were attracted to the social-democratic party's pitch for higher taxes on the wealthy and on corporations as the means to maintain and enrich Canada's social programs. But, by the time of the 1988 federal election, Mulroney appeared to have chosen a neo-liberal issue that would win him re-election: free trade. The Macdonald Commission's report, heavily influenced by business groups, suggested that a free-trade deal with the United States was the answer to Canada's economic woes. Canada, the report argued, should end wasteful expenditures meant to protect Canadian jobs with tariffs and to keep Canadian industries in Canadian hands. The free

but poverty rates remained much higher for elderly women without partners. The Special Senate Committee on Poverty's community-linked standard determined that a third of the elderly in Canada were poor. The Social Planning Council of Metropolitan Toronto calculated that in that city alone, over half of seniors lived in straitened circumstances.[8]

Trudeau's efforts to balance capitalist and popular demands seemed in doubt with the onset of a worldwide recession in 1982. The tight-money policies of the Reagan and Thatcher governments[9] fuelled a massive contraction in international investment and trade. Between 1979 and 1982 unemployment rates almost tripled in Britain, doubled in the United States, and shot up from 8 per cent to almost 13 per cent in Canada. Trudeau clung to tight-money policies while making relatively minor cuts to public expenditures as compared with his American and British counterparts, having little idea about how to reinvigorate the Canadian economy. He appointed a royal commission to plan the path forward, placing at its head Donald Macdonald, a former finance minister who had become a leading figure on Bay Street. Before the royal commission reported, Trudeau retired from politics. His replacement, John Turner, another former finance minister with close connections to Bay Street, called a summer election in 1984.

Both Turner and his principal opponent, the new Progressive Conservative leader, Brian Mulroney, decided that Canadians were not prepared to accept a forthright neo-liberal agenda. Though both promised to decrease government expenditures, they were vague about which programs would be cut. Mulroney, during his run for the leadership of the PCs the year before, had castigated the Trudeau government as "socialist," but during the campaign insisted that a government led by him would not slash social programs established by the Liberals. Universal social programs, proclaimed the would-be prime minister, were a "sacred trust, not to be tampered with."[10] During a national pre-election debate of the party leaders, hosted by the National Action Committee on the Status of Women, all three promised to initiate a federal daycare program that would guarantee subsidized daycare spaces to all working mothers seeking quality child care while they worked. But Mulroney, the ultimate winner of the election, had other priorities.

Neo-Liberalism in Action

Brian Mulroney was the first Canadian prime minister since Louis St. Laurent who was at once a member of both the corporate and political elite. Sharing

market would bring jobs and prosperity to most Canadians if the heavy hand of government regulation were only lifted.[12]

This view was consistent with the view increasingly being expressed by corporate leaders throughout the Western world that government protection of industry and of individuals was hampering economic development. "Globalization" became a buzzword for neo-liberal ideologues who believed that no country should be barring capital or trade from another country to protect domestic companies or workers because this only reduced international economic growth. "Free markets," not governments, could be counted on to dispense economic justice.[13]

Recognizing, however, that some Canadians would continue to fail to meet their economic needs via the marketplace, Macdonald did support reviving the idea of the Guaranteed Annual Income (GAI), but only if it replaced most other social insurance programs. The Canadian Labour Congress (CLC) responded with a proposed program that would strengthen existing social insurance programs and make their benefits available to far more Canadians, using the GAI as a last-resort program for those who received insufficient income from other sources, including social insurance programs.[14]

In the 1988 federal election, both opposition parties opposed the Free Trade Agreement (FTA), arguing that the agreement's provisions against providing unfair advantage to firms in one's own country would place Canada's social programs on the chopping block. The Conservatives responded that social programs were exempt from the provisions of the FTA for fair competition between the two countries.[15] Opponents of free trade won more votes in the 1988 election than its supporters, but the Mulroney government kept its Commons majority. The election over, Mulroney nuanced his argument about how the FTA would affect social programs. The logic of the agreement, though not the letter, argued for Canada to bring its social programs in line with their less generous American counterparts. If Canadian taxes on corporations and investors exceeded American taxes, Canada would lose industry and investors.

Daycare disappeared from the public agenda after the 1988 election, and universality was removed from old age pensions and family allowances, as the government introduced a clawback of part or all of the payments made to individuals netting more than $50,000 a year.[16] Then, in 1990, the government announced a speed-up in the annual decreases to federal transfer payments for health care and post-secondary education, with 2004 targeted as the date when such transfers would end. A limit was also placed on CAP payments to the three wealthiest provinces, while unemployment insurance eligibility rules were

tightened. By the end of the Mulroney years in 1993, federal social spending accounted for 8.5 per cent of the GDP, a decline from 10.5 per cent in 1984.[17]

Cuts to social programs proved unpopular if only because they occurred at the same time that a nasty recession arrived in 1990, causing double-digit unemployment throughout the first half of the decade. Though an international slowdown played a role, Canada's job losses exceeded those in the United States and Europe and the government's tight-money policies, once hardly commented upon, began to draw a great deal of fire. Keynesian ideas still seemed to resonate with Canadians who expressed anger at the government for failing to respond to a recession with low interest rates that would lead businesses to create jobs.

Mulroney's neo-liberal thinking regarding monetary policy was shaped by the Bank of Canada and its governor, John Crow. Crow argued that keeping inflation under control rather than alleviating unemployment must be the government's first order of business, borrowing a term popular with right-wing economists to justify his monetary policies: NAIRU or non-accelerating inflation rate of unemployment. The new orthodoxy at the Bank and in the business community became that, even when the economy was buoyant, monetary and fiscal policy should ensure that 8 per cent of Canadians were both unemployed and recipients of minimal government funding through either unemployment insurance or social assistance. This would moderate the demands for wage improvements on the part of the employed, and allow business profits to rise to levels that had been reduced over a generation because of a combination of inflation and worker militancy. Reducing inflation to the lowest level possible, perhaps eradicating it altogether, became the goal of the Bank of Canada.[18]

RETURN OF THE LIBERALS

The election of NDP governments in Ontario, Saskatchewan, and British Columbia in 1990 and 1991 demonstrated disillusionment with neo-liberalism. However, the NDP governments, while instituting social reforms, largely accepted the neo-liberal thrust in Canadian policy-making. The Ontario NDP government, for example, having promised before its election to spend mightily to restore Ontario's unemployment-ridden economy, soon got cold feet. In his first year in office, Premier Bob Rae expanded social housing, substantially increased daycare spaces and the pay of daycare workers, and increased health care and education spending. By mid-1991, however, faced with business threats of a capital strike, Rae began to emphasize debt reduction over reducing unemployment.[19] He rescinded his promise to nationalize the province's auto insurance industry, and later alienated the public-sector unions by imposing pay cuts of 5 per cent on all public-sector workers earning over $30,000 per year.

The perceived betrayal of Ontario voters by the Rae government gave the Liberals, both provincially and federally, a chance to reassert their reformist credentials. When the election writ was handed down in 1993, the federal Liberals, led by Jean Chrétien, were ready with a Red Book of vague promises that pledged the Liberals would defend the social legislation they had introduced in earlier years. They would end cuts in EPF grants to the provinces, and there were hints that cuts already made would be restored. A national daycare program would be established. Brian Mulroney's successor, Kim Campbell, took up the cudgels for neo-liberalism, but she faced an even more right-wing opponent in the Western-based Reform Party. The Reformers wanted massive cuts in federal spending, and the conversion of the CPP into a program in which individuals would manage their own pension accounts.

The Liberals won a huge victory, winning all the seats in vote-rich Ontario, but they largely ignored their Red Book promises. Reduction in government deficits and debt remained paramount in government policy, resulting in further tightening of UI payments; additional cuts to health care, post-secondary education, and social assistance payments; and an end to family allowances. Paul Martin's budget speech in 1995 slashed government spending by $25 billion in three years, including $7 billion in transfers to provinces. That amounted to a 40 per cent cut in federal transfers.[20] A modest daycare program was announced but then withdrawn when the provinces, which would have to match federal funds, responded unfavourably.

Before facing the electorate for re-election in 1997, the Liberals had completely undone both CAP and family allowances, two programs that were part of the Liberal welfare-state heritage in Canada. CAP had disappeared in 1996 as the federal government, seeking to reduce its overall responsibility in areas of provincial jurisdiction, combined its expenditures in health care, post-secondary education, and social assistance into one cheque called the Canada Health and Social Transfer (CHST).[21] There would no longer be any question of the federal government holding back money from provinces whose welfare regime seemed too restrictive, as there had been with CAP in place. Although the Canada Health Act remained on the books, the Chrétien government continued to allow the federal contribution to the provinces for health care to de-

cline annually. It turned a blind eye to provincial actions that eroded universal access, such as a flat $50 fee for an eye exam conducted by an optometrist in Alberta, and rationed access to psychiatric, physiotherapist and other health services in many provinces.

The Liberals' acceptance of provincial supremacy in the social-welfare field was evident in the Social Union Framework Agreement announced on 4 February 1999. Though Quebec's separatist government refused to be part of the agreement, insisting on provincial sovereignty over its social services, all other provinces and territories signed on with Ottawa. The agreement restricted Ottawa's right to intervene in existing or future provincial programs and guaranteed it would never introduce a program before it had won the support of a majority of provinces and territories. The provinces and territories, in turn, promised to work together to homogenize their social policies as much as possible, and to limit discrimination in the delivery of social provision to migrants from other provinces.[22]

The combination of federal cutbacks and federal unwillingness to impose national standards for social programs could not have come at a worse time, from the point of view of social advocates. The neo-liberal orthodoxy, which regarded deficits and debts as immoral even in times of high unemployment and social need, had gripped most provincial governments. Ralph Klein's government in Alberta, which slashed health spending by almost 20 per cent in 1994, while reducing welfare rolls by over half in a single year, became the poster-boy administration for neo-liberals.[23] Provincial governments in the Atlantic provinces had been administering cuts for years by that time, and Ontario fully joined the neo-liberal column in 1995 after the election of a Progressive Conservative government headed by Mike Harris. Harris, a devotee of tax cuts for the well off, matched and then exceeded Ralph Klein's zeal in cutting social programs.

As the Canadian economy began to recover in the late 1990s, organized public opposition to cuts in social programs forced governments to restore some of the funding cuts of the previous decade. But social advocates were largely on the defensive, trying to restore cuts to programs that still existed, rather than calling for the reinstatement of programs such as CAP and family allowances, or demanding new programs, such as a national daycare program, a guaranteed annual income, or an expansion of medicare's coverage. The right wing's call for tax cuts continued to resonate with many citizens who believed themselves to be overtaxed. Even if the result of tax cuts was that a corporate executive saved about $10,000 while the middle-income taxpayer saved $500, the $500 was much appreciated. The Liberals' tax cuts in the 2001 election, which heavily favoured the rich, seemed to win popular support. They were coupled with promises to increase the annual payout of federal funds to the provinces for health care, though the increases that Jean Chrétien announced did not even restore federal funding to 1993 levels.[24] The next section looks in detail at the role neo-liberalism played in the fate of social programs after 1975.

(UN)EMPLOYMENT INSURANCE

As a result of the 1971 reforms to UI, 96 per cent of unemployed Canadians were eligible to receive insurance when they lost their jobs. Additional changes to the rules in the 1970s and 1980s reduced the eligible group to 85 per cent of the unemployed by 1989. But it was in the 1990s that the rules became especially restrictive and, by 1997, only 41 per cent of the unemployed were eligible for the renamed employment insurance (EI), a figure one percentage point below estimates of the eligible group in 1940 when UI was first introduced.[25] Both actuarial concerns and the government's desire to control wage demands by at once elevating unemployment levels and making the prospect of (un)employment look as grim as possible destroyed the view of (un)employment insurance as social justice for Canadians unable to find work. By 2000, the program looked rather like it did in 1940: primarily a tax grab meant to deal with government deficits in other programs, and very secondarily, a program to help a subset of the unemployed.

When the program was liberalized in 1971, it was estimated that the rate of unemployment would remain at a 5 per cent level, which had been the average in the 1960s. But relative economic stagnation in the 1970s pushed unemployment rates to 8 per cent by the end of the decade. To keep the unemployment insurance fund solvent, the federal government had to increase its share of payments from 19 per cent in 1971 to 51 per cent in 1975. Conservatives argued that UI's availability made it more attractive for workers to leave jobs, but statistics demonstrated that only 10 per cent of people who left jobs voluntarily applied for insurance. Moreover, in 1978, Statistics Canada reported that there were twenty times as many unemployed people in Canada as there were job openings.[26]

Beginning in 1975, the government began to tinker with the 1971 reforms, reducing benefits and increasing the weeks of employment required before an unemployed person could qualify for benefits.[27] But it was Brian Mulroney, in

his second term of office, who was responsible for shredding the philosophy underlining the 1971 changes. During his first term of office, Mulroney had appointed a commission, headed by former Quebec Liberal cabinet minister Claude Forget, to review and make recommendations regarding the UI system. The corporate and trade union representatives on the commission had opposing views, and the commission issued two reports. The majority report, written by Forget and supported by the business representatives, wanted UI returned to its original actuarial principles which excluded insurance for high-risk people. The unions, by contrast, denounced the logic that seasonal, short-term, and part-time workers should be ineligible for insurance because they had such a high likelihood of losing their jobs.[28]

In 1990 the Mulroney government, heeding Forget's advice, increased the number of weeks that a worker had to have worked within the previous year before becoming eligible for UI. So, for example, in Montreal, a high unemployment city where 10 weeks of work in the previous 52 had previously been enough to earn a right to a maximum of 32 weeks of insurance, it was now necessary to have worked a minimum of 16 weeks to collect any insurance, and that could last no more than 27 weeks. The minimum waiting time for eligibility for workers who had left a job or been fired, as opposed to laid off, was increased from 6 to 12 weeks after the employment ended.

Adding salt to the wounds of the unemployed who could not collect insurance, the government announced that it would expand its practice of dipping into the fund to find money for training programs and other "active" programs for the unemployed. Already using 2 per cent of the fund for such purposes, the government envisioned raising that amount to 15 per cent of the payouts from the fund. The trade union movement claimed that this was a raid on monies intended for income support to the unemployed, and that it constituted a subsidy to employers. While the government blamed the unemployed for their own fate—they allegedly lacked the necessary training to be flexible within an economy that required highly skilled labour—and bemoaned "dependency" on UI, social activists noted that the unemployed were the victims of capitalist restructuring. Ironically, they argued, the very people who were tossing workers out of their jobs would benefit from not having to pay to retrain those workers for new jobs in the economy.[29] Study after study would suggest in the years that followed that available training programs provided few skills that workers needed for the jobs that were opening up in Canada." The women's movement argued that most of the jobs that women were being trained for reinforced, rather than reversed, their unequal position in the labour market."

in the late 1990s and the election of opposition members in formerly Liberal ridings in the region in 1997 caused some relaxation of the strict rules governing EI. But, on the whole, changes in UI/EI policy over the post-1975 period represented a victory for neo-liberals.

Housing Policy

Housing policy in the early 2000s also looked a bit more like housing policy in 1945 than in the 1970s. As with UI, the state's move away from public responsibility represented a victory of bourgeois interests over those of the working class and especially the poor. During the 1990s, the tap on social housing was turned off almost as tightly as it had been in the 1940s and 1950s.

The period of liberalism in housing policy lasted throughout the 1970s and for much of the 1980s, but within clear limits. The federal government continued to provide a substantial portion of the funds required for provincial agencies that built and maintained social housing. During these two decades, about 400,000 social housing units were developed, with 91,000 units added by non-profit co-ops and the rest by municipal and private non-profit organizations. This included housing for families and for seniors, though much of the family housing was cheaply constructed and segregated from neighbourhoods of family owned housing. Organizations of the poor sometimes called for rental subsidies as an alternative while others continued to support social housing, but demanded that it be better built, dispersed throughout communities, and run by its tenants. Efforts to turn boarding houses into non-profit permanent homes went awry as developers bought the properties on which they developed condominiums and office towers.[34]

Federal cuts to housing programs began during the late Trudeau period, escalated under Brian Mulroney, and reached their apogee under Jean Chrétien. Sister Monique Picard, assistant to the executive director of Les Oeuvres de la Maison du Père, described the extent of the abandonment in federal help for Quebec at a housing conference in 1990: "In 1979, the federal government was involved in the production of 10,000 public, co-operative or non-profit housing units in the province of Quebec. By 1986, that figure had dropped to 3,000. Yet, more than 35,000 people in Quebec alone are still on public-housing waiting lists."[35]

Cuts in social housing budgets and the relaxation of rent controls hit women hardest. According to Femmes et Logement, a Montreal lobby group for women's rights in housing, half of the province's households headed by

The final Tory reform of UI in 1993 excluded workers who voluntarily left jobs, regardless of the reason for their departure, as well as workers who were fired for misconduct, as judged by the employer. Rates of insurance payouts for those still eligible for insurance were also reduced so that no one could earn more than 57 per cent of their previous income, continuing a decline from the 75 per cent that was possible in 1971.[32] The Liberals cut even further. In Paul Martin's first budget in 1994, the 57 per cent maximum of former earnings was reduced to 55 per cent for 85 per cent of recipients, weeks of work required for eligibility were increased, and only minor adjustments were made to the Tory restrictions on fired workers and voluntary job leavers.

The new Liberal government also continued the former government's policy of at once reducing the government's contribution to the fund and at the same time taking monies away from insurance payments and putting them into "active" programs designed for reintegrating the unemployed into the workforce. Then, in 1995, the government, following the Forget Commission majority's suggestion, began using hours of work rather than weeks of work to determine eligibility for insurance. This removed many part-time workers, mainly women, from the eligibility many had gained for the first time in 1971 for the right to state aid as unemployed workers rather than as social assistance recipients.[33] The result of such policies, which were not accompanied by any lowering of the rates that workers and employers were required to pay into the fund, was that the fund began to accumulate a surplus as the percentage of unemployed able to qualify for EI continued to fall. By the early 2000s, the federal government was using the EI fund much as Mackenzie King used it during the Second World War—as a cash cow to finance other government programs.

There were sporadic workers' protests against growing restrictions on UI benefits. In the late 1970s, a group known as Action-Chômage, organized by left-wing groups in Quebec, counselled workers who had been denied UI and attempted to create a solidarity network among unemployed workers. Quebec's rate of unemployment at the time was consistently about 50 per cent higher than the Canadian average, placing unemployment in the province at about 12 per cent in 1978. It was several points higher in the Atlantic provinces, with Newfoundland consistently posting the country's highest rates of joblessness. But it took the recession of 1982, which pushed national joblessness to 12.8 per cent, to provoke the various provincial federations of labour to establish separate organizations for the unemployed. These organizations made UI a key focus, and their lack of success in influencing government policy testified to labour's growing political weakness. Demonstrations in the Atlantic provinces

women paid between 43 and 46 per cent of their income for housing compared with only 5.5 per cent of families headed by men. Quebec's reduced payments for subsidized housing forced women to live in poorly maintained buildings, and often resulted in frequent moves that left families rootless in their neighbourhoods. Middle-class men became the chief beneficiaries of Quebec's housing programs since "eighty-four per cent of the housing subsidies granted by government go to landlords in the form of tax shelters and assistance to home-ownership or renovation programs."[36] Women in the Atlantic provinces fared even worse than their counterparts in Quebec. Families in New Brunswick on social assistance typically paid 65 per cent of their income on rent, usually for an inadequate shelter.[37]

Poor single men in Canada were also victims of public policies that favoured the interests of the wealthy over the poor in the area of housing. In Vancouver, the Downtown Eastside Residents' Association (DERA) was formed in 1973 to defend the interests of area residents. Most of the community's ten thousand residents were elderly males, half of whom were disabled, and virtually all of whom had monthly incomes of about $425 that permitted them to live only in closet-sized hotel rooms without cooking facilities. Their lives were made even more desperate by constant evictions. DERA had campaigned in the 1980s to prevent EXPO 86, which Vancouver hosted, from precipitating the relocation of poor downtown residents from their homes. Perhaps one thousand residents were evicted during EXPO and, in the next few years, another two thousand lost their homes as developers erected luxury condominiums and high-rise office towers along with parking lots. People in wheelchairs ended up in rooms above the ground floor in hotels or walk-ups that lacked elevators. DERA was able to develop some housing co-ops for area residents, but the developers' policies caused the number of homeless to rise each year.[38]

Aboriginals, both female and male, who lived in urban centres, were especially grimly housed. In Winnipeg, in 2000, a study suggested that the city's fifty thousand Aboriginal residents, while less than 10 per cent of the population, provided half of the city's homeless. Three-quarters lived in substandard housing, and most paid half their income towards rents for their bleak accommodations.[39]

As difficult as the 1980s were for advocates of social housing, the 1990s were worse. In 1993, the federal government cut off all funds for social housing to the provinces, and most provinces simply stopped building social housing altogether. Even the NDP governments elected in Ontario in 1990 and British

Columbia in 1991, though carrying out ambitious housing projects before 1993, largely stopped building new housing once the federal government pulled the plug.[40] Only in Quebec, under the PQ government in the late 1990s, did a modest program of developing new social housing survive.

By 1996, Canada had at least two hundred thousand homeless people, and a significant proportion of tenant households—44 per cent in wealthy Ontario alone—paid more towards rent than the 30 per cent of income that Statistics Canada believed was the upper limit of what households could afford to pay.[41] In 2002, the federal government announced that it would re-enter, in a modest way, the business of sharing social housing costs with the provincial governments, promising to spend $320 million over five years. Social housing advocates hoped that this pittance would encourage the government to resume its social responsibility for sheltering all Canadians.

CHILD CARE

A task force headed by Katie Cooke, established by the Trudeau government in its dying days, demonstrated that provincially approved and licensed daycare spaces remained at a premium in Canada. Only an estimated 8.8 per cent of households where there was no stay-at-home parent had access to such spaces. In Toronto, a survey indicated that 49 per cent of parents regarded a child care centre as the ideal arrangement they would prefer for their children; but only 10 per cent had their kids in daycare. After 1976, mothers' participation rates in the labour force dramatically increased, and by 1986 a majority of mothers with children under twelve years of age, including mothers with preschoolers, were in the labour force.[42]

A national movement for daycare had emerged by the 1984 federal election in the form of the Canadian Day Care Advocacy Association, founded in Winnipeg in 1982. Most daycare advocates campaigned for a national program of publicly operated child care centres, though there were also calls for state support for parent-created, co-operatively run daycares. Daycare advocates were generally united in their support for strict government standards for child care operations and for the banning of private, for-profit centres that, in their view, treated children as commodities. Even Quebec's daycare advocates wanted federal money provided for the support of garderies.[43]

Brian Mulroney's commitment to lower government spending trumped his commitment to a national daycare program. The Macdonald Commission set the pace for the business community's denunciations of plans for an expanded government role in daycare by arguing that such a program would require vastly expanded taxes and thereby restrict Canada's competitiveness in world markets.[44] The Mulroney government established a special committee in November 1985 to consider the extent of the child care crisis in Canada and to make recommendations. Though the committee heard many stories from parents who were unable to find affordable, stable, safe child care while they worked,[45] the Tory majority on the committee endorsed the views of business lobbyists who called for the child care expense allowance to be increased as an alternative to funding daycare directly.[46]

The Liberals, running for election in 1993, promised in the party's Red Book that a Liberal administration would increase the number of daycare spaces in the country by fifty thousand each year that the economy grew by more than 3 per cent.[47] But, although the economy grew by that amount seven times in the following nine years, this commitment was not fulfilled. Human Resources Minister Lloyd Axworthy offered the provinces $700 million in matching grants for adding new daycare spaces, but as it became clear that the monies offered would simply be redistributed from existing shared federal-provincial programs, this initiative was abandoned.

By 2005, there was nothing to show for either the Tory or Liberal promises of a national daycare program, although some progress had been made by a few provinces. Quebec initiated a program in 1997 whose goal was to publicly subsidize and operate daycare for all mothers of children under age twelve. The cost of daycare would be fixed at $5 dollars a day per child. There were several reasons for this bold step. The PQ were aware that women were more cautious about its sovereignty option than men, and so it made an effort to support demands from the women's movement that would establish the party as women-friendly. The women's movement, in turn, made special efforts to convince PQ governments, which were somewhat more progressive than Liberal administrations, to support its agenda. In 1995, a massive March for Bread and Roses, organized by the Fédération des femmes du Québec, emphasized the social power of the women's movement in the province and strengthened feminist forces in the PQ government.

The daycare policy formed part of a family policy that would increase state support for low-income families while providing a large subsidy to daycare centres so that they need charge parents only $5 a day to use their facility. Poor households would receive a subsidy that reduced that rate even further. The gov-

ernment proceeded to build a large number of new child care centres, though this expansion never matched demand, creating some backlash against the PQ from parents whose children were not accommodated. The PQ government also negotiated a contract with unionized child care workers in 1999 that increased pay rates by 38 per cent. That still left this college-educated group with modest salaries, but it gave them higher salaries than daycare workers in the wealthier provinces of Alberta and Ontario.[48] Though $5-a-day daycare soon became a program that no political party dared to attack openly, the provincial Liberals, upon their re-election in 2003, decided that the program would have to be re-examined and later raised the fees.[49] But thanks to a well-organized campaign of feminists and trade unions, the eventual increases proved relatively small despite the neo-liberal inclinations of Jean Charest's administration.

Other provincial governments were largely unfriendly to child care advocates. Alberta had cut its child care subsidies by 20 per cent in 1995, and Ontario and British Columbia also became home to regimes favouring tax cutting and privatization, and with little interest in copying Quebec's approach to child care. In 1998, about 10 per cent of all children in the country under twelve years of age with working mothers were in daycare spaces that had been licensed by their province or territory as meeting government-established standards regarding staff qualifications, staff-to-children ratio, facilities and programs. In Newfoundland that figure fell to 5 per cent, and in Saskatchewan, 3.9 per cent. Interestingly, Prince Edward Island, with spaces available for 15.4 per cent of children in the province, beat the other two Maritime provinces by more than two to one.[50] But only in Quebec was there much of an improvement over the next several years, as the province increased its spending on early childhood care and education from less than $300 million in 1997–98 to over $1 billion in 2001–02.[51] In 2005, the federal government began another round of consultations with the provinces regarding a national daycare program.

In summary, outside Quebec, public support for child care in 2005 was restricted to the poorest families. Governments rejected the view that the state had an obligation to ensure that all families had access to quality child care and that child care workers had a right to a decent wage. Tougher rules for collecting social assistance made labour-force attachments compulsory for most single mothers, but child care subsidies often failed to provide the working poor with licensed daycare spaces. Women in small towns and the countryside, in particular, found that the market did not provide them with good potential daycare arrangements, and they made do as best they could.[52]

PENSIONS AND THE LIVES OF SENIORS

Seniors' groups, women's groups, and labour all campaigned for richer pensions for Canadians. Only 36.8 per cent of employees in Canada were covered by occupational pension plans in 1984, a figure unchanged since 1976. Public pensions provided a large part of the incomes of seniors, particularly women. Unattached elderly women received 53.3 per cent of their incomes from state programs, versus 32.3 per cent for unattached elderly men. This led advocates of greater equity for women to demand that pensions be revisited and payments to the elderly poor be increased.[53]

While popular groups were pressuring the government to enrich public-pension programs, the private-pension industry promoted a focus on employer-based schemes. When the federal government announced its reforms for pension programs in 1987, it was obvious that the interest of business groups had prevailed. Public programs were slightly enriched by bringing in early retirement benefits, at a reduced rate for sixty-year-olds, and improving survivor benefits. But shortly afterwards, the Mulroney government restored the means test to the OAP that had been lifted in 1951, with retirees having an income over $50,000 simply excluded from receiving pensions. Private pensions were reformed to a degree. There would be some coverage for part-time workers, and some provisions for vesting pensions after two years of membership in a plan. Survivor benefits became mandatory and pension benefits were to be split in the case of a marriage or common-law relationship breakdown.[54]

Trade union researcher Rick Deaton sums up the results of the Mulroney pension reforms as follows: "The public policy review of retirement income arrangements in Canada and the remedial reform 'package,' however, failed to expand either the private or the public pension system. As a result of conflicting views and pressures concerning the extent and nature of pension reform based on the opposing class interests of the major actors, the critical issues of coverage, inflation-proofing and an adequate income replacement rate were left unresolved."[55] Nor are the monies collected from working people to fund public pensions used to promote social objectives, either job creation or investment in social infrastructure. Sweden, by contrast, uses pension funds both to promote an industrial strategy meant to ensure low unemployment and to enrich social programs. Canada's private pension schemes are marked by unilateral control by employers, "a reflection of the imbalance in the distribution of power between labour and management under conditions of collective bargaining in capitalist countries."[56]

The government's failure to increase pensions often meant that seniors, who were living longer than ever past retirement, were often without means to purchase home care services as they became less able to care for themselves. Provincial governments established or expanded home care programs that covered both seniors and disabled persons, but often these involved minimal state funding and contracting out of service provision to private firms.[57] As with daycare, the degree of privatization and the question of universal coverage depended upon the ideology of provincial governments, with Manitoba's NDP government deciding in 1974 to operate a universal and completely public program.[58] Most other provinces linked services to income, and gave regional health authorities the right to contract out services, leading the Canadian Association on Gerontology to note in 1999 that "Canada does not have a universally accessible, comprehensive home care policy or program."[59] Families and volunteers, they suggested, provided about 70 or 80 per cent of the care required by seniors, though governments in Canada were spending about $2 billion annually on home care.

Most of the staff hired for paid home care were women, and their wages, like those of child care staff, were at poverty levels. This was particularly the case for women working for subcontractors to regional health authorities, who, unlike Manitoba's government-employed workers, were non-unionized. Competition among potential subcontractors was often based on little more than who could pay the lowest wages and benefits to their casually employed workers. In turn, with most of the unpaid caregiving being provided by women, there was a ripple effect on women's mental health and opportunities for social advancement. Burned out by long hours of care for children and parents, many qualified women were unable to take senior jobs in industry, government, and the professions.[60]

Governments were touchy on the issue of the gendered nature of cutbacks and privatization. It was women who lost state caregiving jobs, women whose jobs were privatized, and women in the home who had to take on the work that state-employed caregivers would no longer provide. When researchers at the University of Alberta concluded that the Klein cuts of 1994 affected women disproportionately, a Conservative MLA demanded that these professors be fired.[61]

POVERTY AND INCOME SUPPORTS

The combination of an increase in GNP per capita, a vast increase in the number of two-income households, and improved social programs reduced poverty levels in Canada from 27 per cent in 1961 to 15.4 per cent in 1975. However, recessions and cutbacks reversed that progress. The Statscan measure of low-income Canadians climbed to almost 20 per cent during the steep recessions of 1982–84, and 1990–93, though the return of an economic boom allowed the rate to drop to 16.2 per cent in 1999.[62] The National Council of Welfare commented in July 2002, "Our patchwork system of social programs is clearly not doing what it takes to seriously address the causes and consequences of poverty. And there is no forum for Canadians outside government, especially for low-income Canadians and hungry children, to come to the table with governments to talk about their own realities, aspirations, priorities and solutions."[63]

As governments began putting the squeeze on social assistance and unemployment insurance, citizens' groups made efforts to deal with the growing problems of poverty and hunger in Canada. Food banks first appeared in Alberta in June 1981. When the economy collapsed in 1982, they spread across the country. Unemployed Action Centres, connected with the trade union movement, operated close to one-third of the food banks in 1986.[64] Many church leaders were also involved in operating food banks, and their disgust that charity was required to prevent Canadians from starving led to the Roman Catholic bishops' condemnation in 1983 of public policies that put corporate profits ahead of the needs of workers and the poor.[65] Half of those being fed were children.

Poverty in Canada was both racialized and gendered. *Nellie's Newsletter* in Toronto reported that, while just over one-fifth of Canadian children lived in poverty according to the 1996 census, that figure increased to 52.1 per cent for Aboriginal children. 42.7 per cent for visible minorities, and 37 per cent for children with disabilities.[66] Women accounted for three-fifths of the adult poor, with single mothers and elderly women without partners experiencing especially high rates of poverty.[67] But it was child poverty that social advocates focused on. In part, this was because efforts to press for policies that recognized the increasing "feminization of poverty" faced a conservative backlash. While social justice advocates demanded equal wages for work of equal value and more income subsidies, their successes were limited. Conservatives, looking at the increasing number of single and divorced mothers, balked at public policies that would contribute to women's independence rather than a return to the "traditional" family. They had the support of industrialists and state employers who benefited from using women as cheap labour. Social advocates de-

cided that they might win more public support if they focused on poor children rather than on their mothers.

This approach seemed to bear some fruit when the House of Commons voted unanimously in 1989 to eliminate child poverty by the end of the century. That year, a year of prosperity, the national child poverty rate was 14.4 per cent, but by 1996, the census reported that the rate had increased to 21.1 per cent. In 2001, there was an encouraging fall to 15.6 per cent,[68] but the decline was the result of a booming economy and there was little to prevent its rising again when the economy stagnated once more. The politicians proved unable to achieve the 1989 goal mainly because social policies that increased poverty among adults inevitably increased poverty for their children. The restrictions on UI pushed many households into poverty; so did provincial efforts to attract employers by raising minimum wages by less than inflation. In 2003, a one income, minimum-wage family of two adults and one child received on average only 40 per cent of a poverty-line income.[69]

The provinces also made it more difficult to collect social assistance and slashed assistance rates, even though they were already quite low. In Ontario, for example, in 1995, the Conservative government of Mike Harris reduced rates by 22 per cent. Welfare recipients who had been unemployed for longer than four months were forced into "workfare" schemes, part-time make-work job schemes meant to subsidize private or public employers while supposedly providing work experience for the unemployed.[70] Ignoring the state of mental health, family responsibilities, and availability of transportation of many aid recipients, provincial governments required them to attend job-training courses, summarily cutting off those who failed to do so. In the country as a whole, income was being redistributed in favour of the wealthy. The net wealth of the top 20 per cent of families with children rose 43 per cent between 1984 and 1999 in Canada, but it only rose by 3 per cent for the middle-income group. For the bottom 20 per cent of Canadians, there was a 51 per cent decline.[71]

The federal contribution to ending child poverty proved feeble, a reflection of its priority of debt and tax reduction over social spending. In 1993, the Liberals followed through on a Conservative plan to end family allowances. They created the New Integrated Child Tax Benefit (NICTB), an income-related benefit meant to assist low-income mothers. However, the small amount of extra income that this benefit directed to mothers living in poverty was largely undone by provincial cuts in social assistance rates. In turn, the federal reduction in transfers to the provinces for all purposes encouraged the provinces to cut welfare spending, the least politically sensitive of all social expenditures. With CAP tossed into the dustbin in 1996, the provinces no longer had to demonstrate that a set portion of their federal funds was being spent to aid the destitute.

In 1997, the federal government replaced the NCTB with the Canada Child Tax Benefit. This benefit to children living in poverty was supposed to free up money for the provinces to spend on such programs as early childhood education for children at risk, child care, pharmacare, and dental health. In practice, the provinces, with federal support, used the monies they received for work incentive payments, often as subsidies to employers. A program whose title implied that it was meant to benefit the children of the poor discriminated against children whose mothers stayed home with them, while leaving mothers well below the poverty line if they chose to accept the provincial work incentives.[72]

Though there continued to be a large community of policy advocates who supported the rights of low-income Canadians, its political power during the 1990s and early 2000s seemed marginal. Although the cutbacks in education and health raised a sufficient ruckus so that most of the funds cut in the 1990s were restored in the early 2000s, there was no parallel enrichment of social assistance budgets, minimum wages, unemployment insurance, or social housing. The poorest Canadians, it seemed, were bearing the brunt of the neo-liberal agenda. Little wonder that there was a revival of militancy among the poor. Organizations of the poor in the major cities sponsored workshops and a variety of political campaigns meant to apply public pressure against recalcitrant politicians. The Ontario Coalition Against Poverty (OCAP), organized in 1995 as the Harris cuts began, proved the most willing to use physical confrontations to challenge government efforts to dispossess the poor. Responding to rising homelessness among those cut off social assistance, OCAP evicted Conservative Finance Minister Ernie Eves from his office in June 2000, with a number of the demonstrators, including OCAP's lead organizer, John Clarke, being arrested as a result.[73]

A summary of OCAP's activities before that time by an activist evokes the state's all-round attack on the most oppressed members of the Canadian working class in the 1990s and the willingness to fight back on the part of some of the victims:

OCAP mounts large collective actions, often with our union allies or the Mohawk warrior society of the Tyendanaga First Nation Reserve, around a specific economic issue such as the withdrawal of provincial and federal governments from public housing, or Toronto's policy, mimicking New York's, for the "social cleansing" of

panhandlers and homeless from the downtown tourist areas. We have picketed and enforced semi-embargos on businesses investing in a redevelopment scheme which, by closing a hostel, threw homeless men back on the street. To enforce specific demands, we have instituted a campaign of continuing "economic disruption"—snake marches, demonstrations, mass panhandling—of bourgeois activities, fairs, festivals, and film shoots. And we have mobilized the larger actions...challenging police power: in Ottawa, a march on Parliament Hill "to persuade the prime minister of the seriousness of the homelessness crisis," interrupted by arrests by the RCMP, whose line we broke; the occupation of a Toronto city park, designating it "safe" from police harassment for the homeless, and holding it for three days until we were violently removed, with arrests, by the police; and most recently, the second, more powerful march on Parliament in November 1999. Each of these was a small, but in our present situation, real victory.[74]

Health Care

Though the poor had always suffered greater problems of health and access to treatment for illnesses than other Canadians, and therefore suffered the most when public health care was undermined, the saving grace of Canadian medicare in neo-liberal times was that all Canadians had access to the public health care system. This meant that middle-class and some upper-class Canadians had considerable affinity for the public health care program that had begun with hospital insurance in 1957 and was enriched with medicare in 1968. Free access to certain medical services became, in most Canadians' minds, a right of citizenship. There was considerable chafing when provincial governments allowed physicians to bill patients directly for services for which the doctors felt governments underpaid them. In Saskatchewan, Premier Ross Thatcher's "deterrent fee" of $2 per visit to a physician helped to defeat his Liberal government in 1971. The Canada Health Act of 1984, which threatened federal financial penalties for provincial violations of the principles of medicare, was immensely popular.[75]

Campaigns to further enlarge medical protection by placing dentists' bills, non-hospital pharmaceutical costs, and eyeglasses within medicare received limited support from the middle class and the unionized working class because many of them already enjoyed these protections from employers. But there was a strong desire to preserve and extend the availability of both physicians' services and hospital care that underlay the prepaid medicare schemes that the provinces had constructed in the spirit of the 1968 legislation.

This did not prevent deep cuts in health care spending in the early 1990s. Health care was rivalling education as the top item in provincial budgets, and deficit-cutting, tax-cutting premiers had no option within a neo-liberal paradigm but to cut health care budgets. While these cuts were proportionately far smaller than the cuts in the programs that targeted the poor, they were significant. In Alberta, the Klein cuts of 1993–96 shaved 17 per cent off the annual health-spending budget over a three-year period.[76] In the Atlantic provinces, where cuts started earlier, annual cuts of 5 to 6 per cent over several years added up to even greater cutbacks than the much-publicized Alberta cuts.

Often, politicians who planned to make drastic cuts in medicare promised voters just the opposite. The federal Liberal Red Book in 1993 promised to halt the bleeding of federal money to the provinces for medicare. But, when EPF was lumped together with CAP in 1995 to form the CHST, the total package was reduced by $7 billion over a three-year period. Conservative Mike Harris, promising to slash "welfare" spending as he ran for election in Ontario in 1995, also assured voters that health care would dodge the bullet. So did the conservative Liberal, Gordon Campbell, running for election in British Columbia in 2001. Once elected, both made deep cuts to the health care system.

Because all polls indicated that over 90 per cent of Canadians wanted to hold on to medicare, and indeed that they regarded Canada's publicly operated health care schemes as superior to American's private medicine, no major politician openly called for an end to the public system. There were, however, calls by Klein and Harris for the private sector to play a major role in the delivery of medical services. Much of the privatization that occurred was at the expense of the lowest-paid hospital workers and of low-income consumers of health services. Food services and maintenance work in hospitals were often contracted out, transforming modest-paying unionized jobs into minimum-wage non-union work. Certain once-free medical services were "delisted," that is removed from a provincial health department's list of services paid for as part of medicare, or were provided in more limited circumstances. Such changes saved provincial medical systems only token amounts, and sometimes resulted in increased costs, for example when provinces contracted out medical services for workers' compensation recipients to for-profit providers.

The decentralization of provincial programs to local health boards, charged with finding slack in the system and cutting it away, also resulted in limited savings. Most of the money in the health care system went to paying fees for physicians' services and salaries for nurses. The political clout of the Canadian

Medical Association and its provincial branches, and the carefully cultivated mystique of the medical profession made an assault on physician control of the medical system too dangerous for any provincial government to seriously consider. While efforts were made to cap payments to doctors, talk of replacing fee-for-service payments with salaries played a minor role in policy discussions regarding the future of medicare. Physicians also successfully resisted most efforts to increase the role of other, less highly paid health professionals within the medical system. Their efforts also resulted in a limited inclusion of non-allopathic practitioners within both state and privately funded health-insurance schemes.[77]

Inevitably, then, much of the initial assault on the costs of the medical system fell upon nursing staff in hospitals. Hospitals sent patients home quickly, and pressured patients' families to carry out tasks in the hospital once carried out by nurses. They attempted to reduce drastically both the numbers of nurses and the wages of the nurses who remained. By 2000, there had been an 8 per cent drop in the number of registered nurses in Canada relative to the population, and a 21 per cent decline in licensed practical nurses. Patients chafed as waiting times for "elective" surgeries increased, and even life-and-death operations seemed to require a waiting period. Families of patients who had been dismissed too early complained bitterly when the result was a death or the need to bring the patient back to hospital within a short time, sometimes in worse shape than when she or he had been sent home.[78] Hospital closings resulted in huge protests.

By the end of the twentieth century, cutbacks in health care were clearly unpopular with voters, and governments began to reinvest in the health system. Medical spending had been cut by 5 per cent per capita in constant dollars in Canada between 1991 and 1996. But, according to the Canadian Institute for Health Information, government health spending in Canada increased by about $20 billion, or 35 per cent, from 1997 to 2003, while inflation during that period was only about 15 per cent.[79] The federal government had gradually increased the size of the CHST. In 2000, after meetings with the provinces, it announced a 35 per cent increase in the CHST over the next five years.[80] That would restore federal funding to about the numbers, with inflation and population increases factored in, in force when the Liberals had taken power.

The federal government's partial turnaround did not create a new consensus regarding medicare. Several provinces, particularly those with NDP governments as well as the PQ government in Quebec, were committed to expanding the services that they provided their citizens in the public system, particularly in such areas as home care and pharmaceuticals. They wanted the CHST to reflect these new obligations. Other provinces, led by Alberta and, before the defeat of its Conservative government in 2003, Ontario, also wanted more funds but wanted Ottawa to permit an expansion of privately run but publicly funded services. The opening of a private hospital in Calgary in 2001, to denunciations from Friends of Medicare, the trade union movement, and the two major opposition parties, seemed to many the thin edge of the wedge of privatization. The Ontario Conservatives had also laid the groundwork for privatization of several hospitals.

In part, the neo-liberal drive towards both cost cutting and privatization within medicare was frustrated by consumer resistance. But, in turn, the role of physicians and nurses in publicizing the dangerous consequences of the changes that were occurring contributed to popular opposition to government cutbacks. Both groups also proved quite militant in defending their economic positions. Nurses had once constituted one of Canada's poorest paid professional groups. Beginning in the 1970s, however, nurses increasingly joined unions, and struck for better wages and working conditions.

A feminist consciousness had emerged in a number of so-called women's professions, including nursing, in the wake of the women's liberation movement of the late 1960s and onwards. "We are not Florence Nightingales," United Nurses of Alberta president Margaret Ethier insisted during the 1980 strike of nurses in that province, the first of three such strikes. These strikes were illegal under Alberta's Essential Services Act and the union paid heavy fines for counselling its members to strike. But the hospitals, in each case, were forced to award handsome settlements to the nurses in order to end the strikes. During the late 1990s, as well, nurses and their unions limited, and sometimes altogether foiled, efforts by provincial governments to erode their wages and working conditions. To the chagrin of many governments, nurses appeared to be able to mobilize significant sections of Canadian society on their behalf.

Because of concerns about the long-term sustainability of medicare, and the perception that various provincial initiatives threatened the guarantee to Canadians of prepaid medical services, the federal government established a one-man commission on medical services in 2001. Prime Minister Chrétien named Roy Romanow, the former NDP premier of Saskatchewan, as commissioner. In hearings across the country, it became clear that, apart from business groups and conservative governments, there was little popular support for

tinkering with medicare. Privatization appealed to chambers of commerce and to potential investors but repelled most Canadians, and particularly the trade unions, members of the health professions (with some ambivalence on the part of physicians), social workers, and the churches. Even in Alberta, the commissioners heard mainly from opponents of two-tier medicine that allowed the wealthy to purchase medical services that were unavailable to the rest of the population.[81]

THE ROMANOW REPORT AND BEYOND

The Romanow Report, while not a radical document, destroyed the arguments of the neo-liberal think tanks and the governments of Alberta and Ontario that medical costs were strangling the national economy and that increased privatization was the solution both to reducing costs and improving national medical standards. Romanow concluded that Canada's health spending was comparable to other countries in the OECD and considerably less than American spending. While the rise in spending was not dramatic, it had increased from 7 per cent of the gross domestic product in 1970 to 9.1 per cent in 2000, a modest amount in light of the aging of the population, the costs of new medical technologies, and the growth of public perceptions of various medical services as a right of citizenship rather than commodities for people with means. Public spending on health care had only increased from 5 per cent to 6.5 per cent of GDP during that period, reflecting a decline in the portion of medical costs covered by public sources, from about 77 per cent in 1970 to 67.6 per cent in 2001–02. That was significantly less than coverage in the Scandinavian countries and the United Kingdom, but somewhat more than the American figure of 60 per cent.

The U.S. figure included expenditures for the minority of Americans who benefited from state programs—Medicare for the aged, and Medicaid for the destitute—and tax deductions for private insurance purchasers. The real losers in the American system were people too poor to carry full insurance (an estimated 44 million Americans had no health insurance at all in 2003, while many others were underinsured) but not poor enough or old enough to qualify for state medical coverage. Provincial spending on health care had increased from 28 per cent of provincial budgets in 1974 to 35 per cent in 1999–2000, most of the increase attributable to the decline in federal grants per capita over that period. Canada's health system, noted the report, was largely a success. In 1999, life expectancy at birth for Canadians was 75.4 years for men and 81.2 years for women, which made Canadians the fifth longest-living people in the world.[82]

Romanow noted that evidence that privatization, delisting, and public–private partnerships improved the efficiency of the medical system "has not been forthcoming." The evidence from the U.S. was that a private system of medicine was far more expensive to administer than a public one. In the U.S., the combination of private insurance systems with systems required to track eligibility for and amounts of tax subsidies accounted for far greater administrative costs per person than in Canada: $1,151 to $325. The Americans also had to pay for the profits of their private-care providers.[83]

But Romanow was critical of gaps in the public health system in Canada. The whole, he wrote, seemed less than the sum of its parts: "We must transform our health care 'system' from one in which a multitude of participants, working in silos, focus primarily on managing illness, to one in which they work collaboratively to deliver a seamless, integrated array of services to Canadians, from prevention and promotion to primary care; to hospital, community, mental health, home and end-of-life care."[84] He proposed that the federal government boost health care spending to the provinces in a targeted manner, with special payments for diagnostic care, services to rural and remote areas, primary health care, home care, and pharmaceutical programs, particularly catastrophic drugs. Altogether, he suggested, that within three years, the CHST should be increased by $6.5 billion to reflect the total number of new dollars needed.[85]

Romanow also noted disparities in services across the country. These were partly the result of philosophical differences and partly the result of poorer provinces and territories being unable to match expenditures on health per capita in wealthier provinces. He proposed a Health Council of Canada that would establish indicators and benchmarks that could be monitored to assess how well governments were doing over time to meet the health needs of Canadians.[86] While the Romanow Report dealt with gender issues only cursorily, it did recommend that home caregivers should receive special benefits under the EI program.[87] He ignored proposals from feminists that family caregivers dealing with individuals who might otherwise require institutional care or paid home care receive a salary for their work.

One area where Romanow believed that special efforts were required was mental health. Deinstitutionalization of mental health patients, which had

begun in earnest in the 1960s, potentially constituted a progressive course of action. It was more just to allow psychiatric patients to remain part of their families and the community than to lock them away from society. But, often deinstitutionalization had been motivated more by cost-saving concerns than by considerations of social justice. Expensive-to-maintain mental institutions were closed or scaled down while their inmates were thrown onto the streets with few services to take the place of the programs that the asylums offered. Romanow agreed with the Canadian Mental Health Association that governments had to offer programs to reduce "barriers to access to community life in areas such as employment, education and housing."[88]

Public reaction to the Romanow Report was overwhelmingly positive, according to opinion polls. Government reaction was more mixed. Poorer provinces welcomed the promise of more federal funds, and Jean Chrétien endorsed the tenor of the report. But the governments of Ontario and Alberta, which were promoting privatization, quickly proclaimed that they would resist any incursion of the federal government in an area of provincial jurisdiction. They wanted more money from the "feds" for health care but with no strings attached as to how it should be spent. Alberta had established an advisory panel on medical care as a rival to the Romanow Commission. It was chaired by former Conservative cabinet minister Donald Mazankowski. Since Mazankowski was a director of several insurance companies and had been Mulroney's minister of privatization, his committee, as expected, supported greater privatization of the delivery of medical services. Romanow bowed at least a little in the direction of the right wingers by suggesting that food and cleaning services for hospitals could continue to be privatized—a suggestion that the unions denounced—and demurring from federal financial penalties for provinces that privatized or created public–private partnerships in the health sector.[89]

A federal-provincial meeting in February 2003 produced the joint responses of the federal and provincial governments to the Romanow Report. The First Ministers' Health Accord promised $17.3 billion in increased health funding over three years and a total of $34.8 billion in five years. The money was meant to fund increases in provincial and territorial spending in the areas mentioned by Romanow. A Health Council "to monitor and make annual reports on the implementation of the Accord, particularly its accountability and transparency provisions" also formed part of the Accord.[90] However, some of the monies promised by the federal government appeared to simply double count funds promised to the provinces in 2000. Nor, in line with the Social Union

Framework of 2000, did the provinces have to account for how they would spend the extra funds they received. Instead, the federal government would rely on the publicity of Health Council reporting to keep premiers and territorial leaders on track with national priorities.

Before year's end, however, Alberta's premier Ralph Klein refused to even have his province participate in the Health Council, which he regarded as an intrusive measure that would meddle into provincial policies. The Accord made no mention of privatization or of public–private partnerships, thus leaving the field open to premiers to continue to contract out various parts of the health system.[91] In 2004, the federal election focused heavily on medicare financing, and Paul Martin, as leader of a minority Liberal government after the June vote, provided another increase in federal funding to provinces for medicare several months afterwards, though again with few strings attached. The funds committed demonstrated the power of the pro-medicare lobbies in Canada, while the successful resistance of several provincial governments to stipulations against privatization and public–private partnerships demonstrated the continued political strength of health entrepreneurs.

FIRST NATIONS AND THE WELFARE STATE

The Romanow Report, following the spirit of the Royal Commission on Aboriginal Peoples (RCAP), noted that the health of Native peoples required a special approach. Native peoples' demands for self-determination, along with federal jurisdiction over registered Indians and Inuit, excluded the possibility of delegating Aboriginal health to the provinces. Yet what Romanow had heard from Native leaders paralleled what the commissioner recommended with respect to Canadians' health generally: a holistic approach to health, one which did not create airtight silos that separated social needs and health. For First Nations, it meant that health was inseparable from the empowerment of its citizens and the strengthening of cultural identity. By 2000, the health of Native peoples had dramatically improved compared with forty years earlier. In 1963, life expectancy for a registered Native person was only half that of other Canadians. By 2000, Native men lived, on average, 7.4 years less than other Canadian men and Native women, 5.2 years less than other Canadian women.[92]

As well, First Nations were increasingly managing their own social affairs. As the residential schools began to close in the 1960s and 1970s, band councils campaigned to have on-reserve schools controlled by First Nations rather than to be forced to send children to off-reserve schools run by non-Natives. By

the 1990s, the on-reserve school controlled by a Native school authority had become the norm. First Nations also turned their attention to gaining control over health services on the reserves. An early precedent was the Kateri Mohawk Hospital Centre, which opened in 1955, the result of a Mohawk women's initiative that secured funding from both the Quebec government and the Mohawk Council of Kahnawake. The James Bay and Northern Quebec Agreement of 1975 created autonomous Aboriginal health and social service boards, though the communities in question struggled to keep the provincial and federal governments from interfering with their new-found authority. Then, in 1979, the Inuit created the Labrador Independent Health Commission in Labrador.[93]

By 2001, an estimated 46 per cent of eligible Native communities had signed agreements with the federal government to manage health services themselves and most other reserves were in the process of negotiating similar arrangements. In addition, Native leaders and various federal government departments had worked together to create programs that would address epidemic problems on the reserves, including the Aboriginal Diabetes Initiative and the National Native Alcohol and Drug Abuse Program. The federal government provided funding to individuals on reserves for prescription drugs, dental treatment, vision care, and transportation to health facilities off reserve as required.[94]

But such services, noted Romanow, did not reflect a clear federal government commitment to providing comprehensive medical services to Natives. Earlier efforts to off-load responsibility for Natives' health onto the provinces continued apace, and the notion remained that the federal government was the "payer of last resort." There had been no repudiation of a 1974 ministerial statement that summarized the federal government's role in the health arena as "giving financial assistance to indigent Indians to pay for necessary services when the assistance [was] not otherwise provided."[95]

Romanow called for an end to the dispersal of responsibility for Native health among federal and provincial government departments. What was required, instead, was to "consolidate Aboriginal health funding from all sources and use the funds to support the creation of Aboriginal Health Partnerships and use them to manage and organize health services for Aboriginal peoples and promote Aboriginal health." "The Partnerships would identify specific health needs of Native communities and make use of community resources to guide health programs. Wherever possible, Native health care providers would be hired, and when non-Natives were hired, Natives would sensitize them to the norms and needs of their communities. In 2002, the percentage of trained Native nurses and physicians in Canada, while much improved compared with a few decades earlier, remained well below the percentage of Natives within the population as a whole—1 per cent versus 3 per cent.[96]

The federal government attempted, in particular, to limit its responsibility for off-reserve Natives, including former reserve residents who had moved to urban locations because of the lack of employment opportunities on reserves. By 2000, about half of all Native peoples lived in cities and towns, and the federal government balked at providing them the autonomous institutions that their reserve counterparts increasingly enjoyed. Organizations of urban Natives placed pressure on governments to recognize that Native peoples who moved to cities should have the right to self-determination. In 2003, there were murmurings about "urban reserves" but no framework for their operation was announced that year, seven years after RCAP had called upon governments to ensure that the needs of all Native peoples, regardless of place of residence, were respected. Federal monies to registered Indians for health purposes covered only reserve residents.[97]

RCAP, which reported in 1996, had provided the comprehensive social policy framework that became the keystone of Native demands. Headed by former Assembly of First Nations (AFN) grand chief Georges Erasmus, RCAP called on governments to make a definitive break with past colonialist and cost-cutting objectives in their dealings with First Nation peoples. The report noted that the goal should be "to pave the way for Aboriginal self-government by enhancing the capacity of Aboriginal citizens to engage in nation building."[98]

This meant ending the control of outsiders over Aboriginal family life. In the postwar period, there had been a drastic increase in intervention by provincial social welfare agencies in the area of Native child welfare. While the social workers sought to protect children from unsafe environments, they operated within a limited framework. Children were seized from Native homes judged by European middle-class standards to be inappropriate and placed in institutional care or adopted out to European families in different provinces from their birth parents and even in the United States. No efforts were made either to involve the Native communities in determining the fate of their children or in working with these communities to create conditions that would make so much intervention into individual households unnecessary. In British Columbia, 34.2 per cent of all children in care in 1964 were Native. By 1981–82, Native children represented 63 per cent of those in care in Saskatchewan and 41 per cent in Alberta. Nationally, 4.6 per cent of Native children were in agency care compared with 1 per cent of non-Native children.[99]

First Nations organizations documented the disastrous impact on many of the children who had been apprehended and on their families and communities. The children grew up in a nether world, discriminated against because of their Native heritage but with no connection to that heritage. Native adults were made to feel that they were inferior parents whose children had to be taken from them, and Native communities were deprived of their young people. In 1981, responding to pressure from the AFN and other Native organizations, the Department of Indian Affairs and Northern Development (DIAND) signed its first agreement with a First Nations agency to deliver child welfare services. Ten years later, there were thirty-six agencies receiving DIAND funding to provide child and family services to 212 bands. By the mid-1990s, several Native child and family agencies in urban centres had signed agreements with the federal government, and Métis agencies began to emerge with the signing of a provincial agreement in Alberta. All three Prairie provincial governments promised to move quickly to implement Native control of the delivery of welfare services to non-reserve Native families.[100]

Though the assimilationist philosophy that once governed relations between the state and First Nations was crumbling, it was unclear that it was giving way to the holistic philosophies espoused by the RCAP and the Romanow Report. Government willingness to fund the programs required to provide Natives with the resources to establish both autonomy for their communities and a standard of living comparable to other Canadians foundered on the neo-liberal rock of government funding. So, for example, as Natives assumed control over medical programs formerly administered by Ottawa, the funds provided were inadequate to integrate medical and social services. Glen Ross of the Cree Nation Tribal Health Centre at The Pas, Manitoba, told the RCAP commissioners: "[Even after transfer], there remain a number of issues which are barriers to providing comprehensive health care services for the Tribal Council membership. Some of these are that we have inadequate community-based mental health programs; we lack adult care; we lack services for the disabled, we have poor, inadequate medical transportation services. Transportation is a non-insured benefit, and we protest that those benefits are not on the table for transfer of control."[101]

Federal resistance to spending new money was particularly evident in the area of housing. While 9.8 per cent of dwellings in Canada needed major structural repairs, the figure for Native accommodations was 19.6 per cent. That figure rose to 26 per cent on reserves and to 33 per cent in Inuit communities. Native families were almost alone among Canadians in still having a substantial group whose homes lacked piped water or bathroom facilities. Valerie Montague, a social service administrator in Christian Island, Ontario, noted: "We have families that are doubled and tripled up. We have up to 18 and 20 people sometimes living in a single unit built for one family."[102]

Many of the homes built with government assistance on reserves in the postwar years had been shoddily constructed. Lack of fire-protection services on reserves led to an average of two hundred reserve dwellings in Canada (out of seventy-four thousand) burning to the ground each year. Solid-waste dumps in the North and inadequate sewage treatment created environmental hazards for the food consumed by Natives in that region. Housing programs implemented in the 1970s and 1980s had alleviated the worst housing conditions of the immediate postwar period. The Rural Housing Program for Aboriginal People added about twenty-five thousand units of Native housing from 1974 to 1994 before the construction of new units was suspended. Native housing co-operatives built another ten thousand units with government financial assistance. Tenant interviews suggested that residents in these co-ops enjoyed a stable environment and a strong cultural identity, but monies for more co-ops disappeared in 1994. RCAP determined that the cost of replacing unrepairable shacks, repairing the homes with structural damage, and building enough new dwellings to ensure adequate housing for all Natives within ten years would be $228 million the first year with costs rising to $774 million by the tenth year. But the payoff would be healthier, more productive communities.[103]

As it was, a large percentage of the monies that governments were spending on Natives in Canada was on funds for their incarceration. Though they made up only 3 per cent of the population, Natives accounted for 17 per cent of the prison population. Before the 1970s, the justice system denied that systemic racism resulted in higher incarceration rates for Native men and women. Pressures from Aboriginal communities after that time resulted in the gradual introduction of Native community policing. Native courts that focused on healing as much as retribution, and rehabilitation programs operated entirely by First Nations or in conjunction with corrections officials. Successful rehabilitation programs "have focused on linking the prisoner with his/her community, e.g., school, family, social service organization, neighbourhood organization."[104]

Corporate Canada, using front groups such as the pseudo-academic "institutes" and aided by a compliant media dominated by a few corporate syndicates, made significant inroads in popular thinking regarding the desirable role

of the state in the last quarter of the twentieth century. Focusing on government deficits and debts, the right wing was able to convince many Canadians that the state interventionism of the previous thirty years was strangling the country's economic potential. This softened up the population for the cutbacks in government programs and spending that marked much of this period. But Canadians' attachment to their social programs, and increasing organization and militancy on the part of opponents of cutbacks, caused politicians to promote "reinvestment" in social infrastructure as the twenty-first century began. This did not mean that the influence of neo-liberal ideology disappeared, particularly with reference to programs affecting the poor. Though a subset of the poorest Canadians remained militant, governments took advantage of the passivity of the majority, a passivity often resulting from fear of state retribution if they participated in political life. The War on Poverty had largely given way to a War on the Poor.

Notes

1 Address by J.M. Keith, Addresses, 29 September 1965, 36th Annual Meeting, Canadian Chamber of Commerce Papers, MG 28, 3, 62, Vol. 4, Library and Archives of Canada (LAC).

2 A trenchant analysis of the move towards neo-liberal thinking on the part of Saskatchewan's NDP is found in Phillip Hansen, Taxing Illusions: Taxation, Democracy and Embedded Political Theory (Halifax, NS: Fernwood, 2003).

3 Michael Mendelson, "Can We Reform Canada's Income Security System?" in The Future of Social Welfare Systems in Canada and the United Kingdom ed. Shirley B. Seward (Halifax, NS: Institute for Research on Public Policy, 1987), 123.

4 The attack on Keynesianism in Canada is documented in Arthur W. Donner and Douglas D. Peters, The Monetarist Counter-Revolution: A Critique of Monetary Policy 1975-1979 (Toronto, ON: James Lorimer, 1979); Harold Chorney and Phillip Hansen, "The Falling Rate of Legitimation: The Problem of the Contemporary Capitalist State in Canada," Studies in Political Economy 4 (1978): 65–98; and Harold Chorney, The Deficit: Hysteria and the Current Economic Crisis (Ottawa, ON: Canadian Centre for Policy Alternatives, 1989).

5 Robert Campbell, Grand Illusions: The Politics of the Keynsian Experience in Canada, 1945-1975 (Peterborough, ON: Broadview Press, 1987); Thomas J. Courchene, The Strategy of Gradualism: An Analysis of Bank of Canada Policy from Mid-1975 to Mid-1977 (Montreal, QC: C.D. Howe Institute, 1977); Harold Chorney, "The Economic and Political Consequences of Canadian Monetarism" (paper presented to the British Association of Canadian Studies, University of Nottingham, Nottingham, UK, 12 April 1991), 31.

6 Malcolm Taylor, "The Canadian Health care System: After Medicare," in Health and Canadian Society: Sociological Perspectives, 2nd ed., ed. David Coburn, Carl D'Arcy, George M. Torrance, and Peter New (Toronto, ON: Fitzhenry and Whiteside, 1987), 84–86.

7 Mike Burke and Susan Silver, "Universal Health Care: Current Challenges to Normative Legacies," in Canadian Social Policy: Issues and Perspectives, 3rd ed., ed. Anne Westhues (Waterloo, ON: Wilfrid Laurier University Press, 2003), 171; Taylor, "The Canadian Health care System," 93–100.

8 Richard Lee Deaton, *The Political Economy of Pensions: Power, Politics and Social Change in Canada, Britain and the United States* (Vancouver, BC: University of British Columbia Press, 1989), 37.

9 Two key works on the New Right of this period in the United States and Britain are Frances Fox Piven and Richard Cloward, *The New Class War: Reagan's Attack on the Welfare State and Its Consequences* (New York, NY: Pantheon, 1982); and Ramesh Mishra, *The Welfare State in Crisis: Social Thought and Social Change* (Brighton, UK: Wheatsheaf, 1984).

10 Sylvia Bashevkin, *Welfare Hot Buttons: Women, Work, and Social Policy Reform* (Toronto, ON: University of Toronto Press, 2002), 28.

11 Monique Simard, "Coalition Politics: The Quebec Labour Movement," *Socialist Studies* 4 (1988): 77.

12 Canada, *Report of the Royal Commission on the Economic Union and Development Prospects for Canada*, vols. 1 and 2 (Ottawa, ON: Supply and Services Canada, 1985).

13 The philosophy of globalization and its impact on social programs are dissected in Gary Teeple, *Globalization and the Decline of Social Reform: Into the Twenty-First Century* (Toronto, ON: Garamond, 2000).

14 Mario Iacobacci and Mario Seccareccia. "Full Employment versus Income Maintenance: Some Reflections on the Macroeconomic and Structural Implications of a Guaranteed Income Program for Canada," *Studies in Political Economy* 28 (Spring 1989): 142; Rodney Haddow, "Canadian Organized Labour and the Guaranteed Annual Income," in *Continuities and Discontinuities: The Political Economy of Social Welfare and Labour Market Policy in Canada*, ed. Andrew F. Johnson, Steven McBride, and P.J. Smith (Toronto, ON: University of Toronto Press, 1994), 350–66.

15 On the contemporary debate regarding the impact of free trade on social policy, see Glenn Drover, ed., *Free Trade and Social Policy* (Ottawa, ON: Canadian Council on Social Development, 1988).

16 John English and William R. Young, "The Federal Government and Social Policy in the 1990s: Reflections on Change and Continuity," in *Canadian Social Policy*, ed. Westhues, 245.

17 Bashevkin, *Welfare Hot Buttons*, 34.

18 Chorney, "The Economic and Political Consequences," 35–39.

19 Support for the pre-election plan of the NDP to focus on unemployment is found in Harold Chorney, "Deficits-Fact or Fiction? Ontario's Public Finances and the Challenge of Full Employment," in *Getting on Track, Social Democratic Struggles for Ontario*, ed. Daniel Drache (Montreal, QC: McGill-Queen's University Press, 1992), 186–201.

20 John Loxley, *Alternative Budgets: Budgeting as If People Mattered* (Halifax, NS: Fernwood. 2003), 9; Bashevkin, *Welfare Hot Buttons*, 82.

21 Anne Westhues, "An Overview of Social Policy," in *Canadian Social Policy*, ed. Westhues, 11.

22 Burke and Silver, "Universal Health Care," 172.

23 On the Klein cuts, see Trevor Harrison and Gordon Laxer, eds., *The Trojan Horse: Alberta and the Future of Canada* (Montreal, QC: Black Rose, 1995); Kevin Taft, *Shredding the Public Interest: Ralph Klein and Twenty-five Years of One-Party Government* (Edmonton, AB: University of Alberta Press, 1997); and Christopher J. Bruce, Ronald D. Kneebone, and Kenneth J. McKenzie, eds, *A Government Reinvented: A Study of Alberta's Deficit Elimination Program* (Toronto, ON: Oxford University Press, 1997).

24 Candace Johnson Redden, *Health Care, Entitlement, and Citizenship* (Toronto, ON: University of Toronto Press, 2002), 71.

25 Georges Campeau, *De l'assurance-chômage à l'assurance-emploi* (Montreal, ON: Boréal, 2001), 117, 153, 281.

26 Ibid, 155, 164.

27 Ibid, 166, 167, 170.

28 Ibid, 179–82,

29 Ibid, 219–21, 231–32.

30 Thomas Dunk, Stephen McBride, and Randle W. Nelson, eds., *The Training Trap: Ideology, Training and the Labour Market* (Halifax, NS: Fernwood, 1996); Marjorie Griffin Cohen, ed., *Training the Excluded for Work: Access and Equity for Women, Immigrants, First Nations, Youth and People with Low Incomes* (Vancouver, BC: University of British Columbia Press, 2004).

31 Submission by the Canada Advisory Council on the Status of Women, September 1980. Canada, House of Commons, Legislative Committee Hearings on Bill C-21, An Act to Amend the Unemployment Insurance Act.

32 Campeau, *De l'assurance-chômage à l'assurance-emploi* 241–45.

33 Ibid, 263–5, 271.

34 Canadian Housing and Renewal Association. *Access to Housing: Proceedings of the Twenty-first Annual Symposium of the Canadian Housing and Renewal Association* (Ottawa, ON: CHRA, 1990), 8.

35 Ibid.

36 Ibid, 23.

37 Ibid, 111.

38 Ibid, 6–8; Tim Falconer, *Watchdogs and Gadflies: Activism from Marginal to Mainstream* (Toronto, ON: Penguin, 2003), 192–96.

39 Lea Caragata, "Housing and Homelessness," in *Canadian Social Policy*, ed. Westhues, 75.

40 Ibid, 79.

41 Ibid, 72, 77.

42 Canada, Status of Women, *Report of the Task Force on Child Care* (Ottawa, ON: Minister of Supply and Services, 1986), 51, 100; Canada, House of Commons, *Report of the Special Committee on Child Care* (March 1987), 8, quoting Statistics Canada, *The Labour Force*, Cat. No. 71-001, May 1982, December 1986.

43 Jane Jenson, "Family Policy, Child Care and Social Solidarity: The Case of Quebec," in *Changing Child Care Advocacy and Policy in Canada*, ed. Susan Prentice (Halifax, NS: Fernwood, 2001).

42: Canada, House of Commons Special Committee on Child Care, 1985–1986, *Hearings and Evidence*, particularly Mrs. Alice Taylor, Director, Holland College Child Study Centre.

44 Canada, *Report of the Royal Commission on the Economic Union and Development Prospects for Canada*, vol. 2, 813.

45 Canada, House of Commons, *Minutes of Proceedings and Evidence of the Special Committee on Child Care, 1985–1986*.

46 So, for example, the Canadian Manufacturers Association, appearing before the committee, claimed that "current government spending on social programs and income support, in total, exceeds what Canada can afford" and recommended an increase in the child care expense deduction as an alternative to government funding of daycares. Canada, House of Commons, *Minutes of Proceedings and Evidence of the Special Committee on Child Care*, May 16, 1986.

47 Liberal Party of Canada, *Creating Opportunity: The Liberal Plan for Canada* (Ottawa, ON: Liberal Party of Canada, 1993). See also Bashevkin, *Welfare Hot Buttons*, 56.

48 The politics of daycare in Quebec is outlined in Jane Jenson, "Family Policy," 49–62.

49 *The Globe and Mail*, 13 October 2003.

50 Child care Resource and Research Unit, *Early Childhood Care and Education in Canada: Provinces and Territories, 1998* (Toronto, ON: Centre for Urban and Community Studies, University of Toronto, 2001), 72, 126.

71 Canadian Council on Social Development, *The Progress of Canada's Children* (Ottawa, ON: CCSD, 2002).

72 Swanson, *Poor-Bashing*, 110–14; Hunter, "The Problem of Child Poverty," 42–44.

73 John Clarke, "Fight to Win," *Labour/Le Travail* 50 (Fall 2002): 383–90.

74 Norman Feltes, "The New Prince in a New Principality: OCAP and the Toronto Poor," *Labour/Le Travail* 48 (Fall 2001): 146.

75 Redden, *Health Care, Entitlement, and Citizenship*, 46–47; Burke and Silver, "Universal Health Care," 171.

76 Simon Renouf, "Chipping Away at Medicare: 'Rome Wasn't Sacked in a Day,'" in *The Trojan Horse*, ed. Harrison and Laxer, 230.

77 Renouf, "Chipping Away at Medicare," 86–92; Roy J. Romanow, *Final Report: Building on Values: The Future of Health Care in Canada*, Commission on the Future of Health Care in Canada (Ottawa, ON: Government of Canada 2002), 136.

78 Romanow, *Final Report*, 128, 174.

79 *Edmonton Journal*, 7 November 2003, 5.

80 Redden, *Health Care, Entitlement, and Citizenship* 71.

81 Romanow, *Final Report*, 17.

82 Ibid., 40, 46, 62, 67, 76.

83 Ibid., 21, 96.

84 Ibid., 19.

85 Ibid., 104.

86 Ibid., 25.

87 Ibid., 32–33.

88 Ibid., 213.

89 Canadian Union of Public Employees (CUPE), *On the Front Line*, 17 February 2003.

90 Health Canada, Health Care System, "2003 First Ministers' Accord on Health Care Renewal" (2003). Retrieved from www.hc-sc.gc.ca/english/hca2003/accord.html.

91 *The Globe and Mail*, 6 February 2003; CUPE, *On the Front Line*, 17 February 2003; *Friends of Medicare*, 6 February 2003.

92 Romanow, *Final Report*, 253.

93 Canada, Royal Commission on Aboriginal Peoples (RCAP), *Final Report*, vol. 3, *Gathering Strength* (Ottawa, ON: Minister of Supply and Services, 1996), chap. 3, "Health and Healing."

94 Romanow, *Final Report*, 248–49.

95 Ibid., 247.

96 Ibid., 34, 255.

97 RCAP, *Final Report*, vol. 3, chap. 3, "Health and Healing."

98 Ibid., chap. 1, section 1, "Social Policy in Context."

99 Ibid., chap. 2.

100 Ibid.

101 Ibid.

102 Ibid., vol. 3, chap. 4, "Housing."

103 Ibid.

104 James S. Frideres and René R. Gadacz, *Aboriginal Peoples in Canada: Contemporary Conflicts*, 6th ed. (Toronto, ON: Prentice Hall, 2001), 125–42; quotation from 136.

---

51 Jocelyne Tougas, "Child Care in Québec: Where There's a Will, There's a Way," a paper of the Child Care Advocacy Association of Canada (n.d.). Retrieved from www.child careadvocacy.ca/resources/pdf/QUE_Child care.pdf.

52 Government of Alberta, MLA Committee to Review Low-Income Programs, *Low-Income Programs Review: What We Heard* (Edmonton, AB: Government of Alberta), November 2001.

53 Deaton, *The Political Economy of Pensions*, 81; Mireille Éthier, "Survey of Pension Issues," in *Income Distribution and Economic Security in Canada*, ed. François Vaillancourt (Toronto, ON: University of Toronto Press, 1985), 220.

54 Deaton, *The Political Economy of Pensions*, 108–14.

55 Ibid., 114.

56 Ibid., 161.

57 Sheila Neysmith, "Caring and Aging: Exposing the Policy Issues," in *Canadian Social Policy*, ed. Westhues, 189.

58 In 2003, this program provided services to 34,300 Manitobans and employed 5,500 casual staff. Though the Manitoba government regarded its program as "universal" and "comprehensive," there were enough gaps to allow private providers to find a market within the province. *Manitoba Health, Manitoba Home Care Program.* Retrieved from www.gov.mb.ca/health/home care.

59 Canadian Association on Gerontology, "Policy Statement: Home Care in Canada" (n.d.). Retrieved from www.cagacg.ca/publications/552_e.php.

60 See the essays in Sheila Neysmith, ed., *Restructuring Caring Labour: Discourse, State Practice and Everyday Life* (Toronto, ON: Oxford University Press, 2000), as well as Jane Aronson and Sheila Neysmith, "The Retreat of the State and Long-Term Care Provision: Implications for Frail Elderly People, Unpaid Family Carers and Paid Home Care Workers," *Studies in Political Economy* (1997): 37–66.

61 Ecumenical Health Care Network, "Home Care: Fact Sheets on Key Health Care Issues" (May 2005). Retrieved from www.united-church.ca/health care/pdf/home care.pdf.

62 Alvin Finkel, *Our Lives: Canada after 1945* (Toronto, ON: Lorimer, 1997), 299; National Council of Welfare, *Poverty Profile 1999* (Ottawa, ON: NCW, 1999).

63 Allyce Herle, acting chair, quoted in "Youngest Canadians at Highest Risk of Chronic Poverty," Press release, National Council of Welfare, 29 July 2002. Retrieved from www.ncwcnbes.net/htmdocument/principales/povertyprog9Press_e.htm.

64 Graham Riches, *Food Banks and the Welfare Crisis* (Ottawa, ON: Canadian Council on Social Development, 1986), 15, 31–32.

65 Canadian Conference of Catholic Bishops, *Ethical Reflections on the Economic Crisis* (Ottawa, ON: Episcopal Commission for Social Affairs, 1983).

66 *Nellie's Newsletter*, August 2002. In possession of the author.

67 In 1993, as in 1982, the ratio of adult women to men who lived in poverty was 1.33 to 1. Andrew Armitage, *Social Welfare in Canada Revisited: Facing Up to the Future* (Toronto, ON: Oxford University Press. 1996), 61.

68 Garson Hunter, "The Problem of Child Poverty in Canada," in *Canadian Social Policy*, ed. Westhues, 32; Social Planning Council of Winnipeg (SPCW), *Children: An Overlooked Investment: Manitoba Child Poverty Report Card 2002* (Winnipeg, MB: Social Planning Council of Winnipeg, 2002); *Toronto Star*, 30 July 2002; *The Globe and Mail*, 25 November 2003.

69 SPCW, *Manitoba Child Poverty Report Card 2002.*

70 Jean Swanson, *Poor-Bashing: The Politics of Exclusion* (Toronto, ON: Between the Lines, 2001), 123.

2
Reframing Justice in a Globalizing World

Globalization is changing the way we argue about justice. Not so long ago, in the heyday of social democracy, disputes about justice presumed what I shall call a "Keynesian-Westphalian frame." Typically played out within modern territorial states, arguments about justice were assumed to concern relations among fellow citizens, to be subject to debate within national publics, and to contemplate redress by national states. This was true for each of two major families of justice claims – claims for socioeconomic redistribution and claims for legal or cultural recognition. At a time when the Bretton Woods system of international capital controls facilitated Keynesian economic steering at the national level, claims for redistribution usually focused on economic inequities within territorial states. Appealing to national public opinion for a fair share of the national pie, claimants sought intervention by national states in national economies. Likewise, in an era still gripped by a Westphalian political imaginary, which sharply distinguished "domestic" from "international" space, claims for recognition generally concerned internal status hierarchies. Appealing to the national conscience for an end to nationally institutionalized disrespect, claimants pressed national governments to outlaw discrimination and accommodate differences among citizens. In both cases, the Keynesian-Westphalian frame was taken for granted. Whether the matter concerned redistribution or recognition, class differentials or status hierarchies, it went without saying that the unit within which justice applied was the modern territorial state.[1]

To be sure, there were always exceptions. Occasionally, famines and genocides galvanized public opinion across borders. And some cosmopolitans and anti-imperialists sought to promulgate globalist views.[2] But these were exceptions that proved the rule. Relegated to the sphere of "the international," they were subsumed within a problematic that was focused primarily on matters of security and humanitarian aid, as opposed to justice. The effect was to reinforce, rather than to challenge, the Keynesian-Westphalian frame. That framing of disputes about justice generally prevailed by default from the end of World War II to the 1970s.

Although it went unnoticed at the time, the Keynesian-Westphalian frame lent a distinctive shape to arguments about social justice. Taking for granted the modern territorial state as the appropriate unit, and its citizens as the pertinent subjects, such arguments turned on what precisely those citizens owed one another. In the eyes of some, it sufficed that citizens be formally equal before the law; for others, equality of opportunity was also required; for still others, justice demanded that all citizens gain access to the resources and respect they needed in order to be able to participate on a par with others, as full members of the political community. The argument focused, in other words, on what exactly should count as a just ordering of social relations within a society. Engrossed in disputing the "what" of justice, the contestants apparently felt no necessity to dispute the "who." With the Keynesian-Westphalian frame securely in place, it went without saying that the "who" was the national citizenry.

Today, however, the Keynesian-Westphalian frame is losing its aura of self-evidence. Thanks to heightened awareness of globalization, and to post-Cold War geopolitical instabilities, many observe that the social processes shaping their lives routinely overflow territorial borders. They note, for example, that decisions taken in one territorial state often impact the lives of those outside it, as do the actions of transnational corporations, international currency speculators, and large institutional investors. Many also note the growing salience of supranational and international organizations, both governmental and nongovernmental, and of transnational public opinion, which flows with

In such cases, disputes about justice are exploding the Keynesian-Westphalian frame. No longer addressed exclusively to national states or debated exclusively by national publics, claims no longer focus solely on relations among fellow citizens. Thus, the grammar of argument has altered. Whether the issue is distribution or recognition, disputes that used to focus exclusively on the question of what is owed as a matter of justice to community members now turn quickly into disputes about who should count as a member and which is the relevant community. Not just the "what" but also the "who" is up for grabs.

Today, in other words, arguments about justice assume a double guise. On the one hand, they concern first-order questions of substance, just as before. How much economic inequality does justice permit, how much redistribution is required, and according to which principle of distributive justice? What constitutes equal respect, which kinds of differences merit public recognition, and by which means? But above and beyond such first-order questions, arguments about justice today also concern second-order, meta-level questions. What is the proper frame within which to consider first-order questions of justice? Who are the relevant subjects entitled to a just distribution or reciprocal recognition in the given case? Thus, it is not only the substance of justice, but also the frame, which is in dispute.

The result is a major challenge to our theories of social justice. Preoccupied largely with first-order issues of distribution and/or recognition, these theories have so far failed to develop conceptual resources for reflecting on the meta-issue of the frame. As things stand, therefore, it is by no means clear that they are capable of addressing the double character of problems of justice in a globalizing age.[10]

In this chapter, I shall propose a strategy for thinking about the problem of the frame. I shall argue, first, that theories of justice must become three-dimensional, incorporating the political dimension of representation alongside the economic dimension of distribution and the cultural dimension of recognition. I shall also argue that the political dimension of representation should itself be understood as encompassing three levels. The combined effect of these two arguments will be to make visible a third question, beyond those of the "what" and the "who," which I shall call the question of the "how." That question, in turn, inaugurates a paradigm shift: what the

supreme disregard for borders through global mass media and cybertechnology. The result is a new sense of vulnerability to transnational forces. Faced with global warming, the spread of HIV-AIDS, international terrorism, and superpower unilateralism, many believe that their chances for living good lives depend at least as much on processes that trespass the borders of territorial states as on those contained within them.[3]

Under these conditions, the Keynesian-Westphalian frame no longer goes without saying. For many, it has ceased to be axiomatic that the modern territorial state is the appropriate unit for thinking about issues of justice, and that the citizens of such states are the pertinent subjects. The effect is to destabilize the previous structure of political claims-making – and therefore to change the way we argue about social justice.

This is true for both major families of justice claims. In today's world, claims for redistribution increasingly eschew the assumption of national economies. Faced with transnationalized production, the outsourcing of jobs, and the associated pressures of the "race to the bottom," once nationally focused labor unions look increasingly for allies abroad.[4] Inspired by the Zapatistas, meanwhile, impoverished peasants and indigenous peoples link their struggles against despotic local and national authorities to critiques of transnational corporate predation and global neoliberalism.[5] Finally, anti-World Trade Organization protestors directly target the new governance structures of the global economy, which have vastly strengthened the ability of large corporations and investors to escape the regulatory and taxation powers of territorial states.[6]

In the same way, movements struggling for recognition increasingly look beyond the territorial state. Under the umbrella slogan "women's rights are human rights," for example, feminists throughout the world are linking struggles against local patriarchal practices to campaigns to reform international law.[7] Meanwhile, religious and ethnic minorities who face discrimination within territorial states are reconstituting themselves as diasporas and building transnational publics from which to mobilize international opinion.[8] Finally, transnational coalitions of human-rights activists are seeking to build new cosmopolitan institutions, such as the International Criminal Court, which can punish state violations of human dignity.[9]

Keynesian-Westphalian frame cast as the theory of social justice must now become a theory of *postwestphalian democratic justice*.

For a three-dimensional theory of justice: on the specificity of the political

Let me begin by explaining what I mean by justice in general and by its political dimension in particular. In my view, the most general meaning of justice is parity of participation. According to this radical-democratic interpretation of the principle of equal moral worth, justice requires social arrangements that permit all to participate as peers in social life. Overcoming injustice means dismantling institutionalized obstacles that prevent some people from participating on a par with others, as full partners in social interaction. Previously, I analyzed two distinct kinds of obstacles to participatory parity, which correspond to two distinct species of injustice.[11] On the one hand, people can be impeded from full participation by economic structures that deny them the resources they need in order to interact with others as peers; in that case they suffer from distributive injustice or maldistribution. On the other hand, people can also be prevented from interacting on terms of parity by institutionalized hierarchies of cultural value that deny them the requisite standing; in that case they suffer from status inequality or misrecognition.[12] In the first case, the problem is the class structure of society, which corresponds to the economic dimension of justice. In the second case, the problem is the status order, which corresponds to its cultural dimension. In modern capitalist societies, the class structure and the status order do not neatly mirror each other, although they interact causally. Rather, each has some autonomy vis-à-vis the other. As a result, misrecognition cannot be reduced to a secondary effect of maldistribution, as some economistic theories of distributive justice appear to suppose. Nor, conversely, can maldistribution be reduced to an epiphenomenal expression of misrecognition, as some culturalist theories of recognition tend to assume. Thus, neither recognition theory nor distribution theory can alone provide an adequate understanding of justice for capitalist society. Only a two-dimensional theory,

encompassing both distribution and recognition, can supply the necessary levels of social-theoretical complexity and moral-philosophical insight.[13]

That, at least, is the view of justice I defended in the past. And this two-dimensional understanding of justice still seems right to me as far as it goes. But I now believe that it does not go far enough. Distribution and recognition could appear to constitute the sole dimensions of justice only so long as the Keynesian-Westphalian frame was taken for granted. Once the question of the frame becomes subject to contestation, the effect is to make visible a third dimension of justice, which was neglected in my previous work – as well as in the work of many other philosophers.[14]

The third dimension of justice is the political. Of course, distribution and recognition are themselves political in the sense of being contested and power-laden; and they have usually been seen as requiring adjudication by the state. But I mean political in a more specific, constitutive sense, which concerns the scope of the state's jurisdiction and the decision rules by which it structures contestation. The political in this sense furnishes the stage on which struggles over distribution and recognition are played out. Establishing criteria of social belonging, and thus determining who counts as a member, the political dimension of justice specifies the reach of those other dimensions: it tells us who is included in, and who excluded from, the circle of those entitled to a just distribution and reciprocal recognition. Establishing decision rules, the political dimension likewise sets the procedures for staging and resolving contests in both the economic and the cultural dimensions: it tells us not only who can make claims for redistribution and recognition, but also how such claims are to be mooted and adjudicated.

Centered on issues of membership and procedure, the political dimension of justice is concerned chiefly with representation. At one level, which pertains to the boundary-setting aspect of the political, representation is a matter of social belonging. What is at issue here is inclusion in, or exclusion from, the community of those entitled to make justice claims on one another. At another level, which pertains to the decision-rule aspect, representation concerns the procedures that structure public processes of contestation. Here, what is at issue are the terms on which those included in the political community air their claims and adjudicate their disputes.[15] At both levels, the question can arise as to whether the relations of representation are just. One can ask: Do the boundaries of the political community wrongly exclude some who are actually entitled to representation? Do the community's decision rules accord equal voice in public deliberations and fair representation in public decision-making to all members? Such issues of representation are specifically political. Conceptually distinct from both economic and cultural questions, they cannot be reduced to the latter, although, as we shall see, they are inextricably interwoven with them.

To say that the political is a conceptually distinct dimension of justice, not reducible to the economic or the cultural, is also to say that it can give rise to a conceptually distinct species of injustice. Given the view of justice as participatory parity, this means that there can be distinctively political obstacles to parity, not reducible to maldistribution or misrecognition, although (again) interwoven with them. Such obstacles arise from the political constitution of society, as opposed to the class structure or status order. Grounded in a specifically political mode of social ordering, they can only be adequately grasped through a theory that conceptualizes representation, along with distribution and recognition, as one of three fundamental dimensions of justice.

Two levels of political injustice: from ordinary-political misrepresentation to misframing

If representation is the defining issue of the political, then the characteristic political injustice is misrepresentation. Misrepresentation occurs when political boundaries and/or decision rules function wrongly to deny some people the possibility of participating on a par with others in social interaction – including, but not only, in political arenas. Far from being reducible to maldistribution or misrecognition, misrepresentation can occur even in the absence of the latter injustices, although it is usually intertwined with them.

At least two different levels of misrepresentation can be distinguished. Insofar as political decision rules wrongly deny

some of the included the chance to participate fully, as peers, the injustice is what I call ordinary-political misrepresentation. Here, where the issue is intra-frame representation, we enter the familiar terrain of political science debates over the relative merits of alternative electoral systems. Do single-member-district, winner-take-all, first-past-the-post systems unjustly deny parity to numerical minorities? And if so, is proportional representation or cumulative voting the appropriate remedy?[16] Likewise, do gender-blind rules, in conjunction with gender-based maldistribution and misrecognition, function to deny parity of political participation to women?[17] And if so, are gender quotas an appropriate remedy? Such questions belong to the sphere of ordinary-political justice, which has usually been played out within the Keynesian-Westphalian frame.

Less obvious, perhaps, is a second level of misrepresentation, which concerns the boundary-setting aspect of the political. Here the injustice arises when the community's boundaries are drawn in such a way as to wrongly exclude some people from the chance to participate at all in its authorized contests over justice. In such cases, misrepresentation takes a deeper form, which I shall call misframing. The deeper character of misframing is a function of the crucial importance of framing to every question of social justice. Far from being of marginal significance, frame-setting is among the most consequential of political decisions. Constituting both members and non-members in a single stroke, this decision effectively excludes the latter from the universe of those entitled to consideration within the community in matters of distribution, recognition, and ordinary-political representation. The result can be a serious injustice. When questions of justice are framed in a way that wrongly excludes some from consideration, the consequence is a special kind of meta-injustice, in which one is denied the chance to press first-order justice claims in a given political community. The injustice remains, moreover, even when those excluded from one political community are included as subjects of justice in another – as long as the effect of the political division is to put some relevant aspects of justice beyond their reach. Still more serious, of course, is the case in which one is excluded from membership in any political community. Akin to the loss of what Hannah Arendt called "the right to have rights," that sort of misframing is a kind of "political death."[18] Those who suffer it may become objects of charity or benevolence. But deprived of the possibility of authoring first-order claims, they become non-persons with respect to justice.

It is the misframing form of misrepresentation that globalization has recently begun to make visible. Earlier, in the heyday of the postwar welfare state, with the Keynesian-Westphalian frame securely in place, the principal concern in thinking about justice was distribution. Later, with the rise of the new social movements and multiculturalism, the center of gravity shifted to recognition. In both cases, the modern territorial state was assumed by default. As a result, the political dimension of justice was relegated to the margins. Where it did emerge, it took the ordinary-political form of contests over the decision rules internal to the polity, whose boundaries were taken for granted. Thus, claims for gender quotas and multicultural rights sought to remove political obstacles to participatory parity for those who were already included in principle in the political community.[19] Taking for granted the Keynesian-Westphalian frame, they did not call into question the assumption that the appropriate unit of justice was the territorial state.

Today, in contrast, globalization has put the question of the frame squarely on the political agenda. Increasingly subject to contestation, the Keynesian-Westphalian frame is now considered by many to be a major vehicle of injustice, as it partitions political space in ways that block many who are poor and despised from challenging the forces that oppress them. Channeling their claims into the domestic political spaces of relatively powerless, if not wholly failed, states, this frame insulates offshore powers from critique and control.[20] Among those powerful predator states and transnational private powers, including foreign investors and creditors, international currency speculators, and transnational corporations. Also protected are the governance structures of the global economy, which set exploitative terms of interaction and then exempt them from democratic control.[21] Finally, the Keynesian-Westphalian frame is self-insulating: the architecture of the interstate system protects the very partitioning of political space that it institutionalizes, effectively excluding transnational democratic decision-making on issues of justice.[22]

From this perspective, the Keynesian-Westphalian frame is a powerful instrument of injustice, which gerrymanders political space at the expense of the poor and despised. For those persons who are denied the chance to press transnational first-order claims, struggles against maldistribution and misrecognition cannot proceed, let alone succeed, unless they are joined with struggles against misframing. It is not surprising, therefore, that some consider misframing the defining injustice of a globalizing age.

Under these conditions, of heightened awareness of misframing, the political dimension of justice is hard to ignore. Insofar as globalization is politicizing the question of the frame, it is also making visible an aspect of the grammar of justice that was often neglected in the previous period. It is now apparent that no claim for justice can avoid presupposing some notion of representation, implicit or explicit, insofar as none can avoid assuming a frame. Thus, representation is always already inherent in all claims for redistribution and recognition. The political dimension is implicit in, indeed required by, the grammar of the concept of justice. Thus, no redistribution or recognition without representation.[23]

In general, then, an adequate theory of justice for our time must be three-dimensional. Encompassing not only redistribution and recognition, but also representation, it must allow us to grasp the question of the frame as a question of justice. Incorporating the economic, cultural, and political dimensions, it must enable us to identify injustices of misframing and to evaluate possible remedies. Above all, it must permit us to pose, and to answer, the key political question of our age: How can we integrate struggles against maldistribution, misrecognition, and misrepresentation within a postwestphalian frame?

On the politics of framing: from state-territoriality to social effectivity?

So far I have been arguing for the irreducible specificity of the political as one of three fundamental dimensions of justice. And I have identified two distinct levels of political injustice: ordinary-political misrepresentation and misframing. Now, I want to examine the politics of framing in a globalizing world.

Distinguishing affirmative from transformative approaches, I shall argue that an adequate politics of representation must also address a third level: beyond contesting ordinary-political misrepresentation, on the one hand, and misframing, on the other, such a politics must also aim to democratize the process of frame-setting.

I begin by explaining what I mean by "the politics of framing." Situated at my second level, where distinctions between members and non-members are drawn, this politics concerns the boundary-setting aspect of the political. Focused on the issues of who counts as a subject of justice, and what is the appropriate frame, the politics of framing comprises efforts to establish and consolidate, to contest and revise, the authoritative division of political space. Included here are struggles against misframing, which aim to dismantle the obstacles that prevent disadvantaged people from confronting the forces that oppress them with claims of justice. Centered on the setting and contesting of frames, the politics of framing is concerned with the question of the "who."

The politics of framing can take two distinct forms, both of which are now being practiced in our globalizing world.[24] The first approach, which I shall call the affirmative politics of framing, contests the boundaries of existing frames while accepting the Westphalian grammar of frame-setting. In this politics, those who claim to suffer injustices of misframing seek to redraw the boundaries of existing territorial states or in some cases to create new ones. But they still assume that the territorial state is the appropriate unit within which to pose and resolve disputes about justice. For them, accordingly, injustices of misframing are not a function of the general principle according to which the Westphalian order partitions political space. They arise, rather, as a result of the faulty way in which that principle has been applied. Thus, those who practice the affirmative politics of framing accept that the principle of state-territoriality is the proper basis for constituting the "who" of justice. They agree, in other words, that what makes a given collection of individuals into fellow subjects of justice is their shared residence on the territory of a modern state and/or their shared membership in the political community that corresponds to such a state. Thus, far from challenging the underlying grammar of the Westphalian order, those who

practice the affirmative politics of framing accept its state-territorial principle.[25]

Precisely that principle is contested, however, in a second version of the politics of framing, which I shall call the transformative approach. For proponents of this approach, the state-territorial principle no longer affords an adequate basis for determining the "who" of justice in every case. They concede, of course, that that principle remains relevant for many purposes; thus, supporters of transformation do not propose to eliminate state-territoriality entirely. But they contend that its grammar is out of synch with the structural causes of many injustices in a globalizing world, which are not territorial in character. Examples include the financial markets, "offshore factories," investment regimes, and governance structures of the global economy, which determine who works for a wage and who does not; the information networks of global media and cybertechnology, which determine who is included in the circuits of communicative power and who is not; and the biopolitics of climate, disease, drugs, weapons, and biotechnology, which determine who will live long and who will die young. In these matters, so fundamental to human well-being, the forces that perpetrate injustice belong not to "the space of places," but to "the space of flows."[26] Not locatable within the jurisdiction of any actual or conceivable territorial state, they cannot be made answerable to claims of justice that are framed in terms of the state-territorial principle. In their case, so the argument goes, to invoke the state-territorial principle to determine the frame is itself to commit an injustice. By partitioning political space along territorial lines, this principle insulates extra- and non-territorial powers from the reach of justice. In a globalizing world, therefore, it is less likely to serve as a remedy for misframing than as a means of inflicting or perpetuating it.

Postwestphalian framing

In general, then, the transformative politics of framing aims to change the deep grammar of frame-setting in a globalizing world. This approach seeks to supplement the state-territorial principle of the Westphalian order with one or more postwestphalian principles. The aim is to overcome injustices of misframing by changing not just the boundaries of the "who" of justice, but also the mode of their constitution, hence the way in which they are drawn. It is to establish a post-territorial mode of political differentiation.[27]

What might a postwestphalian mode of frame-setting look like? Doubtless it is too early to have a clear view. Nevertheless, the most promising candidate so far is the "all-affected principle." This principle holds that all those affected by a given social structure or institution have moral standing as subjects of justice in relation to it. On this view, what turns a collection of people into fellow subjects of justice is not geographical proximity, but their co-imbrication in a common structural or institutional framework, which sets the ground rules that govern their social interaction, thereby shaping their respective life possibilities in patterns of advantage and disadvantage.[28]

Until recently, the all-affected principle seemed to coincide in the eyes of many with the state-territorial principle. It was assumed, in keeping with the Westphalian world picture, that the common framework that determined patterns of advantage and disadvantage was precisely the constitutional order of the modern territorial state. As a result, it seemed that in applying the state-territorial principle, one simultaneously captured the normative force of the all-affected principle. In fact, this was never truly so, as the long history of colonialism and neo-colonialism attests. From the perspective of the metropole, however, the conflation of state-territoriality with social effectivity appeared to have an emancipatory thrust, as it served to justify the progressive incorporation, as subjects of justice, of the subordinate classes and status groups who were resident in the territory but excluded from active citizenship.

Today, however, the idea that state-territoriality can serve as a proxy for social effectivity is no longer plausible. Under current conditions, one's chances to live a good life do not depend wholly on the internal political constitution of the territorial state in which one resides. Although the latter remains undeniably relevant, its effects are mediated by other structures, both extra- and non-territorial, whose impact is at least as significant. In general, globalization is driving a widening wedge between state-territoriality and social effectivity. As those two principles increasingly diverge, the effect is to reveal

the former as an inadequate surrogate for the latter. And so the question arises: Is it possible to apply the all-affected principle directly to the framing of justice, without going through the detour of state-territoriality?[29]

This is precisely what some practitioners of transformative politics are attempting to do. Seeking leverage against offshore sources of maldistribution and misrecognition, some globalization activists are appealing directly to the all-affected principle in order to circumvent the state-territorial partitioning of political space. Contesting their exclusion by the Keynesian-Westphalian frame, environmentalists and indigenous peoples are claiming standing as subjects of justice in relation to the extra- and non-territorial powers that impinge on their lives. Insisting that effectivity trumps state-territoriality, they have joined development activists, international feminists, and others in asserting their right to make claims against the structures that harm them, even when the latter cannot be located in the space of places. Casting off the Westphalian grammar of frame-setting, these claimants are applying the all-affected principle directly to questions of justice in a globalizing world.

Meta-political justice

In such cases, the transformative politics of framing proceeds simultaneously in multiple dimensions and on multiple levels. On one level, the social movements that practice this politics aim to redress first-order injustices of maldistribution, misrecognition, and ordinary-political misrepresentation. On a second level, these movements seek to redress meta-level injustices of misframing by reconstituting the "who" of justice. In those cases, moreover, where the state-territorial principle serves more to indemnify than to challenge injustice, transformative social movements appeal instead to the all-affected principle. Invoking a postwestphalian principle, they are seeking to change the very grammar of frame-setting – and thereby to reconstruct the meta-political foundations of justice for a globalizing world.

But the claims of transformative politics go further still. Above and beyond their other demands, these movements are also claiming a say in the process of frame-setting. Rejecting the standard view, which deems frame-setting the prerogative of states and transnational elites, they are effectively aiming to democratize the process by which the frameworks of justice are drawn and revised. Asserting their right to participate in constituting the "who" of justice, they are simultaneously transforming the "how" – by which I mean the accepted procedures for determining the "who." At their most reflective and ambitious, accordingly, transformative movements are demanding the creation of new democratic arenas for entertaining arguments about the frame. In some cases, moreover, they are creating such arenas themselves. In the World Social Forum, for example, some practitioners of transformative politics have fashioned a transnational public sphere where they can participate on a par with others in airing and resolving disputes about the frame. In this way, they are prefiguring the possibility of new institutions of postwestphalian democratic justice.[30]

The democratizing dimension of transformative politics points to a third level of political injustice, above and beyond the two already discussed. Previously, I distinguished first-order injustices of ordinary-political misrepresentation from second-order injustices of misframing. Now, however, we can discern a third-order species of political injustice, which corresponds to the question of the "how." Exemplified by undemocratic processes of frame-setting, this injustice consists in the failure to institutionalize parity of participation at the meta-political level, in deliberations and decisions concerning the "who." Because what is at stake here is the process by which first-order political space is constituted, I shall call this injustice meta-political misrepresentation. Meta-political misrepresentation arises when states and transnational elites monopolize the activity of frame-setting, denying voice to those who may be harmed in the process, and blocking creation of democratic arenas where the latter's claims can be vetted and redressed. The effect is to exclude the overwhelming majority of people from participation in the meta-discourses that determine the authoritative division of political space. Lacking any institutional arenas for such participation, and submitted to an undemocratic approach to the "how," the majority is denied the chance to engage on terms of parity in decision-making about the "who."

In general, then, struggles against misframing are revealing a new kind of democratic deficit. Just as globalization has made visible injustices of misframing, so transformative struggles against neoliberal globalization are making visible the injustice of meta-political misrepresentation. In exposing the lack of institutions where disputes about the "who" can be democratically aired and resolved, these struggles are focusing attention on the "how." By demonstrating that the absence of such institutions impedes efforts to overcome injustice, they are revealing the deep internal connections between democracy and justice. The effect is to bring to light a structural feature of the current conjuncture: struggles for justice in a globalizing world cannot succeed unless they go hand in hand with struggles for meta-political democracy. At this level, too, then, no redistribution or recognition without representation.

Monological theory and democratic dialogue

I have been arguing that what distinguishes the current conjuncture is intensified contestation concerning both the "who" and the "how" of justice. Under these conditions, the theory of justice is undergoing a paradigm shift. Earlier, when the Keynesian-Westphalian frame was in place, most philosophers neglected the political dimension. Treating the territorial state as a given, they endeavored to ascertain the requirements of justice theoretically, in a monological fashion. Thus, they did not envisage any role in determining these requirements for those who would be subject to them, let alone for those excluded by the national frame. Neglecting to reflect on the question of the frame, these philosophers never imagined that those whose fates would be so decisively shaped by framing decisions might be entitled to participate in making them. Disavowing any need for a dialogical democratic moment, they were content to produce monological theories of social justice.

Today, however, monological theories of social justice are becoming increasingly implausible. As we have seen, globalization cannot help but problematize the question of the "how," as it politicizes the question of the "who." The process goes something like this: as the circle of those claiming a say in frame-setting expands, decisions about the "who" are increasingly viewed as political matters, which should be handled democratically, rather than as technical matters, which can be left to experts and elites. The effect is to shift the burden of argument, requiring defenders of expert privilege to make their case. No longer able to hold themselves above the fray, they are necessarily embroiled in disputes about the "how." As a result, they must contend with demands for meta-political democratization.

An analogous shift is currently making itself felt in normative philosophy. Just as some activists are seeking to transfer elite frame-setting prerogatives to democratic publics, so some theorists of justice are proposing to rethink the classic division of labor between theorist and *demos*. No longer content to ascertain the requirements of justice in a monological fashion, these theorists are looking increasingly to dialogical approaches, which treat important aspects of justice as matters for collective decision-making, to be determined by the citizens themselves, through democratic deliberation. For them, accordingly, the grammar of the theory of justice is being transformed. What could once be called the "theory of social justice" now appears as the "theory of democratic justice."[31]

In its current form, however, the theory of democratic justice remains incomplete. To complete the shift from a monological to dialogical theory requires a further step, beyond those contemplated by most proponents of the dialogical turn.[32] Henceforth, democratic processes of determination must be applied not only to the "what" of justice, but also to the "who" and the "how." In that case, by adopting a democratic approach to the "how," the theory of justice assumes a guise appropriate to a globalizing world. Dialogical at every level, meta-political as well as ordinary-political, it becomes a theory of postwestphalian democratic justice.

The view of justice as participatory parity readily lends itself to such an approach. This principle has a double quality that expresses the reflexive character of democratic justice. On the one hand, the principle of participatory parity is an outcome notion, which specifies a substantive principle of justice by which we may evaluate social arrangements: the latter are just if and only if they permit all the relevant social actors to participate as peers in social life. On the other hand, participatory

parity is also a process notion, which specifies a procedural standard by which we may evaluate the democratic legitimacy of norms: the latter are legitimate if and only if they can command the assent of all concerned in fair and open processes of deliberation, in which all can participate as peers. By virtue of this double quality, the view of justice as participatory parity has an inherent reflexivity. Able to problematize both substance and procedure, it renders visible the mutual entwinement of these two aspects of social arrangements. Thus, this approach can expose both the unjust background conditions that skew putatively democratic decision-making and the undemocratic procedures that generate substantively unequal outcomes. As a result, it enables us to shift levels easily, moving back and forth as necessary between first-order and meta-level questions. Making manifest the co-implication of democracy and justice, the view of justice as participatory parity supplies just the sort of reflexivity that is needed in a globalizing world.

All told, then, the norm of participatory parity suits the account of postwestphalian democratic justice presented here. Encompassing three dimensions and multiple levels, this account renders visible, and criticizable, the characteristic injustices of the present conjuncture. Conceptualizing misframing and meta-political misrepresentation, it discloses core injustices overlooked by standard theories. Focused not only on the "what" of justice, but also on the "who" and the "how," it enables us to grasp the question of the frame as the central question of justice in a globalizing world.

Bureaucratic Disentitlement in Social Welfare Programs

Michael Lipsky
Massachusetts Institute of Technology

Bureaucratic disentitlement is a mode of fiscal and programmatic retrenchment that takes place through obscure and routine actions of public authorities, and through failures to take action, that result in distributive consequences. Drawing primarily upon observations of social welfare programs in Boston over the last five years, this study identifies eight mechanisms by which the relationship of social welfare policy beneficiaries to the state has become attenuated. It emphasizes not only cutbacks in benefits but also retrenchment in opportunities to influence social policy outcomes.

Retrenchment in social welfare policy normally comes to public attention through wholesale legislative cutbacks or highly publicized administrative decisions. This paper, however, draws attention to a mode of fiscal and programmatic retrenchment I call bureaucratic disentitlement. In bureaucratic disentitlement, obligations to social welfare beneficiaries are reduced and circumscribed through largely obscure "bureaucratic" actions and inactions of public authorities.

These obligations involve both benefits to citizens and opportunities to influence government. Thus, they encompass many of the ways social welfare beneficiaries relate to the state. Bureaucratic disentitlement takes place in the hidden recesses of routine or obscure decision making, or the unobtrusive nondecisions of policymakers. Therefore, it tends to allocate entitlements without the accountability that normally restrains government excesses or allows full discussion of critical distributive issues.

Social Service Review (March 1984).

The focus of this article is on the mechanisms by which the social welfare political economy may expand and contract in response to varied and conflicting pressures.[1] I seek to illuminate the process by which macroeconomic pressures to constrain social welfare spending (resonant with antiwelfare ideologies, to be sure) are transformed into the organizationally specific actions of a variety of public officials. It is these actions, in turn, that, when taken together, comprise the patterns that welfare state analysts observe. I also introduce evidence to support the thesis that the relatively low level of mass resistance to large-scale social welfare cuts of the Reagan administration may be sought in the earlier retrenchment experienced by social welfare policy beneficiaries.[2]

Until recently, cutback politics has been treated primarily as a problem of resource allocation for the political system or its chief agencies. Analysts of cutback politics have asked how budget crises arise, and what techniques tend to be employed by public agencies confronted with the need to reduce expenditures. They have tended to focus on the implications of retrenchment as a strategic problem for government, and have concentrated on detailing the structure of government programs before and after retrenchment.[3]

A somewhat different set of concerns arise if we regard cutback politics as a process through which, intentionally and unintentionally, the relationship of the state to welfare state beneficiaries becomes attenuated. Focusing on the relationship of the state to welfare state beneficiaries draws attention to four critical analytic concerns. First, to understand this phenomenon we should look beyond how budget cuts affect individual agencies to look at how budget cuts may affect the targets of agency policies. Indeed, policies that deprive low-income citizens of essential goods and services that they cannot obtain elsewhere, or that deprive them of opportunities to influence the provision of such goods and services, may be said to be so significant that they affect their "constitutional" position.[4]

Second, for our purposes, programs subject to cutbacks are not simply government "outputs." Rather, they structure the relationship of citizens to the state. To say that there is a relationship implies that there are sets of mutual expectations, not necessarily explicit, that establish the ways in which parties in the relationship behave and regard each other.[5] In cutback politics this may take the form of "individual learning," as in the case of a claimant who is put off by three agencies that previously offered services and so never makes a phone call to a fourth. Or it may take the symbolic form of "signaling" low-income citizens that their interests are now of less concern to the general public[6] and thus they should expect less. Cutbacks in one period may reverberate to spur citizen mobilization to resist further changes, or they may have the opposite effect of reducing citizen initiative.

Third, the relationship of citizens to the state consists not only of benefits received ("outputs," if you will), but also of opportunities to influence government. Citizens not only receive the protection of the laws, they also vote. In studying cutback politics, we should be open to recognizing the importance of changes in opportunities for citizen input, as well as understanding reductions in government benefits.

Fourth, relationships between citizens and the state are dynamic and likely to change. It is clear that societies shift between the poles of social welfare generosity and stringency. Thus, we should inquire into the mechanisms whereby societies make such gradual shifts.

The dialectical approaches to fiscal crisis of James O'Connor, and Frances Piven and Richard Cloward, draw attention to the problems posed by growing social welfare expenditures for the managers of welfare state capitalism, even though such expenditures are necessary for managing dependent populations.[7] Other analysts have focused on the need for retrenchment following periods of affluence and the positive responses to high demand provided by liberal societies.[8] Yet political mobilization directed toward changing the balance between social welfare expenditures and responsibilities does not arise overnight. Instead, it more likely develops over time, beginning, perhaps, in a period of mixed support or even hostility to cutback reformation. It follows that one can try to identify the bridges over which periods of generosity are carried to periods of stringency, and to recognize the links between the ebb and flow of the macropolitical behavior of the state and the microbehaviors of public officials who propose, administer, and implement cutbacks.

This paper is concerned with bureaucratic disentitlement, a mode of cutback politics that is more obscure, more indirect, and less decisive as a budgeting tool than the more familiar, highly publicized cutback decisions of legislatures and executives.[9] In part because the identity of the cutback targets is obscure, and the impact of cutbacks is unclear, bureaucratic disentitlement is difficult for the public to apprehend and thus gives rise to little overt opposition. It also tends to be unavailable for inspection by social policy "watchdogs" or, if known to them, is difficult to utilize as a focus for rallying constituency support.

Bureaucratic disentitlement is an "umbrella" term circumscribing a variety of cutback developments that share several characteristics. First, conflict between government agencies and the subjects of their policy decisions tends to take place in bureaucratic rather than public political arenas. Rather than explicitly addressing the value issues of distribution in more visible legislative or high-level executive arenas, these often hidden conflicts tend to be played out in bureaucratic contexts and focus on the process of distributing economic and political resources rather than on the principles governing their distribution.[10]

Second, issues are not only presented and pursued as bureaucratic, but they also arise and are pursued as marginal, incremental, or routine activities.

Third, public officials tend to undertake their actions in the name of other political values, such as the need for efficiency, spending reductions, fairness, or promotion of the work ethic, and to disregard the distributional consequences. Bureaucratic disentitlement represents no less of a political struggle because the conflict is indirect. Power relationships and implicit conflict may be said to exist simply when groups have unequal capacity to achieve goals and are in competition for a limited opportunity to further their interests.[11] Moreover, the fact that public officials are primarily motivated by bureaucratic or budgetary imperatives does not gainsay that they exercise authority in ways that have distributional consequences for their clients.

One form of bureaucratic disentitlement consists of officials acting as if enormous and inescapable forces must inevitably take their toll. Here, public officials' failure to seek to ameliorate the consequences of current policies that involve or affect the availability of resources to low-income communities may be treated as critical nondecisions.[12] In these events, public officials act as if they are not aware that benefits and resources may be reduced by their actions.

Bureaucratic disentitlement is most significant politically in periods in which more overt modes of disentitlement are not prominent. This follows because its manifestations are consistent with policy developments that are pursued in periods of uncertainty over and ambivalence about the social welfare contract, when policy elites favoring a more restricted social welfare state are unable to proceed straightforwardly to realign it. Although instances of bureaucratic disentitlement can be identified throughout the last decade, it is noteworthy that the examples highlighted in this paper precede the Reagan administration's budget cutback initiatives. Drawn primarily from the late 1970s, they may be thought of as having paved the way for later cutbacks made possible by President Reagan's convincing electoral victory.[13] They played this role in part because they prepared the beneficiary population for more extensive and dramatic cuts, and in part because in various ways they disarmed it by withdrawing community resources and opportunities for political influence.

This essay is conceived as an attempt to identify the heretofore neglected relationships between relatively obscure aspects of social policy development and lower-level administration, and the structuring of low-income citizens' relationship to the state. To be sure, no single case study can hope to provide proof of the assertions offered here, nor is it possible to document persuasively all relevant dimensions of these relationships. I hope, however, to make a sufficiently plausible case for the assertions offered here, and provide a coherent framework

for elevating the subject of bureaucratic disentitlement to a level such that others may join in examining this phenomenon and its implications for the American polity.

Forms of Bureaucratic Disentitlement

Critical to a perspective that considers the constitutional relationship of citizens to the welfare state is a focus on citizen contributions to governance as well as state contributions to citizens' welfare. Accordingly, this paper is framed by the recognition that local political structures in the past may be thought of as having extensively organized both the input and output sides of politics for the urban masses. Political machines typically linked people to government by significantly influencing the distribution of political rewards, and also by providing a focus for citizen participation in politics by facilitating access to public officials. The importance of structuring the input and output aspects of citizen relationships to the state was highlighted in the urban crisis of the 1960s and early 1970s when politicians sought to restore and strengthen these linkages by expanding social welfare programs, and by providing increased access to government through broader opportunities for citizen participation and the expansion of individual rights.[14]

Illustrations of bureaucratic disentitlement must draw upon the importance of the dual nature of citizens' relationship to the political system. For just as a person's relationship to the state may be strengthened by expanding social welfare benefits or shoring up opportunities to participate in politics, the relationship may also be weakened if social welfare benefits are cut back or opportunities to influence politics are reduced in scope or significance. In order to demonstrate the wide range of policy areas subject to bureaucratic disentitlement, I consider, first, developments that have conditioned and restricted eligibility and access to social welfare benefits. Then I consider developments in social welfare policies that have affected the ability of low-income people, individually and collectively, to criticize or seek to affect social policies.

While the paper focuses on bureaucratic disentitlement as a general development in welfare state policy, much of the discussion focuses on the effects of city, state, and national politics on neighborhoods of low-income and neighborhood groups in one city (Boston) in which I viewed the[15] matters extensively over a period of years as a participant-observer. This emphasis is called for because the relationship between cutback politics and mass mobilization may be seen most clearly when one observes directly the effect or lack of effect of cuts on individuals and organizations with potential for arousal to action. In other words, when structures for the expression of protest over cutbacks in benefits are circumscribed, compelling questions are raised about the function of such structures for channeling and ameliorating grievances.

Conditioning Availability of Benefits

1. *Rationing access to social welfare benefits.*—Rationing is the most familiar and straightforward approach to bureaucratic restructuring of relations between government agencies and their clients. Faced with high demand and charged with the responsibility of serving people with few alternative resources, public agencies, confronting limited resources themselves, typically develop mechanisms to limit services to eligible citizens while ignoring the costs to clients of the new administrative arrangements.[16]

Implemented indirectly through budgetary stringency or as side-effects of fiscal cutbacks, rationing tends to be inconspicuous as policy. Its effects are usually diffuse, and it makes its impact through imposing costs and inconvenience on clients as individuals rather than on identifiable groups. Rationing results in the maintenance of previous policy in form, with reduction of policy outputs in practice. It is often hard to resist because, as a result of widespread media attention, in the public mind the need to cut back is widely believed to be great, whereas the agency's need for the marginal dollar or amenity is generally believed to be low because of popular characterizations of social welfare agencies as wasteful.

During the period under discussion, rationing effectively reduced citizen access to Boston social welfare programs by imposing costs and inconvenience on clients, and by changing the operating ideology of the system toward one in which workers were less helpful and recipients were more apprehensive. For example, increased regimentation and surveillance in welfare eligibility claims, undertaken in the name of reducing fraud, generated fear and uncertainty among welfare recipients. Forbidding and threatening notices were sent to recipients whose names came up in computer matches of welfare and social security rolls, although only a small minority of those receiving the notices were likely to be withholding information. Requirements for photo identifications for check cashing and new, burdensome verification requirements all contributed to a more heavily policed system in which recipients had to work harder to establish or maintain eligibility, were made less secure, and in which workers' skepticism of recipient eligibility tended to drive out concern for the clients' destitution. Agency officials explained these developments as a tightening up of routine surveillance mechanisms with which honest people should be happy to comply. From the bottom up, however, the developments looked like increased

harassment and the addition of degrading difficulties in maintaining eligibility.

Some of these examples of rationing resulted from state policy decisions that received some press coverage after they were announced, so that attentive followers may have been appraised of the changes. However, no publicity attended the more ubiquitous, low-level rationing that resulted from maintaining inadequate welfare staffing levels, burgeoning staff responsibilities, and an inability to solve fundamental administrative problems such as inadequate record keeping.[17]

Efforts to consolidate offices were prominent and remained prominent with welfare administrators because of the cost savings implied. In two major initiatives involving office consolidation—an abortive effort to create a single welfare applications center for Boston, and district office closings that have proceeded throughout the last four years—the costs to recipients as a result of additional travel and office inaccessibility were not calculated or publicly discussed.

The subject of rationing directly bears on a discussion of the structuring of relations between poor people and public agencies. Bureaucratic rationing conveys the message that government is incapable of providing services, or does so under duress. Rationing not only reduces the number of people who seek services, it also transforms entitlement programs into conditionally restricted programs. The more difficult it is to pierce the bureaucratic veil, the more luck, persistence, or the ability to manipulate public workers determine whether aid is forthcoming. Thus rationing not only reduces entitlements; it also teaches political lessons contributing to future political expectations.

2. *Rationing benefits: the growing gap between need and "slots."*—Rationing can take place not only when bureaucracies become less accessible, but also when the availability of material assistance is reduced. To be sure, there have never been enough summer jobs for teenagers, training programs for aspiring craftworkers, or subsidized housing to go around. (For that matter, income support programs typically have not provided "sufficient" support.)[18] However, as living costs increased and continued to rise unabated, as they did throughout the 1970s, and as fiscal retrenchment began to occur throughout the social welfare policy network, more people sought assistance, and every benefit became less and less available to people in need.

From the street-level point of view, this implies, most obviously, that services and benefits are reduced. It also means that the gap between the apparent availability of assistance and actual help increases. Further, it reinforces the view that aid from the welfare state depends on luck, "connections," persistence, or other factors over which people have little control.

The severity of this problem is graphic in the area of housing policy. Low-income families in Boston and elsewhere find it virtually impossible to find housing they can afford.[19] The Section 8 "as is" rental subsidy program is a fitting programmatic response to the problem of rising housing costs and relatively fixed incomes.[20] The problem with the Section 8 program is that it is so scarce a resource relative to the need.[21]

A similar, immense gap exists between the number of people who seek legal services and those who actually can be represented or receive the services of a lawyer. While not everyone who inquires actually ought to have the services of a lawyer, the number of people whose cases could be taken is much larger than the number actually getting helped.[22] Subsidized day-care for working mothers is another resource in short supply.

Potential users of these services, of course, are even greater than the number who apply for them. But because of the difficulty or improbability of getting help, the expectations of needy and eligible people have been dampened; they believe that they are not likely to be aided and therefore that the effort to apply may not be worth the cost.

The formal availability of programs to meet needs, which in reality can meet only a small proportion of the need, conditions people's claims on government and the society. Poor people in need of housing are told on the one hand that they should apply for Section 8 housing, and on the other hand that they are not likely to get it. It is not that public policy has failed to recognize the need; there is no policy to meet the need. Thus requests or demands for assistance or relief, righteously expressed, become transformed into measures of frustration or resignation as people realize that, although their needs have been recognized, no resources are available to help them.

The importance of social programs that formally address but fail to meet need is that they give rich and poor alike the appearance of systemic responsiveness while implicitly signaling people who remain dependent that they are unlucky or somehow at fault for failing to take advantage of these programs. Such approaches to social policy are consistent with the ambivalence toward programs for the poor that characterizes the American welfare state. In contrast, the Reagan administration's categorical disentitlements at least reflect no similar ambivalence, being directed relatively singlemindedly to altering the share of national resources that support low-income people.

3. *Letting "natural" forces have their way.*—A special but related case of rationing benefits through reduced programmatic commitments is provided by the role of social and economic conditions regarded as "natural" or uncontrollable parts of the environment. Inflation, when regarded as a condition rather than a problem, poses such difficulties. With rapid inflation, benefit programs that are not tied to the cost of living become less and less helpful, although the programs ostensibly

continue. Long before the Reagan administration "tightened" up AFDC, this program had been effectively diminished by the failure of most states to raise grant levels as living costs rose.[23]

Failure to increase AFDC grant levels in an inflationary period represents a critical nondecision by social welfare policymakers and may be distinctly analyzed as an exercise of power operating against the interests of recipients. Political scientists have explored at length the critical significance for power relationships of the failure to make critical decisions. Some have been wary of this concept of "nondecisions" because it is often difficult to know when and why a decision is not made.[24] However, the utility of nondecisions as an analytic tool is enhanced in this case because normal policy guidelines call for welfare grant level adjustments through periodic reassessments of the "standard of need." The failure of states to provide for periodic and adequate recalculation of the need standard directly contradicts a prominent, express program requirement. Thus legislative and administrative leaders, seeking to constrain budgets and failing to perceive significant pressures to the contrary, may be seen as having determined not to maintain welfare grant parity.

The housing issue also helps illustrate the effect on poor people of regarding problems as beyond the ability of society to solve them. The housing crisis in many older American cities is significantly exacerbated by condominium conversion, rent increases occasioned by renewed interest in urban living by the middle class, and conversion of public buildings into luxury housing. Elected officials generally favor this development in a time of fiscal strain because it promises to increase the tax base. Just as watching inflation proceed without adjusting income support programs erodes the value of the programs, watching rents increase and rental units being removed from the rolls without intervention drives low-income people out of the city or forces them into crowded or unsanitary living conditions.

Although one is a national and the other a local policy matter, it is important to recognize that inflation and the housing market are far from "natural" forces. They are both powerfully affected by governmental and institutional decisions—the supply of money in the case of inflation, for example, and in the case of housing, the degree of development, for example, and in the case of housing, the degree of local subsidy for low-income units, infrastructure development, or the promotion of luxury housing.

While inflation has eroded the value of public welfare in the absence of decisions to adjust its grant levels periodically, it has crosscutting implications for other social welfare programs. Food stamps and Section 8 housing, for example, are structured to maintain their value with inflation. From the point of view of program recipients, however, these programs contain their own self-limiting logic. Programs responsive to inflation come under pressure to be "capped," therefore serving fewer clients (as in Section 8), or if they are entitlement programs, come under pressure to reduce eligibility or increase client contributions (as with Medicaid). The significance of this "logic" is to help transform debate over social welfare policy into conflicts over fiscal capacity. This decisive transformation makes social welfare programs particularly vulnerable to the persuasive decision rules of the budgetary process, such as the "level funding" rule under which agencies in periods of inflation receive only as much as they did in the previous year, thereby forcing service reductions.

4. Changing the balance between discretion and bureaucratic accountability.— In many policy areas involving professionals and lower-level "gate-keepers," managerial reforms in periods of retrenchment focus on reducing workers' discretion and increasing accountability through time studies, more thorough reporting requirements, quotas, and other bureaucratic control mechanisms. In no area has this been more apparent than in the Aid to Families with Dependent Children program (AFDC). Developments in AFDC over the past fifteen years in this area include: consolidating emergency grants into the general grant in order to alleviate recipients' pressure on the welfare system; separating social services from financial assistance payments, in part in order to limit workers in making eligibility and grant calculations free from concerns for recipients' ability to cope; and downgrading the job of welfare grant administrators from social workers to clerical employees. Whatever the origins of these developments, they substantially reduced workers' discretion and their ability to offer or provide helpful responses when confronted by recipients in need.

The campaign to reduce the "error rate" in AFDC has been the most comprehensive and far-reaching effort to turn welfare workers into bureaucrats responsive only to (increasingly stringent) agency directives.[25] In 1979, in response to sanctions threatened by the federal government for continued high error rates, Massachusetts welfare officials introduced a variety of measures to try to bring the error rate down.[26] Starting with AFDC, this federal initiative has also been adapted by the federal government for food stamps and Medicaid reimbursement controls.

These campaigns in AFDC, following federal guidelines that specified what quality control errors were, focused attention exclusively on errors associated with excessive leniency. Significantly, they ignored errors of equal magnitude that were inappropriately restrictive (i.e., wrongly disqualifying eligible claimants or underpaying grants).[27]

When workers and their supervisors come under administrative scrutiny or are sanctioned because of errors associated with laxity or excessive leniency, they tend to focus their efforts on correcting these faults at the expense of helping clients. While responsible critics hardly advocate an error-rich welfare program, the issue is not so simple. If

workers are exclusively concerned with one kind of error, their activities will be devoted to reducing that error at the expense of other demands of the job. In the case of welfare administration, workers concerned with reducing positive case errors become less concerned with rendering assistance to recipients, and have fewer tools with which to be helpful.

Consider the example of the mother who applies for aid in Boston and has difficulty in obtaining her children's birth records from Puerto Rico. In the past, she might have had her application continued beyond the statutory limit for responding to requests for aid, or she might have received help from her social worker in obtaining verification by alternate means. Indeed, welfare workers were and continue to be positively obliged to assist applicants in such circumstances.[28] Under pressures to reduce error rates, however, exclusive concern with quality control errors resulted in diminished attention to helping recipients or concern about whether they fully received all to which they were entitled. Remarkably, quality control sometimes resulted in stringent policies that made accountability of workers easier but violated departmental regulations.[29]

Evidence that the error-rate campaigns tended to have this effect may be inferred not only from the testimony of caseworkers, but also from two other sources: the relatively high level of reversal of caseworkers' decisions by hearing officers in the rare instances in which recipients appealed workers' decisions, and the high number of cases that were reinstated retroactively to the day they were dropped. These are indirect indicators of continued substantive eligibility despite bureaucratically determined ineligibility.[30]

It is no accident that federal and state welfare regulations require workers both to control expenditures and be helpful to recipients. These venerable twin objectives are not mutually exclusive. Quality control, in its single-minded focus on positive case errors, changes the constitutional relationship between the welfare system and recipients. Demand for quality control and error-rate reduction, as currently designed, weights the tenuous balance between helpfulness and distrust in favor of distrust. Quality control and error-rate reduction campaigns, as implemented, result in hardships on eligible recipients who must accept increased burdens of interactions with the welfare system, or inappropriate rejections. The final outcome of excessive concern about quality control and error-rate reduction is a change in the relationships of poor people to the state. To recipients, this change has come about through obscure federal regulations, while they and many social welfare advocates remain ignorant of the underlying bureaucratic mechanisms accounting for these developments.

Conditioning Access to the Political Process

One response to the political mobilization of the 1960s was the creation of a variety of mechanisms to direct the expressions of political protest into legitimate channels where they could be responded to in an orderly fashion, and in which they would likely become moderated through direct experiences with other powerful interests. Urban politicians of the 1960s, recognizing the gaps in governing new urban populations, often used federal program funds to reincorporate poor people into the political process through political organizations.[31] These attempts took many forms: encouraging citizen participation on local boards, establishing neighborhood outreach centers to receive complaints and expedite services so that credit accrued to City Hall, and creating complaint bureaus and ombudsmen to receive expressions of grievance, agency by agency.

These developments were tacit forms of exchange. People implicitly agreed to express themselves on policy matters through the media of citizen participation; public officials implicitly agreed to take some notice of their activities, to respect if not act upon their expressed sentiments, and to regard their message as legitimate. However minimal implicit exchanges are, they present government with obligations to heed and maintain the legitimate channels of citizen expression in a policy world that calls for at least the registration of citizen view. Citizens may have other avenues of influence open to them, but they will be pressured to use these mechanisms if conflict over policy emerges.[32]

Bureaucratic disentitlement occurs not only when benefits are conditioned or reduced, but also when opportunities to affect government policy are circumscribed or limited as well. I refer here not to the opportunities of interest groups, such as city-wide housing coalitions, that represent the concerns of poor people in policy formation, but to the day-to-day incorporation of low-income people into the politics of policy delivery. If poor people most certainly "experience" government when they receive services or benefits or are directly involved in public policy, it follows that the ways they are incorporated into policy processes affect not only their involvement in particular policy arenas but also their general perception of the possibilities of contributing to political life. Thus we should pay particular attention to the ways in which people participate in the policy worlds to which they have most direct access.

5. *Individual grievance processing: shadow and substance.*—Virtually every administrative agency develops a means to reduce citizen grievances and to accept appeals from the decision of lower-level workers. This is organizationally necessary wherever worker abuse of discretion may occur. It is also a primary way that citizens may seek to affect policy delivery. Appeals processes play a variety of functions, including providing agencies with feedback on policy implementation, assuring agency clients that they can be heard, and serving agencies as "safety valves" so that disruptive clients can be granted hearings without interruption of agency routines.

Although in many cases citizens can realize substantial benefits simply by making an appeal (e.g., in welfare administration filing an appeal results in the continuation of benefits until the appeal is heard), relatively few people take advantage of appeal opportunities. In the late 1960s and through the early 1970s, there was almost a total lack of appeals from welfare decisions, although federal law required each state to establish an appeals procedure.[33]

Familiarity with appeals and requirements that welfare administrators better inform recipients of their right to appeal have somewhat changed the situation, but appeals in welfare are still uncommon. For example, from 1978 to 1980, 1,024 "fair hearings" involving AFDC cases were held in Boston.[34] With approximately 27,500 AFDC cases in the city, this breaks down to an annual appeal rate of approximately 1 percent. Similarly low appeal levels during this period were being recorded in Boston for rent control, public housing, and special education decisions.[35]

Two straightforward reasons for the low ratio of appeals are that not every program beneficiary experiences a new determination on case status each year, and most, presumably, are processed correctly. However, with persistent high error rates in some programs (such as AFDC) and palpable administrative disarray and eligibility ambiguities in others (such as rent control and special education), one should look further to understand low appeal rates.

Effective participation requires both able communicators and receptive and potentially responsive receivers. If the difficulties of negotiating the appeals process affect the former, the irrelevance of appeals for social welfare agencies characterizes the latter. Generally, appeal procedures have little impact on the individual worker or on the agency as a whole. Workers whose decisions are overturned on appeal suffer no significant penalties.

To return to fair hearings in welfare, successful recipient appeals have no significant impact on the Department of Public Welfare because fair hearings do not establish precedents for future decisions. Moreover, fair-hearing decisions in welfare are not published or publicized. Indeed, rarely is information about fair-hearing activities even circulated.[36] One of the most common barriers to participation is the belief that success is unlikely. Yet this need not be a barrier to filing appeals, since more than half the appeals filed during this period in Massachusetts were resolved in favor of the recipients.[37]

The terms of participation through fair hearings, then, are skewed in ways that minimize their potential as resources. Their possible impact on clients can be substantial, but the likelihood that they will result in corrective action for the agency is remote, as is the chance that similarly situated recipients will learn from them how to take effective action.

An interesting variation on the opportunity to obtain a hearing occurs in several other places where citizens may have their disputes heard. The Housing Court of the City of Boston, for example, employs "housing specialists" who are charged with working out settlements between landlords and tenants to attempt to avoid the necessity of appearing before a judge.[38] The Department of Public Utilities conducts hearings that function similarly to attempt to resolve disputes between the gas company and consumers.[39] In both cases, the mediators pay primary attention to obtaining a settlement, often oblivious to the obvious discrepancies in power and legal competence of the contending parties.

To utilize appeal opportunities most effectively, citizens must know that they exist and know the laws and regulations that constrain administrative practice. In actuality, citizens are often informed of dispute-resolution mechanisms, if at all, without command of this information. It is not surprising that those who make it to the hearing stage without expert help are at a great disadvantage.[40]

A primary difficulty in mounting appeals is the need for experts and expertise in pursuing grievances. Legal services for the poor, even before their decimation during the Reagan years, were less and less available in proportion to need. In addition, while legal services offices experienced more and more resource shortages, they also came under increased pressure to emphasize case work rather than class actions or group representation. Thus in a sense individuals' needs competed with collective interests for this important community resource.

6. *The fading significance of citizen advisory boards.*—In urban public administration the great legacy of the 1960s has been the incorporation of requirements for citizen participation in governance of social welfare programs. There is hardly a social policy area in which citizen participation is not officially mandated and solicited. In Massachusetts, even in 1980, more than 3,000 people, including many community service providers, still served on citizen advisory boards of four state agencies: the departments of Public Welfare, Social Services, Mental Health, and the Office for Children.[41] This only begins to account for citizen participation structures in the Commonwealth.

Although the agencies they serve and the structure of these boards are often quite diverse, the following generalizations concerning the relationship between public policies and boards' effectiveness may be suggested. Notably, these relationships became more and more attenuated during the late 1970s as the administration of Governor Edward King attempted to reorganize and constrict state social welfare policy.

a) One of the crucial determinants of citizen board effectiveness is staff assistance in helping to keep board members informed, and in serving as liaison with agency staff and following through on board initiatives. Yet these boards have no staff or little staff assistance. It is not surprising that without staffing only a small number of the forty welfare community services area boards were even moderately active.[42] One of the most vigorous citizen advisory boards in the state (Roxbury Crossing) was one of the only boards to have a full-time staff liaison.

Its activities and influences declined when the staff member was transferred to another position in the department, and despite promises to the contrary, not replaced.

Staffing for citizen boards is sometimes withheld in accordance with the self-fulfilling prophecy that boards do not require assistance because they are ineffective. The decline of court-ordered Racial/Ethnic Parent Councils in Boston schools, a result in part of inadequate staffing, led to a decision to reduce the amount of staff available to them.

b) The advisory nature of most of these boards remains a source of great frustration. Moreover, their views tend to be solicited on matters affecting individual local offices but not on the major structural policy decisions that affect the constituents (e.g., categorical eligibility for Medicaid). Their ability to sustain membership and members' interest declined as the state increasingly ignored the statewide councils established to aggregate clients' points of view.

c) Although various citizen boards may be relatively inactive, the boards constitute the official vessels through which participation is expected to be channeled. With formal, official channels to receive citizen input, administrators of these programs often insist that these channels should be used when issues arise. Moreover, policy advocates, forced to respect the legitimacy of this point, partially structure their efforts to affect policy through these mechanisms. Thus a variety of mechanisms exist that serve to channel policy advocates' energies, yet diffuse pointed discontent if it is articulated. It is predictable that if another period of urban unrest soon ensues, these structures will be dusted off and recommended as the "proper" place to lodge grievances.

7. *Problems of building a policy "community".*—Prerequisite to the effective functioning of any political community is potential members' belief that political activity can effectively solve common problems. This proposition is at the root of difficulties with citizen participation in policy area governance. People do not believe, and they are often proved correct, that their participation makes a difference.

Another prerequisite is potential members' identification with the community. Official efforts to solicit citizen participation in social policy governance appear to assume that people have or can develop a sense of themselves as "policy citizens." Yet such efforts neglect some of the things it takes to develop the necessary sense of political or community citizenship.

For example, one of the reasons that clients have not flocked to join citizen boards is that people rarely identify themselves primarily with any one policy service area. In contrast to a comprehensive government or quasi-governmental agency whose scope of powers corresponds to issues bearing on people's daily life experiences, these citizen boards in a sense ask people to isolate or fragment their interests in ways that fit the needs and contours of service-delivery agencies.

Contrary to the views of many critics of welfare, people who receive public assistance do not establish primary identification as welfare recipients.[43] Neither do they think of themselves primarily as constituents of schools, which in Boston and other cities may be located far from home.[44] Thus, even if people were inclined to involve themselves in political activity connected with service agencies, it is not clear that they would seek to do so in terms of the categories and labels established by government policy.

Policy is further fragmented by the absence of coherence in policy jurisdictional boundaries. At least in Boston there is virtually no center to urban service delivery and no common boundaries around areas served by various agencies. There is no central location for administration of social policy; fragmentation is the rule. In the relatively large Jamaica Plain neighborhood, for example, the following are the places one would go in 1981 to discuss service-delivery problems: for schools, one of two district offices; for welfare, one of three services centers; for social services, one of two area offices; for police matters, one of two precinct stations; for legal matters, one of three district courts, including the housing court, located downtown.

Additionally, each policy area is administered by an agency that has its central offices—city or state—elsewhere, and may have an intermediate regional office as well. Also to be considered are the large number of private agencies, such as home-care and day-care providers, performing public functions on contract. This is not simply a matter of Jamaica Plain, to its misfortune, being on the border of various jurisdictional lines; the entire city is carved up like this.

Services could be fragmented in terms of office locations and still be unified by the fact that these offices serve the same community. Not so in Jamaica Plain, or Boston generally. There is no overlap among school districts, police districts, court service areas, and welfare/social service districts. There is no identity between officially designated electoral wards and any service-delivery areas. On this subject, the one bright spot is the effort at the state level, over a period of years, to bring social service districts in line with the catchment areas of the Department of Mental Health.[45]

Delivering services in nonintegrated geographic patterns ensures fragmentation of community.[46] It is important that, for this analysis, there is no historic basis for this fragmentation; it is a relatively modern creation. Most Boston neighborhoods have their own "municipal buildings" from which many services at one time were dispatched. Still later, the recently abandoned Little City Hall Program made efforts to better focus citizen access to services.[47] Finally, the state plan to provide various social services through congruent service districts indicates additional official recognition of the problem of jurisdictional fragmentation and the desirability of making service delivery more coherent. We may conclude that the jurisdictional incoherence ex-

perienced by the service consumer is, in a sense, an issue on the public policy agenda, but one that is considered of too low priority to generate a response or mobilize support to overcome agency resistance to consolidation.

8. *Interdependencies of community groups and governmental agencies.*— Community groups and neighborhood-based agencies have become clients of local, state, and national governments. Many of the funds that have been allocated for urban development and urban services are designated for spending by neighborhood groups and agencies that often attract the most active and committed community leaders. Whatever the liabilities, this is one area in which national policy developments would appear to have strengthened community groups in the 1970s.

This trend began in the 1960s with the federal antidelinquency program, the War on Poverty, and Model Cities. Community groups and agencies remained important in the Nixon adminstration. The Law Enforcement Assistance Adminstration (LEAA), the Community Development Block Grant (CDBG) program, and the Social Security Administration under Title XX (social services) all provided support for local groups and agencies to carry out policy through grants and contracts. This has enriched neighborhood groups and agencies and encouraged their expansion.

However, grants to neighborhood groups are not provided without reciprocal expectations. These include not only the obvious obligation to perform the tasks specified in contracts or grants, but also include expectations of more diffuse sorts.

Nonprofit service agencies, supposedly a bulwark of private initiative arrayed against the dominance of the public sector, recognize that their existence depends on the support of public officials with shifting policy agendas. Therefore, they are constantly forced by their desire to maintain service contracts to anticipate and accommodate changes in policy fashion as well as in real demand. The discovery of every new social policy problem—street children, battered women, abused children, battered elderly, to name a few recent ones—evokes new demands for community-based services, draws funds away from ongoing policy initiatives, and creates turmoil in the social agency network.

The pivotal effort of the Nixon administration to bring urban policy spending under the control of elected officials through block grants has succeeded, particularly in cities, such as Boston, in which the mayor exerts a high degree of control. In Boston, community groups receiving federal funds dispensed by mayoral appointees regularly refrain from challenging mayoral plans, or moderate their criticism, to avoid a future "freeze out" by City Hall.

These organizations, having failed to establish independent financial bases or having let them atrophy because of the enticement of public monies and the general difficulties of fund raising, are particularly vulnerable in times of fiscal cutbacks. As a result, neighborhood groups become more and more narrow in the scope of their advocacy. They do this, understandably, so as not to jeopardize their funding and to maintain vital community services. This is even more the case with the many neighborhood organizations that, as one analysis phrases it, "define themselves according to the federal program from which they emanated or the agency with which they work."[48] Both groups are unwilling to challenge decisions outside their narrow spheres that would give them reputations as "troublemakers."

Still another aspect of the co-optation of neighborhood groups relates to the competition they must engage in to obtain their share of community funding. The competition for inclusion in the favored network of social agencies and the need to maintain one's position within the competition provide incentives for groups to resist the entry of new organizations and services to consolidate their relations with existing funding sources at the expense of new agencies and services.

From the point of view of the city or the providing agency, this relationship to neighborhood groups and agencies encourages a predictable effort to distribute funds in such a way as to minimize bad feeling and maintain organized support. The city and the contracting agencies, confronted with many organizations with claims on their support, are provided all the more with incentive to allocate resources in patronage fashion.

This dynamic is particularly evident in the CDBG program, which requires cities to engage in an annual planning process to establish community priorities and designate recipients of neighborhood-focused funds. The CDBG "process" has encouraged current grantees of their program to resist the emergence of new organizations because of their dependence on limited, and from year to year decreasing, funds for their well-being.[49]

Discussion

This discussion has focused on a form of policy retrenchment I call bureaucratic disentitlement. It is characterized by low-level, marginal decisions or nondecisions of low visibility that nonetheless have sustained implications for the relationship of poor people to the state.

What do these developments tell us more generally about the politics in the American welfare state? Analytically, bureaucratic disentitlement represents developments, intended or unintended, that erode the position of relatively powerless groups without arousing them or their watchdog allies. The ways in which these developments come to public

attention make them difficult to hold up as targets of countermobilization. They represent issues of policy implementation rather than executive or legislative decision making, and appear to involve technical and managerial rather than political matters. They sometimes seem to represent side effects of enormous, almost "natural" forces that government could not expect to control. They often foist obligations on subordinate groups and low-status people that continue to bind them to the institutions that are simultaneously diluting their benefits and influence. Throughout, they appear to leave the structure of policy in place, while indirectly diluting its substantive value.

These developments fit the contours of a political arena in which fiscal stringency was increasingly regarded as a priority and the distributional consequences of social welfare spending were increasingly visible to a mobilized middle class. They took place in a period in which the size of the public sector and allocations within the public sector were under increasing scrutiny among policymakers.

However, there were crosscutting developments during the period in which bureaucratic disentitlement became manifest. Relatively powerless groups and individuals to some degree had institutionalized their influence. Not only did entitlement programs expand and individual rights receive protection in some fashion, but low-income advocacy groups, such as the Food/Research Action Council and the Children's Defense Fund, also emerged to protect those advances. In addition, as a legacy of the 1960s, individuals entered public service who to some degree continued to endorse those social welfare initiatives. Congressmen and state legislators who championed these developments continued to occupy seats of power. And important centers of electoral influence, such as large cities with significant black populations, continued to provide a base of support for expanded social welfare programs and entitlements. In short, these developments fit a political arena in which there remained at least some support for ameliorative social welfare policy.[50]

Moreover, these developments fit a political arena ideologically (even if loosely and ambiguously) committed to extended welfare state benefits. Thus there remained during this period wells of support for protection of people in need, for due process in the event of administrative error, and for citizen participation in decision making. This does not mean that the American populace burned to protect entitlements. On the contrary, this diffuse social welfare constituency is generally inattentive to program developments that fall below the waterline of high-level policy. It is a constituency that can be mobilized, but only by great events, dramatic circumstances, or to protect symbolic commitments. So long as nothing is apparently happening, and decisions rest or appear to rest with lower-level officials, or policy decisions appear to be focused on structure rather than substance, this constituency remains relatively unaffected. In the meantime, public managers experience enormous pressure to keep budgets down and conduct the processes of government expeditiously. They may experience little effective pressure to extend the benefits of their programs to clients, while they are likely to be under great pressure to withhold benefits or make them difficult to access. One need not posit a structurally determined bias in favor of elites to see that without support to the contrary from a powerful and active constituency, bureaucrats may have plenty of reasons and opportunities to develop policy in ways that withdraw resources from constituents, and may be inclined to be receptive to policy initiatives that direct them to do so.

Bureaucratic disentitlement consists of structural imperatives in public agencies that narrow the range of resources available to lower-status members of society. It permits the expression of structural biases against the interests of social welfare clients while maximizing the likelihood that potential opponents of these biases will remain quiescent, and that separate costly community cleavages will be avoided. The problem is not that bureaucratic disentitlement contributes to a declining social welfare sector. It is that its contribution to the decline is unheralded and unavailable for public inspection.

Bureaucratic disentitlement helps explain a dimension of cutback politics that is not well addressed either by dialectical or managerial approaches to retrenchment. It is an intermediate stage, consistent with a complex reality, in which fiscal pressures begin to be experienced, but also in which support for social welfare programs has not yet been eroded or undermined by elites.

In this paper I have tried to examine, from the perspective of cutback politics, an aspect of retrenchment that has thus far evaded scrutiny. It has evaded scrutiny in part because by definition it includes cutbacks that rarely surface to a level where they can be observed, and that are not promulgated as retrenchment. It has also evaded scrutiny because social policy analysts have paid insufficient attention to the overall implications of reducing citizen benefits as citizen holdings, and the implications of reducing constituent's opportunities for affecting benefit outcomes for the relationship of citizens to the state. The eight forms of bureaucratic disentitlement I have tentatively identified, however, represent only the beginning of a systematic effort to understand how isolated, low-level, and marginal decision making and non-decision making can add up to patterns of retrenchment that deserve serious attention alongside more dramatic episodes of cutbacks.

Notes

An earlier version of this paper was delivered at the Annual Meeting of the Western Political Science Association, Seattle, March 26, 1983. I am grateful to Evelyn Brodkin,

Emma Jackson, John Kirlin, David J. Olson, Clarence Stone, and Martha Weinberg for helpful comments on the earlier draft.

1. On social welfare expansion, consider that in the years from 1965 to 1975, the AFDC population more than tripled. One million five thousand people were served in 1965; 3.49 million were served in 1975 (Arthur Spindler, *Public Welfare* [New York: Human Services Press, 1979], p. 88). Two-thirds of the increase in the AFDC rolls from 1967 to 1971, the years of greatest concern over rising welfare costs, is attributable to increases in the rate of participation of eligible families. During this period participation rose from 2.2 million families (63 percent of the eligibles) to 3.0 million families (94 percent of the eligible families) (Lester Salamon, *Welfare: The Elusive Consensus* [New York: Praeger Publishers, 1978], p. 22). For increases in participation in noncash programs such as food stamps and school lunch benefits, see U.S. Bureau of the Census, *Characteristics of Households Receiving Noncash Benefits* (Washington, D.C.: Government Printing Office, November 1981), as reported in the *New York Times* (November 3, 1981), p. B12. On contraction, see John Palmer and Isabel Sawhill, eds., *The Reagan Experiment* (Washington, D.C.: Urban Institute, 1982); John Ellwood, ed., *Reductions in U.S. Domestic Spending* (New Brunswick, N.J.: Transaction Books, 1982).

2. See Frances Piven and Richard Cloward, *The New Class War* (New York: Pantheon Books, 1982).

3. See, e.g., the writings of Charles Levine, "Organizational Decline and Cutback Management," *Public Administration Review* 38 (July/August 1978): 316–25; "More on Cutback Management: Hard Questions for Hard Times," *Public Administration Review* 39 (March/April 1979): 179–83; also, Levine, ed., *Managing Fiscal Stress: The Crisis in the Public Sector* (Chatham, N.J.: Chatham House, 1980).

4. Constitutional relationships are fundamental, sustained, mutual expectations on which societies are ordered and through which political systems are legitimized. They may involve relationships between institutions, institutions and citizens, and citizens and citizens. See Theodore Lowi, *American Government: Incomplete Conquest* (Hinsdale, Ill.: Dryden Press, 1976), p. 90; see also Michael Lipsky, *Street-Level Bureaucracy* (New York: Russell Sage Foundation, 1980), chaps. 1, 5.

5. A growing body of literature has assumed the task of better comprehending the significance of citizen encounters with government. See, e.g., the collection of articles in Charles Goodsell, ed., *The Public Encounter* (Bloomington: Indiana University Press, 1981); Herbert Jacob, "Contact with Government Agencies: A Preliminary Analysis of the Distribution of Government Services," *Midwest Journal of Political Science* 16 (February 1972): 123–46, and *Debtors in Court* (Chicago: Rand McNally & Co., 1968); Bryan Jones et al., "Bureaucratic Response to Citizen Initiated Contacts: Environmental Enforcement in Detroit," *American Political Science Review* 71 (March 1977): 148–65; Michael Lipsky, *Street-Level Bureaucracy*, chap. 1. Barbara Nelson has made a particularly useful start in analyzing citizens' decisions to seek government benefits and services as political participation. See Nelson, "Help Seeking from Public Authorities: Who Arrives at the Agency Door," *Policy Sciences* 12 (August 1980): 175–92. Most analyses of the expansion of social welfare policies treat these developments as benefits and outcomes of the political system. They reserve the term "political participation" for actions taken to affect governmental decisions. See, e.g., Sidney Verba and Norman Nie, *Participation in America* (New York: Harper & Row, 1982), p. 2. In contrast, Robert Alford and Roger Friedland treat consumption of government services as a form of "bureaucratic participation without power." See their essay, "Political Participation and Public Policy," *Annual Review of Sociology* 1 (1975): 429–79, esp. 455–64.

6. Generally, see Murray Edelman, *Politics as Symbolic Action* (New York: Academic Press, 1971).

7. James O'Conner, *The Fiscal Crisis of the State* (New York: St. Martin's Press, 1973); Frances Piven and Richard Cloward, *Regulating the Poor* (New York: Pantheon Books, 1971).

8. See, e.g., Lester Thurow, *The Zero-Sum Society* (New York: Basic Books, 1980); Hugh Heclo, "Toward a New Welfare State," in *The Development of Welfare States in Europe and America*, ed. Peter Flora and Arnold Heidenheimer (New Brunswick, N.J.: Transaction Books, 1981).

9. The study of bureaucratic disentitlement in some respects resembles the study of policy implementation. Initial efforts to study policy implementation took a top-down

approach in which policy was conceived as "flowing" through hierarchical organizational layers from decision maker to implementor. For a summary, see Erwin Hargrove, *The Missing Link* (Washington, D.C.: Urban Institute, 1975). More recent conceptualizations recognize the critical significance of lower-level implementors in determining policy outcomes and have styled their inquiries accordingly. See, e.g., Richard Elmore, "Backward Mapping: Implementation Research and Policy Decision," *Political Science Quarterly* 94 (Winter 1979–80): 601–16. Bureaucratic disentitlement also allots primary attention to lower-level, relatively obscure decision making.

10. For example, although local officials often possess considerable leeway in administering federal policy, they often describe themselves as bound by federal requirements or helpless in the face of federal pressures or federal inactions, implying that they have no room for discretion in responding to federal requirements. The wholesale purging of the Supplementary Security Income rolls in Massachusetts by state-appointed examiners following guidelines based on federal directives is illustrative. Their actual leeway is indicated by the fact that their decisions are regularly overturned on appeal (see, e.g., *New York Times* [August 23, 1982], p. B12). On the symbolic functions of bureaucracy in political conflict, see Murray Edelman, *Political Language* (New York: Academic Press, 1977).

11. Clarence Stone, "Systemic Power in Community Decision Making: A Restatement of Stratification Theory," *American Political Science Review* 74 (December 1980): 978–90. See also Ralf Dahrendorf, *Class and Class Conflict in Industrial Society* (Stanford, Calif.: Stanford University Press, 1969), chap. 5; and William Gamson, "Stable Unrepresentation in American Society," *American Behavioral Scientist* 12 (November–December 1968): 15–21.

12. For an excellent recent explication and application of non-decision making, see John Gaventa, *Power and Powerlessness* (London: Oxford University Press, 1980).

13. See Piven and Cloward, *The New Class War*; Thomas Ferguson and Joel Rogers, eds., *The Hidden Election* (New York: Pantheon Books, 1981).

14. The significance of this point for contemporary urban affairs is noted by Ira Katznelson, "The Crisis of the Capitalist City," in *Theoretical Perspectives on Urban Politics*, ed. Willis Hawley and Michael Lipsky (Englewood Cliffs, N.J.: Prentice-Hall, Inc., 1976), p. 224.

15. From January 1979 to September 1981 I served as a staff member of the Legal Services Institute, a legal services agency and training center, in Jamaica Plain, a low-income and working-class Boston neighborhood. I am greatly indebted to my colleagues at LSI, with whom many of these observations were formed and refined. Approximately 37,900 people, down from 46,100 in 1970, live in the neighborhood designated by the City of Boston as Jamaica Plain. Fourteen percent are black, and 7 percent are "others," mostly Hispanic (Research and Policy Analysis Division, Boston Redevelopment Agency, "Preliminary Population Counts and Racial Composition 1980," mimeographed [April 8, 1981]; generally, see the discussion of Boston's political environment [pp. 99–102] in Martha Wagner Weinberg, "Boston's Kevin White," *Political Science Quarterly* 96 [Spring 1981]: 87–106). Because many of the observations reported in this paper are derived from the experience of a single city, care should be exercised in generalizing to the American experience as a whole. However, while the details of bureaucratic disentitlement undoubtedly vary from place to place, the models of retrenchment described here are likely to apply in a wide variety of policy arenas.

16. On rationing, see Lipsky, *Street-Level Bureaucracy*, chap. 7; also, Jeffrey Prottas, "The Cost of Free Services," *Public Administration Review* 41 (September–October 1981): 526–34. On cutbacks through rationing, see Charles Levine et al., *The Politics of Retrenchment*, Sage Library of Social Research, vol. 130 (Beverly Hills, Calif.: Sage Publications, 1981), p. 39.

17. For details on welfare administration in Boston during this period, see Evelyn Brodkin, "The Error of Their Ways" (Ph.D. diss., Massachusetts Institute of Technology, 1983).

18. All states are required to establish a "standard of need" in AFDC, defined as the amount necessary to sustain a family at a subsistence level. Although states are not required to pay recipients that amount, Massachusetts has always done so. However, the state has effectively avoided this requirement by inconsistently determining the standard and "losing track" of the basis on which the standard was determined (see

Ellen Epstein, "The AFDC Standard of Need in Massachusetts," mimeographed [Office of Research and Evaluation, Massachusetts Department of Public Welfare, December, 1980)].

19. The average vacancy rate for the Boston metropolitan area according to real estate specialists is approximately 2 percent. It is even lower when one excludes from calculation the high-rent units that tend to be rented at a slower pace. Moreover, the figure does not reflect variation within individual neighborhoods, where the problem may be much greater. According to the mayor's housing advisor, the private market may not be able to house even moderate-income people anymore (see *Boston Globe*, [April 2, 1981], p. 22).

20. Those who are accepted into the Section 8 program are entitled to find an apartment anywhere in the city. The government pays the difference between the rent and 25 percent of the participant's income. Because this program is (currently) geared to the fair market value of the apartment, it is particularly valuable to be a Section 8 recipient in a period of inflation.

21. Illustratively, when the Boston Housing Authority allocated 125 rent-subsidy certificates in the summer of 1980, 9,000 people applied for them. On another occasion, when a neighborhood developer in Boston's South End announced that applications would be taken for 190 subsidized units, the 5,000 people who showed up formed such a "throng . . . that the center's door literally could not be opened." Several people were injured in this incident (*Boston Globe* [July 6, 1980], p. 26; [April 29, 1981], p. 40). According to the *New York Times*, "housing officials say that in almost every part of the country, they are inundated with applications when they announce the availability of subsidies. The officials say that housing assistance is available to less than 20 percent of those who need it. Inflation, budget cuts, a slowdown in new construction, and the conversion of rental apartments to condominiums are all factors that are said to contribute to the shortage of low-cost housing" (*New York Times* [March 16, 1981], p. A13).

22. At the Legal Services Institute, approximately 30 percent of eligible people seeking help were accepted as clients through 1981. This ratio is undoubtedly very favorable to clients compared to most legal services offices, except for offices that heavily ration access to services. At the national level, according to one estimate, only 20 percent of the poor who face a civil legal problem receive legal assistance (*New York Times* [April 8, 1981], p. A27). Drastic cuts in funding for the Legal Services Corporation in FY 1982 greatly exacerbate this problem.

23. From 1970 to 1980, the AFDC standard of need in Massachusetts, which determines the grant level, increased by 30 percent. At the same time, the Consumer Price Index for Boston increased by 107 percent. While the CPI doubled, the grant increased by less than one-third. In other words, the purchasing power of the AFDC grant declined over the period by 37 percent. If food stamp benefits are included, the welfare grant package increased over the decade by 51 percent, a decline of 27 percent in purchasing power (Epstein, pp. 5–6). New York welfare recipients, without an increase in benefit level since 1974, had it worse. By 1980 their standard of living had been cut in half (Daniel P. Moynihan, "Opening Statement," *How to Think about Welfare Reform in the 1980's: Hearings before the Subcommittee on Public Assistance, Committee on Finance, U.S. Senate*, 96th Cong. [February 6 and 7, 1980], p. 6). For a review at the national level, see "Welfare Benefits Quietly Decreasing," *Boston Globe* (July 7, 1980), p. 5. For a discussion on the overall effects in inflation on AFDC, see Paul Peretz, *The Political Economy of Inflation in the United States* (Chicago: University of Chicago Press, 1983), chap. 3.

24. See, e.g., Raymond Wolfinger, "Nondecisions and the Study of Local Politics," *American Political Science Review* 65 (December 1981): 1063–80; Frederick Frey, "Comment," ibid., pp. 1081–1101; and references in Gaventa (n. 12 above).

25. On the development of quality control and error-rate reduction as federal policy, see Robert Randall, "Presidential Power versus Bureaucratic Intransigence: The Influence of the Nixon Administration on Welfare Policy," *American Political Science Review* 73 (1979): 795–810. For elaboration of the points in these paragraphs, see Evelyn Brodkin and Michael Lipsky, "Quality Control in AFDC as an Administrative Strategy," *Social Service Review* 57 (March 1983): 3–34.

26. The state, e.g., feared a loss of $8 million in 1980 (*Boston Globe* [March 6, 1980], p. 20; also, *Boston Globe* [August 8, 1980], p. 16). In addition to paying greater attention

to worker training and updating and revising the worker's manual, the department sought to tighten welfare policy by episodic campaigns to root out case file errors (such as the lack of a WIN registration form in the file) and to "clarify" the kind of verifications that would be accepted as proof of the validity of claims (John D. Pratt, "State Agencies Can Be Managed: The Massachusetts Experience with Reducing AFDC Error Rates," *New England Journal of Human Services* 1 [Spring 1981]: 20–26; also, interview with John Pratt, June 18, 1981).

27. The federal rationale for this approach is that the government can only sanction the states when the states fail to spend money according to their official state plans. Since the federal government cannot withhold matching funds for monies never spent, there can be no federal sanctions of negative case errors. This approach has been pursued despite the lack of sound information on the extent to which zealous reduction of overpayments also affects the degree of underpayment to eligible recipients and wrongful denials (see Randall, pp. 799–806).

28. See, e.g., 106 C.M.R. §302.210; see also 106 C.M.R. §302.130(E).

29. See Brodkin (n. 17 above).

30. Ibid.

31. See Ira Katznelson, "Urban Counterrevolution," in *1984 Revisited*, ed. Robert Paul Wolff (New York: Alfred A. Knopf, Inc., 1973), pp. 139–64; and Eric Nordlinger, *Decentralizing the City* (Cambridge, Mass.: MIT Press, 1972).

32. These precepts of pluralism, descriptive of at least a part of the political world occupied by relatively powerless groups, are evaluated in Stephen Lukes, *Power: A Radical View* (London: Macmillan Co., 1974). See also Michael Lipsky, *Protest in City Politics* (Chicago: Rand McNally & Co., 1970), chap. 1, pp. 201–3.

33. The appeal rate in public assistance programs in the first six months of 1971 was approximately 2 percent, with more than half the appeals coming from three states (Jerry Mashaw, "The Management Side of Due Process: Some Theoretical and Litigation Notes on the Assurance of Accuracy, Fairness and Timeliness in the Adjudication of Social Welfare Claims," *Cornell Law Review* 59 [1974]: 784). As Mashaw observes (p. 811), ". . . in a program which is reasonably well-known for its error rate, which has a complex set of standards to apply, and which involves decisions of great importance to its claimants, a negligible appeal rate is troubling."

34. Betsy Hecker and Theresa Nelson, "AFDC Fair Hearings: A Study of Administrative Due Process" (unpublished paper, Legal Services Institute, May 1981), pp. 6–9. The fact that over the 1978–80 period hearing examiners increasingly found in favor of recipients is one reason for believing that quality control pressures in welfare drove workers increasingly to make errors negatively affecting recipients. For a discussion of the impact on organizations that deprive themselves of 'feedback opportunities, see Donald Schon, *Beyond the Stable State* (New York: Random House, 1971), chap. 2.

35. Out of approximately 154,000 Massachusetts pupils provided special education services during the period 1978–80, school departments experienced on the average fewer than four appeals per year. In Boston, where 13,000–14,000 children received special services during this period, less than 1 percent of the parents appealed their children's placement ("Contents of Special Education Master File" [undated document produced for the Division of Special Education], Department of Education, Commonwealth of Massachusetts, 1981).

36. See Stan Altman et al., "The Use of State Fair Hearing to Monitor Performance of the AFDC Program," *Administrative Law Review* 31 (Fall 1979): 463–84.

37. See Heckler and Nelson.

38. For a description, see Paul Garrity, "The Boston Housing Court: An Encouraging Response to Complex Issues," *Urban Law Annual* 17 (1979): 15–26. In FY 1981, the court processed 5,208 civil actions, almost all involving landlord-tenant disputes (Annual Report Information FY 1981, Housing Court Department, City of Boston Division).

39. Near the end of the heating season, almost one of every ten of the Boston Gas Company's 500,000 customers were more than three months behind in their bills (*Boston Globe* [March 24, 1981], p. 1).

40. In disability insurance appeals, an applicant represented by a lawyer is three times more likely to succeed than one who is not (*New York Times* [April 7, 1981], p. B9; see also Jan L. Hagen, "Justice for the Welfare Recipient: Another Look at Welfare Fair Hearings," *Social Service Review* 57 [June 1983]: 177–95). This is not universally

the case, as some adjudicators will try to assist unknowledgeable citizens acting on their own behalf, but will treat represented citizens in an adversarial way.

41. "Volunteers in a Bureaucracy: Unmet Potential," *Beacon Hill Update* 5 (September 15, 1980): 1.

42. Ibid. For a review of the literature on citizen participation, see Alford and Friedland (n. 5 above).

43. For one thing, again contrary to the popular view, AFDC recipients do not necessarily stay on the rolls for long. The average one-parent (typical) recipient family in Massachusetts receives aid for less than four years. One-third are recipients for two years or less. The average two-person (AFDC-UP) family receives aid for less than two years (Roger Wirt, "Cash Benefits Primer: A Summary of Massachusetts' Financial Assistance Programs for Low-Income Families," mimeographed [Office of Research and Evaluation, Massachusetts Department of Public Welfare, December 1980], p. 60). On the rarity of policy consumers organizing to achieve objectives, see Erwin C. Hargrove and Gillian Dean, "Federal Authority and Grass-Roots Accountability: The Case of CETA," *Policy Analysis* 6 (Spring 1980): 127–49.

44. Ira Katznelson discusses the political disjuncture of home and community in *City Trenches* (New York: Pantheon Books, 1981). In this discussion we may speculate further about the significance of geographical fragmentation of community activities alone.

45. There is overlap between welfare and social services because the Department of Social Services is a recent spin-off of the welfare department.

46. On the importance of geographic coherence for group solidarity in welfare and social services, see Morris Janowitz, *Social Control of the Welfare State* (New York: Elsevier, 1976), pp. 126–33.

47. Starting in 1968, Boston eventually established seventeen neighborhood little city halls in order to provide a central focus for citizen complaints and expressions of concern. These innovations in decentralization were relatively successful in evoking and focusing additional citizen complaints (Nordlinger [n. 31 above]). In June 1981, the little city halls program was phased out (*Boston Globe* [June 17, 1981], p. 24).

48. Norman Fainstein and Susan Fainstein, "Bureaucratic Enfranchisement and the Politics of Neighborhood Development" (paper prepared for the 1980 annual meeting of the American Political Science Association, Washington, D.C., August 28–31, 1980).

49. For an excellent analysis of the CDBG process that strongly supports this view of the role of neighborhood groups, see ibid. Fainstein and Fainstein point out that neighborhood groups play their greatest role in debating the distribution of funds for social services, although this represents a minority of CDBG funds. Generally, see Paul Dommel et al., *Targeting Community Development* (Washington, D.C.: Department of Housing and Urban Development, January 1980), and *Dividing the Pie: Resource Allocation to Urban Neighborhoods* (Boston Neighborhood Development Agency, City of Boston, November 1980).

50. See Piven and Cloward, *The New Class War*, chap. 5.

Chapter 11

Homelessness, Employment, and Structural Violence

Exploring Constraints on Collective Mobilizations against Systemic Inequality

Vincent Lyon-Callo

Jonathan,[1] now twenty-eight years old, stayed at a homeless shelter in Northampton, Massachusetts, during the autumn and winter of both 1993 and 1994. Struggling to survive while working food-service jobs, he relocated to western Massachusetts hoping to attend the University of Massachusetts. As a bright and articulate young, white man, he was quickly able to secure employment while trying to save money for housing and school. He was a model guest during both of his stays at the shelter, frequently helping insightfully to mediate disputes between guests around the shelter. Despite his wealth of skills and consistent efforts, he was never able to locate housing he could afford in the city.

During his first stay, Jonathan worked both as a cashier in a local supermarket and conducting telephone surveys. In 1994, he found a job washing dishes in an upscale local restaurant. Both times the shelter staff were supportive of his efforts, extended his stays, and suggested all "available options" they could think of to help Jonathan locate income and housing. The wages paid in the service work available were just not enough, however, to secure housing.

Jonathan and I discussed his plans one evening during the autumn of 1994. He had been working for the past two months, washing dishes five nights a week. About a month and a half previously he began to look for an apartment with another shelter resident, Tom, who worked with him in the restaurant. They wanted to avoid living in rooming houses because they felt them to be unsafe and inhumane. Instead, they had been saving their

tural inequalities in the United States during this historical period of neoliberalism. An argument could be put forth that widespread homelessness is simply the result of changing material conditions of life for many people in terms of income and housing costs. That understanding would resonate with much recent work by scholars who emphasize the impact of recent economic restructuring and altered political and cultural conditions on the lives of residents of the United States.

Increased disparity in the distribution of wealth and income[4] (U.S. Bureau of the Census 1996; Albelda et al. 1996) has resulted from the decline in higher-paying manufacturing jobs in much of the country, a growing temporary labor industry, urban gentrification (Williams 1996), corporate conglomeration, increased globalization of capitalist production, the decreased strength of unions in the United States, altered tax policies,[5] and other, related conditions.[6] This restructuring has led both to the rewards of increased wealth for those enacting policies that contribute to homelessness at home and abroad and to a drastic increase in the incidence of chronic unemployment and underemployment (Hardin 1996) in low-paying, part-time, temporary employment for many people[7] (Economic Policy Institute 1997). Homelessness is further exacerbated by policies and practices that have created an increasing shortage of affordable housing units in the nation[8] (Lazere 1995; Kaufman 1996; Kaufman 1997; O'Flaherty 1996) and by political decisions regarding taxation policy, funding for housing, labor laws, and international trade. Domination through processes of class exploitation, racial injustice, unequal educational opportunities, and gendered inequality are also all fairly easy to document components of homelessness.

Historical and material conditions clearly contribute to producing homelessness in the United States. I would argue, however, that this knowledge alone is inadequate for understanding the phenomenon of widespread homelessness here. We also need to analyze how such economic restructuring is allowed to occur.[9] We need to account for issues of human agency and strive to comprehend the seeming acquiescence or consent to political-economic conditions that result in inequality and homelessness. Without such an analysis, one is left with the impression that oppression acts solely as overt coercion and domination. The subtle, more insidious ways in which what is taken for granted as normal, natural, or uncontestable helps produce and maintain inequality are left unexamined.

Examinations of how it has become "common sense" to condone homelessness might entail questioning how "average" citizens consent to the

money for an apartment. That night, Jonathan told me he was planning to relocate to South Carolina, with the hope of finding cheaper rents during the winter. As he put it, "Minimum wage is just about the same everywhere. I can get an apartment for half-price there during the off-season." His "solution" to his homelessness in Massachusetts was to leave town, give up on school for the moment, and try to locate housing further south, where he envisioned less costly rents.

Jonathan's experience is far from unique. The number of people living on the streets and in homeless shelters throughout the United States continues to increase despite the widely reported flourishing economy of the late 1990s (Burt 1997; National Coalition for the Homeless 1997; Dowdy 1998; Waxman and Hinderliter 1996). In a situation that is sometimes seen as paradoxical, a growing number of people who find themselves homeless are, like Jonathan, employed in the "booming" economy (Hardin 1996; National Coalition for the Homeless 1997). In Northampton, I found that over one-third of the single, adult homeless people staying in one emergency shelter were employed in the years 1994–1996. In 1995, 116 of 193 people utilizing the shelter received income from either paid employment or social security disability insurance (SSI) payments.[2] Many others were involved in training programs or self-reform to prepare for work. Despite some popularly held beliefs about the laziness or learned dependence of "the homeless," many of the people I worked with were working quite hard and were desperate to locate better jobs and more income. As in Katherine Newman's research on the working poor in New York City, I found that the income from available employment did not enable people to escape poverty or homelessness.[3] For example, less than one-third of the employed workers I worked with moved into permanent housing when they left the shelter. How does it make sense that so many people continue to be homeless despite their active participation in the "strong" national economy?

There are several possible ways of understanding these dynamics. One possibility is to interpret homelessness as the result of shortcomings in some people that make them unable to compete effectively in the market economy. Another possibility would be to examine homelessness in relation to recent material and historical conditions that have contributed to vastly increased social inequality. As wealth has been increasingly concentrated in the hands of a small percentage of the population over the last two decades of the twentieth century, homelessness for many extremely poor people has also become an almost routine feature of life in the United States. In that light, the statistics cited above could be read as the result of increasing struc-

structural violence of homelessness, why so few practices by people working within the homeless sheltering industry challenge systemic conditions, how popular imaginings about homeless people are discursively produced, and how people who find themselves living on the streets come to understand that situation and respond to that experience. As part of that effort, this chapter attempts to make sense of why it is so difficult to find organized, collective movements of homeless people working to challenge systemic inequality in the United States at the beginning of the twenty-first century.

As recent ethnographic work by Talmadge Wright (1997) and David Wagner (1993) demonstrates, homeless people are not simply passive victims. Some people living on the streets or in shelters do engage in organized mobilizations, even if these efforts most often focus on organizing for improved living conditions in shelters or on the streets. Other ethnographies of poverty in the United States, by Alisse Waterston (1993), Jagna Sharff (1998), Gwendolyn Dordick (1997), and Philippe Bourgois (1996), for example, account for issues of human agency by analyzing drug and alcohol abuse, mental illness, membership in gangs, and similar coping behaviors that are commonly portrayed as symptoms of disorders that cause people to live in poverty. They interpret their ethnographic data to argue that such practices are actually strategies to cope with historical exploitation and structural inequality. What these ethnographies fail fully to explain, however, is how it makes sense to particular social actors to "choose" coping strategies that accommodate homelessness instead of collective work challenging the material and discursive conditions that produce or justify the social relations that result in many people being homeless despite the vast wealth in the United States. As Joel Blau argued, it still remains much more difficult to find collective mobilizations *of homeless people* than to locate charity and advocacy efforts *for the homeless* (1992:93). Blau suggests that this results from how homeless people have been politically disabled by their internalization of dominant images toward them. As he puts it, "The message is a simple one: someone without a home is an inconsequential person, and the actions of an inconsequential person cannot have political consequences" (1992:94).

In a slight contrast to Blau's argument, I argue that to understand seeming popular consent, it is necessary both to critically analyze individual and collective practices and to investigate how engaging in casual resistance and compliance comes to make more sense to many homeless people than does working to foster opposition. Utilizing five years of ethnographic research,

I show in this essay how many of the people living in shelters are not passive and do act to "resist" homelessness. To locate such resistance, however, it is often necessary to look at subversions, self-constructions, individual acts of subterfuge, seeming resignation, and behind-the-scenes complaints, rather than only at large-scale, collective insurrections aimed at overthrow or emancipation (Scott 1990; Kondo 1990).

Individual acts of resistance occurred on a daily basis in the Massachusetts shelter I examined. Often, as I show later in the chapter, these acts take the form of individual efforts that largely accept hegemonic explanations of homelessness as being the result of individual shortcomings or deviancy. Examples include practices such as a homeless person trying for a better job or engaging in self-reform through job training or therapy. Alternative efforts that seemingly reject the notion that the solution to homelessness is to be found in reforming homeless people also took place. Some homeless people I worked with actively avoided participation in what they saw as exploitative labor conditions, moved to another community in the hope of finding more favorable wages and housing, or engaged in racist and sexist blaming of other poor people. Sometimes these efforts were confined to complaints and noncompliance with shelter rules and "helping efforts." Very few homeless people whom I knew passively accepted their conditions, but even fewer engaged in collective mobilizations or acted in opposition to systemic inequities.

While being cognizant of such demonstrations of agency, we must avoid romanticizing the often individualized strategies of coping or accommodation. Analyzing the resistance acts that do take place, however, allows us to analyze more precisely power relations in particular settings and at precise historical moments. To understand the conditions maintaining homelessness, it is imperative to contemplate the subtle, insidious nature of how certain social conditions come to be taken for granted as normal, natural, or uncontestable. We need to understand how particular conditions promote particular actions while constraining the possibility of more collective mobilizations against structural inequities. Rather than simply reading "the homeless" as passive victims of misguided social and economic policies or as suffering from the debilitating effects of "false consciousness,"[10] I suggest that the often paradoxical ways in which people see themselves and society helps explain why particular strategies of coping, defiance, or accommodation are employed while other possibilities are marginalized as "unrealistic" or "impractical."

As Lila Abu-Lughod writes, "Where there is resistance, there is power"

(1990:42). Thus, it is imperative to analyze the effects of such power relations if we hope to understand the maintenance of homelessness despite the vast wealth in the United States. To do that, I explore how particular material and discursive conditions set conceptual parameters constraining the possibility of collective mobilizations by homeless people against recently increasing systemic inequalities. What factors, material and discursive, function to constrain these social actors' collective resistance against social inequality and homelessness?

Exploring Homelessness within a Thriving Economy

In an effort to analyze the dynamics described above, I conducted ethnographic research at a homeless shelter in Northampton, Massachusetts, between 1993 and 1997. In this research, I spent between forty and sixty hours each week at the shelter or in public meetings, taking note of the concrete, everyday practices that various agents enacted in response to homelessness. While actively participating in shelter routines, shelter meetings, staff hirings and trainings, public forums, and community planning efforts, I observed and engaged with staff members, people who were homeless, policymakers, and local advocates. In particular, I engaged in dialogue with homeless people as they applied for jobs, tried to be "reformed" by social service workers, and attempted to resolve homelessness through a wide range of actions. Taking part in shelter meetings, discussions, and loosely structured interviews, I also engaged in debates, dialogues, and discussions with people regarding both our perceptions and our practices. In these discussions, I urged those I had close relationships with to critically evaluate the effects of our routine practices and to explore the possibilities of expanding the range of permissible responses. Through these dialogical relationships, I gained enhanced access to information regarding the subtle, sometimes hidden strategies and tactics that people I worked with utilized and the ideological and material constraints on collective resistance to systemic inequality.

Conducting such ethnographic research within a homeless shelter in the city of Northampton provided an ideal setting for analyzing seemingly acquiescence to social inequality. Northampton is a small city of approximately thirty thousand people, located along the Connecticut River in the more rural, western section of Massachusetts. Having undergone much gentrification in the 1980s and 1990s, the city has managed to avoid the phenomenon of empty storefronts that plague nearby communities and is widely portrayed as a model of how to thrive despite recent deindustrialization. For example, a 1996 *Boston Globe Magazine* article applauded Northampton as an unusual story of success in the postindustrial, mall-driven economy of 1990s New England (Roche 1996), and the acclaimed 1999 book focused on Northampton, *Hometown,* by Pulitzer Prize–winning author Tracy Kidder, invokes an image of Northampton as the type of successful small city other communities and citizens can only emulate (Kidder 1999).

With four elite colleges and the University of Massachusetts located close by, Northampton attracts many visitors. Urban gentrification has produced a busy Main Street full of art galleries, coffee shops, and upscale restaurants, which ends at the gates of Smith College. Avoiding the trend toward malls and national chains, the downtown area features locally owned movie theaters, bookstores, and a range of shopping options. A thriving arts and music community draws even more consumers to the city. Despite appearances, however, there is another side to the Northampton area: that of increasing poverty and homelessness.

The work experiences of Jonathan reflect an overall economic shift in the region. The entire region has witnessed major political-economic restructuring in recent years. For example, 20 percent of workers in the county were employed in manufacturing in 1980. By 1990, this figure had dropped to 15 percent. By 1991, 51.12 percent of jobs countywide were located in either wholesale and retail trade or services (Market Street Research 1994:60). A 15 percent decrease in manufacturing jobs and a 12 percent increase in service-sector jobs occurred countywide during the 1980s as manufacturing plants were replaced by restaurants, coffee shops, galleries, and large retail chains (Market Street Research 1994:14). This trend continued during the 1990s.

On October 10, 1996, Kellog Brush announced that they would be closing down their manufacturing plant in Easthampton and laying off 220 workers. Kellog Brush had been manufacturing goods in western Massachusetts since 1924. This layoff came on the heels of business decisions by National Felt to lay off one hundred workers in 1994; by Stanley Home Products to lay off sixty employees while eliminating manufacturing operations in western Massachusetts, where they had been manufacturing goods since 1947; and by the Lesnow Manufacturing Company to close its factory in 1995, ending employment for 230 workers. Nine months later, during July 1997, another six hundred jobs (many of them in manufacturing) were lost in the western Massachusetts region due to businesses closing or moving. As a result of these tactical business decisions, 42 percent of all jobs in Northampton in 1998 were located in the service sectors, according to the Northampton Chamber of Commerce. Similarly, 45 percent of new jobs projected to be developed in the region over the next ten years are expected to pay wages below the federal poverty level for a family of two (Turner 1998).

Changes in employment and wages alone, however, do not adequately explain the political-economic conditions in the region. One needs to consider also housing availability and cost. In 1990, the median gross monthly rent for an apartment in Hampshire County was $526 per month (Market Street Research 1994:53). In April 1996, I surveyed the cost of apartments listed for rent in the community and found that the average rent of listed apartments was $665 (or $410 per bedroom). A 1996 study conducted by the University of Massachusetts Off Campus Housing Office found similar rents, with the average one-bedroom apartment costing $650 per month without heat (Watson 1996:16). Coupled with the high rents is an occupancy rate for apartments that routinely exceeds 95 percent.

Given that the income available to many working people in Northampton is inadequate to pay "market rate" rents, the only affordable housing option for many is to move into a rooming house or subsidized housing. Even these options are out of the range of many people. As of May 1996, there were 259 single-room occupancy (SRO) units in the city. This represents only slightly more than one-half the number of units in the city twenty years ago. The loss of SRO housing in Northampton is reflective of an overall trend throughout the nation. "Urban renewal" efforts contributed to eighteen thousand SRO units being lost between 1973 and 1984 in Chicago, more than half the SRO units in Los Angeles being demolished between 1970 and 1985, and Boston losing 94 percent of its rooming houses by the mid-1980s (Burt 1997:34).

A second type of low-income housing once available to poorer members of the society involved government subsidies for apartments. Unfortunately, the waiting list for Housing and Urban Development (HUD) Section 8 housing certificates or subsidized rooms and apartments in the city is virtually closed to anyone not categorized as "disabled" or elderly. Even these people often have to wait several years for a subsidy, and then they need to locate an available apartment and a willing landlord.

For three days during September 1996, the neighboring town of Amherst opened its Section 8 housing subsidy waiting list for applications. These had

been the only days that they even took applications during the previous two years. In 1997, the nearby city of Springfield opened its waiting list for three days. More than ten thousand different people placed their names on the waiting lists for Section 8 subsidies in the four-city Springfield HUD region in those days. Workers at the shelter informed current and former guests and helped them fill out many applications, knowing there was very little chance that space for even qualified applicants would become available in the next several years. One housing advocate, Elizabeth, explained this strategy in the following manner: "It's just something to do in case it ever comes through."

Again, the local situation is a reflection of national trends. A 1995 report by the U.S. Conference of Mayors reported that the average wait for Section 8 housing subsidies was thirty-nine months. Applicants had to wait an average of seventeen months from the time they applied until they received assistance (Waxman and Hinderliter 1997). In 1993, 1.4 million households nationally were on waiting lists for housing subsidies for privately owned housing, and 900,000 households were on waiting lists for public housing (Lazere 1995:4). As many housing authorities do not even take new applications, these numbers underestimate the demand for housing assistance.

Despite these dynamics, organized responses by homeless people to homelessness that challenge the availability of affordable housing or the wages paid in local jobs have been difficult to locate in western Massachusetts. This does not mean, however, that homeless people do not understand the impact of recent restructuring or that they have simply been passively acquiescing to those conditions. As I show in the next section, in working closely with homeless people over a several-year period I uncovered myriad ways in which people living at the shelter acted in response to the conditions of their lives and their community.

Responding to Homelessness in Northampton

In Northampton, approximately three hundred people stayed at the shelter where my work was focused during each of the years of this study.[11] In addition, over one-third of the people staying at the shelter during 1994, 1995, and 1996 were employed. Fewer than 20 percent, however, moved into nonsheltered housing after leaving the shelter. Many left town, moved to a different shelter, moved to some type of treatment program, lived in the woods surrounding the city, or doubled up with family and friends. This can partly be explained by the fact that the vast majority of these workers found themselves in low-paying food-service or retail trade jobs. For example, forty-two of the sixty-nine employed people staying at the shelter during 1995 worked in either food or retail trade for near minimum wage with no benefits.

Clearly, Jonathan's case of working for wages inadequate to afford housing is far from unique. Questions remain, however, regarding how homeless people respond to such dynamics and why some strategies make sense and are enacted while others are nearly silenced by being deemed impractical or unreasonable.

I worked with more than six hundred different homeless people in the course of this research. They exercised a variety of strategies in the effort to end their homelessness. Many of these people attempted to work their way out of poverty through paid employment. Others looked for more education or training. Some people tried to work hard at their job, hoping their skills would be appreciated while fearful of being fired if they spoke up. Still others moved from town to town, looking for housing they could afford with available wages. The vast majority of people also engaged in some type of self-reform. Yet these strategies almost always remain individualized, based on largely accepted, dominant notions about homeless people, and rarely challenged systemic inequality.

Through engaging with shelter residents as they negotiated the local political economy and housing market, and through participating in the daily workings of the local sheltering industry over a five-year period of time, it became quite clear to me that the dominant responses involved a great deal of self-government.[12] I uncovered a hypothesis of deviancy dominating within the homeless sheltering industry (Lyon-Callo 1998a). Based on discursively produced, prototypical conceptions of "the homeless" as alcoholics or mentally ill, discourses of self-help and bio-medicalization dominate in the shelters. These discourses and resultant practices combine to reproduce a conceptual framework in which homelessness is understood and responded to, by many homeless people, shelter staff members, shelter administrators, and funders, as being the result of shortcomings or pathologies within each homeless person. In such a setting, it comes to make sense to many homeless residents of the shelter to reform the self.

I found that an assumption that guides the preponderance of shelter "helping" practices is that, through a bio-medicalized search for symptoms, staff and guests can discover why one particular person became homeless. This is hardly surprising, given the dominance of bio-medicalized and in-

dividualized explanations for social problems in the United States during recent years. In fact, many of the people I worked with came to the shelter already blaming some type of disorder for their homelessness. For example, when asked what caused their homelessness, over 35 percent of the people who stayed at the shelter between 1994 and 1996 chose "substance abuse."

As one woman, Ariel, put it, "I was always blaming myself. Thinking that there must be something wrong with me. Other people have houses. How did I screw up my life to become homeless for so long?" This self-blame is not simply the result of false consciousness but rather the result of being entwined within the dominant discourses operating in the shelter and in the society at large. Homeless people often hold a deep-seated belief in the myth of the American Dream. Many homeless people also remain deeply committed to concepts of individual responsibility and pulling oneself up by one's bootstraps.

Examining shelters' routines, including case management, counseling sessions, staff decisions about how long to allow someone to remain at the shelter, and the response to violations of shelter rules and regulations, I found that shelter helping practices reinforce feelings of self-blame and the need for self-help by training homeless people to look for and treat disorders within themselves as the appropriate way of responding to homelessness. Homeless people are encouraged to look for "the cause" of their homelessness within themselves through self-reflection. They are urged to consider "what did I do to become this way." Each person is understood to have become homeless because he or she has a problem (a biological disorder, an attitude toward life, mental illness, a lack of self-discipline, or an addictive personality, for example) that is within the self.

Through routine practices of detecting and treating pathology, statistical record keeping, maintaining case histories, and self-help efforts, a homeless person becomes a subject who was inclined to be homeless because of something within the self. Routine shelter practices serve to produce "the homeless" and homeless subjects, reinforce social policy based on managing these presumed pathological "others," and hegemonically marginalize alternative resistance possibilities by reconfirming "common sense." Subjectivities are created through the widespread languages of self-empowerment and self-improvement and through diagnosing "disorders" in individuals. The "solution," then, is to treat those disorders through retraining, discipline, confession, punishment, or therapy. Self-governing homeless subjects are often produced.

Having subordinated people believe that they are a danger to themselves proved unsuccessful, Jonathan displaced the blame from himself by blaming other marginalized groups of people. He came to place much of the blame for his inability to find housing on preferential treatment for students, "minorities," and the "disabled." He stated, "They [the shelter staff, local politicians, and employers] don't want to help anybody in this town unless they're lesbian or Puerto Rican. These people just want to get a check. It takes about two minutes to get a job in this town if you want one. They [minorities] just don't want to work and they get all the help."

Jonathan was far from alone in expressing such sentiments at the shelter. Men and women staying at the shelter quite frequently asserted their whiteness by scapegoating minorities. They voiced their beliefs that "minorities" or "welfare queens" were taking resources and causing them to be homeless. As Susan, a woman in her mid-fifties, told me, "This town isn't a place for someone like me. They only build affordable housing for those 'Spanish' people." Other young white men at the shelter began to openly discuss the need for organizing in militia-like organizations to protect the "rights of real Americans" who were suffering because of government favoring of "minorities." Such sentiments were expressed so frequently at the shelter that some staff members proposed rules banning guests who used such "disrespectful language." These racist responses to poverty by some homeless people are hardly surprising. Despite the extensive historical roots of contemporary state-sanctioned and institutionalized white privilege in the United States (Lipsitz 1995; Sacks 1994; Page 1998), there is also a long history in the nation of poor white citizens embracing racist notions of perceived privileges for nonwhite others as a rationalization of their own less-privileged class position.[14]

While quite disturbing, the blaming of other marginalized or poor people was often combined with other responses. During another discussion, Jonathan mentioned that his bosses at the restaurant where he was working at the time were trying to get Tom (a co-worker who was also living at the shelter) and him to continue working instead of leaving town. "They're trying to get us to stay, but there's nothing they can do. This town hates homeless people. Everywhere else I've been people are more willing to help you. Some places people even help without you asking. Here they just don't want to see you."

I suggested that there was something his bosses could do. "Well, they could pay you enough to live on. How about paying you $7 an hour instead of $5?"

without self-reform works quite effectively in producing what appears to be acquiescence. This is precisely where the more insidious forms of self-government come into play. Shelter guests govern themselves (through self-help efforts) and other homeless people (through discussing the benefits of self-help and self-empowerment groups). Suggested remedies for the disorders that lead to homelessness include attending the local skills center and workshops at the shelter, accessing public education, attaining a GED, developing a mentoring program, and attending classes at the local literacy project. Those shelter guests who embrace such responses are often rewarded with extended stays, increased staff attention, and similar privileges, while noncompliance is often diagnosed as a symptom of why those who do not participate remain homeless and used as a reason to make someone leave the shelter. Given these dynamics, it is hardly surprising that there are very few large-scale collective resistance struggles by homeless people against economic or racial inequality and housing policies. Self-blaming and self-governing subjects who are rewarded for looking within their selves for the solution to their individual homelessness can scarcely be expected to spend time organizing collective mobilizations against structural inequalities.[13]

Despite these dynamics, however, not everyone staying at the shelter voiced agreement with the representations of homelessness as the result of inadequacies or pathologies within particular homeless people. People staying at the shelter did articulate concerns regarding costs of housing, wages available at local jobs, and similar concerns about economic restructuring on almost a daily basis. As one young, employed, homeless man argued, "If this was the 1950s I wouldn't be homeless. My father graduated from high school and got a job right away in doing tool and dye work. They gave him good pay and benefits and on-the-job training. There just aren't good jobs like that anymore." Many people shared that sentiment, but they still often engaged in individual attempts to resolve homelessness. To examine more fully how these people did respond to homelessness in the face of such dynamics, let me return to Jonathan.

Jonathan, like many other people I have come to know, utilized individual strategies of hard work and self-responsibility as the pathway toward "success." He always was employed, often worked two jobs at a time, never missed a day of work, and hoped to work his way out of poverty. Yet he continued to be homeless. When his individual strategy of trying to work his way out of homelessness through being a responsible, hard-working person

Jonathan did not think that was possible. He replied, "They can't do that. They won't stay in business. They could give me 40 hours every week, but I still won't be able to afford an apartment."

Jonathan could not envision his food-service job paying a decent wage. Like many other homeless and housed people, Jonathan represented as "natural" that such jobs must remain low-paying for the very survival of the business, and that decisions about distribution of the surplus naturally are the province of the employer. The possibility that food-service jobs can become "good" jobs, with high pay and benefits, remains outside the realm of even being imagined. He felt powerless to change the pay in these jobs and instead blamed "minorities" for his homelessness.

Again, Jonathan's feelings of powerlessness to alter conditions of work were widely shared by those people living at the shelter. Many of the people I worked with stated that they were powerless to change the wages paid at local jobs or the local cost of housing. When I brought up such concerns, the most frequent response was "That's the way things are. We don't have any power to change it." This feeling of powerlessness to make any substantive changes in systemic conditions is a frequently articulated explanation for homeless people not participating in "politics" at many levels. As neoliberal, market-oriented policies and practices are taken for granted, structural inequities often seem so all-encompassing and overwhelming that many homeless people believe they can do nothing to alter those conditions. It thus appears to be a more reasonable approach to focus on how to do well individually. As one example of many, Howard, an African American male in his early twenties, came to the shelter when he could no longer afford to remain housed or continue paying to attend the University of Massachusetts. Despite being an academic success throughout high school and his two and one-half years at the university, he had become homeless due to financial aid difficulties. Howard had been staying at the shelter for several months when he complained to me about how he had been working at a local supermarket for over six months and still could not afford to move out of the shelter. Despite a near-perfect work record, he was still stuck with a part-time and inconsistent schedule and minimum wage pay, and he felt powerless to alter those conditions of employment except through possibly demonstrating his reliability and efficiency as an individual employee.

I asked if he had requested more hours. Howard replied that he was told that "you don't get to work full time until you've been employed for a year." What was most frustrating to Howard was seeing the "Help Wanted" sign in the front of the store and seeing management hire people for more part-

time jobs but remain unwilling to give him enough hours so that he could afford to become housed. When I asked why he thinks they did not simply offer him full-time hours, Howard replied, "'Cause they don't want to pay for benefits and they want to have you able to be at their call. Like yesterday. I wasn't scheduled, but they called me in to fill for someone else. They know you'll come because you're desperate for hours."

Adding to Howard's frustration was the inability of his union representative from the United Food and Commercial Workers Union to understand his desperation for more hours and greater pay. As Howard explained, "All they [the union stewards] do is tell me that we have a contract. That doesn't help me get money for a place to live." When I asked union leadership at his local about the practice, they argued that they got the best contract possible considering competition from nearby nonunion supermarkets. The "need" for large corporate profits and exorbitant salaries for top management went unchallenged in the union's effort to work cooperatively with management or in any of Howard's practices.

The supermarket where Howard (and Jonathan at one time) worked was part of a chain of 128 supermarkets that employed more than forty-eight thousand people throughout New England in 1995. That year the company reported $73 million in net income on sales of close to $4 billion. The chief executive officer received $1,198,153 in compensation (Spain and Talbott 1996:1351). Yet, despite the profits and high executive salaries, many workers continued to be paid wages inadequate to afford housing. Of course, it was understood as "unreasonable" for homeless people or many of the workers to challenge that tactical business decision.

When I asked what he could do about this, Howard said, "I just go to work and hope that I'll be able to save up enough money to find a place to live before I run out of time here [at the shelter]. You don't want to be thinking about it all the time or else you couldn't go to work. There doesn't seem to be much you can do anyway. . . . You can't make too much of a fuss because none of us who want to work full time are able to risk being fired." Despite the presence of a union, which is an increasingly rare condition in private-sector employment, Howard still could not imagine collective action aimed at challenging structural inequalities. Like many poor or homeless people, Howard (perhaps rightly) came to believe that his most rational move was to individualize his response to his homelessness and his working conditions. Instead of working with fellow employees toward gaining a more equitable distribution of the value of their labor, many workers cope by putting on blinders regarding the exploitative conditions of their work while being virtually forced to compete with fellow part-time workers for hours.

I found that establishing an awareness and mode of action outside set parameters is often seen as too overwhelming for many homeless people. Many people consider this sense of too much awareness as a way of numbing their own professional agency. As one homeless woman, Susan, stated, "Yes, what you say makes sense. Of course the problems are with the economy. I'm not stupid, but thinking about changing the wage structure or getting more housing is just too much. I have no idea of where to even start. I only have so much time here and I have to figure out how to cope with the reality of the situation."

Eventually, Jonathan, Susan, and Howard all left the city, hoping for better luck elsewhere. Jonathan headed south, hoping to find housing in South Carolina. Like 10 percent of those people who stayed at the shelter during 1994–1996, he decided that the only solution to his problem was to leave Northampton and hope for better luck somewhere else. He wanted to improve his income potential and job skills through education but couldn't afford to attend college. He worked hard but became extremely frustrated by his inability to afford decent housing. Feeling that he was powerless to alter the wages paid locally, the cost of housing, or any systemic conditions, he "chose" to leave town and try his luck elsewhere when his time at the shelter ran out.

An alternative response sometimes employed by a few homeless people is that demonstrated by Anthony. A white man in his early forties, Anthony, stayed at the shelter on three different occasions during the five years of my research. Most frequently he traveled throughout the country trying to survive. He offered a rarely articulated perspective on the link between employment, wages, and homelessness. His coping techniques for dealing with homelessness, however, remained an individualized strategy.

Anthony argued that much homelessness was caused by economic restructuring leading to declining real wages for many workers and the effects of unequal opportunities for success in the United States. He argued, "I don't have the opportunities because of how I grew up. All my father's relatives were very rural Appalachian Mountain folk doing logging or agriculture. I certainly did not have any Mom and Dad down in Connecticut or southern California like you were saying. [I had suggested that one explanation for why he was homeless and I was not was that I had a relatively well-off fam-

ily.] It's more than just getting the hair cut and putting on the three-piece [suit] and here's the training position working for some stock exchange.

"I have certainly worked all my life. I worked, coming home from junior high school, feeding thirty head of beef cattle. I grew up working constantly on my parent's farm, but that was cool. My father worked at nights at the steel mill. I bought my own school clothes. I do have a work ethic. At times I rebel considering that I have three and a half years of college education and I can't get a decent job. I rebel against the fact that I've never made more than $5.50 an hour, except for when I fought fires for the fire service." Significantly, though, he does not rebel by organizing collectively with other homeless people. Instead, he simply does not work for wages for long periods of time.

Unlike Anthony and a few others, however, the vast majority of homeless people I worked with shared many of the ideological norms and cultural values of dominant U.S. culture. Many who believe most strongly in survival of the fittest, patriotism, white male genetic superiority, and individual responsibility can be found practicing these beliefs at the shelters. Other people use sheltering industry representations of Horatio Alger–type stories, of the rare homeless person who has "succeeded" in pulling him- or herself out of homelessness, as a model to emulate. If a few model shelter guests managed to become "housed," then it must be possible. Therefore, there is no need for anything as drastic as organized, collective mobilization to challenge increasing inequality.

Likewise, it is understood that there is little that can be done about the cost and availability of local housing within the assumed "reality" of the current climate. Efforts at building a social movement to make permanent housing a right for all or even to limit the amount of rent a private landlord can charge are similarly minority efforts. Even when nondominant discursive efforts raise the possibilities of such resistance, they are marginalized by being deemed unrealistic and not worth pursuing. Possible collective resistance against systemic inequality is severely constrained when social agents understand current political-economic relations and class processes as inevitable, natural, or too overwhelming to ever change. Collective mobilization often is also almost mind-numbing to consider and understood as too risky to undertake, thus interfering further with personal agency. There is often little need for explicit coercion. Efforts are focused on how to cure, control, or manage the "disease" of homelessness, which is not at all construed as a problem with any racial, gendered, or class dimensions.

Homelessness persists in part because the material and discursive conditions causing it remain largely uncontested in daily practices.

Many of these social actors do articulate some degree of implicit awareness of the systemic and class nature of homelessness. Yet the possibilities for how they struggle against homelessness are constrained by how local actors understand the impediments to housing homeless people in relation to their own community. In Northampton, it appears that prevailing economic practices are not considered a variable to be contemplated in developing strategies to confront homelessness. Instead, it is taken as a given that decisions about production, appropriation, and distribution of the local surplus will remain in the hands of a few. Resistance to the discursive and systemic dimensions of homelessness will not be organized or amplified. Consequently, it is accepted that food-service employers will pay low wages, offer no benefits, and offer most workers only part-time work, even if this means that homeless people will not be able to afford a place to live in the community. These conditions are tolerated because of the combined impact of prevailing assumptions that there is nothing that can be done to alter structural violence; that market capitalism is natural, or at least inevitable; and that other subordinated people are to blame for homelessness. Added to these are the subject effects of a dominant individualized hypothesis of deviancy and self-government.

Is the Shelter a Possible Site for Collective Mobilization?

Routine, everyday practices by which homeless people, shelter staff, or homeless advocates respond to homelessness rarely include collective mobilization. Rarer still are collective strategies of resistance aimed at responding to homelessness through altering the prevailing conditions of systemic inequality in the United States. In Northampton, I found that interrelated understandings and practices connected with feelings of powerlessness to alter socioeconomic conditions, with individualized self-blame and self-government, and with blaming other oppressed people functioned to marginalize the very possibility of collective action. Although such understandings and practices were dominant, however, they were never total. As Raymond Williams so clearly emphasized, hegemony is always a process and is never all-encompassing (1977).

Particular social and ideological conditions working together produced understandings whereby some responses to homelessness were marginal-

ized as unrealistic while other possibilities became common sense. Yet alternative and counterhegemonic possibilities, while marginalized, nonetheless existed in the shelter. Dominant ways of knowing and being were contested on a daily basis. As noted earlier, the majority of these contestations took the form of alternative approaches or subterfuge, sometimes as coping strategies, rarely as oppositional challenges. Rather than pointing out the inevitability of existing conditions (i.e., the sentiment often expressed at the shelter that "we need to work within the reality of these conditions"), I propose that such dynamics contain the possibilities of potential collective and oppositional mobilization. For such mobilization to emerge, however, the social conditions need to be created where collective understandings and practices become imaginable, are fostered, and are allowed to emerge. Just such a moment was created in one shelter in Northampton, Massachusetts, for a short period of time in 1995 and 1996.

The staff and regular volunteers working at this shelter began to explicitly challenge routine, everyday practices in a variety of ways. As part of my ongoing ethnographic research, I began to engage in increased dialogical exchanges with shelter staff members and with the people living at the shelter about my analysis of the effects of routine shelter practices. I shared the results of archival research and statistical compilations regarding local wages and housing costs, the number of employed people residing at the shelter, the extreme rarity of someone locating housing in the community on the basis of income received through low-paid employment, and how I analyzed shelter helping practices as teaching individualized responses.

None of this information was regularly compiled or publicly available at the shelter prior to my research. Once available, however, this information provided new possibilities for some of the staff to think about their own work at the shelter. This critique resonated well with sentiments that several staff members were concurrently developing. A newly hired staff member frequently articulated a Marxist-feminist critique of what she read as the medicalization of homeless people. Other staff were questioning how to do their work more effectively in the face of an unprecedented local demand for shelter. They were struggling to align their own self-proclaimed progressive, anarchist, socialist, and/or feminist political sentiments with an increasing awareness of how very little their helping practices were doing to decrease homelessness. The disjunction between their stated theoretical understandings and their actual practices in the shelter was articulated, acknowledged, and problematized. The culmination of these convergent practices was an expressed and enacted desire among the vast majority of these shelter workers to contemplate how to approach working in the shelters and with homeless people in new ways. Almost all staff members at this moment embraced a desire to rethink routine understandings and practices.

As those conditions came together, new practices began to emerge, creating discursive space for those staying in the shelter to think and act in new ways. All the shelter staff agreed to dedicate one hour of each weekly staff meeting toward discussing how to work in new ways. Staff debated their roles, their positions in the broader community, the effectiveness of prevailing practices, and the impact of existing hierarchical, distanced relationships with homeless people living in the shelter. Some staff began to discuss these issues with current and former residents of the shelter. Some significant changes in practices resulted from these discussions. One such change was the establishment of a weekly "community organizing" meeting at the shelter.

All staff of the shelter, any current or former guest of the shelter, and invited community members came together at this weekly meeting to discuss how to address homelessness. No set agendas were imposed, and the only rules of the meeting were that there be no physical violence and that anyone could say anything without fear of future reprisals from the staff. The stated intention of the meeting was for staff members and homeless people to begin listening to one another and to begin contemplating how they could work together in collaborative efforts. An institutionally sanctioned practice encouraging collective understandings and actions, rather than individualized strategies, emerged.

Preliminary discussions began to take place at this meeting regarding such practices as the developing and enforcing of shelter rules, funding the shelter without being beholden to state welfare agencies, and determining who would have access to producing the official summary of guest behavior in the daily logs, how intakes would be conducted, what statistical and demographic information would be compiled, and how such data would be conveyed to both the local community and government sources. After a few weeks, several homeless people began to use these meetings to discuss their frustrations with finding employment that paid more than minimum wage or with locating housing they could afford. I, in turn, shared data I had compiled on wages and housing costs in the community, the nation, and around the globe, so that those staying at the shelter could contextualize their struggles within a broader political-economic framework. When people raised racist or sexist arguments to explain their low wages or inability to find

housing (and, as people were explicitly told they were free to do or say anything at these meetings except use physical violence, many did just that), staff and other guests began to openly challenge one another to think more critically about both the articulated assumptions and their broader effects. When some people argued that we were powerless to alter systemic conditions, other guests could now engage in dialogue. Often this involved raising historical examples of people who had managed to organize collective mobilization for dramatic changes.

Over time, many staff members and shelter residents began throughout the day, in most of their interactions with each other, to discuss and debate power relations within the shelter, employment issues, and the availability of affordable housing in the city. Dialogue about the connections between systemic inequalities and homelessness were now encouraged rather than being seen as misplaced, a waste of time, or a symptom of the disorder of "denial." After weeks and months of discussion and collaborative learning, more staff, guests, and a few shelter administrators began to attempt to enact new practices. New practices and resistance strategies aimed at possibly altering both the material and discursive dimensions of homelessness began to emerge. The culmination of these converging social conditions was such that collective mobilization became possible for a short moment in this shelter and this community.

Throughout these discussions, I continued to suggest that people could begin to work together collaboratively at the grassroots level to begin thinking and working toward more equality. The discursive parameters of what was thinkable and doable in this situation began to be stretched and altered. Some homeless people and some shelter staff began to consider the commonality of their experiences. Collaborative coalitions began to emerge between local organized labor, activist church members, local youth groups, welfare rights activists, and those working in the homeless sheltering industry. As one example, a living-wage movement was developed and organized from the discussions in the community organizing meetings at the shelter. Other people worked to organize a community center focused on community organizing and a collectively run business venture to provide nonexploitative local employment. Additionally, a coalition focused on issues of affordable housing, an effort to counteract popular imaginings about homeless people through producing a film at the shelter for local cable access television, and increased engagement with the local news media came out of these meetings. Several homeless and formerly homeless people were at the center of organizing these collaborative movements.

Unfortunately, this reflective moment and the related collective efforts lasted less than two years. When these nascent social movements moved into actual practices aimed at challenging inequities, shelter administrators, those funding the shelter, and local politicians became quite upset. It was made explicitly clear that the actions were jeopardizing support and the future economic viability of the shelter.[15] Shelter administrators were told to make their staff behave and return to their "proper" job of reforming homeless deviants. A new staff conduct policy was implemented that mandated a detached and professional relationship between staff and homeless "clients." As staff increasingly felt devalued and unable to work in the way they felt was necessary, many took jobs elsewhere or pursued more education. A new director was hired, who did not support or attend the community organizing meeting. Eventually the meeting was eliminated entirely.

Although short-lived, the practices that emerged out of this set of discursive conditions at this shelter in this community suggest that collective mobilizations of homeless people are possible. Previously accepted restrictions on what is possible and acceptable for both staff and homeless guests may be stretched and challenged. Shelter staff and homeless people can learn to rethink their established and habitual roles, including how they work with one another and the broader community. With these practices, different types of subjectivities might be produced within the homeless sheltering industry. A renewed sense of potential in collectively working together to challenge increasing systemic inequalities might become possible. New knowledge may provide the possibility for producing new kinds of subjects who undertake different resistance strategies aimed at altering structural conditions such as housing costs, housing availability, wages paid, the distribution of wealth and income, and racial inequalities. For such collective mobilizations and resistance to emerge or be sustained, the social conditions where such strategies are thinkable need to be in place. To allow such practices to become thinkable, let alone doable, critical reflections and transformations regarding the discursive and material conditions of homelessness must be established and enacted.

NOTES

1. The names of all participants in this study have been changed to protect their confidentiality.

2. Sixty-nine (38 percent) of the people staying at the shelter during 1995 worked at least part time.

3. See Katherine Newman, *No Shame in My Game: The Working Poor in the Inner City* (New York: Alfred A. Knopf and The Russell Sage Foundation, 1996).

4. The growth in homelessness has taken place within a two-decade period that is also characterized by an increasingly polarized distribution of wealth. The number of people with incomes at or below the federally defined poverty level increased from 22,973,000 (11.1 percent of total population) in 1973 to 39,265,000 (15.1 percent) in 1993 (Center on Budget and Policy Priorities 1994:11; U.S. Bureau of the Census 1996).

5. Due to the restructured tax code, the percentage of total federal tax revenue from corporate taxes decreased from 23 percent in 1960 to 10 percent in 1995 (Albelda et al. 1996:21).

6. The distribution of aggregate household income in the United States documents this trend toward increased inequality. In 1993, the wealthiest 5 percent of the population received 20 percent of the nation's total income, while the poorest 40 percent received only 12.7 percent. Twenty years earlier, the distribution was 16.6 percent for the top 5 percent and 14.7 percent for the lowest 40 percent of families (Center on Budget and Policy Priorities 1994:57). This trend has continued in recent years. According to U.S. Bureau of the Census data, real median income in 1995 fell to 3.8 percent below that of 1989 (U.S. Bureau of the Census 1996).

7. The Census Bureau reported that the proportion of full-time workers with earnings too low to lift a family of four out of poverty rose from 12.1 percent in 1979 to 16.2 percent in 1993, an increase of one-third (Lazere 1995:18).

8. In 1970, after several years of increased government expenditures on housing as one component of the "war on poverty," the 7.4 million low-cost rental units in the United States represented an abundance of 900,000 more units than the number of low-income renters (6.5 million). In 1973, there were 5.1 million nonsubsidized rental units with costs of $300 per month or less (in 1993 dollars). By 1993, however, the number of low-rent units fell to 6.5 million (only 2.9 million of which were nonsubsidized) while the number of low-income potential renters increased to 11.2 million people. A shortage of 4.7 million units was the result (Lazere 1995:2).

9. The articles in the edited volume *More than Class: Studying Power in U.S. Workplaces* (Kingsolver 1998) spell out related arguments about relationships within the United States under contemporary capitalism.

10. By "false consciousness" I am referring to the notion that ideological or structural conditions obfuscate the truth from people, thus resulting in mystification of their essential interests. Following Michel Foucault (1991), I am suggesting that there is no essential consciousness, but rather all human subjects are always produced through the relations in which they are enmeshed.

11. An additional 100–250 other people were turned away, due to a lack of shelter space, each year during 1995–1997.

12. For related arguments about the growth of self-government as the most

reasonable and practical way of responding to social problems, see the work of Nikolas Rose (1996) and Barbara Cruikshank (1996).

13. For a more detailed argument on the effects of the medicalization of homelessness, see my forthcoming article in *Medical Anthropology Quarterly* (Lyon-Callo, 2000).

14. See, for example, the work of Pem Davidson Buck (1992).

15. For a further discussion of the impact that funding considerations played in constraining resistance, see my article in *Human Organization* (Lyon-Callo 1998b).

REFERENCES

Abu-Lughod, Lila. 1990. "The Romance of Resistance: Tracing Transformations of Power through Bedouin Women." *American Ethnologist* 17(1):41–55.

Albelda, Randy, Nancy Folbre, and the Center for Popular Economics. 1996. *The War on the Poor.* New York: New Press.

Blau, Joel. 1992. *The Visible Poor: Homelessness in the United States.* New York: Oxford University Press.

Bourgois, Philippe. 1996. *In Search of Respect: Selling Crack in El Barrio.* Cambridge: Cambridge University Press.

Buck, Pem Davidson. 1992. "With Our Heads in the Sand: The Racist Right, Concentration Camps, and the Incarceration of People of Color." *Transforming Anthropology* 3:13–18.

Burt, Martha. 1997. "Causes of the Growth of Homelessness during the 1980s." In *Understanding Homelessness: New Policy and Research Perspectives.* Washington, DC: Fannie Mae Foundation.

Center on Budget and Policy Priorities. 1994. *1993 Poverty and Income Trends.* Washington, DC: Center on Budget and Policy Priorities.

Cruikshank, Barbara. 1996. "Revolutions Within: Self-Government and Self-Esteem." In *Foucault and Political Reason: Liberalism, Neo-Liberalism, and Rationalities of Government.* Edited by Andrew Barry, Thomas Osborne, and Nikolas Rose. Chicago: University of Chicago Press.

Dordick, Gwendolyn. 1997. *Something Left to Lose: Personal Relations and Survival among New York's Homeless.* Philadelphia: Temple University Press.

Dowdy, Zachary R. 1998. "Homelessness Rising despite Brisk Economy." *Boston Globe*, 10/12, B1.

Economic Policy Institute. 1997. *Nonstandard Work, Substandard Jobs: Flexible Work Arrangements in the US.* Washington, DC: Economic Policy Institute.

Foucault, Michel. 1991. *Conversations with Duccio Trombadori.* New York: Semiotext(e).

Hardin, Bristow. 1996. "Why the Road Off the Street Is Not Paved with Jobs." In *Homelessness in America.* Phoenix: Oryx Press.

Kaufman, Tracy. 1996. *Out of Reach: Can America Pay the Rent?* Washington, DC: National Low Income Housing Coalition.

———. 1997. *Out of Reach: Rental Housing at What Cost?* Washington, DC: National Low Income Housing Coalition.

Kidder, Tracy. 1999. *Hometown.* New York: Random House.

Kingsolver, Ann. 1998. *More than Class: Studying Power in U.S. Workplaces.* Albany: State University of New York Press.

Kondo, Dorinne. 1990. *Crafting Selves: Power, Gender, and Discourses of Identity in a Japanese Workplace.* Chicago: University of Chicago Press.

Lazere, Edward. 1995. *In Short Supply: The Growing Affordable Housing Gap.* Washington, DC: Center on Budget and Policy Priorities.

Lipsitz, George. 1995. "The Possessive Investment in Whiteness: Racialized Social Democracy and the 'White' Problem in American Studies." *American Quarterly* 47(3):369–87.

Lyon-Callo, Vincent. 1998a. "Hegemony and the Construction of Selves: A Dialogical Ethnography of Homelessness and Resistance." Unpublished Ph.D. dissertation, University of Massachusetts, Amherst.

———. 1998b. "Constraining Responses to Homelessness: An Ethnographic Exploration of the Impact of Funding Concerns on Resistance." *Human Organization* 57(1):1–7.

———. 2000. "Medicalizing Homelessness: The Production of Self-Blame and Self-Governing within Homeless Shelters." *Medical Anthropology Quarterly* 14(3):328–45.

Market Street Research Inc. 1994. *Health and Human Service Needs of Hampshire County Residents: Need Assessment Report.* Northampton, MA: Market Street Research Inc.

National Coalition for the Homeless. 1997. *Homelessness in America: Unabated and Increasing.* Washington, DC: National Coalition for the Homeless.

O'Flaherty, Brendan. 1996. *Making Room: The Economics of Homelessness.* Cambridge: Cambridge University Press.

Page, Helan. 1998. "Understanding White Cultural Practices." *Anthropology Newsletter* 39(4):58–60.

Roche, B. J. 1996. "Balancing Act: Northampton Is a City That Works." *Boston Globe Magazine*, 8/21, 20–29.

Rose, Nicholas. 1996. "The Death of the Social? Re-figuring the Territories of Government." *Economy and Society* 25(3):327–56.

Sacks, Karen Brodkin. 1994. "How Did Jews Become White Folks?" In *Race*. Edited by Steven Gregory and Roger Sanjek. New Brunswick: Rutgers University Press.

Scott, James. 1990. *Domination and the Arts of Resistance: Hidden Transcripts.* New Haven: Yale University Press.

Sharff, Jagna Wojcicka. 1998. *King Kong on 4th Street: Families and the Violence of Poverty on the Lower East Side.* Boulder: Westview Press.

Spain, Patrick, and James Talbott. 1996. *Hoover's Handbook of American Businesses 1996*. Austin: Reference Press.

Turner, Maureen. 1998. "The Division of Labor: Employment Numbers Look Good on Paper, but They Hide Serious Weak Spots in the Market." *Valley Advocate*, 2/26, 20–22.

U.S. Bureau of the Census. 1996. *Poverty in the United States: 1995*. Washington, DC: U.S. Bureau of the Census.

Wagner, David. 1993. *Checkerboard Square: Culture and Resistance in a Homeless Community*. Boulder: Westview Press.

Waterston, Alisse. 1993. *Street Addicts in the Political Economy*. Philadelphia: Temple University Press.

Watson, Bruce. 1996. "Tight Rental Market Aggravates Annual Housing Scramble." *Daily Hampshire Gazette*, 8/28, 15–16.

Waxman, Laura, and Sharon Hinderliter. 1997. *A Status Report on Hunger and Homelessness in America's Cities: 1996*. Washington, DC: U.S. Conference of Mayors.

Williams, Brett. 1996. "There Goes the Neighborhood: Gentrification, Displacement, and Homelessness in Washington DC." In *There's No Place like Home: Anthropological Perspectives on Housing and Homelessness in the United States*. Edited by Anna Lou Dehavenon. Westport: Bergin and Garvey.

Williams, Raymond. 1977. *Marxism and Literature*. Oxford: Oxford University Press.

Wright, Talmadge. 1997. *Out of Place: Homeless Mobilizations, Subcities, and Contested Landscapes*. Albany: State University of New York Press.

April 2009

CANADA'S QUIET BARGAIN
The benefits of public spending

By Hugh Mackenzie and Richard Shillington

Growing Gap .ca

CANADIAN CENTRE FOR POLICY ALTERNATIVES

ISBN 978-1-897569-39-9

Canadian Centre for Policy Alternatives

2 Carlton Street, Suite 1001, Toronto, Ontario
(416) 263-9896
www.GrowingGap.ca

Acknowledgements

The authors wish to thank the organizations that provided core funding for this project. The authors are also indebted to Statistics Canada, whose database on government revenue and expenditures enables consistent comparison of public revenue and expenditures across Canada and whose Social Policy Simulation Database and Model and Survey of Labour Income Dynamics supports the distributional analysis which forms the core of this study. Trish Hennessy, Armine Yalnizyan, Bruce Campbell, Kerri-Anne Finn, Tim Scarth, Andrew Jackson, Stan Marshall, Toby Sanger, Howie West, John Staple, Ian Boyko, Larry Brown, Sheila Block, Charles Pascal, Marc Lee and Seth Klein all provided helpful guidance, advice and encouragement as the project proceeded. None of the above is responsible for any errors, omissions or disagreeable opinions presented in this paper. The findings reflect the work of the authors and do not necessarily reflect the views of the Canadian Centre for Policy Alternatives or of the funding organizations.

Financial assistance for this project was provided by:
The National Union of Public and General Employees, The Public Service Alliance of Canada, The Canadian Union of Public Employees, The Canadian Teachers' Federation, The Canadian Labour Congress and the Canadian Federation of Students.

About the Authors

Hugh Mackenzie is a Research Associate of the Canadian Centre for Policy Alternatives and part of the research team of the CCPA Inequality Project. He has written reports and backgrounders for the CCPA on a wide range of issues including his July 2006 CCPA study of the public economy in Canada, "The Art of the Impossible: Fiscal Federalism and Fiscal Balance in Canada" which serves as the macroeconomic counterpart to the distributional analysis in the current report. He created the CCPA's popular "gas gouge meter" and conceived and writes the CCPA's annual review of executive compensation in Canada. He is principal in Hugh Mackenzie & Associates, which provides economic consulting services to the trade union movement and the not-for-profit sector. He co-chairs and is principal economist for the Ontario Alternative Budget project. He has written extensively on a wide range of budgetary issues in Ontario, including tax and fiscal policy, elementary and secondary education finance and postsecondary education finance. From 1991 to 1994, he was Executive Director of the Ontario Fair Tax Commission. He was one of the founders of the Alternative Federal Budget project of the Canadian Centre for Policy Alternatives.

Richard Shillington is a Senior Associate of the Ottawa-based economic consulting firm Informetrica Ltd. and principal of his consulting business, Tristat Resources Ltd. He has post-graduate degrees in statistics from the University of Waterloo and has been engaged in the quantitative analysis of health, social and economic policy for the past 30 years. His research has covered several policy fields; health manpower planning, program evaluation, income security, poverty, tax policy and human rights. He has worked for several provincial and federal departments as well as commissions studying the economy, unemployment insurance, human rights and tax policy. Richard has been an active participant in policy and public debates concerning the relationship between the tax system and the retirement income system in Canada. He has also contributed his statistical and analytical talents to a number of CCPA projects, most notably the analyses of the growing gap published by the CCPA's Inequality Project.

Summary

THIS STUDY ADDS a dimension that has been missing to the public debate over taxes and public spending in Canada. It weighs the benefits of public services provided by federal, provincial, and municipal governments against the benefits of recent tax cuts.

Using a sophisticated array of data sets and analytical tools from Statistics Canada, this study concludes that Canadians depend to a significant extent on public services such as education, health care, child care, public pensions, employment insurance, and family benefits for their living standard.

In fact, this study puts a number on it: Canadians enjoy an average $17,000 benefit from the public services which our taxes fund — about the same amount a Canadian working full-time, full-year at the minimum wage would earn.

The results of this study show the vast majority of Canadians are getting a quiet bargain by investing in taxes that produce enormous public benefits.

For the vast majority of Canada's population, public services are, to put it bluntly, the best deal they are ever going to get.

More than two-thirds of Canadians' benefit from public services adds up to more than 50% of their household's total earned income.

Looking at Canadians in median income households, their benefit from public services amounts to $41,000 — equivalent to roughly 63% of their total income.

Overall, the average per capita benefit from public services in Canada in 2006 came to $16,952. Approximately 56% of that benefit comes from health care, education and personal transfer payments.

137

The benefit middle-income Canadians receive from public services represents a significant proportion of the total resources available to them. Even in the $80,000 to $90,000 household income range — just below the richest 20% — the benefit they receive from public services is equivalent to about half of their private income.

No matter how you cut it, the data in this study shows how powerful a role public spending plays in ensuring the majority of Canadians enjoy a better quality of life.

The paper also shows that the vast majority of Canadians would have been better off if the fiscal capacity lost through tax cuts had instead been invested in improving public services.

It estimates that an astounding 80% of Canadians would have been better off if the Harper government had transferred money to local governments to pay for more and better public services instead of cutting the GST by 1%.

Similarly, 75% of Canadians would have been better off if their provincial governments had invested in public health care and education instead of administering broad-based income tax cuts in the late-1990s and early-2000s.

And had the federal government invested in improved federal public services instead of cutting capital gains taxation by one third in the early-2000s, 88% of Canadians would have been better off.

This path-breaking study raises serious questions about continuing Canada's tax cut agenda and provides robust evidence that the taxes Canadians pay contribute substantially to their standard of living by providing them with some of the best public services in the world.

Introduction

. . . .

OVER THE PAST 30 YEARS, and particularly since the early-1990s, public debate over broad fiscal issues in Canada has been dominated by tax cuts, without reference to the services for which taxes pay.

The tax and service debate in Canada in the past 15 years has been almost completely one-sided, and has created a political atmosphere in which tax cuts have become the default answer to virtually every political question.

The overall impact of tax cuts — and the cuts in public services that accompany them — has not been addressed in any substantive way.

At the philosophical level, opponents of widespread tax cuts often make arguments that are a variant of the oft-quoted view of former US Supreme Court Justice Oliver Wendell Holmes that "taxes are what we pay for civilized society", although this leaves open the questions of how we define civilized society and how much of civilized society we actually want to buy.

Another approach is to list services that are dependent on revenue from the tax system for their existence. While this serves politically and rhetorically to remind advocates for tax cuts that there is another side to the question, it doesn't actually provide a meaningful measure of the benefits we receive from public services or address directly the trade-off between the taxes that we pay and the benefits we receive from the services those taxes fund. This paper provides answers to these questions.

Using data and analytical tools from Statistics Canada, we estimate that Canadians enjoy an average $17,000 benefit from the public services which our taxes fund — roughly equivalent to the annual earnings of an individual working full-time at the minimum wage.

Lower-income Canadians benefit more from personal transfer payments (most of which are income-related) but middle- and upper-income Canadians benefit fairly equally from all public services. The public services we use and benefit from change as we go through the life cycle. Seniors, for instance, benefit less directly from public education than they do from public health care — but when they were young parents raising children, the opposite was true.

No matter how you cut it, the data in this study shows how powerful a role public spending plays in ensuring the majority of Canadians enjoy a better quality of life.

For the vast majority of Canada's population, public services are, to put it bluntly, the best deal they are ever going to get. The median Canadian household income (half of Canadians live in households with incomes below that amount; half live in households with incomes above that amount) is approximately $66,000 in a 2.6 person household. That median household realizes a $41,000 benefit from public services. That is equivalent to roughly 63% of that household's private income.

More than ⅔ of Canadians' benefit from public services which are worth more than 50% of their household's total earned income.

This paper also shows that the vast majority of Canadians would also be better off without tax cuts. Our analysis estimates that 80% of Canadians would have been better off if, instead of cutting the GST, the Harper government had transferred the money to local governments to pay for more and better public services.

Compared to the broad-based income tax cuts implemented by provincial governments in the late-1990s and early-2000s, 75% of Canadians would have been better off if their provincial governments had spent the money on health care and education.

And had the federal government invested in improved federal public services instead of cutting capital gains taxation by one third in the early-2000s, 88% of Canadians would have been better off.

In other words, the tax cuts made to sound like free money to middle-income Canadians are anything but. Indeed, the tax cuts implemented in Canada in the last 15 years have had the net effect of reducing the living standards of most Canadians.

What this study measures

THIS STUDY MEASURES the value of public services received by households in each household income group, in the aggregate as well as disaggregated by level of government and type of public service. This in turn supports an exploration of such issues as:

- the distribution of the benefit from public services, by household income group;

- the relative distributive impact of public services based on level of government;

- the size of the social wage — the value of public services received — by household income, in the aggregate and in relation to income and total tax incidence;

- the distributive impact of various types of tax cuts matched by marginal reductions in public services spending; and

- the fiscal bargain — the balance between taxes and public services benefit, by household income.

COMPOSITION OF PUBLIC SPENDING

Chart 1 shows the distribution of public spending in Canada for all three levels of government and C/QPP combined.

Education, social services (including all personal transfer payments) and health together account for about 64% of consolidated public spending in Canada. The

CHART 1 **Distribution of consolidated public spending** Canada, 2006

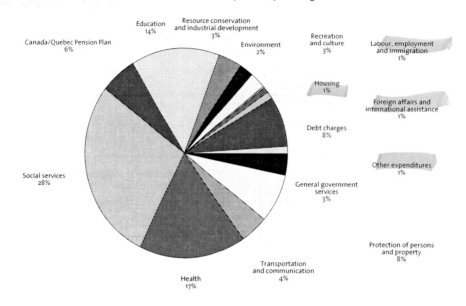

Education
14%

Resource conservation
and industrial development
3%

Canada/Quebec Pension Plan
6%

Environment
2%

Recreation
and culture
3%

Labour, employment
and immigration
1%

Housing
1%

Foreign affairs and
international assistance
1%

Debt charges
8%

Other expenditures
1%

Social services
28%

General government
services
3%

Protection of persons
and property
8%

Transportation
and communication
4%

Health
17%

CHART 2 **Households and population by household income range** 2006

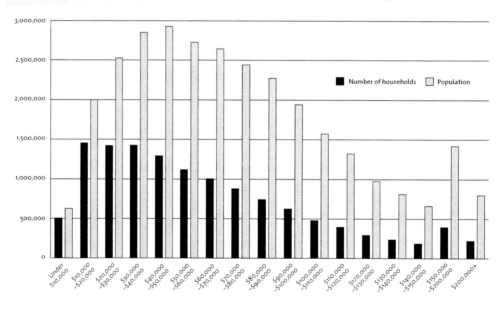

Number of households   Population

only other categories that approach 10% are protection of persons and property and public debt charges.

Statistics Canada's government revenue and expenditure accounts provide data on public spending, by category of public spending and by level of government.[1]

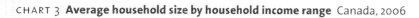

CHART 3 **Average household size by household income range** Canada, 2006

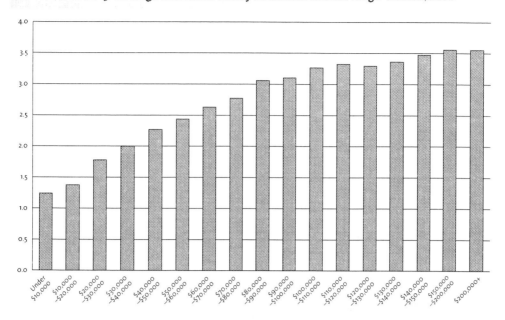

CHART 4 **Distribution of households, population and income**
Canada, 2006, cumulative %

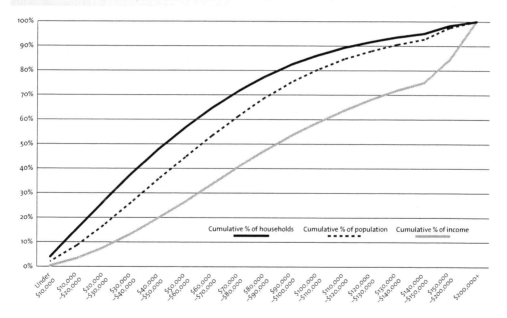

Cumulative % of households   Cumulative % of population   Cumulative % of income

HOUSEHOLD INCOME

Chart 2 shows the number of households for Canada by household income range. Because households vary in size, and because average household size varies systematically with income, we also show the total population of the households in each income range.

Household size increases as household income increases, as chart 3 illustrates.

Chart 4 shows the cumulative percentage of all households and population in households, as income increases.

Households with incomes of less than $80,000 per year represent 72% of households comprising 61% of Canada's population, but account for only 41% of total income.

ESTIMATING THE BENEFIT FROM PUBLIC SERVICES

With detailed data on public spending as a base, we draw on three public data sources to estimate the distribution of benefits by household type and household income level from each category of public spending. Health care utilization data measured by age and household income from the Canadian Institute for Health Information are used to estimate the value of health care services provided to households. Statistics Canada's Social Policy Simulation Database and Model (SPSD/M) and Statistics Canada's Survey of Labour Income Dynamics (SLID) database generate information about household characteristics and expenditure patterns, by household income, which in turn is used to estimate the distribution of benefit from other types of public services.

Details of the allocation methodology are presented in Appendix 2.

It should be emphasized at the outset that by virtue of our use of Statistics Canada's government expenditure data as the basis for the analysis, we are following the convention in public accounting of valuing public services at their cost. To the extent that public programs are supported by a cost-benefit analysis, our implicit assumption is that the net benefit from public services is zero — an extremely conservative assumption.

For the purposes of the analysis, public services are divided into four broad categories. The first category consists of public services for which the allocation of benefit to family types by income can be measured directly using Statistics Canada data series and analysis tools. This category consists primarily of direct personal transfer payments, which make up 21% of public spending.

The second category consists of services for which there are direct proxy measures that closely approximate direct measurement. For example, elementary and secondary education expenditures are allocated based on the number of school-age children in the household. Postsecondary education expenditures are allocated based on the presence of postsecondary students in the household. Health and hospital expenditures respectively are allocated from measures of physician and hospital visits prepared by the Canadian Institute for Health Information. This category accounts for about 36% of public spending.

The third category consists of services for which there are indirect proxy measures for benefit from the service. For example, expenditures on roads and traffic were allocated based on expenditures on motor vehicle fuel and lubricants. Similarly, expenditures on sewer and water services were assumed to be distributed to households on a per capita basis. This category accounts for about 26% of public spending.

The fourth category consists of broadly-based public benefits that are indivisible and cannot be isolated to any individual characteristic or behaviour. Examples include environmental protection, national defence and foreign affairs and international development. These expenditures, accounting for 18% of public services spending, were allocated on a per-capita basis.

The allocation methods set out above generate a distribution of public expenditures, by category of expenditure and by household private income. For the purposes of the analysis, households are grouped by income in $10,000 increments, from $0 to $150,000, for the income range $150,000 to $200,000 and for incomes over $200,000.

Results of the analysis

....

DATA ARE PRESENTED for all income ranges. It should be noted, however, that the characteristics of households with incomes in the ranges $0 to $10,000 and, to a lesser extent $10,000 to $20,000, are somewhat unusual and should be interpreted with caution.[2]

In accordance with the paper's analytical framework, the value of each category of public spending is determined for each household income group using the specific data series selected to estimate each household's benefit from that category of spending. As noted above, public spending is broken down by level of government as well as by type of public service.

These disaggregated amounts are then added together to produce an estimate of the total benefit from public services provided by all governments together, and for each level of government separately.

Chart 5 presents the distribution of per capita benefits from public services, by household income range. Spending is broken down by level of government.

Two patterns are apparent from this chart. First, once household income rises above the median of $50–60,000 per year, benefit from public spending is remarkably evenly distributed on a per-capita basis in households in all income ranges.

Second, it is apparent that the distribution of benefit from public services differs notably among the levels of government. This is illustrated in charts 6, 7 and 8 following.

As one might expect given the important role the federal government plays in the personal income transfer system, the per capita value of federal public services declines, in absolute dollar terms, as income increases to a household income of

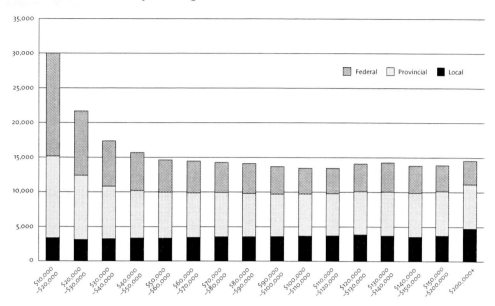

CHART 5 **Per capita benefit from public spending by household income**
Canada, 2006, by level of government

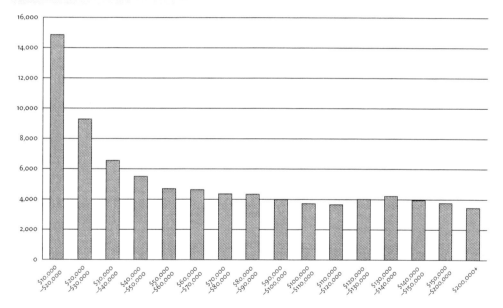

CHART 6 **Per capita benefit from public spending by household income**
Canada, 2006, federal government

approximately $100,000, above which Canadians benefit on consistent per-capita basis. The higher values at low income are due to transfers (OAS/GIS, C/QPP, EI and the Child Tax Benefit).

Provincial spending shows a similar downward slope as income increases, reflecting the provincial governments' responsibility for social assistance benefits. Given the tighter targeting of provincial income assistance programs, benefit from

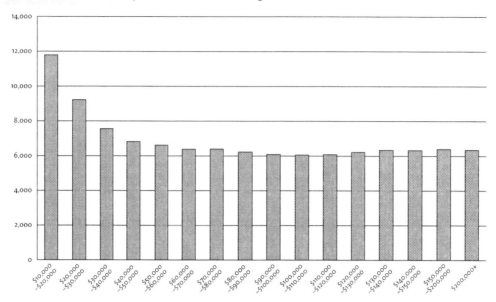

CHART 7 **Per capita benefit from public spending by household income**
Canada, 2006, provincial and territorial governments

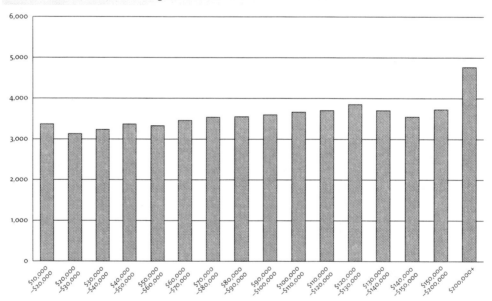

CHART 8 **Per capita benefit from public spending by household income**
Canada, 2006, local governments

public services declines to a relatively stable per capita average at a lower income range — below $40,000.

The higher values at low income are due to transfers (social assistance), postsecondary education (attributed to students) and health care for seniors.

The pattern of benefit from the spending of local governments is quite different from that of both the federal or provincial governments. The per capita absolute dollar benefit from public services delivered by local governments actually increases as household income increases. Two factors explain this phenomenon. First, some of the services delivered by local governments are related in one way or another to consumption, which tends to increase as household income increases. Second, the proportion of a household's population that consists of children increases as income increases. That will tend to produce per capita spending that increases as income increases because of the importance of elementary and secondary education as a local service. More than 40% of local spending is for elementary and secondary education.

For higher-income households, local government is actually more important than it is for households with lower incomes. In fact, measured benefit from local services for high-income households exceeds the measured benefit from federal government services.

There is relatively little variation in the benefit from public services as income increases. Without reference to the revenue sources from which the services are funded, this would appear to suggest that public services do not play a significant role in greater equality. But when you measure public services as a share of income rather than in absolute dollar terms, it becomes clear that public spending does, indeed, play a major redistributive role in Canada.

These findings are fully consistent with the results of an analysis of the impact of public services on the distribution of income in selected industrialized countries conducted by the Organization for Economic Cooperation and development and published in 2008.[3] In the summary of its chapter on public services, it observed:

> Public services to households significantly narrow inequality, although this reduction is typically lower than that achieved by the combined effect of household taxes and public cash transfers. This inequality-reducing effect results mainly from a relatively uniform distribution of these services across the population, which implies that they account for a larger share of the resources of people at the bottom of the distribution than at the top. [OECD 2008, p. 223]

Chart 9 shows how benefit from public services varies as a share of household income, by household income range.

The chart above shows the relationship between benefit from public services and household income. It also illustrates the relationship between public revenue, which is roughly constant as a share of income, and benefit from public services. It illustrates how public services funded from general revenue that deliver equal benefits to all Canadians have a powerful redistributive effect.

This effect is most evident in the middle of the income distribution — the approximately 50% of Canadians that live in households with total incomes between $30,000 and $100,000, in Chart 10.

The benefit middle-income Canadians receive from public services represents a significant proportion of the total resources available to them. Even in the $80,000 to $90,000 household income range — just below the richest 20% — the benefit received from public services is equivalent to about half of the household's private income.

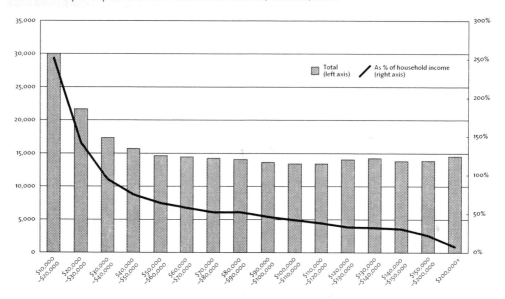

CHART 9 **Benefit from public services and household income**
$ per capita and % of household income, Canada, 2006

Total (left axis) — As % of household income (right axis)

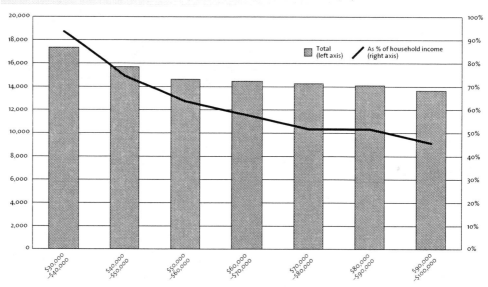

CHART 10 **Benefit from public services and household income** Canada, 2006,
$ per capita and % of household income, middle 50% of population in households

Total (left axis) — As % of household income (right axis)

wow!

In other words, an upper-middle income Canadian household would have to devote half a year's wages to pay for the public services their taxes provide.

The population-weighted median household (half of Canadians live in households with incomes below this level, half in households with incomes above this level) has an income of $66,000 and derives a benefit of $41,000 from public services — equivalent to more than 63% of its income. With an average household size of 2.6 persons per household, the benefit per capita in the median household is $15,724.

CHART 11 **Major categories of public expenditure** Total

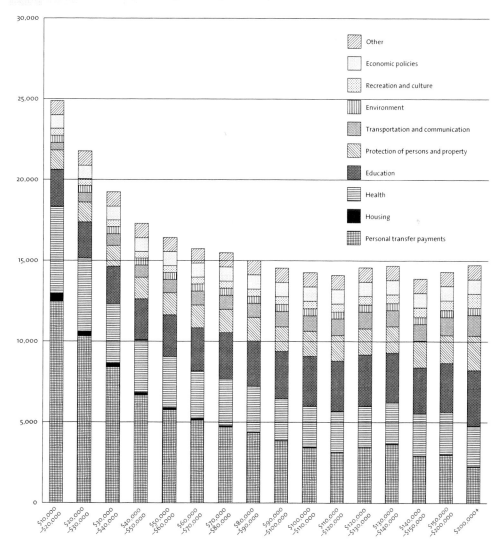

More than two-thirds of Canadians' live in households whose benefit from public services exceeds 50% of the household's private income.

Along with the variations in total benefits from public spending, the composition of benefit from public spending also varies across income ranges.

Chart 11 shows graphically the composition of benefits from public services as it varies from income group to income group. This chart breaks down the benefit from public services per capita in household income ranges into broad categories of public benefit.

Personal transfer payments and health care are relatively more important as sources of benefit from public spending in lower-income ranges than in higher household income ranges, although that effect is partially offset by the greater relative importance of education in public services benefit as income increases. This chart underlines the fact that, for spending in areas other than personal transfer payments, per

TABLE A **Average and Distribution of Benefit from Public Services by Family Type**

	% of Population	Per capita benefit	Education	Health	Transfers	Other
Total	100%	16,527	16%	19%	21%	44%
Couples with only older Kids	11%	14,758	17%	23%	7%	53%
Families with Kids	41%	13,332	29%	15%	13%	43%
Lone Parents with Kids	6%	20,416	28%	12%	24%	37%
Non-Senior Couple: no Kids	15%	15,407	8%	25%	10%	57%
Other	2%	16,740	17%	17%	28%	38%
Senior Couple	12%	21,199	1%	21%	43%	34%
Single Senior	4%	25,386	0%	22%	50%	28%
Single non-seniors	10%	21,929	10%	24%	9%	57%

capita benefit from public services is relatively evenly distributed across household income ranges.

PUBLIC SPENDING CATEGORIES AND FAMILY TYPES

As one might expect, the value and composition of benefit from public services varies across public spending categories and family types.

For example, seniors derive significant benefit from personal transfer payments like Old Age Security, the Guaranteed Income Supplement and the Canada/Quebec Pension Plans. As they age further, they realize increasing benefits from the health care system.

Families with young children will tend to benefit relatively more from the health care system, whereas families with older children will tend to benefit from the public education system to a greater extent than other types of families.

Overall, the average per capita benefit from public services in Canada in 2006 came to $16,952. Approximately 56% of that benefit is derived from expenditures on health and education and personal transfer payments.

Although the average benefit from public services falls within a relatively narrow range, the source of that benefit varies significantly depending on family type.

Not surprisingly, families with children derive a relatively high proportion of their benefit from public services from education, whereas seniors' public services benefit comes predominantly from transfer payments and health care.

Because single seniors tend to be older than senior couples, they derive greater benefit in both absolute and relative terms from health care than senior couples. Lone parents with children derive greater benefit from transfers than families with children generally because lone parent households tend to be lower-income than two-parent households.

That the range of variation in the aggregate is relatively small indicates Canadians draw remarkably similar levels of benefit from public services in the aggregate over their lifetimes, although the specific types of public services that are the source of that benefit vary over their lifetime.

Implications of the analysis
for the tax cut debate

RESULTS FROM THIS STUDY indicate that the movement for tax cuts in Canada has been the political equivalent of a bait-and-switch sales campaign. The populist rhetoric about the tax burden on the ordinary family has given way to actual tax policy changes that have overwhelmingly benefited only a very small proportion of the population — Canada's richest taxpayers.

A recent comprehensive study of tax incidence in Canada conducted by Marc Lee of the Canadian Centre for Policy Alternatives makes it clear that, taken together, tax changes at all levels of government in Canada since the early-1990s have delivered virtually no benefit to most Canadians. They have delivered substantial benefits to those Canadians at the top of the income scale. And they have transformed a mildly progressive tax system into a regressive one. Thanks to the tax cuts of the 1990s, the tax system is now no longer alleviating relative market income inequality in Canada — it is exacerbating inequality.[4]

A significant study from Statistics Canada that focused on income growth at the top end of the income scale in Canada between 1982 and 1992 and between 1992 and 2004 adds considerable detail to the picture. It finds that the income distribution was relatively stable between 1982 and 1992 but that income inequality exploded between 1992 and 2004. It shows that gains in individual real incomes since the early-1990s have gone entirely to Canadians in the top 10% of the income scale and that the resulting increase in the share of total income going to the richest 10% of Canadians has in fact gone predominantly to the richest 1% of Canadians.[5]

tax cuts overwhelmingly benefitted Canada's richest families!!

inequality is exacerbated

Looking at income taxes and CPP premiums, the Statistics Canada study found that while effective tax rates for most Canadians had been relatively stable between 1992 and 2004, effective tax rates on Canadians at the very top of the income scale had come down dramatically.[6] Effective tax rates dropped by three percentage points for the richest 1%; five percentage points for the richest 0.1%; and eleven percentage points for the richest 0.01%.

To look at it another way, roughly 70% of the gains of the richest 10% of tax filers went to the richest 5%; more than 70% of the gain made by the richest 5% went to the richest 1%; nearly 65% of the gains of the richest 1% went to the richest 0.1%; and 80% of the gains of the richest 0.1% went to the top 0.01%.

More than 25% of the tax savings realized by the richest 10% of Canadian tax filers actually went to the richest 1/100 of 1% of tax filers.

Arguments for tax cuts avoid like the plague any reference to their implications for public spending. With good reason. In the real world, budgets have to be balanced and a dollar less revenue means a dollar less to pay for public services. The key question is: with a tax cut balanced off against the corresponding reduction in funding available for public services, who wins and who loses?

For the two main sources of revenue raised from individuals, sales taxes and personal income taxes, the data demonstrate that, regardless of the form of the tax cut or the category of public spending offset against it, the majority of Canadians lose when these broad-based taxes are cut.

To illustrate the point, we look at three political trade-off decisions between tax cuts and public spending made in the past 10 years: the decision of the federal government to cut the GST rather than transfer the equivalent revenue to support program spending by local governments; the decision by all provincial governments to cut personal income taxes and make up for the lost revenue by cutting back on their major spending areas in health care and education; and the decision of the federal government to reduce the inclusion rate for capital gains taxation from 75% of the gain to 50%.

There has been an ongoing public discussion for several years concerning the idea of transferring a point of the GST to local governments to ease their collective financial difficulties. That question surfaced most recently in the debate following the federal mini-budget of October 2007. Municipal leaders argued that if the federal government didn't need the revenue it should transfer the revenue to the level of government that has the most pressing need. The Harper government decided instead simply to cut the GST by 1%.

Chart 12 shows the net impact of a cut in the GST rate by 1% offset against a reduction in spending on public services by local governments across Canada. It shows the per capita net impact of this trade-off, by household income class.

The 1% cut in the GST reduced revenue by a total of $5.7 billion. The alternative in this comparison is to transfer that amount to local governments for spending on local government services generally.

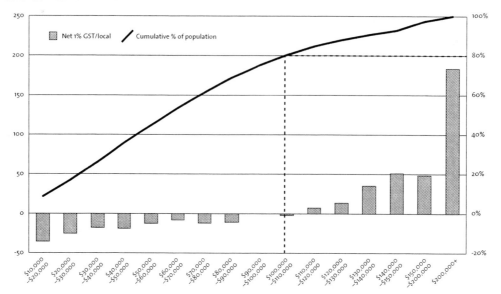

A trade-off of a GST cut against local government services leaves 80% of Canadians worse off. Households with incomes under $110,000 would have been better off had the federal government not cut the GST and instead had transferred the money to local governments to support local services. For households with incomes between $110,000 and $200,000 the net gain never exceeds $50 for a year. For households with incomes over $200,000 the net gain averages $200.

From the mid-1990s until the early-2000s, provincial governments across Canada introduced competitive personal income tax cuts, paid for largely by artificially constraining their spending on education and health. The effect of those spending constraints has been readily visible in the financial pressures on school boards across the country, in large and growing amounts of student debt and deteriorating standards of postsecondary education, and in the crisis in health care at the turn of the 21st century.

Chart 13 illustrates the net effect of this kind of political choice, looking at the net effect of a 1% cut in each personal income tax rate combined with an equivalent reduction in spending on health care and education.

Such a cut would have reduced personal income tax revenue across Canada in 2006 by $7.2 billion.

75% of Canadians would lose as a result of a 1% income tax cut forcing an equivalent reduction or constraint on education and health services spending. Most of those who gain from the trade-off — households earning between $90,000 and $150,000 — gain less than $200 per person from the trade-off. The exception is households with incomes over $200,000 which gain more than $600 per person from the trade-off.

GROWING GAP PROJECT

people would rather have a cheque so they can see where their money is going — forget that many services we use require funding $$ because we expect these services. as Canadians

156

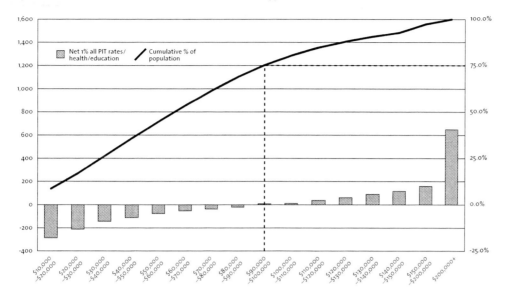

CHART 13 **A 1% cut in each personal income tax rate offset by cuts in education and health services leaves 75% of Canadians worse off**

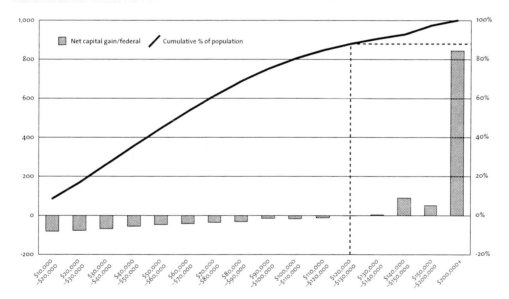

CHART 14 **Reducing the capital gains inclusion rate from 75% to 50% and paying for it with reduced federal public services spending left 88% of Canadians worse off**

In its first two budgets of the 21st century, the federal government introduced the most regressive change in the personal income tax system in Canadian history by reducing the rate of tax on capital gains. Instead of the pre-existing system, in which 75% of realized capital gains were required to be included as income, the government introduced a new regime under which only 50% of gains were included as income.

To illustrate the political choice involved, Chart 14 shows the net impact of a trade-off between federal government services and this one-third cut in the effective tax rate on capital gains.

The gain from the capital gains tax cut is so heavily concentrated at the top of the income scale that households with incomes of less than $130,000 are net losers from the trade-off. Households with incomes between $140,000 and $200,000 gain less than $100 per person in the household. The net gain for households with incomes over $200,000 is nearly $900 per household member.

Fully 88% of Canadians would have been better off if the government had left capital gains taxes where they were, at an inclusion rate of 75%, and allocated the revenue instead to public services.

Conclusion

....

THE RESULTS OF THIS STUDY demonstrate that what passes for public policy debate on tax cuts ignores a significant part of the story. For most Canadians, the benefit they receive from tax cuts is outweighed by a significant margin by their losses from accompanying cuts in public services.

Public services spending improve the quality of life for most Canadians and make Canada a more equal society.

Lower-income Canadians benefit more from transfer payments to people — such as Employment Insurance, social assistance, child benefits, and pensions .

Provincial and local spending has a powerful impact on middle-income Canadians, thanks to public services such as education and health, roads and sewer and water services.

Depending on the type of tax cut, 75% or more of Canadians are net losers when the gains from tax cuts are offset by reductions in public services.

What the findings of this study demonstrate is that public policy debate over taxes without reference to the public services impact of tax cuts is like shopping without looking at the price tags. Just as some Canadians can afford to shop without looking at price tags, some Canadians' incomes are high enough that they can buy into tax cuts and remain confident that their private gains will be greater than their public services losses. But the vast majority of Canadians can't or shouldn't shop without looking at the tags.

1

Desperately Seeking a Successor to the Welfare State

The social welfare state that once prevailed in Canada is no more. During the three decades from the mid-1940s to the mid-1970s, a loose set of social policies and programs labelled "the Keynesian welfare state" (KWS) provided most Canadians with a modest level of economic security and social support.[1] Since the mid-1970s, the Canadian version of the KWS has been dismantled, piece by piece, through a combination of funding cutbacks, program restructuring, and adoption of new social policy assumptions by both federal and provincial levels of government. Even the one aspect of the welfare state not yet dismantled – universal public access to medical and hospital care – has come under extreme pressure across Canada due to insufficient funding. In provinces such as Alberta and Ontario work is underway to turn potentially profitable parts of health care over to private-sector operators and insurers.

None of our politicians have publicly announced the dismantling of the welfare state. Campaigning as the new Conservative leader in the 1984 federal election campaign, Brian Mulroney stated that social programs were a "sacred trust." What the Tories under Mulroney had in mind for social programs, though, was substantial downsizing and a shift from universal to targeted programs. When governing, they had to back away from some of their goals after they encountered strong public opposition. The Liberals under Jean Chrétien came to power in 1993 with a promise to revitalize the social programs that had been launched by their party in the postwar era, but as it turned out they only accelerated the further dismantling of the KWS.

Taking the demise of the KWS[2] as my point of departure, then, I intend in this book to focus on current efforts to rethink and refashion the concept of social welfare in Canada: specifically, the questions of if, how, and to what extent social movements and progressive organizations based in civil society and committed to greater economic and political equality have undertaken the tasks of rethinking "social welfare" in a broad, "philosophical" sense.[3] I will also examine the extent to which social movements and progressive organizations have begun to address practical questions concerning the structure and delivery of social welfare programs[4] so that those programs might better meet the needs and aspirations of Canadians in the new millennium.

The modern concept of social welfare, and its practical expression in the Canadian state's social policy and social programs, have roots that go back to the Elizabethan Poor Law of 1601 (Splane 1965; Guest 1997). The transformation of social welfare in industrial countries – from a charity-based model of providing assistance to the most destitute into a set of state-sponsored programs and entitlements for broad segments of the population – began in the late nineteenth century. In the two and a half decades following World War II, advanced industrial countries launched and expanded publicly provided social welfare programs on a variety of fronts. KWS programs included contributory and universal public pensions, allowances for families with children, better access to health services and post-secondary education, child-care provisions, social housing, and improvements in financial assistance to the poor. These programs worked in combination with state intervention in the economy based on Keynesian principles, aimed at evening out the booms and busts of the capitalist business cycle, and government job-creation initiatives to combat unemployment. Variations on the theme of the Keynesian welfare state emerged in advanced capitalist countries in North America, Western Europe, Australia, and New Zealand.[5]

The high point of development, in terms of resources spent and coverage provided, was reached in the early to mid-1970s, with a subsequent decline in the 1980s and 1990s (Loney 1986; Whitaker 1987; Block et al. 1987; Marchak 1991; McBride 1992; Teeple 2000). The sustained and in the end successful attack on the KWS was waged by a combination of neo-conservative and neo-liberal ideological forces.[6] The resulting retrenchment of social welfare might, perhaps, lead to the conclusion that the KWS was a thirty-year aberration in the longue dureé of unfettered and vicious capitalism to which we have now returned – an analysis very much at variance with the optimistic postwar view (for example, Wilensky and Lebeaux 1958; Marshall 1964; Titmuss 1968) that the welfare state was a new and permanent fixture resulting from the "natural" evolution of capitalism, now tamed and made more "just."

In large part, in Canada, the values and activism of social democrats and organized labour helped to shape the social welfare project in the postwar period. During its tenure, this social welfare project was a success in many ways. The KWS kept income inequality from becoming markedly greater. It ameliorated the problem of poverty among specific groups such as the elderly. It provided virtually the entire population with comprehensive and publicly funded health care. It fostered a substantial degree of upward social mobility through higher education and an expanding labour market for those born into the middle and working classes.

In the last two decades of the twentieth century, given the increasing global power of transnational corporations, social-democratic approaches to social welfare and social equality became increasingly ineffective. The growing reach of global capital over and against public-policy formulation and Keynesian economic measures at the national level brought to an end the social-democratic welfare state project. What John McMurtry (1998) describes as a fundamentalist and rigid "market theology," which deifies private enterprise and the quest for profit, has gone a substantial distance towards replacing popular faith in collective welfare measures and the "civil commons."

The dismantling of the KWS was initially advocated in Canada by organizations representing the interests of large corporations, such as the Business Council on National Issues (BCNI) (Langille 1987). This attack on the welfare state was subsequently taken up by political forces on the right,[7] including the federal Conservative party during its time in government from 1984 to 1993 (McQuaig 1993). The BCNI and the Tories fashioned their strategy and policies in many ways after those of formations of business and the political right in Britain (under Prime Minister Margaret Thatcher) and in the United States (under President Ronald Reagan). Still, as Reg Whitaker (1987) argues, the Canadian new right of the 1980s was not able to reshape the welfare state as quickly or as radically as its British and U.S. counterparts did.

The Canadian state's efforts to scale down and dismantle social programs[8] have frequently provoked strong and widespread opposition. Among other things, the critics have called into question the motives behind government efforts to dismantle the KWS. On at least some occasions, social program cuts have also forced progressive constituencies to scrutinize their own positions in regard to the strengths and weaknesses of the KWS. On one hand the corporate media, the economic elite, and politicians of all stripes (including many social-democrats)[9] have been promoting "restructuring" and "rethinking" of social programs with a view to rationalizing and legitimating the right's attack on the welfare state. On the other hand, groups struggling for economic justice and social equality have responded to attacks on the welfare state by engaging, at least in some cases, in new and more or less radical discourses[10] on the future of social welfare.

During the early phases of the new right's attack on the KWS, many progressive organizations and movements (representing constituencies such as labour, feminists, and social policy advocates) and parties on the left (especially the New Democratic Party) argued that the programs and entitlements of the KWS needed to be preserved and consolidated. Gradually, though, the attempts to defend the KWS were de-legitimated and marginalized. A new "hegemonic discourse"[11] pointed to the unfettered marketplace as the mechanism best suited to generate economic growth and distribute wealth efficiently and fairly. This new discourse was linked to the increasingly powerful mythology of social spending as the root cause of growing government deficits and debt.[12] This mythology in turn added to the credibility of pressure coming from business groups and the media for cuts to social programs.

Of course, this radical shift in discourses on social welfare did not occur in an economic and political vacuum. From the late 1970s onwards came dramatic economic restructuring, sometimes described as a transition to post-Fordism,[13] which has resulted in the decline of the relative security of middle-class incomes and a growing gap between the poor and the wealthy (Yalnizyan 1998). In Canadian politics at the national level, the dramatic shift to the right begun by the Mulroney Conservative government was continued and entrenched after the election of the Chrétien Liberal government in 1993. The strongly neo-conservative Reform Party became the Official Opposition in the House of Commons as a result of the 1997 federal election. Early in the year 2000 the Reform Party evolved into the Canadian Alliance in an effort to bring right-wing Tories into the fold, capture voter support in Ontario, and obtain greater financial backing from big business.

Rightward shifts also occurred in provincial politics over the 1980s and 1990s, with the election of neo-conservative/neo-liberal governments such as Sterling Lyon's Conservatives in Manitoba, Grant Devine's Conservatives in Saskatchewan, Bill Vander Zalm's Social Credit in British Columbia, Ralph Klein's Conservatives in Alberta, and

Mike Harris's Conservatives in Ontario. Even NDP provincial governments under Glen Clark in British Columbia, Roy Romanow in Saskatchewan, and Bob Rae in Ontario retreated from their former level of support for social programs. They adopted a more business-friendly tone and abandoned their party's traditional willingness to intervene in the economy in the interests of social equality and planned development.

By the late 1980s and early 1990s, parties all across the political spectrum, along with broad sections of civil society, had joined the new hegemonic discourse calling for the deconstruction of the KWS. What was largely absent was a counter-hegemonic discourse emanating from the left, from labour, and from equality-seeking social movements – a discourse capable of articulating new social welfare programs, policies, and paradigms. But by the end of the 1990s and as the new century dawned, counter-hegemonic voices on social welfare were becoming more prominent.

Progressive Theories of Social Welfare

Practical struggles to build a viable alternative to the postwar welfare state in the interests of economic justice and social equality must be rooted in a sound intellectual understanding of social welfare. Theoretical work on social welfare should reflect on lessons of the past, accurately analyse present circumstances, and set out a workable vision for the future.

Several writers have set out what I would call "critical-left-progressive" perspectives.[14] In his typology of welfare state theories, James Struthers (1994) outlines three such perspectives: the social-democratic model, Marxist and neo-Marxist theories, and gender analysis of the welfare state.[15] Christopher Pierson (1991) identifies two additional categories: the anti-racist critique and the green critique of the welfare state. Glenn Drover and Patrick Kerans (1993) and Jürgen Habermas (1989) identify one other useful theoretical perspective in understanding social welfare: what might be (somewhat clumsily) labelled the emancipatory needs-articulation approach.

We will examine each of these six theoretical vantage points in turn as keys to a general retheorization of social welfare.

1. Social-Democratic Perspectives

Struthers (1994: 8) describes the social-democratic model of the welfare state as the result of "pressure from the left":

"The level of any nation's or region's social policy development reflects the extent to which the working class, through trade union organization and political organization, can move the state to meet its needs rather than those of capital."

Walter Korpi pioneered this view in his highly influential power-resource model of welfare state development.[16] Korpi (1983: 15) defines power resources as "characteristics which provide actors – individuals and collectivities – with the ability to punish or reward other actors." Of prime importance as power resources in this scheme are "capital and control over the means of production" and "human capital,' i.e., labour power, education and occupational skills" (p.16). Compared to the business interests, which control capital, the owners of labour power – that is, the wage-earning members of the working class – are inherently at a disadvantage in regard to the exercise of power. By organizing their efforts in trade unions and political parties on the left, however, wage-earners can make use of the distribution of power more equal. They can make use of tripartite societal bargaining among the state, labour, and capital in order to achieve redistribution of wealth, protection in the workplace, and programs of social insurance and social support for working people.

The power-resource model portrays the state as a site of struggle between labour and capital, and as a somewhat neutral and potentially friendly arbitrator on behalf of the working class in relation to capital. The model assumes that the state can and will do the "right" things, from the point of view of workers, if only social-democratic parties and organized labour can achieve and maintain electoral power. This theorization of politics and the welfare state is at variance with the neo-Marxist conception of the capitalist state (Miliband 1969; Poulantzas 1973; Panitch 1977), which sees the governments in capitalist societies as having an unwavering commitment (regardless of which electoral party achieves power) to the processes of capital accumulation, to the legitimation and reproduction of these arrangements, and if necessary to the use of coercive power to maintain them.

Power-resource theory assumes more or less *zero sum* bargaining between capital and labour. Coming out of a neo-Marxist background, Claus Offe (1984: 194) argues that under the particular conditions of Keynesianism, the welfare state was a *positive sum* arrangement for both capital and labour. This situation changed, however, when Keynesian economic policies were abandoned and the KWS entered a period of

protracted crisis, with the globalization of capital and the transfer of employment to low-wage newly industrializing countries – when unions and social-democratic parties arguably came to play a *negative sum* game. Organized labour and the electoral left began to focus on minimizing losses in a context of adverse economic and political circumstances.

Gosta Esping-Andersen (1990) developed the highly influential typology of national welfare state regimes, classifying specific national versions of them as liberal, conservative-corporatist, and social-democratic.[17] He remains an influential social-democratic theorist of social welfare. He argues that, despite the end of the "golden age" of postwar growth and prosperity, "the degree of welfare state roll-back, let alone significant change, has so far been modest" with the two exceptions of Britain and New Zealand. Nonetheless, he also argues: "Marginal cuts [to social welfare programs] today may have long-term cumulative effects of a quite radical nature. If social benefits gradually fall behind earnings, those who can seek compensation in private insurance will do so, thus weakening broad support for the welfare state" (Esping-Andersen 1996: 10).

According to Esping-Andersen (1996: 10-20), governments have made three general responses to the economic and social changes that have occurred since the end of the golden age.[18] Firstly, Scandinavian countries have (until recently) compensated for rising unemployment with the expansion of public-sector jobs, and have (more recently) emphasized social investment strategies to better equip working age persons for the labour market. In the Scandinavian context there is a need to revitalize the "consensus building infrastructure" of a corporatist nature (p.15).

The second adaptation to economic restructuring, which has been taken by English-speaking democracies (to a greater or lesser extent), is "the neo-liberal route" of deregulating labour markets and the private sector, and allowing wage structures to become more "flexible." While this approach does lead to the expansion of employment, Esping-Andersen (1996: 17) cites evidence that it also "nurtures employment growth in low-productivity 'lousy jobs' where even full-time, all-year employment results in below-poverty income." The outcome is "rising inequality and poverty" (p.16).

Countries in continental Western Europe have shown the third response to economic and social restructuring: that of labour-force reduction through measures such as early retirement, and denying or withdrawing supports for women, such as maternity benefits and child care, that facilitate their participation in the labour market. While this approach keeps unemployment rates low, it also makes the cost of social insurance very high, fosters the underground economy, and creates an insider/outsider problem. The approach protects male participants in the primary labour market, but marginalizes and excludes women, youth, and those not covered by social insurance (Esping-Andersen 1996: 18-20).

Esping-Andersen (1996: 20-24) analyses how other countries in East-Central Europe, East Asia, and Latin America are taking different routes to constructing social welfare infrastructure, and points out the similarities and differences in their approaches compared to the longer-established welfare states in Western Europe, North America, Australia, and New Zealand. For instance, in East-Central Europe, Chile, and Argentina, liberal social welfare regimes feature the privatization of social insurance (p.20). Still, some countries such as Brazil and Costa Rica have "so far shunned neo-liberalism" and have "taken some steps towards strengthening their public social safety nets" by extending universality of coverage (p.21). Finally, East Asian countries tend to develop a hybrid welfare regime premised on traditional gender roles in the family and featuring (in the conservative-corporatist welfare state model) state provision of social benefits for privileged workers in the public sector and military, and (in the liberal welfare state model) occupational welfare provisions for private-sector workers who are fortunate enough to be situated in the primary labour market.

2. Marxian and Neo-Marxian Approaches

According to Struthers (1994: 10), Marxist and neo-Marxist theorists of the welfare state "argue that the welfare state is an instrument of social control, or that it reflects more contradictory purposes of serving the needs of both capital accumulation and state legitimation."

Neo-Marxian theoretical streams understand the Keynesian welfare state as something of a paradox (Gough 1979; Therborn 1984; Finkel 1977). On the one hand, the KWS was the product of the struggle by labour and other social movements against capital in order to obtain a modicum of economic security and social equality. On the other hand, the KWS was also a set of economic and political arrangements that served the interests of capital in a particular set of economic and political circumstances. The KWS secured peace with labour and ensured the

conditions for rapid capital accumulation during the thirty-year economic boom following World War II. As a compromise between labour and capital, the KWS was both a result of class struggle and a means of containing class conflict.

Offe (1984) presents a useful analysis of the Keynesian welfare state's contradictions, which have led to its deterioration since the mid-1970s. Following in the theoretical traditions of Marx and Polanyi, he argues that the capitalist economy treats living labour as if it were an inert commodity. But he also argues that the welfare state to some extent sets in place programs that decommodify labour and take workers out of the nexus of wage dependence and reliance on the capitalist labour market. This contradiction was sustainable during the long postwar boom, when economic growth not only generated a tax dividend to finance the welfare state but also limited demand on welfare state entitlements by keeping unemployment relatively low. The welfare state was also enabled by governments' Keynesian commitment to maintain consumer demand through transfer payments to individuals and families. When economic growth faltered and governments abandoned Keynesian economic policies for monetarist measures starting in the mid-1970s, two legs (high levels of employment and consumer demand, both premised on strong economic growth) of the three-legged KWS stool became wobbly. The third leg (social programs) came under stress and was considerably weakened.

Offe does not take the position that the welfare state is on the brink of extinction. He argues that the welfare state is "irreversible" (Offe 1984: 287) and adds:

> The "dismantling" of the welfare state would result in widespread conflict and forms of anomic and "criminal" behaviour that together would be more destructive than the enormous burdens of the welfare state itself. The welfare state is indeed a highly problematic, costly and disruptive arrangement, yet its absence would be even more disruptive. Welfare state capitalist societies simply cannot be remodelled into something resembling pure market societies. (Offe 1984: 288)

Offe also points to other inherent contradictions. For instance, he accepts the prima facie arguments of the right that welfare programs create disincentives for investment and work and diminish profits margins, al-

3. Feminist Perspectives

According to Struthers (1994: 15), the gender analysis of the welfare state emphasizes the dependency of women and children on the male breadwinner, the bifurcation of social welfare into insurance-based entitlements for men and needs-tested and stigmatizing programs for women, and the activity of women as "clients, reformers, and state employees" in the welfare state.

In a relatively early call to bring gender into welfare state analysis, Caroline Andrew (1984: 667) argued, "The relations between women and the welfare state...are ambiguous, perhaps even contradictory, but they are vital." Andrew contends that in both pluralist and Marxist conceptions of the welfare state, "the broad concentration on economics and production has meant that gender has not been given a central importance in analyses" of welfare state development (p.669). Looking at things historically, Andrew further contends that "the reform era from 1880 to 1920" helped to "set the stage for the later development of the fully-formed welfare state," and that "women's organizing and women's organizations are crucial to the developments of this period" (p.670). She also points to the central roles of women in the welfare state as workers and as clients (pp. 676-82).

Jane Ursel (1992: 9-11) puts consideration of welfare in the broader context of "state mediation of the restructuring of production and reproduction," which she divides into three different periods. The first period (1884-1913) saw measures by the state (at the federal and provincial levels in Canada) aimed at addressing "the use of women and children in the labour force and the consequent disruptions of family dynamics." Through the adoption of labour and family laws, the state provided "legislative and social discouragement of women's employment in combination with the legislative enforcement of men's role as providers [which] created the support-service marriage structure, the male-breadwinner, female-home-maker division of labour" (p.10). Restriction of women's and children's participation in the wage-labour market, however, created "an income crisis for the family." This crisis led to a second period of state intervention in the family (1914-39), characterized by "the development of more systematic structures for the support of the family (welfare law), while extending the limitations on female and child labour (labour law) and elaborating on legislation to ensure familial support of its members (family law)" (p.11). Finally, in the third period (1940-68) the state had to respond to "an income shortage at the household level" and "a la-

though he adds that these criticisms ignore "inherent crisis tendencies of the capitalist economy such as overaccumulation, the business cycle, or uncontrolled technological change" (pp.149-52). He also posits as valid the arguments of the left that the capitalist welfare state is ineffective, inefficient, and repressive, and performs a political-ideological control function (pp.154-57). He postulates that efforts to reshape the welfare state in the post-Keynesian era have three possible outcomes:

· i) a "neo-laissez-faire coalition, based on an alliance of big capital and the old middle class";

ii) "the 'right dose' of welfare state expansion," which "would involve the extensive reliance on 'neo-corporatist' or 'tripartite' models of decision-making," but would exclude the old middle class and unorganized sections of the working class; and

iii) "a non-bureaucratic, decentralized, and egalitarian model of a self-reliant 'welfare society'" brought about through efforts of working-class organizations, elements of the new middle class, and new social movements (Offe 1984: 158-59).

Scott Lash and John Urry (1987) set out one way of conceptualizing the post-Keynesian transformation. They argue that we have moved from "organized" to "disorganized" capitalism. A characteristic of organized capitalism was the "development of class-specific welfare-state legislation" in conjunction with "the increased representation of diverse interests in and through the state" (Lash and Urry 1987: 3). The stage of disorganized capitalism manifests "the breakdown of most neo-corporatist forms of state regulation of wage bargaining" and "challenges from left and right to the centralized welfare state" (pp.5-6). They argue that, although welfare expenditures will not grow, the welfare state can be preserved through efforts of various social movements and interests (pp.230-31). At the same time, they foresee "less bureaucratized, more decentralized and in [some] cases more privatized forms as the welfare state of organized capitalism makes way for a much more varied and less centrally organized form of welfare provision in disorganized capitalism" (p.231).

education, and maintain their rights and benefits despite conservative and religious backlash. This new way of looking at women and welfare must "expand...women's choices beyond the alternatives of dependency (on men or the state) or inferior employment" (p. 195). These normative claims amount to a "new welfare politics." Gordon (p. 195) states:

The transformation of welfare into a non-stigmatizing, empowering system, one that encourages independence rather than dependence, must include a higher valuation of the work of child-raising and nurturance of dependants, an end to discrimination against women and minorities in the labour force, *and a* radical increase in employment opportunities overall.

Ann Orloff (1996) argues that an analysis of the impact of welfare state measures on women must move beyond the simplistic bifurcation of welfare programs as either a means of reproducing the oppression of women by men or a means of ameliorating gender inequality. She outlines the contradictory effects of maternalism discourses on the establishment of social welfare programs (Orloff 1996: 57-63). She also calls for comparative international case studies of welfare states as a way of understanding "the mutual effects of gender relations and welfare states" (pp. 73-74). In a similar vein, Julia O'Connor (1996) argues that it is necessary to move beyond analysing women *in* the welfare state to an understanding of the "gendering of welfare state regimes."

4. The Anti-Racist Critique of the Welfare State

Pierson (1991: 80) points to the "double process of disadvantage" that racial and ethnic minorities confront in relation to welfare state apparatuses: "First, their economically and socially less privileged position tends to make them more reliant upon provision through the welfare state. Secondly, this welfare state very often treats them on systematically less favourable terms than members of the majority community."

Frances Fox Piven and Richard A. Cloward (1987) point out that the ideological attack against social welfare entitlements in the United States "has veered away from programs where the idea of economic rights is most firmly established" (such as social security), which mostly benefit the white middle class. Instead, the attack on the U.S. welfare state has centred on "welfare and the nutritional subsidies for the poor" and par-

---

bour shortage at the production level." During this period, "The central task of the state became one of realignment of income and labour flows between the two spheres [of household and wage labour market] and a restructuring of the state to accommodate the increasing demand to so-cialize costs of reproduction (p.11). According to Ursel, this last stage completed "the transition from familial to social patriarchy."

Isabella Bakker (1996: 32) looks at the situation of women in the more recent period of welfare state shrinkage, pointing to "the dual pressures of women's increased labour-force participation and the simultaneous contraction of the Keynesian welfare state." Furthermore, reflecting on the macroeconomic framework within which social welfare policy and programs operate, she argues:

Macro-economics is androcentric because the male worker/con-sumer/citizen is often assumed to be the norm (that is, the policy target). The interactions between paid and unpaid labour are left out of modelling considerations, as indeed are any observations from the "soft" disciplines (that is, not math and statistics) about social networks and people's personal histories.... The macro level is conceived...as dealing with aggregates and not talking about men or women. (Bakker 1996: 32)

Nancy Fraser (1989: 144-60) points out the bifurcated structure of so-cial welfare programs based on gender. Male wage-earners are the ben-eficiaries of rights-based, non-stigmatizing, contributory social insur-ance programs such as unemployment insurance and public pensions. Women are assumed to be dependent on male breadwinners, and the so-cial welfare programs set up to provide for women (social assistance, for instance) are needs-tested, more subject to bureaucratic discretion, and premised on implicit and sometimes explicit forms of stigmatization and moral correction.[19]

Linda Gordon (1990) sets out an explicitly socialist-feminist perspec-tive on the welfare state. She argues for a "new welfare scholarship," which would encompass "racial and gender relations of power," "the agency of these subordinated groups in the construction of programmes and policies," and a recognition of the welfare state as "a complex, multi-layered and often contradictory cluster" (Gordon 1990: 192). She also calls for scholarship that situates women's welfare in relation to their ability to make reproductive choices, obtain employment and higher

ticularly on the (now completely defunct) federal social assistance program called Aid to Families with Dependent Children (AFDC). As Piven and Cloward (1987: 48) argue:

Singling out AFDC inevitably becomes an attack on minorities. A majority of the women and children on AFDC are blacks and Hispanics; the charges [of critics of the welfare state] are not so much against "dependent Americans" as against "dependent minority Americans." Race is a deep and fiercely divisive factor in this division and draws strength from it.

Writing on the experience of people of African ancestry with the British welfare state, Fiona Williams (1987: 18) argues:

What is needed for social policy...is an approach which is formulated according to the experiences of Black people as workers (including welfare workers), as consumers of welfare, and those engaged in struggles over welfare. It has to be based on an historical analysis of racism, imperialism, and neo-imperialism, in their articulation with the main goals of the welfare state: accumulation, reproduction, control [through] legitimation/repression.

Social policy's role in reflecting and reproducing racial inequality is also evident in the Canadian context. The Report of the Royal Commission on Aboriginal Peoples documents the systematic abuse and resulting social dysfunction visited upon Native peoples when they were sent as children to government-funded residential schools run by Christian churches (Canada 1996a: 333–409). The Royal Commission also documents the social, economic, and cultural devastation of First Nations communities that were forcibly relocated by the federal government (pp. 411–543). More generally, the Royal Commission points to:

the process by which Aboriginal peoples were systematically dispossessed of their lands and their livelihood, their cultures and languages, and their social and political institutions.... This was done through government policies based on the false assumptions that Aboriginal ways of life were at a primitive level of evolutionary development; and that the high point of human development was to

be achieved by adopting the culture of European colonists. (Canada 1996b: 2)

The outcomes of these "ethnocentric and demeaning attitudes" are that "Aboriginal people in Canada endure ill health, insufficient and unsafe housing, polluted water supplies, inadequate education, poverty and family breakdown" (p.1). Looking to the future, the Royal Commission argues that the solution to "the painful legacy of displacement and assimilation policies that have undermined the foundations of Aboriginal societies" lies in the "redistribution of power and resources so that Aboriginal people can pursue their social and economic goals and regain their health and equilibrium through means they choose freely" (p.2).

In her study of community employment services for immigrant women, Roxanna Ng (1988) uses a theoretical framework that synthesizes a Marxist understanding of class with sensitivity to oppression based on gender and ethnicity. She provides a useful example of how such a holistic and critical theory can be applied to the analysis of community programs, including the racist aspects of human services. Daiva Stasiulis (1997: 159) argues in a more general way that the official multiculturalism of the federal Canadian state has not only failed to make "palatable for ethnic minorities their exclusion from the settler-society construct of a 'bilingual and bicultural' Canada," but has also enabled state officials and elites to hide behind "the antiquated white, Christian definitions of the country." The policy has thus indirectly contributed to greater restrictions on entry, eligibility for citizenship, and access to public services for "the multitude of racialized and ethnic 'Others.'"

5. The Green Critique of the Welfare State

Pierson (1991: 92–95) argues that a green critique consists of two general thrusts. On one hand, the "welfare state and the logic of industrialism" critique puts forth the position that welfare provision is "embedded in an industrial order which itself is premised upon economic growth" that is no longer environmentally sustainable. Regardless of the sanguine outcomes of the welfare state in terms of economic security or redistribution, it depends on an expanding economy based upon overproduction, resource depletion, pollution, and the environmentally irrational use of the factors of production. These costs make the capitalist welfare state insupportable in ecological terms in the long run. Pierson (p. 94) argues that the social-democratic version of the welfare state "means 'bracketing out' a whole range of radical issues (including socialization of production, workers' control, quality of life, planning) which were a part of the traditional ideological baggage of pre-welfare state socialism." He also points to the problem that "the welfare state represents a national rather global response to the problem of reconciling general social welfare with economic growth."

The other thrust to the green critique, according to Pierson (1991: 94-95), is the "welfare state as social control" argument. The focus here is on "the exercise of 'micro-power' over the individual" through "disabling professions," transformation of citizens into consumers, and the displacement of democratic process with bureaucratic administration: "Insofar as social welfare is a response to real needs – and not simply to the 'false needs' created by the requirements of industrial capitalism – these can only be satisfactorily met by small scale, co-operative, 'bottom up' self-production and self-management" (p. 95).

6. The Emancipatory Needs-Articulation Approach to Social Welfare

Drover and Kerans (1993) have put forward an innovative approach to social welfare theory. They argue for the necessity of moving beyond utilitarian and contractarian concepts of welfare, and beyond the supposedly objective notions of need as determined by experts, which have permeated thinking in social policy circles and on much of the political left. "The welfare state has not broken past the assumption that people are infinite consumers of utilities," they say (Drover and Kerans 1993: 5-6). They advocate the reformulation of welfare as "the development of human capabilities" and point out the "duality of welfare": it comprises not only autonomy based on a stable social order and an ideal of universal justice, but also emancipation, which works through never-ending claimsmaking to achieve a more satisfactory set of social arrangements. This duality sets up "a series of dialectical tensions...between the self and society, between justice and the good life, and between a 'thin' and a 'thick' understanding of need" (pp. 8-9).

According to Drover and Kerans, it is necessary to make "the shift from compensatory welfare to empowering welfare."

Welfare as the reallocation of resources gives rise to a deficit model of the welfare state: those who fall below some agreed-upon community standard – for instance a poverty line – are construed as deficient and should be compensated by the rest of us who are its ben-

eficiaries. Welfare as the development of human capacities, by contrast, is empowering. It implies that society is not divided into those who can cope and those who are deficient; rather, everyone requires the help of others in order to develop. (Drover and Kerans 1993:6)

The second implication is: "Welfare as empowerment entails a profound diversity or pluralism in people's understanding of their needs and therefore of their welfare. What is central is the struggle over the interpretation of needs" (Drover and Kerans 1993: 6).

Certainly, a commitment to empowerment and choice in the interpretation of human need and in claims-making processes, at both individual and collective levels, must be at the heart of reformulating our concept of social welfare for the years ahead. At the same time we need to situate this commitment to emancipatory needs-articulation, and its ideological and practical corollaries, within a clear and evolving understanding of how political-economic power is exercised at all levels of society. The power of capital in relation to economic processes and political discourses can constrain the articulation and achievement of pluralistic and "thick" visions of social welfare. This constraint seems to be particularly true in the present era, when the power of transnational corporations reaches around the globe and limits the ability of democratically elected governments and international bodies representing the public good to act effectively.

Habermas (1989: 292-95) is one critic who has discussed the potential for emancipatory reimagining of social welfare, while situating this potential within actually existing political and economic forces. He points out the emergence of three bodies of opinion regarding the welfare state. The social-democratic "legitimists" are today's "true conservatives." They argue for the need "to find a point of equilibrium between the development of a welfare state and a modernization based on a market economy" (Habermas 1989: 293). The "neo-conservatives" argue for "supply-side economic policy" to "set the process of capital accumulation back in motion," while calling for "definite reductions in social welfare services" (Habermas 1989: 293). The third group represents a challenge to both of these conventional ways of thinking about the welfare state. The "critics of growth" have "an ambivalent attitude toward the welfare state." This "antiproductivist alliance" is composed of "minorities of the most diverse origins" and includes "the old and the young, women and the unemployed, gays and the handicapped, [religious] believers and non-believers" (Habermas 1989: 294). These critics of growth

> start from the premise that the lifeworld is equally threatened by commodification *and* bureaucratization; neither of the two media, money and power, is by nature "more innocent" than the other.... Only [critics of growth] demand that the inner dynamic of subsystems regulated by power and money be broken, or at least checked, by forms of organization that are closer to the base and self-administered. In this context, concepts of a dual economy and proposals for the decoupling of social security and employment come into play. (Habermas 1989: 295)

Habermas goes on to combine elements of the green critique of social welfare with neo-Marxist and emancipatory needs-articulation perspectives. He says that the "dissident critics of a growth-oriented society" must take the lead so that:

> The welfare state project [is] neither simply maintained nor simply terminated but rather continued at a higher level of reflection. A welfare state project that has become reflective, that is directed not only to restraining the capitalist economy but to controlling the state itself, would, of course, lose labour as its central point of reference. (Habermas 1989: 296)

He points out that the introduction of a guaranteed minimum income in a "reflective" welfare state that is no longer built around the labour market would be "revolutionary, but not revolutionary enough":

> Modern societies have at their disposal three resources...money, power, and solidarity. The respective spheres of influence of these three resources would have to be brought into a new balance. By this I mean that the integrative social force of solidarity would have to be able to maintain itself in the face of the "forces" of the other two regulatory resources, money and administrative power. (Habermas 1989: 296)

Habermas (1989: 297) sees this reflection upon and reformulation of a more solidaristic version of social welfare as occurring in an arena of

non-elites, which operates independently of (and perhaps in opposition to) "identifiable political elites within the state apparatus," and powerful interest groups, which "control access to the means of production and communication" and thereby shape decisions of the political elite.

Towards a Theoretical Synthesis

The traditional social-democratic strategies for achieving equality and well-being that characterized the KWS are no longer adequate. Social-democratic theoretical approaches no longer adequately address, conceptually or programmatically, the questions of how to curb the power of transnational capital, how to reorganize economic activities for the public good, or how to ensure that politicians and bureaucrats (including those directly involved in social welfare) are working in the interests of those citizens rather than working to protect and enhance accumulation of wealth by economic elites.

If the social-democratic social welfare project is theoretically exhausted and practically immobilized, then other theories of social welfare are more likely to point us in productive directions. Neo-Marxian theoretical approaches unmask and specify the structure and dynamics of transnational capital, and the reproduction of capitalist hegemony through social institutions such as the welfare state. Feminist and anti-racist critiques of the welfare state point to intersecting and frequently compounding forms of domination, based on gender differences or ethno-cultural identity, that contribute to the structuration of social inequality in the era of global corporate rule. The green critique of social welfare challenges the productivist ethic and the bureaucratic and technological forms of social control that are deeply inscribed in social policy formulation and social program delivery in the capitalist welfare state. Finally, the emancipatory needs-articulation perspective points the way towards more democratic, inclusive, and nuanced processes for defining and realizing social welfare in innovative and radical senses of the term.

What remains to be seen, in the attempt to chart ways forward beyond the social-democratic welfare state, is how the ideas and efforts of social movements can guide us in specific ways in reimagining social welfare.

From Theory to Issues

The theoretical perspectives pertaining to social welfare point us towards a set of four contested issues and fundamental debates in social policy. First of all, the development of welfare programs has always been intimately connected to changing structures and processes of people's work. In simple terms, the question might be asked, "What counts as real work that is valued both socially and economically?" Therefore, any reimagining of social welfare must tackle the issue of

• how to broaden our understanding of **socially necessary and useful work** in all its forms in Canadian society, including paid work in the labour market, unpaid caring work in the family, and various forms of service in the community. All of these different forms of work contribute to social welfare broadly defined (chapter 2).

The question of how we understand and financially recognize work in all its forms is closely tied to people's level of economic security. In industrial capitalist economies most people have to sell their labour power in the labour market in order to survive economically. Welfare state programs in their most highly developed forms have served only to supplement or temporarily replace (at a very minimal level) labour-market incomes. Therefore, building on an expanded and enriched understanding of work, we will also focus on the question of

• how to ensure an **adequate economic livelihood and material standard of living for all**, given labour-market restructuring over the last quarter of the twentieth century, the shrinking levels of social support through programs that comprised the Keynesian welfare state, rising economic inequality, and the fundamental questions of economic redistribution raised by these changes (chapter 3).

In a fundamental sense, the welfare state project has always been about trying to achieve a greater degree of social equality in democratic societies. Often, however, social policy discourse has restricted the goal of "equality" to the reapportionment of economic resources and the standardized delivery of a limited set of services. The approach pays insufficient attention to how to make equality concrete in regard to diverse individual and collective identities, and in regard to the distinctive social characteristics of persons and communities. The understanding of social welfare as "one size fits all" has been profoundly challenged by the rise of "new social movements" and identity politics in recent decades, and we

must now rethink social equality and social welfare in ways that take us beyond the redistribution of economic resources, as important as this is. We face the challenge of

• how to extend our understanding of **social equality** beyond access to economic resources, in order to incorporate the rich **diversity of human capabilities and needs**, and the variegated nature of **individual and collective identities** (chapter 4).

Another necessity is to explore the relationship of social welfare policy to a broadened conception of citizenship in our communities, our nation, and our world. Citizens are more often than not excluded from having a genuine and effectual role in defining social policy goals and in overseeing and influencing efforts to reach these goals. If we are genuinely committed to the democratic process, then we must come up with practical ways for citizens to be significantly involved in formulating their own conceptions of social equality and economic justice, and in translating these conceptions into reality.

Our understanding of citizenship can also be strengthened by situating it within growing concerns about local and global environmental sustainability. Environmental concerns have given rise to "green" politics in recent years, and to a growing awareness of the need to change our economic assumptions, expectations, and behaviours if we are to survive and flourish in the fragile and threatened environment of our biosphere. The challenge here, then, becomes

• how to extend and reshape our understanding of **citizenship**. We face the challenge of **building on the concept of social rights** of citizens to welfare programs that was an innovation of the Keynesian welfare state. We must extend our notion of citizenship to include the **democratization of social policy** debate and formulation in both the state and civil society. We must also extend our notion of citizenship to take collective and individual responsibility to ensure **ecological sustainability**, both locally and globally (chapter 5).

In considering these four critical issues in social welfare policy, we will examine the views of selected social movements and constituencies engaged with these matters, considering critical discussion of unresolved and emerging issues related to broad questions of social policy. Sometimes fundamental disagreements exist about how the questions should be formulated and how the debates should be framed. The challenge is to grapple with questions and debate issues in these four broad areas, as opposed to dealing with categorical, well-formulated "answers."

Finally, as in any investigation of contested social policy terrain, we must also analyse struggles over the use of language and discourses, as well as the possibilities and limitations of political coalescence among groups wanting to achieve more or less similar goals (chapter 6). This analysis entails a consideration of the issues of strategy formulation (including the question of ideological hegemony in social policy debates) and the process of coalition-building among social movements as they attempt to reshape social welfare in Canada. Building on the key themes and issues discussed in the previous four "substantive" chapters, we will revisit the discussion of theoretical frameworks with a view to contributing to a retheorization of social welfare for the twenty-first century.

The Social Movements and Organizations

The following study focuses primarily upon the work of five constituencies that are active players in social policy debates in Canadian society. The first constituency is the **Canadian labour movement**, as it finds expression in both central labour organizations (especially the Canadian Labour Congress) and in specific unions (including private-sector unions such as the Canadian Auto Workers, and public-sector unions such as the Canadian Union of Public Employees).

The second constituency consists of various **social policy advocacy organizations (SPAOs)**, which include a variety of not-for-profit, non-governmental organizations (NGOs) that are players in the social policy arena. Some of these organizations represent the viewpoints and interests of the voluntary sector of human service delivery. Other SPAOs advocate on behalf of particular constituencies, such as poor people or the elderly. Still other organizations could be characterized as "think tanks," whose primary role is research, consultation, and the development and marketing of social policy proposals and social program models.

SPAOs include organizations whose *raison d'être* is engagement in social policy questions (for example, the Caledon Institute of Social Development, the Canadian Council on Social Policy), and organizations that address social welfare issues as an integral part of a broader focus on

---

public policy (for example, the Council of Canadians, the Canadian Centre for Policy Alternatives).

The third constituency is the **women's movement**, which includes a broad swath of informal groups and formal organizations working for equality and more specific feminist goals. In English-speaking Canada, this multifaceted constituency is brought together in a national-level umbrella organization, the National Action Committee on the Status of Women (NAC). For purposes of this study, NAC will serve as a proxy for the broader women's movement in Canada outside of Quebec. To be sure, feminism has many currents, and a broad range of groups are struggling for women's equality. These groups address many different issues or sometimes embrace differing principles and priorities. Still, NAC's ability since 1972 to advance sophisticated and relatively high-profile feminist positions on a broad range of public policy questions makes it the pre-eminent women's organization with the left in English Canada.

The fourth constituency is the loose amalgam of **faith communities and religious denominations** that over the years have attempted to translate their religious values into social policies and programs reflecting ideals of social and economic justice. The social gospel movement, which emerged in Protestant churches in the late nineteenth and early twentieth centuries, and elements of the Roman Catholic Church that have advocated for public policies and social practices consistent with Catholic social teaching, are of particular historical significance. Both of these tendencies in the Christian faith are still evident in current debates on the future of social welfare. The contemporary positions of non-Christian faiths also play a part in social policy in Canada.

The fifth constituency consists of **Aboriginal peoples** and their organizations. First Nations, Métis, and Inuit, as well as Native people outside these officially recognized categories, have a unique perspective on social programs. Native peoples live with the aftermath of conquest.[20] They have had their traditional land base and way of life taken away from them and their cultures and spiritual beliefs attacked by conquering European powers.

In contrast, the non-Native constituencies considered here are historically rooted in and express certain values and beliefs of dominant European cultures. Although their goals as social movements have been egalitarian and progressive, these non-Aboriginal constituencies are nonetheless rooted in European social traditions and institutions. But Native peoples have been and to a significant extent still are excluded from participation in Euro-Canadian social institutions and discourses related to social welfare. For example, the welfare state has been a means of cushioning waged workers and their families from the exigencies of employment in a capitalist labour market. Native peoples until quite recently were largely denied opportunities to participate in this labour market, and even today they remain highly disadvantaged in terms of levels of employment and labour-market income.

Not only have Aboriginal peoples been excluded from the benefits of the welfare state related to labour-market participation, but they have also been the deliberately targeted victims of social welfare services aimed at controlling and assimilating them. Child welfare and education programs have taken Native children away from their communities. Schools have tried to strip Native young people of their languages and cultural knowledge. Government officials have placed Native families in abominable housing. Social assistance programs have contributed to cycles of impoverishment and hopelessness in Native communities. For all of these reasons, Native peoples have every right to be suspicious of social welfare as a Euro-Canadian institution. Still, it may be their very experience of colonialism and subjugation at the hands of those who "meant them well" and those who wanted them "to develop socially" that makes Native peoples fundamentally important critics of the welfare state. They form a constituency that can make important contributions to reimagining social welfare in Canada in the twenty-first century.

Certainly, other categories of social movement organizations and progressive groups beyond those mentioned in the pages that follow have also been advancing a broad conception of social welfare, and they have a potential contribution to make in the rethinking of social welfare. For instance, recent years have seen a resurgence of student activism as postsecondary education becomes increasingly economically inaccessible and more and more aligned with corporate interests. I can only hope that at least some of the concerns and views of the "absent progressive voices" are reflected, if indirectly, in what follows.

Dealing with Issues in the "Real World"

In any discussion of theoretical frameworks or bold conceptual visions, including ones pertaining to social welfare, it is possible to draw up models that are intellectually coherent, and perhaps even elegant and highly persuasive. In the practical struggles of flesh and blood human actors in the social policy arena, however, limited resources and conflicting

priorities often have a more immediate impact upon these actors than whatever excitement they may feel about new or worthwhile ideas in regard to social policy. Individual and collective players in social welfare debates tend not to deal in neat and tidy conceptual frameworks. They engage in the complex, often frustrating, and occasionally rewarding business of working towards their social policy goals, often in adverse economic, political, and ideological contexts. Their particular set of policy goals as movements and organizations may be more or less explicit, complete, internally coherent, or consistent in relation to the broader alliances or coalitions to which they belong.

Methodology

This study of possible directions in social welfare employs three general sources of data. First of all, **key informant interviews** were conducted with individuals from the five constituencies being examined (see Appendix I for a complete listing of the key informants). These individuals were selected for interviews because they were part of organizations with a recognized interest in social policy questions, and because their particular role in the organization put them in a position to exercise leadership in this area. **Documentary sources,** such as policy papers and briefs to government prepared by the organizations examined, provide a second source of data. **Media reports** on social policy questions and the positions and activities of the constituencies being examined provide a third.

This study will focus for the most part on national-level organizations and efforts intended to influence social policy debates at the level of the federal state. The term "national" in this context refers to actors and campaigns based in English Canada (that is, all of the country outside of Quebec). This study posits the linguistic, cultural, and social distinctiveness of Quebec in relation to the rest of Canada. It also recognizes that at least three of the five constituencies examined (labour, SPAOs, and the women's movement) have different organizational structures, agendas, and cultures in Quebec than they do in English Canada.[21] The question of shifting conceptions of social welfare inside Quebec is a very important one, but goes beyond our boundaries here.

It is also the case, of course, that national debates on social policy in Canada inevitably have to include an analysis of the role of the provincial governments. This level of the state has constitutional jurisdiction for "on the ground" delivery of most health, education, and welfare programs. In addition, in recent years the federal government has been shedding its postwar commitment to sharing the cost of social programs with provinces, and to setting national standard based on its fiscal support. The resulting political vacuum has increased the ability of provinces (and especially those committed to dismantling the welfare state) to play a prominent role in the social policy arena. Our discussion must to some extent, then, move back and forth between national and provincial levels of analysis.

Activist Research Contributions To Shutting Down A Welfare Snitch Line

Marge Reitsma-Street [1]

ABSTRACT

An approach to activist research is presented, illustrated, and evaluated using three criteria. Did the research promote change, help participants learn, and theorize change processes?

RÉSUMÉ

Présentation, démonstration et évaluation d'une approche de recherche activiste selon trois critères. La recherche a-t-elle encouragé des changements, aidé les participants/tes à apprendre et a-t-elle favorisé l'émission de théories concernant les processus de changement?

INTRODUCTION

This paper emerged from a nagging uneasiness that stemmed from experiences I and other activist researchers encounter using the feminist, collaborative participatory action research approach to social justice practice (Ng, 1990; Pulkingham, 1993; Shakespeare, 1993). In activist research, researchers lose the privileged position to control method, timing, and interpretation of data and action. This leaves us less certain of what we are responsible for, or how to evaluate success. We can be pulled in several directions, and placed in conflicting situations, unclear how best to discharge our responsibilities. What do we actually do? What can we best contribute? What did research add? Could not the social justice practice have carried on just as well without research? Alary (1990) wonders if activist research is just a sophisticated form of good works. Even when activist research is relevant and trustworthy, I am troubled by how little is generalized or written up for community or refereed academic journals: elephantine effort for such mousy results.

This paper explores the practice and value of activist research, developed during a decade of anti-poverty work. I work from my position as a white, female social work professor in a regional university serving a geographically dispersed, multicultural population. After presenting an approach to the practice of activist research, the approach is illustrated with the examples of research initiatives made during a successful effort to shut down a welfare snitch line. The paper ends with an evaluation of this case of activist research using three criteria.

AN APPROACH TO ACTIVIST RESEARCH

Research is about asking questions, collecting data, and proposing explanations to make sense of the data. Activist researchers, however, search for particular questions, data, and explanations: those that promote liberating action for the dispossessed. The approach I use to action-promoting questions, data, and explanations is summarized in the figure below.

An Approach to Activist Research

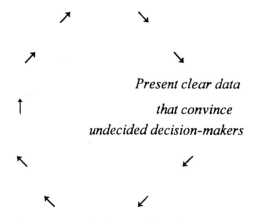

Pose timely questions
that mobilize activists' energy

Present clear data

that convince
undecided decision-makers

Propose competing explanations
that demonstrate value conflicts

One element of the approach is to select timely questions that can mobilize the energy of a particular group of people who may find the energy to act. What are simple but sharp questions that do not just shock people but go deeper to shatter ethical "frames" that people use to make sense of their world and place within it (Argyis et al, 1985, p. 79)? How can one avoid those paralysing questions that are too big or horrible to face in one chunk, or too dense, hiding the ethical debates about justice that spur people to engage in action? Activist researchers pose questions that not only disrupt the status quo but also release energy to think and act differently.

To maintain the energy released by mobilizing questions, the activist researcher uses another element of research: collection of data from many sources and several time periods. To promote action, the data need to go beyond reliably demonstrating injustices. The data must demonstrate that the status quo is not inevitable, and the situation can change (Townsend, 1993). There are variations over time and place, and the situation could change again provided decision-makers act. When trying to abolish injustices or create alternatives it helps to collect reliable data about policy variations within the influence of a group of decision-makers. What is within someone's control that could make a difference? Action-promoting data needs to challenge undecided decision-makers about the wisdom of the status quo, and to suggest the value of exploring new possibilities.

Action-promoting questions and data need to be debated by those who make decisions, and by those who can push decision-makers to act differently. But, energy for action can stall if the debate stays at the level of description. "Isn't it awful" and "it used to be better, or others have it better" must be replaced with "we could make it better here."

Activist researchers add depth and

creativity to the debates by a third element of research: uncovering competing, but equally plausible explanations for the injustices and the variations over time and place (Dobash & Dobash, 1988; Mathieson, 1974). If there are several explanations for welfare fraud, for instance, then decision-makers cannot avoid debate that evaluates the value of one explanation and its implications versus another explanation. The status quo is only one option and it can no longer be taken for granted; there are other options that may be better.

Explanations can challenge the orthodox, victim-blaming, apolitical understanding of poverty or welfare fraud, by revealing the values upon which the competing explanations are based. It is important to unmask who are the few that benefit and who are the many who pay in the different but equally plausible explanations of an injustice. Debating the fundamental value conflicts within competing, contradictory explanations for injustices helps to maintain energy needed for action by opening up the space to imagine remedies for the injustice (Jenson, 1993). Thus, activist researchers work to uncover the competing explanations and values within most people, a struggle that is the source of creative debate and imaginative options.

A CASE OF ACTIVIST RESEARCH: SHUTTING DOWN A WELFARE SNITCH LINE

The elements of this approach to activist research are illustrated in the following case study on shutting down a welfare snitch line in a Northern Ontario district with over 160,000 native, francophone, anglophone, and immigrant citizens. Shutting down the snitch line did not begin as a research project, nor did

an established group formally invite a researcher to help out. The case exemplifies the evolving (and unfunded) nature of activist research in social justice practice and possible points of entry for activist researchers to contribute action-promoting questions, data, and explanations.

In January 1994, the administrative board responsible for municipal social assistance approved the installation of a "fraud hotline." The hotline, labelled a welfare snitch line by its opponents, is a telephone line with a widely advertised phone number dedicated to receiving reports from citizens willing to report, often anonymously, cases of suspected welfare fraud. Each report is investigated by welfare authorities.

Within two months, vivid street protests of a new coalition of welfare recipients and professionals, two pieces of investigative journalism, letters to the editor, and radio and T.V. talks by myself and others broke open the dominant discourse (St. Louis, 1994). Was the snitch line just? Was welfare fraud a problem? Why do "dozens of welfare recipients live under [a] cloud of suspicion?" (Lowe, 1994a). What about the "cost of running [a] welfare snitch line adding to burden on taxpayers" (Lowe, 1994b) and to "destroying solidarity of community" (Plouffe, 1994). Why were citizens asked to snitch anonymously on each other, especially when trained professionals could not easily establish eligibility given the complicated mass of rules? The language in the popular media had shifted by the fall of 1994 from discussing the hotline as an efficient, rational activity that recovered taxpayers' money to a moral debate about a snitch line that could divide a community and prey upon the poor.

A network of anti-poverty professionals under the guidance of myself and the Laurentian University School of Social Work timed the release of an in-depth, longitudinal research report on poverty in the area to feed the poverty and welfare fraud debates. In November and December of 1994, we used press conferences, radio engagements, and speaking occasions to publicize the variations in poverty rates over time and place. To challenge the arguments of snitch line proponents we focused on the competing explanations for the high costs of welfare, such as high poverty rates and women's low wages, and presented research results that disproved the efficacy of anti-fraud measures, like snitch lines (Reitsma-Street, 1994). Despite the need for complex responses to poverty, we looked at some simple, inexpensive solutions within the power of local people, including shutting down the snitch line and voting for politicians who worked for social justice.

Early in 1995, I convened the first meeting of an ad hoc group committed to the line's abolition and representative of a wide range of professional, anti-poverty, and cultural groups. At the same time a class of 33 upper year social work students under my supervision chose to prepare position papers for and against the snitch line as a term assignment. Several students who strongly opposed the line chose to add their research and energies to the ad hoc group.

At this point in the story research contributions included a search for who had the power to abolish the line and what opportunities were there for shutting it down. The next step was to research how to get a review on the decision-makers' agenda. Clear, prompt answers to these questions quickly mobilized and focused energy. The anniversary of its installation was selected as a natural date, and letters and briefs were sent to the chair and members of the administration board to argue the review was timely and in the community's interest. Data on the inhumane costs and procedures comparing alleged income tax evasion and welfare fraud were selected to help convince those decision-makers most opposed to the line that a review was necessary. After hotly debating whether to put a review of the snitch line on the agenda, the board finally did so in their February 16, 1995 meeting.

This done, the activist researchers among the ad hoc group members gathered solid data that might sway the wavering or undecided decision-makers, including the powerful bureaucrats who served the board. The ad hoc group broadcasted the evidence and the morality underlying explanations of fraud to the decision-makers, and to individuals and organizations, including the press, with the suggestion that decision-makers be made aware of community concerns before the March meeting.

Another wave of letters and briefs were sent to decision-makers; the papers carried new investigative media reports (Lowe, 1995); undecided decision-makers were visited. The research in these broadcasting strategies focused on the ethical debates behind the explanations for and against a snitch line. We also broadcast research that compared the lack of savings before compared to after installation of the snitch line, and the absence of differences in rates of welfare abuse in those communities with versus those without a snitch line. In addition, we clearly exposed the systematic, false inflation of savings and the invisible financial as well as human costs associated with a snitch line. On March 16, 1995, the board passed a motion to discontinue the welfare snitch line.

EVALUATION OF ACTIVIST RESEARCH

Did the research contributions to mobilizing questions, comparative data, and competing explanations help shut down the snitch line? I am not sure how much the decision-makers would admit to being swayed by the data. Without pressure from citizens and organizations using the data and arguments, however, the issue may not have been put on the decision-maker's agenda.[2] The questions, data, and alternative explanations were used to support first a coalition of recipients and professionals, and later to mobilize an ad hoc group and a class of social work students. The activist research focused limited personal and non-existent financial resources on strategic actions that put pressure on decision-makers.

But an uneasiness about activist research remains. There are standards to ensure the validity and reliability of activist research including the familiar triangulation of sources, audit trail of procedures, and repetitive participant check of data (e.g Kreftig, 1991). Feminist, cross-cultural, and postmodern researchers have proposed other intriguing standards such as the relevant, catalytic, ironic, and voluptuous tests of validity (Brown, 1994; Lather, 1993). But even if activist research is valid and reliable, is it always necessary and worthwhile? How can its value be assessed? Three criteria may help in evaluating the worth of activist research contributions in this case, and in others.

If we accept that "social change is the starting point of science" (Cook & Fonow citing Mies, 1990, p. 80), then the first criterion is whether the activist research contributes to changes in policies, programs, and individuals. Does the research promote social justice? Is the welfare snitch line abolished?

Even if the answer is yes, and in this case the activist research helped to close the snitch line, more study is necessary to understand precisely how the specific research contributions assist social change. It is hypothesized, for example, that without extensive dissemination of research, or what Sutherland (1994/95) calls broadcasting, the questions, data, and explanations of activist research will not make significant contributions to social justice. Greenberg and Mandell (1991) compared the powerful impact on American decision-makers of the successful broadcast strategies of work-for-welfare researchers to the unsuccessful, muddled dissemination efforts of those evaluating progressive income assistance experiments. In this case study on the welfare snitch line, participants thought carefully how to broadcast mobilizing research questions, data, and explanations in clear language, not only for popular multi-media venues, but also for the newsletters and occasions accessible to bureaucrats and professionals. Sommer (1987) hypothesized that when senior policy-planners participate in designing and disseminating research, they are more likely to implement research implications compared to those who do not participate. In this case study, the researchers connected to the November 1994 poverty reports sought and accepted invitations for meetings with social assistance bureaucrats and other decision-makers to look at poverty and solutions.

The second criterion to help evaluate activist research is transferability of knowledge and skills to participants and other communities. In activist research, the transfer must first be to people within the community that is being researched, especially to those most on the margins, to help with future struggles (Kirby & McKenna, 1989; Fetterman & al, 1996). Cook and Fonow state unequivocally that knowledge from activist research may not be withheld from participants (1990, p.78). Later, if research results are valid and reliable, they may be shared with other people in other communities who will pick what is helpful and congruent with their situation (Krefting, 1991).

Even if the first criterion of change has not been met--as is all too common given that many social justice struggles go on for years--the second criterion stands alone. Activist research is valuable if it brings change to at least some of the research participants. Evaluation of this criterion means exploring the extent to which participants in the activist research absorb sufficient information, skills, and confidence to engage more fully in liberating activities, within their own families and communities. In this case study, members of the Bleeding Heart Coalition and the ad hoc group fighting the snitch line used the November 1994 poverty report and snitch line fact sheets prepared with the help of the activist researchers to build their arguments, legitimacy and confidence. In one instance I was called by a woman who said she represented the low-income mothers in her housing unit. She told me how important the anti-snitch line talks in the popular media were to them.

We are afraid of the snitch line, and you big shot professors in that university up the hill made us feel not so stupid and alone.

Seven of the 33 students decided to send their term assignments to decision-makers, stating their opposition to the snitch line backed up with evidence and arguments. The brief of an eighth student ended up as an editorial in a local newspaper. The work of a ninth student was used by the board of directors of the organization in which she worked on placement to send a protest letter. Six of these nine students had never done something like this before. In their evaluation of the course, students spoke passionately about the welfare snitch line assignment. One student said:

I hate you. We talk all the time about the snitch line. Before I knew what I thought, but now I am not so sure the line is a good idea.

Another student added that she had not known municipal politics was important, or that "me, a poor mother, could meet a politician and help to change her mind."

These changes in participants exemplify the second criterion. I am not certain that the activist research contributions to shutting down the snitch line met the third criterion relevant to the evaluation of activist research--understanding change processes to feed the imagination about alternatives. Good activist research not only uncovers difficult facts but also helps participants enter what Westkott calls a "dialogue with a future...free of domination" (Westkott, 1990, p.65). Once injustices are uncovered, it becomes less important to dig up similar types of facts, and more important to discover how systems or individuals change. Understanding the change processes promotes the possibility of moving towards an alternative to the current injustice.

To analyze how unjust initiatives emerge, and to imagine alternatives, it is necessary to engage directly in change, or be very close to the action.

> If you want to know a thing, you must change it.... we have to start fighting against women's exploitation and oppression in order to be able to understand the extent, dimensions, and forms and causes of this patriarchal system (Mies, 1993, p.40).

What are the privileges, and resistances woven deep in the bowels of a person or a system? One encounters them when trying to change the rules, as we found out in trying to end the snitch line. Thus, action is absolutely essential to understanding deeply, and to constructing new theory.

Participation and empowerment of the dispossessed is a core concept that activist research can help to understand and to imagine alternatives (Heyworth, 1991; Fetterman et al, 1996; Stanley & Wise, 1990; Whyte et al, 1991). An approach to theorizing empowerment is to reflect on initiatives that increase the engagement of marginalized people within their various cultural groups--in learning about injustices, fighting them, and imagining other possibilities (e.g. Kuhlmann, 1992). Another approach theorizes how serious participation in community work or political arenas is systematically discouraged, constrained, limited, even punished. The processes that create, and those that resist repressive constraints, such as the snitch line, cry for investigation. As Chruikshank (1994) argues, activist research would search for alternative conditions that energize people and

groups to resist the systematic forces that disempower an increasing number of women, men, and children.

In sum, key responsibilities of activist researchers are to pose questions, collect data, and suggest explanations that mobilize energy for social justice practice. There also needs to be a commitment to participate from the beginning to the end of a particular phase of social justice practice, caring enough to monitor the impact of research processes, and making adjustments when necessary. It is not yet clear under which conditions activist research can best occur, nor when it is least helpful. Posing the criteria of promoting change, helping participants learn, and theorizing change processes may assist in evaluating the practice of activist research.

ENDNOTES

1. Marge Reitsma-Street, Ph.D., is an Associate Professor at the School of Social Work, Laurentian University, Ramsey Lake Road, Sudbury Ontario Canada, P3E 2C6. E-mail address MREITSMA@NICKEL.LAURENTIAN.CA
An earlier version of this paper was presented January 20, 1996 at "Praxis♀Nexus: Feminist Methodology,Theory, Community" international conference sponsored by the Humanities Centre at the University of Victoria, British Columbia, Canada. This paper is supported in part by the Social Sciences and Humanities Research Council of Canada---Women and Change Network Grants, No

816-94-0003. Thanks to Sheila
Neysmith, Harry Street, and Karen
Swift for thoughtful comments on
earlier versions of this paper.

2.   See also minutes of the District of
      Sudbury Social Services
      Administration Board for March 16,
      1995. Attached to the report on the
      snitch line by the bureaucrats were
      many of the letters, briefs, and
      newspaper articles, mostly
      opposing the snitch line.

BIBLIOGRAPHY

Alary, Jacques (Ed) with Susan Usher
(Trans.) (1990). Community Care and
Participatory Research. Montreal: Nu-age
Editions.

Argyis, Chris, Robert Putnam & Diana
McLain Smith (1985) Action Science. San
Francisco & London: Jossey-Bass.

Brown, Pamela Ann (1994). Participatory
research: A new paradigm for social work. In
L. Gutierrez & P. Nuriua (Eds.) Education
And Research for Empowerment Practice
(Monograph No. 7, pp. 293-303). Seattle:
Centre for Policy and Practice Research,
School of Social Work, University of
Washington.

Chruiksank, Barbara (1994). The will to
empower: Technologies of citizenship and
the war on poverty. Socialist Review 23(4),
29-55.

Cook, Judith A. & Mary Margaret Fonow
(1990). Knowledge and Women's Interests.
In J.McCarl Nielsen (Ed) Feminist Research
Methods (pp. 69-93). Boulder, San
Francisco, & London: Westview Press.
(Reprint from Sociological Inquiry 56(1),
1986, 2-29.)

Dobash, R. Emerson & Russell, R. Dobash
(1988). Research as social action, the
struggle for battered women. In Kerst Yllo &
Michele Bograd (Eds.) Feminist Perspectives
On Wife Abuse. (pp.51-74). Newbury Park:
Sage.

Fetterman, David M., S.J. Kafterian, & A.
Wandersman (Eds.) 1996. Empowerment
Evaluation Thousand Oaks, Ca. Sage.

Jenson, Jane (1993). "De-constructing
dualities; Making rights claims in political
institutions," In G. Drover & P. Kerans
(Eds.) New Approaches to Welfare Theory
(pp. 127-142). Aldershot, Hants: Gower
House.

Greenberg, D.H. & Mandell, M.B. (1991).
Research utilization in policymaking: A tale
of two series of social experiments. Journal
of Policy Analysis and Management 10(4),
633-656.

Heyworth, Elspeth (1991). "Town"/"gown"
and community relations: Case studies of
social empowerment. In Peter Harries-Jones
(Ed.) Making Knowledge Count Advocacy
and Social Science (pp. 100-118). Montreal:
McGill-Queen's University

Kirby, Sandra & K. McKenna (1989).

Experience Research Social Change: Methods From the Margins. Toronto: Garamond Press.

Krefting, Laura (1991). Rigour in qualitative research: The assessment of trustworthiness. The American Journal of Occupational Therapy 45(3), 214-222.

Kuhlmann, Annette (1992). Collaborative research among the Kickapoo Tribe of Oklahoma. Human Organization 51(3), 274-283.

Lather, Patti (1993). Fertile obsession: Validity after postmodernism. The Sociological Quarterly 34(4), 673-693.

Lowe, Mick (1994a) Dozens of welfare recipients live under cloud of suspicion. Northern Life (Sudbury), June 19, pp. A4,A7.

Lowe, Mick, (1994b). Charges only tell part of story about welfare fraud cases. Northern Life (Sudbury). June 12, p. A4.

Lowe, Mick (1995) Still think snitch line is a good idea? Northern Life, March 5, p. A4.

Mies, Maria (1993). Feminist research: Science, violence and responsibility. In M. Mies & V. Shiva (Eds.) Ecofeminism (pp.36-54). Halifax: Fernwood.

Mathiesen, Thomas (1974). The Politics of Abolition (Oslo: Universitagaet).

Ng, Roxana, Gillian Walker & Jacob Muller (Eds.) (1990) Community Organization and the Canadian State. Toronto: Garamond Press

Pender, Terry (1994) Child poverty rate high in Sudbury. The Sudbury Star Nov. 24, 1994, A1.

Plouffe, Kim-Dominique (1994). Welfare snitch line destroying solidarity of community prof. Northern Life (Sudbury). April 3, p. A3.

Pulkingham, Jane 1993. Community development in action: Reality or rhetoric. Canadian Review of Social Policy, 32, 29-42.

Reitsma-Street, M. (Ed.) (1994). Child and Youth Poverty: A Follow-Up Study. Sudbury: School of Social Work, Laurentian University.

Reitsma-Street, M. & Robert Arnold (1994). Community-based action research in a multi-site prevention project: Challenges and resolutions. Canadian Journal of Community Mental Health 13(2), 229-240.

St. Louis, Pierre (1994) Sudbury area's poor fight propaganda war. Sudbury Star, April 15, p.1.

Shakespeare, Pam, Dorothy Atkinson, & Sally French (Eds.) (1993). Reflecting on Research Practice. Buckingham, Philadelphia: Open University Press.

Sommer, R. (1987). An experimental investigation of the action research approach. The Journal of Applied Behavioural Science,

23(2), 185-199.

Stanley, Liz (Ed.) (1990) Feminist Praxis:
Research, Theory and Epistemology in
Feminist Sociology. London and New York:
Routledge.

Sutherland, Dawn (1994/95). Speaking truth
to power: Oppositional research practice and
colonial power. Resources for Feminist
Research 23(4), 46-52.

Townsend, Peter (1993). The International
Analysis of Poverty. New York: Harvester
Wheatsheaf.

"Welfare snitch line to be reviewed" (1995)
The Northern Life (Sudbury). March 15, p.
A5

Westkott, Marcia (1990). Feminist criticism
of the social sciences. In J. McCarl Nielsen
(Ed.) Feminist Research Methods (pp.58-93).
Boulder: Westview Press. (Reprint from
Harvard Educational Review, 49(4), 1979,
422-430.)

Whyte, William Foot, D.J. Greenwood, P.
Lazes (1991). Participatory action research
through practice to science in social
research. In W. F. Whyte (Ed) Participatory
Action Research (pp. 19-55). Newbury Park.
Ca.: Sage.

CHAPTER 2

Policy Controversies
as Frame Conflicts

This chapter presents the framework for reflection on intractable policy controversies that we propose as an alternative to the three we have discussed in the previous chapter. We see policy positions as resting on underlying structures of belief, perception, and appreciation,[1] which we call "frames." We see policy controversies as disputes in which the contending parties hold conflicting frames. Such disputes are resistant to resolution by appeal to facts or reasoned argumentation because the parties' conflicting frames determine what counts as a fact and what arguments are taken to be relevant and compelling. Moreover, the frames that shape policy positions and underlie controversy are usually tacit, which means that they are exempt from conscious attention and reasoning.

FRAMES AND GENERATIVE METAPHORS:
AN EXAMPLE FROM URBAN HOUSING

The issue domain of urban housing is a good one in which to explore policy frames. Over the last sixty years or so, people have held very different views about urban housing. The issue has provoked extensive controversy in both developed and developing countries, and there have been some very dramatic shifts in ideas in good currency about the problem.

The examples with which we begin are drawn from the rather distant past—the debates about urban renewal policy in the United States in the late 1950s and early 1960s.[2] Yet, as we shall see, the frames underlying these debates are still alive and well.

The first piece of writing we shall examine is drawn from Justice William Douglas's opinion, handed down in 1954, on the constitutionality of the Federal Urban Renewal Program in the District of Columbia.

> The experts concluded that if the community were to be healthy, if it were not to revert again to a blighted or slum area, as though possessed of a congenital disease, the area must be planned as a whole. It was not enough, they believed, to remove existing buildings that were unsanitary or unsightly. It was important to redesign the whole area so as to eliminate the conditions that cause slums—the overcrowding of dwellings, the lack of parks, the lack of adequate streets and alleys, the absence of recreational areas, the lack of light and air, the presence of outmoded street patterns. It was believed that the piecemeal approach, the removal of individual structures that were offensive, would be only a palliative. The entire area needed redesigning so that a balanced, integrated plan could be developed for the region including not only new homes but also schools, churches, parks, streets, and shopping centers. In this way it was hoped that the cycle of decay of the area could be controlled and the birth of future slums prevented.[3]

It is useful, in order to construct the frame underlying this paragraph, to consider it as a story—a story told about a troublesome situation—in this case, the presumed plight of older urban neighborhoods—in which the author describes what is wrong and what needs fixing. In this story, the community itself is one main character, and the planner, or expert, is another. The community, once healthy, has become blighted and diseased. The planner, beholding it in its decayed condition, conceives the image of the community become healthy once again, with "new homes . . . schools, churches, parks, streets and shopping centers." But this can be achieved only through redesign of the whole area, under a balanced and integrated plan. Otherwise the area will "revert again to a . . . slum area, as though possessed of a congenital disease."

According to a second story, however, the places called slums are not all the same. Some of them are, indeed, decadent and impoverished, the victims of cycles of decay exacerbated by federal policies of "immuring" and of "urban renewal." Others, such as the East Village in New York City, or Boston's West and North Ends (of which Jane Jacobs said, "If this is a slum, we need more like it!"), are true low-income communities that offer their residents the formal services and informal supports that evoke feelings of comfort and belonging. The task is not to

redesign and rebuild these communities, much less to destroy buildings and dislocate residents, but to reinforce and rehabilitate them, drawing on the forces for "unslumming" that are already inherent in them.

This story can be made out in Peggy Gleicher and Mark Fried's summary of their study of West End residents.

> In summary, then, we observe that a number of factors contribute to the special importance that the West End seemed to bear for the large majority of its inhabitants. . . . Residence in the West End was highly stable, with relatively little movement from one dwelling unit to another and with minimal transience into and out of the area. Although residential stability is a fact of importance in itself, it does not wholly account for commitment to the area. . . . For the great majority of the people, the local area was a focus for strongly positive sentiments and was perceived, probably in its multiple meanings, as home. The critical significance of belonging in or to an area has been one of the most consistent findings in working-class communities both in the U.S. and in England. . . . [Patterns] of social interaction were of great importance in the West End. Certainly for a great number of people, local space . . . served as a locus for social relationships. . . . In this respect, the urban slum community also has much in common with the communities so frequently observed in folk cultures. . . . These observations lead us to question the extent to which through urban renewal we relieve a situation of stress or create further damage. If the local spatial area and orientation toward localism provide the core of social organization and integration for a large proportion of the working class and if, as current behavioral theories would suggest, social organization and integration are primary factors in providing a base for effective social functioning, what are the consequences of dislocating people from their local areas? Or, assuming that the potentialities of people for adaption to crisis are great, what deeper damage occurs in the process?[4]

These are powerful stories, powerful in the sense that they have shaped public consciousness about the issue of urban housing. Each in its time guided the writing of legislation, the formation of policy, the design of programs, the diligence of planners, the allocation of funds, the conduct of evaluation. Each, moreover, has had its period of dominance. The story of blight and renewal shaped public policy in the 1950s, when the idea of urban renewal was at its height. In the 1960s, the story of natural community and its dislocation expressed the negative reactions to urban renewal. In the later 1960s and 1970s, the furmiliar come to be seen in new ways. One thing is seen as another—A is seen as B—just as in the familiar drawings of the Gestalt psychologists a figure may be seen as a vase or the conjunction of two profiles, as a young woman or an old one, as a duck or a rabbit. When A is seen as B, the existing description of B is taken as a putative redescription of A.

In the first of our stories, the urban housing situation is seen as a disease that must be cured and, in the second, as the threatened disruption of a natural community that must be protected or restored. In both cases, the constellation of ideas associated with B is inherently normative. In our ideas about disease and about natural community, there is already an evaluation—a sense of the good to be sought and the evil to be avoided. When we see A as B, we carry over to A the evaluation implicit in B.

Once we are able to see a slum as a blighted area, we know that blight must be removed ("unsanitary" and "unsightly" buildings must be torn down), and the area must be returned to its former state ("redesigned" and "rebuilt"). The metaphor is one of disease and cure. Moreover, the cure must not be a "mere palliative"; a particular, holistic view of medicine is involved in this metaphor. It would not be enough, the experts said, to remove the offensive structures piecemeal. "The entire area needed redesigning so that a balanced, integrated plan could be developed for a region. . . In this way it was hoped that the cycle of decay of the area could be controlled and the birth of future slums prevented." Effective prophylaxis requires an integrated and balanced plan. Just as in medicine one must treat the whole person, so in urban renewal one must treat the whole community.

Once we are able to see the slum as a "natural community" (Gleicher and Fried's "folk community" or Herbert Gans's "urban village"), then it is also clear what is wrong and what needs doing. What is wrong is that the natural community, with its homelike stability and informal networks of mutual support, is threatened with destruction—indeed, by the very prophylaxis undertaken in the name of "urban renewal." We should think twice, as Gleicher and Fried put it, about dislocating people from their local areas; natural communities should be preserved.

Each of these generative metaphors derives its normative force from certain purposes and values, certain normative images, that have long been powerful in our culture.[5] We abhor disease and strive for health. The disease metaphor is discernible not only in frames associated with urban blight but also in human service professionals' use of the term "problem families," which connotes a social pathology that calls for therapeutic intervention. It is equally discernible in the assertion of a

ther history of urban renewal in Boston bore the marks of both of these stories. Under the leadership of Edward Logue, the powerful director of the Boston Redevelopment Authority, the elimination of crowded and dilapidated buildings continued, justified in considerable measure by the need to preserve the city's housing stock from blight and decay, and new housing, schools, parks, and shopping centers were developed. But this later urban renewal proceeded with the addition of carefully orchestrated community-based participation, motivated in no small measure by the horrible example of the destruction of Boston's old West End.

Each story conveys a very different view of reality and represents a special way of seeing. From a problematic situation that is vague, ambiguous, and indeterminate (or rich and complex, depending on one's frame of mind), each story selects and names different features and relations that become the "things" of the story—what the story is about. In the first, for example, they are community, blight, health, renewal, cycle of decay, integrated plan; in the second, home, spatial identity, patterns of social interaction, informal networks, dislocation. Each story places the features it has selected within the frame of a particular context—for example, of blight and the removal of blight; of natural communities, their threatened dissolution, and their preservation.

Each story constructs its view of social reality through a complementary process of naming and framing. Things are selected for attention and named in such a way as to fit the frame constructed for the situation. Together, the two processes construct a problem out of the vague and indeterminate reality that John Dewey calls a "problematic situation." They carry out the essential problem-setting functions. They select for attention a few salient features and relations from what would otherwise be an overwhelmingly complex reality. They give these elements a coherent organization, and they describe what is wrong with the present situation in such a way as to set the direction for its future transformation. Through the processes of naming and framing, the stories make the "normative leap" from data to recommendations, from fact to values, from "is" to "ought." It is typical of diagnostic-prescriptive stories such as these that they execute the normative leap in such a way as to make it seem graceful, compelling, even obvious.

How are such functions carried out?

In our two stories, the naming and framing of the urban housing situation proceeds through generative metaphor—a process by which a familiar constellation of ideas is carried over (meta-pherein, in the Greek) to a new situation, with the result that both the familiar and the unfa-

genetic predisposition to criminal behavior, where it is the genetic stock itself that is seen as either "healthy" or "diseased." Indeed, popular culture seems often to identify the good life with the healthy life and to make progress synonymous with the eradication of disease.[6]

Just as we strive for health and abhor disease, we have a strong affinity for the "natural" and a deep distrust of the "artificial." The idea of the natural, with its Romantic origins in the writings of Rousseau and its deeper sources in pantheism, still works its magical appeal. One can also discern the workings of a powerful metaphor of wholeness, which may be associated with the healthy and the natural. When we define the problem of a social service system as fragmentation, for example, and prescribe the remedy of coordination, it is as though we thought of the service system as a shattered vase. The metaphor of wholeness and fragmentation also underlies the familiar call for an integration of medical services currently delivered by a wide range of medical specialists, no one of whom sees the whole patient, as the general practitioner of a bygone era is supposed to have done.

In such examples it is possible to see the workings of a metaphor, or myth, of a Golden Age, according to which present problems are understood as a falling away from a more ideal state attributed to the past. This image underlies both the metaphor of fragmented services, which are seen as having once been whole, and the metaphor of natural communities, which are seen as having been disturbed by such artificial interventions as urban renewal. It is plausible, we believe, although we shall not try to prove the point here, that the number of metacultural frames at work in a society and, even more, the number of generative metaphors underlying these frames are relatively small and constant over long periods of time.

A situation may begin by seeming complex, uncertain, and indeterminate. However, if we can once see it in terms of a normative dualism such as health/disease, nature/artifice, or wholeness/fragmentation, then we shall know in what direction to move. Indeed, the diagnosis and the prescription will seem obvious. This sense of the obviousness of what is wrong and what needs fixing is the hallmark of policy frames and of the generative metaphors that underlie them, and it is central to our account of the intractability of the frame conflicts implicit in policy controversies.

FRAME CONFLICT AND POLICY CONTROVERSY

In a policy controversy such as the continuing controversy over urban renewal and the treatment of urban housing, two or more parties con-

tend with one another over the definition of a problematic policy situation and vie for control of the policy-making process. Their struggles over the naming and framing of a policy situation are symbolic contests over the social meaning of an issue domain, where meaning implies not only what is at issue but what is to be done.

Typically, the contestants in a symbolic contest enter into it on the basis of their interests in the policy situation. For example, they may be representatives of existing communities threatened with dislocation, real estate developers attracted by an opportunity for profitable development, or representatives of an urban regime committed to promote the physical rehabilitation and economic revitalization of the inner city. There is a reciprocal, but nondeterministic, relationship between the actors' interests and their frames. Frames and interests are logically independent concepts; they are by no means identical. Nevertheless, interests are shaped by frames, and frames may be used to promote interests. One might say, for example, that real estate developers and urban planners favor the language of "blight" and "slum clearance" because these names are linked to a frame that prescribes actions favorable to increases in real estate profits and the urban tax base. One might say, with equal validity, that how actors understand their interests is shaped by their frames—that advocates for working class neighborhoods, for example, have an interest in neighborhood preservation because they see neighborhoods as natural communities, very much as Fried and Gleicher do.

The political interpretation of policy controversies, discussed in the previous chapter, treats controversies as disputes among actors who hold conflicting interests and use their respective powers to promote their interests, thereby initiating a win-lose political game. But it is the frames held by the actors that determine what they see as *being in* their interests and, therefore, what interests they perceive as conflicting. Their problem formulations and preferred solutions are grounded in different problem-setting stories rooted in different frames that may rest, in turn, on different generative metaphors.

Frames are not free-floating but are grounded in the institutions that sponsor them, and policy controversies are disputes among institutional actors who sponsor conflicting frames. The actors are in contention with one another; the frames they sponsor are in conflict, in the sense that they represent mutually incompatible ways of seeing the policy situation. Just as we cannot see the familiar Gestalt figure at one and the same time as both an old woman and a young one, so we cannot see the urban housing situation at one and the same time as both prophylactic slum clearance and the preservation of natural communities. One person's blight is another's folk community. What one person sees as unsanitary and unsightly another may find comfortable, homelike, or even picturesque.

Evidence that one party regards as devastating to a second party's argument, the second may easily patch his or her argument so as to incorporate the second may dismiss as irrelevant or innocuous. Or the new evidence within it. So, for example, when Gleicher and Fried call attention to the rich networks of social interaction that filled the old West End, a partisan of urban renewal might point out that the new, high-rise, upper-middle-class development that replaced the old West End has its own networks of social interaction, or might point to the fact that the working-class people displaced by urban renewal in the West End were subsequently able to create new social bonds in the inner-city suburbs to which many of them moved (a possibility also recognized by Gleicher and Fried).

For all these reasons, there is no possibility of *falsifying* a frame; no data can be produced that would conclusively disconfirm it in the eyes of all qualified, objective observers. The reason for this is that if *objective* means frame-neutral, there *are* no objective observers. There is no way of perceiving and making sense of social reality except through a frame, for the very task of making sense of complex, information-rich situations requires an operation of selectivity and organization, which is what "framing" means.[7] As we have illustrated above, those who construct the social reality of a situation through one frame can always ignore or reinterpret the "facts" that holders of a second frame present as decisive counterevidence to the first.

When we attribute the stubbornness of policy frames resistant to conflicts of policy frames resistant to refutation by appeal to evidence, we come very close to the position Thomas Kuhn has advanced in the philosophy of science.[8] Kuhn distinguished periods of normal science, in which scientists operate within a shared paradigm and agree on the rules of the game for settling their disagreements, from periods of scientific revolution, in which disputes cut across scientific paradigms and there is no agreed-upon framework for reaching agreement. In periods of scientific revolution controversies are not resolved by reasoned appeal to evidence, although they may fade away because the holders of a competing paradigm suffer a conversion experience, or because those individuals simply die out and are not replaced.

In his *Philosophy and the Mirror of Nature*, Richard Rorty generalizes Kuhn's distinction, differentiating normal from abnormal discourse in science as well as in other fields of inquiry. By "normal" Rorty means

discourse that proceeds under a shared set of rules, assumptions, conventions, criteria, and beliefs, all of which tell us how disagreements can be settled, in principle, over time. Here, even though a dispute may in fact persist, there is a belief—perhaps illusory—that it can be settled through reasoned discourse, a belief based on the assumption that the ordinary rules of discourse "embody agreed-upon criteria for reaching agreement."[9] This description would apply, in our terms, to policy disagreements. Abnormal discourse occurs, by contrast, when agreed-upon criteria for reaching agreement are not present as a basis for communication among the contending actors. Such situations are not defined by the participants in terms of an objective framework within which disagreements can be arbitrated or managed. This is, in our terms, the realm of discourse that revolves around conflicts of frames in policy controversies.

KINDS, LEVELS, AND SOURCES OF FRAMES

Part II describes how frame conflicts arise in policy debate and practice and explores the prospects for their resolution through policy inquiry. In order to set the stage for these explorations, however, we must introduce certain terms and distinctions to be illustrated and discussed in greater detail: policy discourse and its several types; rhetorical and action frames; and the several levels of frames, which we call policy, institutional action, and metacultural frames.

POLICY DISCOURSE

By *policy discourse* we mean verbal exchange, or dialogue, about policy issues. The root sense of this term probably lies in the experience of a literal conversation between individuals. When we speak of discourse within or across institutions, we metaphorically extend the meaning of the term.

Because there are no institutional vacuums, interpersonal discourse must have an institutional locus within some larger social system. Even a chat between close friends occurs in the institutional setting of someone's house or a walk around the park. This institutional embedding is important to the nature of discourse in several ways. The institutional context may carry its own characteristic perspectives and ways of framing issues, or it may offer particular roles, channels, and norms for discussion and debate.

When discourse is public, it takes on the special properties of the

POLICY, INSTITUTIONAL ACTION, AND METACULTURAL FRAMES

Action frames operate at different levels of specificity, as the image of the policy ladder suggests. We distinguish three levels of action frames: policy, institutional action, and metacultural frames.

A policy frame is the frame an institutional actor uses to construct the problem of a specific policy situation. For example, in the mid-1970s the Boston Redevelopment Authority (BRA) framed the problem of low- and middle-income housing mainly in terms of the need to "preserve the city's healthy housing stock," which led the BRA to adopt policies that gave priority to the rehabilitation of existing stock and the clearer separation of "decayed" from "healthy" stock.[10] This policy frame did not lead to policies that emphasized either the income level of the occupants of rehabilitated housing or the shortfall between the need for affordable housing and the available supply.

An institutional action frame is the more generic action frame from which institutional actors derive the policy frames they use to structure a wide range of problematic policy situations. As agents of thought and action, institutions possess characteristic points of view, prevailing systems of beliefs, category schemes, images, routines, and styles of argument and action, all of which inform their action frames.[11] It is in this sense that, in a given policy environment, people learn what to expect from a development authority, a tenant advocacy group, a real estate firm, or a city government.

Institutional action frames tend to be complex and hybrid in nature. They do not usually consist in a single, coherent, overarching frame, but in families of related frames. For example, the same development authority that in one situation sponsors the preservation of healthy housing stock may, in a situation of a different sort, frame policy issues in terms of landlord neglect and tenant disaffection. Moreover, the action frames held by individuals may be only loosely coupled to the action frames of the institutions of which they are members. Individuals' frames may represent selections from or variations of the institution's larger store. For example, individuals closer to street-level operations tend to see problems and respond to them differently than individuals closer to the agency's top and center. Individuals, at whatever level, may differ in their ways of interpreting the action frames that prevail within the agency, or in the degree to which they conform to the agency's prevailing line of thought and action.

Institutional action frames are local expressions of broad, culturally shared systems of belief, which we call metacultural frames. The oppositional pairs disease and cure, natural and artificial, and wholeness and

institutions reserved in our society for dialogue about issues of public concern. These are *policy forums* that serve as institutional vehicles for policy debate. They include legislative arenas, the courts, public commissions, councils of government and political parties, the editorial pages of magazines and newspapers, and radio and television programs, as well as the seminar rooms and lecture halls of academia. Policy forums have their own rules, and discourse tends to conform to the norms of the forum in which it occurs. In a court of law, for example, where people expect to engage in an adversarial process, they tend to keep to themselves whatever doubts they may feel about their own positions. At the bargaining table, each utterance tends to be construed as a move in the bargaining game. In all such forums, individual utterances are likely to have meanings and consequences that go beyond the interpersonal context in which they occur. For example, if there is a possibility that words uttered in a forum may be released to a larger public, who knows how that public may respond?

RHETORICAL FRAMES AND ACTION FRAMES

There is a discourse of policy debate and a discourse of policy practice. In policy debate, policy stories and the frames they contain serve the rhetorical functions of persuasion, justification, and symbolic display—the functions to which Deborah Stone alludes when she asserts, in the passage quoted, that "groups . . . portray issues deliberately in certain ways so as to win the allegiance of large numbers of people who agree (tacitly) to let the portrait speak for them." In policy practice, on the other hand, policy stories influence the shaping of laws, regulations, allocation decisions, institutional mechanisms, sanctions, incentives, procedures, and patterns of behavior that determine what policies actually mean in action.

We distinguish between rhetorical and action frames. By the former we mean frames that underlie the persuasive use of story and argument in policy debate; by the latter, frames that inform policy practice. Sometimes the same frames serve both functions. More often, frames implicit in the language used to "win the allegiance of large groups of people" differ from the frames implicit in the agreements that determine the content of laws, regulations, and procedures. For example, in the field of welfare policy in the United States, the rhetoric of the "safety net," which figured prominently in speeches on welfare policy by officials of the Reagan and Bush administrations, was accompanied by changes in regulations that seemed mainly intended to crack down on "welfare cheaters."

fragmentation belong to the realm of metacultural frames. Metacultural frames, organized around generative metaphors, are at the root of the policy stories that shape both rhetorical and action frames. For example, the debate between Wilson and Herrnstein and Leon Kamin, referred to in the previous chapter, is a contemporary version of the nature vs. nurture debate that flourished at the turn of the century, suggesting that in the policy domain of crime—or, more broadly, social pathology—cultural metaframes of nature and nurture remain powerful for thought and action in our society. The nature frame lends itself to prescriptions that favor restraint and segregation of criminals, swift and sure punishment, and (at worst) attempts to control the reproductive behavior of people who are believed to carry the wrong kinds of genetic material. The nurture frame suggests policies that remove or mitigate environmental factors presumed to be conducive to criminality or other forms of social pathology.

Traditionally, liberals in American society have tended to favor the nurture frame, which is consistent with the idea of a public responsibility for the improvement of environmental conditions judged to be conducive to social pathology. It is among conservatives (though not of all types) that the nature frame is held, in conjunction with a broad prescription of social control: rigorous law enforcement coupled with "more and better prisons."[12] While both liberalism and conservatism in our society are so complex and multilayered that one cannot uniquely attribute a pure metacultural frame to either view, versions of particular metacultural frames clearly tend to be associated with traditional political-economic perspectives.

THE DIFFICULTIES OF FRAME CONSTRUCTION

The frames that shape policies are usually tacit, which means that we tend to argue *from* our tacit frames *to* our explicit policy positions.[13] Although frames exert a powerful influence on what we see and how we interpret what we see, they belong to the taken-for-granted world of policy making, and we are usually unaware of their role in organizing our actions, thoughts, and perceptions. In order to reflect on the conflicting frames that underlie policy controversies, we must become aware of our frames, which is to say that we must construct them, either from the texts of debates and speeches or from the decisions, laws, regulations, and routines that make up policy practice.[14] But frame construction is difficult, for both practical and theoretical reasons.

In terms of practical methodology, it may be difficult to tell, in an

actual policy situation, what frame really underlies an institutional actor's policy position. First, the rhetorical frames that shape the public utterances of policy makers may be incongruent with the frames implicit in their patterns of action. In their public utterances, policy makers may hitch on to a dominant frame and its conventional metaphors (the free market, privatization, and "community empowerment," for example), hoping thereby to purchase legitimacy for a course of action actually inspired by different intentions. When policy antagonists challenge one another's legitimacy, they may begin gaming, seeking deliberately to obscure the action frames that underlie their stated positions.

Second, the same course of action may be consistent with quite different policy frames. In American welfare policy, for example, there was a marked continuity in the policy actions taken by the Ford and Carter administrations, even though the two administrations espoused very different views of welfare policy. Conversely, the same frame can lead to different courses of action. Liberals, who advocate the same welfare policies, when such policies are expressed at a high level of generality, tend to disagree among themselves about the proper treatment of ineligibles on the welfare rolls.

Third, as Pressman and Wildavsky showed, the meanings of policy made by a central governmental body in the early stages of policy formation may be transformed at local levels at the stage of policy implementation. Even at the local level, the frames implicit in the discretionary judgments made by street-level bureaucrats, such as housing managers or welfare officials, may differ from the policy frames espoused by state legislators.

Fourth, it may be difficult to distinguish between conflicts within a frame and conflicts that cut across frames. Our judgments on this score may differ depending on how we construct the more generic institutional action and metacultural frames that underlie conflicting policy positions.

Finally, it may be difficult to distinguish between real and potential shifts of frame. The introduction of a new piece of legislation may signal the potential for a reframing of national policy (as the introduction of supplementary security income, SSI, suggested a reframing of American policy toward the poor), but that potential may lie dormant because other reforms, essential to the activation of that potential, are not forthcoming. Conversely, even in the absence of formal deliberations and decision, policy may be reframed as a result of cumulative, incremental adaptations to a changing situation.

These practical difficulties in constructing policy frames may be overcome, at least in principle, by carefully nuanced observations and analyses of the processes by which policy utterances and actions evolve over time and at different levels of the policy-making process. Sophisticated frame construction must attend to the differences between central and local policies, potential and actual changes of frame, the rhetorical frames implicit in espoused policies and the action frames implicit in policy-in-use,[15] formal policies and the policies implicit in the practices of street-level bureaucrats, and visible shifts of policy and the cumulative effects of small changes of policy made in response to changing situations.

In contrast to practical difficulties of frame construction, there is a generic, theoretical difficulty that does not yield in any obvious way to careful methods of observation and analysis. Frames must be constructed by someone, and those who construct frames (the authors of this book, for example) do not do so from positions of unassailable frame-neutrality. They bring their own frames to the enterprise and, what is more, they may be unaware of doing so. For example, a policy analyst who shares the Wilson-Herrnstein position on criminality might go about the task of constructing the frames implicit in that debate very differently than would an analyst who shared Kamin's position.

If we are right in our approach to frame construction, then any given construction of a policy frame can be tested against relevant data—for example, the texts of policy debates or the artifacts and routines of the policy-making process. Frame-critical analysts can and should ask whether these constructs fit the data, exploring, for example, whether these constructs account adequately for the things and relations the frame sponsor singles out for attention or selectively ignores, or for the way in which the frame sponsor's policy story executes the normative leap from facts to recommendations. In spite of the availability of such tests, it is quite possible that frame-critical analysts who proceed from different frames of their own may disagree about the nature of a particular frame conflict, and may be unable to resolve that disagreement through reasoned evidence and argument alone. In such an eventuality, we glimpse an epistemological predicament, to which the following chapter turns.

CHAPTER 30

DISTRIBUTIVE AND REDISTRIBUTIVE POLICY

TOM SEFTON

1. INTRODUCTION

Whenever a government pursues a course of action towards a specific goal, there will inevitably be winners and losers, even if these distributional effects are unintended. In this broadest sense, virtually all government policy can be termed redistributive (Tullock 1997). But for the purposes of this chapter, the focus is on social and welfare[1] policies, where the redistributive motive is most prominent (Hills 2004). Most of the literature in this area is concerned with taxation and spending on cash transfers or in-kind services, though "legal welfare," such as minimum wage legislation, can also have significant distributional effects.

Social and welfare policies are often assessed as if their only purpose were to redistribute from rich to poor. If so, the effectiveness of welfare systems as a whole could be assessed by looking at their impact on overall inequality and poverty. Similarly, in assessing a particular policy or program, the crucial question would be which income groups benefit most. In common with most of the literature on redistributive policy, this chapter is largely concerned with these two types of question.

* I am grateful to the ESRC for funding for part of his time preparing this chapter and to the editors and to John Hills for very helpful suggestions and comments on an earlier draft.

[1] The word "welfare" is used here in the broader sense of social welfare policies, including cash and in-kind transfers from government, not just in the narrower sense often applied in the USA referring only to assistance for certain poor groups. Similarly "social security" refers to all cash transfer programs, not just those for the elderly.

However, it is also important to recognize that redistribution from rich to poor is only one of several dimensions along which redistribution may occur and furthermore, that policies with redistributive effects may have dominant objectives other than redistribution. These issues are discussed briefly in the next section along with some of the implications for the analysis of redistributive policy.

In understanding empirical analysis of the redistributive effects of policy, it is also important to realize that this will entail an (often implicit) comparison with a counterfactual world where the policy was not applied. The use of different counterfactuals will change the results. One important aspect of this is that if one is looking at the impact of government spending, one usually has to ask which taxes would be lower in its absence. The answer may be crucial, but not obvious. But beyond this, many other aspects of behaviour may change too: without social insurance systems covering health care, individuals would make more use of private health insurance, with many knock-on effects through the economy. What economists call the "final incidence" of a tax or spending item is very difficult to measure, but cannot be assumed simply to equal the "first round" measurement of who administratively is the recipient or liable (Pechman and Okner 1974).

2. ALTERNATIVE FORMS OF REDISTRIBUTION

Low incomes are not the only reason for receiving cash benefits or services in kind. Many welfare policies provide insurance against adverse risks, such as unemployment or ill health, and provide a mechanism for smoothing income over the life cycle—what Barr (2001) refers to as the "Piggy Bank" function. This has received relatively little attention in the literature compared with the "Robin Hood" function (i.e. redistribution from rich to poor), but is arguably as, if not more important. Barry (1990) argues that whilst there is no reason for expecting the welfare state to have a single rationale, if it is to be identified with one objective, it is that of income *maintenance* rather than the relief of poverty.

This has several implications for analysis of redistributive policy. First, a snapshot picture of redistribution can be misleading. Education goes disproportionately on the young, health care and pensions on the old, while the taxes that finance them come mostly from the working generation. Much of the redistribution that appears to be taking place at a given point in time will be canceled out over people's lifetimes. According to Hills and Falkingham (1995), between two-thirds and three-quarters of welfare state spending in the UK in the 1980s and 1990s was life-cycle redistribution—redistribution of individuals' own lifetime incomes across different stages in their own lives, as opposed to redistribution between the "lifetime rich" and "lifetime poor."

Secondly, it may not always be appropriate to judge a particular benefit or service according to whether it benefits the poor more than the rich. Many public health care systems, whether social insurance based or tax funded, seek to provide equal treatment for equal need: as such, they are primarily designed to achieve horizontal redistribution between people with similar incomes, but different medical needs, as opposed to vertical redistribution between people with different incomes, but similar medical needs. Similarly, certain social welfare policies are designed to provide for the extra needs of families with children, to meet the additional costs incurred by disabled people, or to help counter the effect of other forms of disadvantage relating to age or race, for example. The key distributional question in these cases is whether the benefits people receive match their respective needs, irrespective of whether they are rich or poor—or possibly whether they compound disadvantage. Studies of the distributional effects of programs or policies may therefore emphasize the impact on different ethnic groups, age and/or gender groups, geographic areas, or some other relevant breakdown of the population, rather than, or as well as the impact on different income groups (Danziger and Portney 1988).

Nonetheless, even policies that are not primarily designed to redistribute from rich to poor can have a significant redistributional impact for a variety of reasons. Lower socioeconomic groups generally face a greater risk of experiencing the adverse events that social insurance schemes are designed to protect them against: they are more likely to experience extended spells of unemployment, to suffer ill health, or to be injured at work (Burchardt and Hills 1996; Ferrarini and Nelson 2003). Thus, even if all citizens were to participate in these schemes on equal terms (though as we see later on, social insurance schemes and universal public services almost invariably incorporate progressive elements), they would still involve redistribution from higher- to lower-income groups.

Furthermore, poverty alleviation is a *byproduct* of a "well-ordered" welfare state, even if that is not the primary objective of most of the individual policies that make up that system (Barry 1990). In a welfare state that provides a continuing income (above the poverty line) for the unemployed, the sick or disabled, and the retired; that provides an income for those not expected to work because they are looking after young children or adults who need constant care; that offers a universal child benefit set at a level sufficient to meet the costs of raising children; and that covers special expenses associated with personal misfortune, almost all the job of relieving poverty will be done by policies whose rationale is in fact quite different.

Thus, at the very least, redistribution from rich to poor is an important side effect or secondary objective of many social and welfare policies and collectively, they should ideally ensure that poverty is kept to a minimum, even if that is not their primary motivation. On this basis, it is often important to assess such policies in terms of their redistributive impact.

3. OTHER AIMS

Two further points should be borne in mind in reading this chapter. First, redistribution is not only about redistributing incomes, but also about redistributing opportunities: access to better education, better job opportunities, and better health that may lead to greater equality in incomes in the long term, as well as being an end in themselves. The appropriate balance between more traditional tax-transfer forms of redistribution and what has been variously termed an "equal opportunity" or "active" welfare state has been the subject of a long-running debate among policy makers and academics (e.g. Haveman 1988; HM Treasury 1999). Most countries still rely mostly on the former to achieve their distributional objectives, but have over time attempted to shift the balance more towards the latter.

Secondly, social spending and taxation are not only (or even primarily) about redistribution in whatever form and therefore, should not be judged solely against this criterion. In particular, there is an efficiency, as well as an equity function to the welfare state. Even if all poverty could be eliminated, there would still be a need for institutions to enable people to insure themselves and to provide important services, such as health care and education. Uncertainty and other forms of imperfect information on the part of insurers mean that important areas of private insurance are likely to be inefficient or non-existent and external benefits may also mean that certain goods or services would be under-provided in a free market. In cases where market failure is costly and government is effective, state intervention can increase efficiency (Barr 2001).

Browning (1975), however, challenges the presumption that in-kind transfers are necessarily more efficient than cash transfers as a method of redistribution whenever there are external benefits associated with the consumption of particular goods. More generally, economists often maintain that the market system is a superior mechanism for allocating resources as there will always be a way of combining the price system (to achieve efficiency) with lump-sum transfers (to achieve distributional objectives). But as Weitzman (1977) points out, this is typically not very useful for policy prescriptions, because the necessary transfers are almost never paid. Furthermore, Arrow (1963) uses the example of the medical care industry to show that in some cases market conditions deviate markedly from those under which the "competitive model" (or free market) can be assumed to produce an efficient allocation of resources.

Another rationale for the in-kind provision of certain goods or services is that taxpayers have an altruistic, but paternalistic concern for the welfare of others; they may be prepared to pay for some kind of redistribution to the poor, but only if it takes the form of providing them with specific services, such as health care, food stamps, or subsidized housing (Le Grand 1982). This is sometimes referred to as the "merit good" argument. Similarly, Weitzman (1977) discusses a particular class of good or service, such as housing, whose just distribution to those having the greatest need for them might be viewed by society as a desirable end in itself. Tobin (1970) refers to this as "specific egalitarianism:" the view that certain commodities should be distributed more evenly than the ability to pay for them. Weitzman argues that the price mechanism of the market will be comparatively less effective in achieving an appropriate distribution of these goods (compared with a crude form of state rationing) when income inequality is relatively high, because those with larger incomes will tend to monopolize consumption of the goods in question.

Whilst these principles help to differentiate between in-kind and cash provision on "efficiency" or other grounds, the patterns of provision observed in different countries are also likely to be strongly influenced by historical circumstances and the power of different actors in the policy process.

4. Approaches to Redistributive Policy

Esping-Andersen (1990) provides a useful, though contested typology of welfare states with distinct approaches to redistribution, based on a broader conceptualization of the welfare state which recognizes that the level of social expenditure does not necessarily provide an accurate indication of a state's redistributive effort. This sets redistributive policy into an institutional context, helping to explain the political and economic values that underlie different welfare states. In the context of this chapter, the focus is on the notion of equity that underlies these welfare regimes and how this is reflected in different approaches to redistributive policy.

Liberal welfare regimes look to the market as their primary source of "welfare." The main role of the state is to ensure the smooth operation of the market, implying a minimalist role for redistributive policy. The state assumes responsibility only when the family or the market fails and seeks to limit its commitments to providing a safety net for marginal and deserving groups. Entitlement rules should be strict, and benefit levels modest and time limited so as not to crowd out private provision or charity, whilst guarding against the danger of cultivating a dependency culture.

Social democratic welfare regimes give a much more prominent role to redistributive policy. Unlike the liberal regime, the underlying assumption is that the outcomes of unfettered capitalism are unfair and, therefore, social democrats are much more prepared to manipulate the market economy to social ends (e.g. via strong employment protection and minimum wage legislation) even at some cost to overall productivity. Redistribution is also to be achieved by taking certain goods and services, such as health, education, and housing out of the capitalist realm and ensuring they are distributed more equally than income or wealth ("decommodification"). Entitlement to certain state benefits is seen as part of the "rights of citizenship" and insurance systems are usually broad and universal. Benefits are typically graduated in proportion to accustomed earnings in order to ensure high replacement rates, even for relatively high earners. Since state services and benefits are tailored to the expectations of middle-income groups, the market is largely crowded out of the welfare sector.

Corporatist welfare regimes seek to preserve the existing order and the patterns of distribution within it, in contrast to the social democratic state's explicit attempt to alter the distribution between rich and poor. The corporatist approach to welfare relies on mutual aid to take care of those who fall upon hard times. Social programs are generous, but are funded largely by contributions made over recipients' own working lives. Social entitlements derive principally from employment rather than citizenship (as in the social democratic model) or proven need (as in the classic liberal model). The primary role of the state is to underwrite and facilitate group-based schemes of insurance and arrange residual insurance pools for those who are not part of an established occupational group. The state's emphasis on upholding status differentials dampens its distributional impact (over complete lifetimes, at least), though most corporatist systems contain some weakly redistributive elements.

Such differences are not only seen in the structures that emerged between different nations' welfare regimes in the third quarter of the twentieth century, but also in their responses to fiscal pressures at the end of the century. Such pressures—from aging and slower growth—may have been greater in the more extensive social democratic or corporatist regimes, but so was their political entrenchment, leading to varied responses (Pierson 2001).

Esping-Andersen and others have attempted to classify countries into one of these three regimes, using a whole range of indicators. In practice, few countries match these descriptions in every respect, though most countries tend towards one or other of them. The USA is the clearest example of a liberal welfare regime, the Scandinavian countries come closest to the social democratic model, and the continental European countries, including France, Germany, and Italy, are commonly cited as examples of corporatist regimes.

4.1 Universal versus Targeted Welfare

One of the key distinctions between the liberal and social democratic regimes is that the former favors targeted welfare on the poor, whereas the latter favors universal provision of welfare. In practice, however, all welfare states contain a mixture of targeted and universal welfare provision.

"Universalists" advance many reasons for regarding the targeting of welfare as bad policy. Means testing often involves an intrusive enquiry into people's personal and financial circumstances; it can stigmatize the recipients and may be socially divisive; targeted welfare payments may tend to become less generous to the poor over time, because they generally command less political support than universal programs; many of those in need may miss out, because need is often difficult to identify; non-take-up is a greater problem with means-tested benefits, in part because of the stigma or time cost attached to claiming these benefits; means-tested benefits are generally more difficult and expensive to administer; means testing can create a "poverty trap," because benefits are withdrawn as incomes rise; and, since means tests only make sense when applied to the family, they run counter to the desire to have a social security system that promotes greater independence for women (Atkinson 1983, 1993, 1995, part III; Cornia and Stewart 1995).

Supporters of more targeted welfare argue that it is a more efficient way of combating poverty and can be equally effective. By definition, a greater proportion of any expenditure goes towards helping those below the poverty line. Social transfers impose costs on the economy, which are minimized through better targeting. They also dispute or downplay some of the arguments against means testing. Mitchell, Harding, and Gruen (1994), for example, have argued that a well-designed means test need not be stigmatizing; that non-take-up is generally greatest among those entitled to only small amounts; and that the disincentive effects generated by means testing may not be as great as might be thought.

4.2 The Efficiency–Equity Trade-off

Another key distinction between liberal and other welfare regimes is that they are more concerned about the potential trade-off between equity and economic efficiency. The principal idea behind the neoclassical critique of the welfare state is that social programs with high replacement rates constitute a powerful disincentive for people to work and to save for old age or insure against other adverse events. These disincentives are expected to reduce employment rates and increase welfare dependency, which are in turn a drag on economic growth (cf. Goodin et al. 1999). At the same time, greater income inequality is a spur to economic growth, because it rewards innovation and effort and increases savings and investment as those with higher incomes tend to save a larger share of their income (see, for example, Welch 1999).

On the other hand, there are theoretical arguments for why greater equality may be good for economic growth. Higher tax rates can increase work effort if there is a large enough "income effect," whereby individuals have to work harder to achieve a given level of post-tax income. Some economists also argue that more equal pay can help to suppress unwanted (but unobservable) uncooperative behaviour at work, such as shirking. More generally, Haveman (1988) argues that the redistribution system reduces economic insecurity and uncertainty, increases economic stability, and facilitates economic change and the production of human capital. As he puts it, each of us feels better knowing we live in a society which protects the weak and moderates the extremes in income and economic power that accompany the operation of free markets. Though harder to quantify, these efficiency gains need to be set against the economic losses generated by any adverse incentives and distortions that the redistribution system creates.

Whilst it is a commonplace contention that high taxes and generous transfers produce work disincentives, a comprehensive review of research on Denmark, Sweden, Germany, and the UK demonstrates that the empirical evidence is much more mixed (Atkinson and Mogensen 1993). Generous early retirement pensions do appear to induce early exit from the labour market; otherwise, the negative effects on labour supply are generally small or insignificant and positive effects are not infrequent for some subgroups such as prime age men. Moreover, findings for one country do not necessarily hold for another, so it is hard to generalize.

Empirical evidence on the relationship between inequality and growth is also inconclusive. Some studies find that countries with more inequality tend to have slower rates of economic growth, whilst others find precisely the opposite, depending on the countries included in the study, the period covered, and the methodology used. Kenworthy (2004), for example, carries out a cross-country analysis and a cross-state analysis (for the USA) and shows that in both cases there is a possible negative effect of inequality on growth, but that the association is weak at best and very sensitive to one or two outliers. He concludes that "although there is surely a point at which the distribution of income might be too egalitarian to be compatible with desirable rates of economic growth, the experience of the past two decades suggests that such a point has yet to be reached." Particular institutions or policies may have growth-impeding effects, but there is no evidence of a general equity–efficiency trade-off over this period.

Similarly Atkinson reviews ten econometric studies of the relationship between the level of social spending in different countries and their economic performance. For comparability, he takes the results of each study to produce its prediction of what would be implied for a country's rate of economic growth if its social spending was smaller as a share of GDP. Four of the studies fitted suggestions that a smaller welfare state would be associated with faster growth. But two found no significant relationship, and four suggested that growth would be *slower* if social spending were reduced. He concludes, "studies of the aggregate relationship between economic performance and the size of the welfare state do not yield conclusive evidence" (Atkinson 1999, 84). The question itself may not be the right one to ask—instead we should be looking at the structure and design of the components of social spending: some may have positive effects on economic performance, for instance education and training; others may have negative effects, for instance because of damaging incentive effects.

5. Effectiveness of Redistributive Policy

The effectiveness of redistributive policy can be examined on two levels: macro-level comparisons of different welfare regimes across countries and micro-level analyses of individual social policies and programs within countries. These two strands of literature are discussed in turn.

5.1 Cross-country Comparisons

The effectiveness of different welfare regimes is usually judged in terms of their impact on inequality and poverty, though some of these analyses also take into account other criteria, such as economic efficiency.

Smeeding (2004) compares the level of inequality before and after taxes and benefits in thirteen OECD countries using the most recent data from the Luxembourg Income Study for 2000 (or the mid–late 1990s for some countries). His analysis shows that the high-spending countries in northern and central Europe and Scandinavia have the greatest impact on inequality—a reduction of between 40 and 48 per cent in the Gini coefficient. The Anglo-Saxon nations, excluding the USA, are next with reductions of 24 to 31 per cent; the USA with an 18 per cent reduction is the lowest of the rich OECD nations.

The anti-poverty effect of taxes and transfers shows a similar pattern. In all countries, taxes and transfers reduce income poverty, but the reduction is greater in both absolute and proportional terms in countries with high levels of social spending (as in Scandinavia and northern Europe) or more careful targeting of government transfers on the poor (as in Canada, for example). The USA shows the least anti-poverty effect of these countries—poverty is reduced by 28 per cent in 2000 (from 23.7 to 17.0 per cent), compared to an average reduction of more than 60 per cent for the eight countries included in this analysis.

The Dutch welfare regime—used in Goodin et al. (1999) as an "imperfect" example of a social democratic regime—is also more effective at reducing the length and recurrence of poverty spells through its public transfer program, as well as minimizing the number of such spells in the first place. On an annual basis, around 18 per cent of the US population were poor, whereas it was less than a third of that in the Netherlands (during the late 1980s and early 1990s). These differences are even greater when looked at over an extended time period. Dutch poverty rates dropped to around 1 per cent if incomes are averaged over a five-year period, whereas American rates remained at around 15 per cent. The US welfare regime has no impact (or even a slightly negative one) on working age households. The only sort of poverty the US regime helps to alleviate is among the elderly—and it removes only about half of that, compared to around 90 per cent in Germany and the Netherlands.

Hicks and Kenworthy (2003) use regression analysis to examine the relationship between the characteristics of welfare regimes and various outcome measures, including redistribution. They find that those characteristics associated with "progressive liberalism" (which broadly equates to Esping-Andersen's social democratic model) have a strong and positive effect on inequality and poverty reduction. The estimates for "traditional conservatism" (which broadly equates to Esping-Andersen's corporatist model) are also positive in both cases, but the impact on inequality is not statistically significant and its impact in reducing poverty is weaker than that of progressive liberalism.

5.2 Paradox of Redistribution

Contrary to common wisdom, it is now well established that systems which target narrowly to the most needy generally perform rather badly in terms of redistribution or poverty alleviation (Esping-Andersen 1996). Korpi and Palme (1998) called this the "paradox of redistribution:" the more benefits are targeted at the poor, the less likely this is to reduce poverty and inequality. While a targeted program may have greater redistributive effects per unit of money spent, other factors are likely to make universalistic programs more redistributive.

Korpi and Palme put forward several explanations for this counter-intuitive finding. First, an emphasis on targeting may over time undermine broad-based support for social security, because it largely benefits the politically weak poor, and may therefore lead to lower levels of social security expenditure and ultimately to more, not less inequality. Second, the institutional welfare state may "crowd out" even more inegalitarian private alternatives. This might explain, for example, why the lowest inequality in the incomes of older people occurs in the four countries with the most unequal public pensions—Finland, Sweden, Norway, and Germany. Third, most earnings-related social insurance programs have some, often a strong element of redistribution built into them. In a "pure" earnings-related scheme, contributions and benefits are both proportional to earnings, but in practice most schemes have a "floor" below which benefits are not allowed to fall and a "ceiling" above which the percentage of earnings replaced is gradually reduced, favouring lower earners.

Goodin et al. (1999) offer a slightly different explanation for why liberal welfare regimes are less effective at combating poverty. While liberals want their welfare state to help the poor and only the poor, they also want it to do so efficiently and at least cost to overall macroeconomic performance. This "big trade-off" causes them to temper their pursuit of poverty alleviation. Whereas social democratic welfare regimes "err on the side of kindness," the liberal US system is "lean and mean." US welfare programmes are over-tightly targeted, so many poor people receive less than they need and a substantial proportion do not receive any transfer payments.

5.3 Caveats

In summary, the evidence strongly suggests that comprehensive, universalistic, and more generous welfare states of the Scandinavian type are considerably more egalitarian in outcome than others. By contrast, the same studies invariably show that the USA, and to a lesser extent other more "liberal" regimes, perform relatively poorly in terms of reducing inequality or poverty compared to other OECD countries. However, there are several caveats which need to be borne in mind.

First, even in the USA, the tax-transfer system has been a powerful instrument for reducing poverty and inequality. Absolute poverty (as measured by the official US poverty line) was between 40 and 60 per cent lower in the mid- to late 1980s than it would have been in the absence of government transfers (Haveman 1988; Danziger 1988). Federal taxes are also progressive, though only mildly so (Pechman and Mazur 1984; Haveman 1988). In a historical context, the period 1960–80 saw the US government transformed from a traditional defense–transportation–natural resources enterprise to a major engine for poverty reduction. Social policies that are redistributional by nature grew from about a quarter to nearly half of federal activities over this period (Haveman 1988). Nevertheless, as he also points out, in spite of the massive increase in taxes and spending, inequality was no lower in 1988 (and is probably higher now) than it was in 1950, because of rising inequality in market incomes.

Secondly, as argued by Alesina and Angeletos (2003), redistribution from rich to poor is more limited in the USA than in continental Europe at least in part because of differences in public attitudes towards the source of income inequality. In a society like the USA, people are much more likely to believe that individual efforts determine income and that poverty is due to lack of effort rather than bad luck or social injustice. Americans accept a larger measure of inequality and choose less redistribution, because they believe that the distribution of incomes produced by the market is closer to what they consider to be a fair outcome. Schwabish, Smeeding, and Osberg (2003) offer a different perspective on the relationship between income inequality and social spending. They argue that cross-national differences in social expenditure are associated with and according to their theory, may be driven by the degree of inequality in the top half of the income distribution, because political influence is concentrated among the rich who stand to benefit less (or lose more) from social and welfare programs the more unequal the society.

Thirdly, and related to the previous point, many defenders of American economic and political institutions argue that inequality plays a crucial role in creating incentives for people to improve their situations through saving, hard work, and investment in education and training. According to this line of argument, wide income disparities may be in the best long-term interest of the poor themselves as the benefits of higher economic growth "trickle down" to the poor. However, Smeeding, Rainwater, and Burtless (2000) conclude that the supposed efficiency advantages of high inequality do not appear to have accrued to low-income residents of the USA, at least so far, but rather to those further up the income scale. Kenworthy (1998) assesses the relationship between the "extensiveness" of social welfare policies and overall poverty rates in fifteen developed countries over the period 1960–91, allowing for the possible impact on long-run economic growth. The results of his multivariate analysis, though not conclusive, suggest that social welfare policies do significantly help to reduce absolute and relative poverty, even when possible indirect, dynamic effects on long-term economic growth are taken into account.

Finally, there are various ways in which the methodology used in comparative studies may exaggerate the differences between countries, making simple comparisons of pre- and post-transfer poverty or inequality potentially misleading. This relates to the problem with establishing incidence discussed at the start. For example, in countries with generous earnings-related social insurance schemes, older people will have had less need to make private provision for their retirement, so they are more likely to have relatively low pre-transfer incomes. A simple comparison of pre- and post-transfer poverty rates will show that government transfers are lifting many older people out of poverty. But, this implicitly assumes that people would not alter their behavior in the absence of social insurance or other government transfer schemes. In practice, many of these older people would have made alternative arrangements and would not in fact have been poor in the absence of government transfers. Similarly, by deducting taxes and national insurance contributions, but not private pension contributions, the "standard approach" to the analysis of income data will exaggerate the disposable incomes of middle- and higher-income groups in countries where pensions are more private than public (Whiteford and Kennedy 1995).

Studies based solely on cash incomes may also give a distorted picture of the impact of social and welfare policies, because governments may seek to achieve their redistributive goals through programs which provide non-cash benefits rather than just through tax-transfer mechanisms. Smeeding et al. (1993) find, however, that the ranking of countries according to levels of cash and non-cash transfers is similar (with the exception of Canada whose non-cash ranking is well above its cash transfer ranking), suggesting that governments have not used cash transfer and non-cash benefit programs as substitutable methods of achieving their social objectives. Non-cash incomes appear to reinforce the distributional impact of conventional tax-transfer mechanisms, rather than acting to offset them in any major way.

5.4 Analysis of Individual Programs

Twenty years ago, in his book *The Strategy of Equality*, Julian Le Grand (1982) reached the striking conclusion that "almost all public expenditure on the social services [in the UK] benefits the better off to a greater extent than the poor." Goodin and Le Grand (1987a) extended this analysis to other countries and to include examples of cash payments, as well as in-kind services. Their conclusion has been widely, though not universally accepted. Esping-Andersen (1996), for example, states that "it is now well-established that huge areas of welfare state activity, especially in education and the other in-kind services, are probably of greatest benefit to the middle classes."

If this is so, a large part of social policy would have failed in what many would see as one of its main aims. As we shall see below, this conclusion depends critically on a series of assumptions about how to analyze the distributive impact of social welfare programs, and more fundamentally, on the meaning attached to their redistributive role.

Le Grand (1987) examined the use of various social services in the UK in the 1970s and found that people from lower social classes used fewer health services per ill person, benefited less from subsidies to owner-occupiers and transport-related subsidies, and that their children were less likely to stay on in post-compulsory state education. Of the services he looked at, only subsidies to council tenants and rent rebates were directed primarily at the poor (though his analysis did not cover social care or cash transfers, both of which are also pro-poor). Goodin and Le Grand (1987b) used the example of the Australian social security system to argue that even programs that are tightly targeted on the poor at their inception may, over time, be "infiltrated" by the non-poor, defeating or at least defusing their redistributive aims—what they term "creeping universalism." At the same time, those services targeted at the poor have a tendency to be cut first when budgets are under pressure. Hanson (1987) argued that state-funded programs in the USA are particularly vulnerable to these kinds of pressures because "footloose" businesses lobby them to keep taxes low. The neglect of social assistance is easily carried out simply by not adjusting benefit levels for inflation—as a result, the entry point for social assistance (i.e. the maximum permissible income to qualify for AFDC payments) fell from 80 per cent of the official US poverty line in 1968 to 57 per cent in 1981. Thus, governments appear to favor public services that are extensively used by the middle classes and to neglect spending areas that are targeted at the poor.

The authors offered several possible explanations for "middle-class capture." The better off, being generally better educated and more articulate, are more able to manipulate the system to their advantage: to ensure, for example, that their doctor refers them to a specialist or that their children go to the right schools. They are also likely to face lower costs in using services and have greater political influence.

To some extent at least, therefore, inequality in health care and other services reflects inequality in society more generally. On this basis, they argue that governments should intervene directly in the market to ensure it produces the "right" income distribution in the first place, rather than relying on fiscal transfers or in-kind provision of social services to "patch up" the secondary income distribution.

These conclusions have been challenged on at least two grounds. First, some have argued that universal programs are a good thing per se, because they foster social cohesion, whereas targeted programs can be socially divisive. This view seems to be consistent with the founding principles of the British welfare state. According to Marshall, "universal benefits symbolise the fact of social equality by conferring on everyone a badge ... of citizenship." If equality is seen in terms of a common system of provision for all, then equality of entitlement is more important than equality of use or equal use for equal need (Powell 1995). Taking measures to reduce the participation of the middle classes would involve lowering the quality of services to deter middle-class users and/or tightening the conditions for access and risking stigmatizing low-income users, neither of which would seem to be of benefit to the poor.

Secondly, subsequent analyses of the distributional effects of welfare programs—both cash and in-kind—have found that they involve substantial redistribution from low- to high-income groups. It is important to be careful in specifying the precise distributional question being asked. For instance, poorer groups may receive fewer (or lower-quality) services *relative to their* needs than higher-income groups, but may still receive the largest aggregate amounts, simply because their needs are so much greater. Sefton (2002) examines the UK distribution of what he calls the "social wage" (benefits in kind from health care, education, social housing, and social care) between income groups between 1979 and 2000. The results show that the poorest fifth of households receive, on average, around twice the value of services that the richest fifth of households receive. Part of this pro-poor bias is accounted for by the demographic composition of income groups: older people and children, who are the most intensive users of welfare services, are disproportionately represented among lower-income groups. But, a significant pro-poor bias remains even after controlling for demographic factors, because certain services are targeted at poorer households, some services are strongly needs related (which skews them towards lower-income groups), and higher-income groups are much more likely to use private education and health care. Calero (2002) comes to very similar conclusion using Spanish data for 1994. He finds that age determines a considerable part of the distribution of spending on cash benefits and benefits in kind, but that social spending also leads to significant reductions in inequalities between social classes.

Furthermore, neither of these studies takes into account the distributional effects of taxation. Most social spending is financed from general taxation so it is difficult to say definitively which taxes are used to pay for which services. However, on plausible assumptions, allowing for taxation will substantially strengthen the redistributive impact of welfare policies. This is because most forms of taxation are proportional to incomes or progressive. Thus, even if spending on welfare programs were equal across income groups, those on lower incomes would still be net gainers, simply because they pay less tax into the system.

Having said this, some studies of individual policies or programs have shown these are less redistributive than they may appear at first. Gustman and Steinmeier (2000), for example, show that the US social security benefit system is not nearly as progressive as a point-in-time examination of the benefit formula would suggest. Replacement rates are considerably lower for those with relatively high average annual earnings over their lifetime than for those with low average earnings (ranging from 15 up to 90 per cent in 2000), implying substantial redistribution from high to low earners—and indeed this is the case at the level of the individual. However, about half of this redistribution is *within* families—from men to their spouses, especially those who have spent large amounts of time out of the labor market. There is much less redistribution from high- to low-income families. Similarly, Liebman (2002) finds that the extent of income-based redistribution is fairly modest compared to the benefits paid out by the social security system—only between 5 and 9 per cent of the total. Much of the intra-cohort redistribution is related to factors other than income, including from people with low to people with high life expectancies and from single workers and two-earner couples to one-earner couples. Since high-income families tend to have higher life expectancies and receive larger spouse benefits, a substantial part of the progressivity implicit in the basic benefit formula is offset.

6. CONCLUSIONS

Whilst nearly all acts of government have redistributive effects, most are not primarily about "traditional" redistribution from rich to poor. Even redistributive policies are often concerned with different forms of redistribution and have other objectives besides redistribution. Nonetheless, government tax and transfer policies substantially reduce inequality and poverty in all rich OECD countries, though with varying degrees of success. The outcomes in different countries are shaped by differences in political and economic values, including judgements about the trade-offs between equity and efficiency and the merits of targeted versus universal support, as well as considerations of political economy.

In a broader context, the politics of important areas of public policy may depend as much on who gains from government's activities and their financing as on their success against other, often primary objectives. This is not only true of cash transfer or taxation policies, but applies across most areas of government. When reform is proposed, debate often focuses on who are the losers from any transition from the status quo, rather than on assessing any new structure in its entirety. However, determining who the losers and gainers are usually depends on particular and contestable assumptions about how the world would be in the absence of policy change, as well as the time period over which comparisons are made. Empirical studies in the last twenty or so years have helped to shed light not only on what the redistributive impact of government is, but also on the most appropriate ways of framing the questions.

REFERENCES

ARROW, K. 1963. Uncertainty and the welfare economics of medical care. *American Economic Review*, 53 (5): 941–73.

ALESINA, A., and ANGELETOS, G. 2003. Fairness and redistribution: US versus Europe. NBER Working Paper 9502. Cambridge, Mass.: National Bureau of Economic Research.

ATKINSON, A. 1983. *The Economics of Inequality*. Oxford: Clarendon Press.

—— 1993. On targeting social security: theory and Western experience with family benefits. Welfare State Programme Discussion Paper 99. London: STICERD, London School of Economics.

—— 1995. *Incomes and the Welfare State: Essays on Britain and Europe*. Cambridge: Cambridge University Press.

—— 1999. *The Economic Consequences of Rolling Back the Welfare State*. Cambridge, Mass.: MIT Press.

—— and MOGENSEN, G. (eds.) 1993. *Welfare and Work Incentives: A North European Perspective*. Oxford: Clarendon Press.

BARR, N. 2001. *The Welfare State as Piggy Bank: Information, Risk, Uncertainty, and the Role of the State*. Oxford: Oxford University Press.

BARRY, B. 1990. The welfare state vesus the relief of poverty. In *Needs and Welfare Provision*, ed. A. Ware and R. Goodin. London: Sage.

BROWNING, E. 1975. The externality argument for in-kind transfers: some critical remarks. *Kyklos*, 28: 526–44.

BURCHARDT, T., and HILLS, J. 1996. *Private Welfare Insurance and Social Security: Pushing the Boundaries*. York: York Publishing Services for the Joseph Rowntree Foundation.

CALERO, J. 2002. The distribution of public social expenditure in Spain: a general analysis with special reference to age and social class. *Social Policy and Administration*, 36 (5).

CORNIA, G., and STEWART, F. 1995. Two errors of targeting. In *Public Spending and the Poor: Theory and Evidence*, ed. D. Van de Walle and K. Nead. Baltimore: Johns Hopkins University for the World Bank.

DANZIGER, S. 1988. Recent trends in poverty and the antipoverty effectiveness of income transfers. In *The Distributional Impacts of Public Policies*, ed. S. Danziger and K. Portney. Basingstoke: Macmillan in association with the Policy Studies Organization.

—— and PORTNEY, K. (eds.) 1988. *The Distributional Impacts of Public Policies*. Basingstoke: Macmillan in association with the Policy Studies Organisation.

ESPING-ANDERSEN, G. 1990. *The Three Worlds of Welfare Capitalism*. Cambridge: Polity Press.

—— 1996. Positive-sum solutions in a world of trade-offs? Pp. 256–67 in *Welfare States in Transition: National Adaptations in Global Economies*, ed. G. Esping-Andersen. London: Sage.

FERRARINI, T., and NELSON, K. 2003. Taxation of social insurance and redistribution: a comparative analysis of ten welfare states. *Journal of European Social Policy*, 13 (1).

GOODIN, R., and LE GRAND, J. et al. 1987a. *Not Only the Poor: The Middle Classes and the Welfare State*. London: Unwin Hyman.

—— —— 1987b. Creeping universalism in the Australian welfare state In R. Goodin and J. Le Grand et al. 1987a.

—— et al. 1999. *The Real Worlds of Welfare Capitalism*. Cambridge: Cambridge University Press. Cambridge.

GUSTMAN, A., and STEINMEIER, T. 2000. How effective is redistribution under the social security benefit formula. NBER Working Paper No. w7597. Cambridge, Mass.: National Bureau of Economic Research.

HANSON, R. 1987. The expansion and contraction in the American welfare state. In R. Goodin and J. Le Grand et al. 1987a.

HAVEMAN, R. 1988. *Starting Even: An Equal Opportunity Program to Combat the Nation's New Poverty*. New York: Simon and Schuster.

HICKS, A., and KENWORTHY, L. 2003. Varieties of welfare capitalism. *Socio-Economic Review*, 1 (1).

HILLS, J. 2004. *Inequality and the State*. Oxford: Oxford University Press.

—— and FALKINGHAM, J. 1995. *The Dynamic of Welfare: The Welfare State and the Life Cycle*. Hemel Hempstead: Prentice Hall.

HM TREASURY 1999. *Tackling Poverty and Extending Opportunity*. The Modernisation of Britain's Tax and Benefit System No. 4. London: HM Treasury.

KENWORTHY, L. 1998. *Do Social-Welfare Policies Reduce Poverty? A Cross-National Assessment*. Luxembourg Income Study Working Paper No. 188.

—— 2004. An equality–growth trade-off? Ch. 5 in *Egalitarian Capitalism*. New York: Russell Sage Foundation.

KORPI, W., and PALME, J. 1998. The paradox of redistribution and strategies of equality: welfare state institutions, inequality, and poverty in the western countries. *American Sociological Review*, 63 (5): 661–87.

LE GRAND, J. 1982. *The Strategy of Equality: Redistribution and the Social Services*. London: Allen and Unwin.

—— 1987. The middle-class use of the British social services. In R. Goodin and J. Le Grand et al. 1987a.

LIEBMAN, J. 2002. Redistribution in the current US social security system. NBER Working Paper No. w8625. Cambridge, Mass.: National Bureau of Economic Research.

MITCHELL, D., HARDING, H., and GRUEN, F. 1994. Targeting welfare. *Economic Record*, 70 (210): 315–40.

PECHMAN, J., and MAZUR, M. 1984. The rich, the poor and the taxes they pay: an update. *Public Interest*, 77.

—— and OKNER, B. 1974. *Who Bears the Tax Burden?* Washington, DC: Brookings Institution.

PIERSON, P. (ed.) 2001. *The New Politics of the Welfare State*. Oxford: Oxford University Press.

POWELL, M. 1995. The strategy of equality revisited. *Journal of Social Policy*, 24 (2).

SCHWABISH, J., SMEEDING, T., and OSBERG, L. 2003. *Income Distribution and Social Expenditures: A Crossnational Perspective*. Luxembourg Income Study Working Paper No. 350.

SEFTON, T. 2002. Recent changes in the distribution of the social wage. CASE Paper 62. London: London School of Economics.

SMEEDING, T. 2004. Public policy, economic inequality, and poverty: the US in comparative perspective. Paper presented at the "Inequality and American politics" conference, Syracuse University, 20 Feb.

—— RAINWATER, L., and BURTLESS, G. 2000. *United States Poverty in a Cross-National Context*. Luxembourg Income Study Working Paper No. 244.

SMEEDING, T., SAUNDERS, P., CODER, J., JENKINS, S., FRITZELL, J., HAGENHAARS, A., HAUSER, R., and WOLFSON, M. 1993. Poverty, inequality, and family living standards impacts across seven countries: the effect of non cash subsidies for health, education and housing. *Review of Income and Wealth*, 39: 229–54.

TOBIN, J. 1970. On limiting the domain of inequality. *Journal of Law and Economics*, 13: 263–78.

TULLOCH, G. 1997. *Economics of Income Redistribution*. London: Kluwer Academic.

WEITZMAN, M. 1977. Is the price system or rationing more effective in getting a commodity to those who need it most? *Bell Journal of Economics*, 8: 517–24.

WELCH, F. 1999. In defence of inequality. *American Economic Review, Papers and Proceedings*, 89 (2).

WHITEFORD, P., and KENNEDY, S. 1995. *Incomes and Living Standards of Older People*. Department of Social Security Research Report No. 34. London: HMSO.

CHAPTER SIX

TOWARDS A CONCLUSION: COMMUNITY ORGANIZING AND SOCIAL CHANGE

During the time I have been writing this book, I have renewed my involvement in community organizing and become more focussed on the world of practice. The book began as a critical reflection, coloured by pessimism about the contribution of community organizing practices to wider struggles for social justice and progressive social change. The problems and conditions that community organizations face on a daily basis are shaped by the inequalities of wealth and power and the relentless pressures of an unregulated marketplace to increase these inequities. Those in the community sector face difficult challenges as they balance the demands of people asking for help and services with those of funding bodies, while understanding that underlying all of these is the necessity for basic social change. However, influenced by those I interviewed and by a chance to involve myself in new forms of engagement, my perceptions have shifted, and I have become more optimistic about the future.

Today's activists and organizers, stimulated by the anti-globalization movement, articulate a political vision for their work, tying their practices directly to a process of social change. Whereas one of the biggest problems with the professionalization of organizing is the lack of commitment to mobilizing people in order to build a collective voice, those I interviewed believe that priority should be given to such mobilization and to taking action into the streets. For them, service provision, although present, is secondary and is linked to an educational agenda. They share an analysis of power in society—who has it and how it is used to maintain oppression. In addition, they have shifted away from the identity politics that dominated the 1980s and 1990s. Although most have a strong sense of personal identity shaped by gender, ethnicity, or disability, their organizing approaches and practices have gone beyond it to build common cause with many groups.

Identity politics begins with the individual and her/his specific group. For example, Irshad Manji's book *Risking Utopia: On the Edge of a New Democracy* (1997) opens with a discussion of who she is: a Moslem, a woman, and a lesbian. At the same time, she rejects the categories of feminism and socialism to describe her stance. The book parodies the left and travels down the road from identity politics to a politics of self in a world in which tolerance is the main challenge. Manji argues that identity has become so fragmented that the only category that remains is the individual and that we live in a society of individuals. Everything becomes relative in a world of trade-offs. She posits a society no longer shaped by interest and power, but one in which "nobody is 'given' justice. Everybody has the right and responsibility to bargain for it. To ensure that diversity is respected—a condition of belonging—patient negotiation must supplant instant gratification" (p. 139). In her world, as opposed to any kind of collective interest, the individual is the basic unit, and everything is negotiated from there. She states:

my adaptation of radical democracy emphasizes the individual infinitely more than the institution.... That focus on the personal relationship is intentional. The age of institutions, from the family to the company, has died. In trying to update the concept of radical democracy, I treat it as a set of values that takes root with the individual and radiates out. (p. 155)

Identity politics has always played an ambiguous role. Many new groups have asserted their rights and demanded representation in the political sphere, insisting that their voices be heard. Beginning with the women's movement and followed by gays and lesbians, the disabled, and so on, these groups have challenged the orthodoxy of the traditional left and have created new opportunities for opposition. They made gains and in the process, contributed to a new politics of the left that was more inclusive, acknowledged difference, and created opportunities for new actors on the political scene.

In the period from the 1980s until recently, those working toward social change put a great deal of emphasis on identity as a way of revealing and reacting to conditions of oppression. Despite gains made, the emphasis on identity has acted to fragment opposition. As Andrea Levy (1994) argues:

Identity politics represents not only the balkanization of the remnants of the left but also the abandonment of a larger vision or project of social transformation; taken to its logical extremes, the elevation of difference as the sole thing which defines us renders the idea of commonly held values on which such a vision can be based not only theoretically dubious but nefariously homogenizing. We appear to be on the verge of forgetting ... that commonality does not imply the obliteration of diversity, that the opposite pole of difference does not have to be sameness but solidarity. (p. 19)

Recognizing this, the people I interviewed have moved beyond identity politics and argue for a return to a broad opposition movement based on the common interest of those facing social and economic inequality. The women describe themselves as feminists. Those of minority ethnic or cultural communities understand their unique historical experiences and struggles but, at the same time, acknowledge their connection to others and to common experiences as the basis for a wider social and political solidarity. The challenge for this generation of organizers is, according to John Anner (1996):

A reinvigorated social justice Movement with capital "M" will have to develop mechanisms of reconnecting identity politics with class issues, putting matters of economic justice on the front burner while showing how a racist and sexist power structure—now some—what more integrated—works to deny most people a decent life. (p. 11)

The interviews demonstrate that this challenge has been taken up through a reinserting a broad political vision and the struggle for basic social change within local organizing practice.

NEW PRACTICES

THE IMMIGRANT WORKERS' CENTRE

As I mentioned at the beginning of this chapter, I have become involved again in several organizations that do contribute to processes of social change. The Immigrant Workers' Centre (IWC) was founded in 2000. (Two of the people I interviewed were key in its development.) The idea for the centre grew out of the frustration of two immigrant union organizers with the difficulties of organizing immigrant workers and with the limits to conventional union approaches. They believed that the actual workplace presented many obstacles, such as intimidation by bosses, to bringing people together. Further, in order for workplace struggle to succeed, broader support was necessary, along with ongoing education and analysis. The IWC acts primarily as a place for immigrants to Canada to meet and learn about labour rights and to organize themselves on work-related questions. The community centre is a safe place to meet outside of work and brings together workers of different backgrounds with union and community activists. The IWC's program is formed by the issues brought by workers coming into the centre, such as participation in a campaign against the expulsion from Canada of a domestic live-in caregiver and her son. The case received a lot of coverage and raised

not only the specific issues this woman faced but a critique of the wider situation of how immigrant labour is brought to Canada and the lack of rights in live-in conditions. Another campaign, launched in alliance with others, aims to improve the Labour Standards Act in Quebec. It grew out of the situation of several women who were laid off from a company and were unable to defend themselves because of large loopholes in the Act. In addition, the IWC has become a gathering place for many different groups, such as a Filipino youth group that is challenging the harassment many immigrant youth suffer at the hands of the police and lobbying for recreational and sports facilities to counter gang membership.

Organizationally, the IWC has a board and charter, but it functions more informally with a paid (badly and sometimes irregularly) coordinator and a loose, core group of activists. Specific working groups and campaigns have attracted both immigrant workers and allies, including student activists. Building an organizational structure is not given as high a priority as working directly on campaigns, education, and mobilization. The practice of the IWC contrasts significantly with the majority of service and development organizations. It is explicitly political in the sense that its leadership understands its work as linking local struggles to global concerns and other international social movements and as making sure that political education is always present. Further, building a bridge between workplace and community organizing has always been a huge challenge for both unions and the community. The different cultures and styles of organizing are not easy to overcome. However, several unions have given financial and other support to the IWC and have collaborated with it on specific activities.

The IWC is firmly in the social action tradition, fighting on labour issues through mobilizing people and their allies. Because it is a relatively young organization and because it does not fall into traditional categories, it has not received funding from government agencies that support community organizations. With its support from unions, it has been able to carry out its activities without having to compromise its mission or orientation. However, the IWC is financially unstable and has had to live with a very limited budget.

This seems to be the new reality for groups that do not fall into government-defined service and development categories. The IWC combines intervention on the specific issues of immigrant workers with a broader socio-political analysis and mobilization for social justice. In addition, it has made connections between local and global action, establishing links with a new generation of activists in the struggle against corporate power.

ECO-INITIATIVES

Eco-Initiatives is an organization in my neighbourhood that promotes urban agriculture. It comes out of an ecological tradition and combines community development with collective gardens. The gardens are a place for residents to meet and work collectively to produce fresh organic produce for themselves and for local organizations that provide food for low-income people. It began as part of a municipal recycling program; its role was to educate and to encourage participation in the program. Because of increased bureaucratic pressures and controls exerted by the city, the organization decided to break from this relationship and pursue only the urban agriculture agenda. As a consequence, it is financially less stable, but more autonomous in pursuit of its goals. It is also involved in a wider network of organizations that examines the issue of food security.

Eco-Initiatives practice can be described as within the community development approach. It does not engage in action strategies nor mobilize people to make demands for social change. Its politics are carried out in different ways. The gardens are a place of social solidarity where people gather to produce food in a way that is different from the one dominated by corporations. In one of the interviews in Chapter 5, a young woman employed there talks about community gardens as a place for political education. Since the gardens are not individual plots but collective, they encourage a culture in which direct participation in a collective is an important objective. Politics are expressed through the understanding that organic urban agriculture opposes corporate-dominated food production and distribution and creates an alternative to it. In this aspect, Eco-initiatives is part

of a movement that preserves heritage seeds discarded by mass production. For example, a variety of melons known as Montreal Melons had disappeared. Eco-Initiatives workers tracked down the seeds from a small producer in the United States and reintroduced this melon to its own gardens as well as selling the seeds to private gardens. An ecological consciousness is promoted through these types of activities. Further, community gardens belong in the movement toward more sustainable neighbourhoods, which redefines what functions can be carried out locally and contributes toward greater collective self-reliance. Creating alternatives to capitalism through even small activities like the gardens contributes to building a new political and social culture at the local level.

THE POPULAR ARCHIVES OF POINTE ST. CHARLES

The third organization with which I have become involved was founded in order to keep alive the traditions of community organization practice. The Popular Archives of Pointe St. Charles is located in a working-class neighbourhood with a long history of militant community organizing and alternative organizations. It was the birthplace of the first CED organizations in Montreal, community health and legal clinics. Many organizations have worked in the struggle against poverty in the area, providing services and education, and these groups continue to mobilize locally. In addition, the residents have mobilized effectively to defend their clinics against government attempts to take them over or close them. The ratio of French-speakers to English-speakers is 60 to 40; both groups have their own organizations and histories and have worked together in major struggles. Because of the high percentage of social housing—non-profits, cooperatives, and public—the community has limited the pressures of gentrification. As a consequence, many older activists have remained, and there are some new projects created by younger residents. At the same time, because no one organization has systematically gathered the traditions together, there has been a loss of the history of these organizing efforts. Documents, photos, and videotapes of these earlier periods are decaying, unsorted, and stored in basements. One goal of the Popular

Archive is to reclaim these materials; another is to use these materials for popular education, linking past traditions to present struggles.

The Popular Archive has created a video and film festival, featuring more than 40 videos and films made on community life and organizing. An after-school program introduces young children to community organizations and their history. A large exhibit on the role of women in the community and how this role has changed over the last 50 years was prepared for the World March of Women in 2000. Interviews with women active in the community were used to construct the exhibit. Following its success and the demand in both the local and wider community for its display, a wider project celebrating the contribution of women to the development of community organizing was initiated under the leadership of a Ph.D. student. Entitled "Tissons une courte pointe: L'histoire de l'action communautaire à travers les histoires de vies de femmes de Pointe-St-Charles" (Weaving a quilt: History of community action via the life stories of women from Point St. Charles), this project was made up of two groups of women, one French and the other English-speaking. All of the women had participated in a variety of ways in the neighbourhood and shared not only their stories but also the impact of their participation on their lives. Out of this project came the production of a book and video. In the long-term, an inter-generation project is planned.

The board of the Archives is small with the leadership coming from people who have been leading activists in the community over more than 25 years. The idea of the archive is to promote a consciousness of struggle and opposition within the area and to celebrate these traditions—to make history real and link it to present struggles. It is easy for history to disappear with the loss of documents and the death or disengagement of older activists and organizers. Connecting generations provides continuity and gives those involved in the daily struggles support and insights.

As with the other two organizations, the Popular Archives faces a difficult time financially. The Quebec government's funding programs specify sectoral categories. Organizations that fall outside of these categories have trouble receiving support. The Archive is perceived neither as a formal archive nor as a specialist in popular edu-

cation. Therefore, the main source of its support has come from a foundation, but this is time-limited. The lack of a proper funding base has created internal stress and has limited the potential of the organization to expand its archiving and educational activities.

I describe the archive because it is an example of how the traditions of a district have been preserved. In Chapters 3 and 4 two approaches to community organizing were discussed—action and development. I argued there that the political and economic context and external pressures have contributed to the shaping or recasting of practice. With the restructuring of the 1980s, many of the older action traditions were abandoned for moderation, partnerships, and development. Pointe St. Charles was also subjected to these pressures, and its CED organization has gone that route. However, the tradition of mobilization and action is still alive and well. The Archives supports this tradition and contributes to this continuity.

These three examples contribute to a process of social change. They do so in different ways, linking action and education and a vision of community as a place for the mobilization of political struggles and the creation of social alternatives. A couple of lessons come out of these experiences. First, social change is not necessarily linked to a particular model of practice. Second, organizations that bring people together and that provide activities connected to their daily lives and linked to broader political questions and traditions can be the basis for building local activism and for wider movements for social change.

TOWARDS A CONCLUSION: REVISITING COMMUNITY ORGANIZING MODELS

Each of these three organizations has within its practice and wider orientation elements of a struggle for basic social change. Although the practices can also be viewed as constrained by the system, the tension lived in these organizations is between performing specific activities that are within the boundaries and simultaneously working beyond those limits. The tension—and how organizations and organizers work with it—is the key dilemma.

In Chapter 2, I cited the work of Rothman (1999) and Minkler and Wallerstein (1999) to examine the action and development models or approaches. Here, I will revisit them with a priority given to the question of social change as the starting point in exploring a different approach to community organizing practice.[1] The action and development models and the literature concerning them examine practice elements and strategies. The politics tends to be limited to what can be described as "pragmatic reformism," that is, improving social conditions within the boundaries of what exits. I have raised the question of how community organizing can move beyond this and contribute to basic social change. The issue is complex; it is not easy to separate limited gains from long-term social change because engagement in the "real world" inevitably leads to pushing for specific victories. The difference between those practices that are limited to specific gains only and those that see practice as part of a process of wider social change is due to factors such as intention, vision, process, and alliances. Both action and development can contribute to social change or can play a role in maintaining the status quo by not moving beyond specific local gains; both can also have a lasting impact by changing the consciousness of the groups they serve, thus creating conditions for mobilization for social and political change.

The table below expresses the relationship between the development and action approaches and the question of social change. I have used the terms integration and opposition in order to contrast the politics of practice. Integration strategies are used to increase people's participation in the system as it is or to enlarge resources or distribute some goods a little more fairly without challenging the basic assumptions of the system itself. This can happen either through pressure group tactics or through a variety of social programs. For example, local organizing to pressure the municipal government to improve traffic patterns or garbage pick-up can better the quality of life in a neighbourhood but does not challenge the domination of the

[1] Thanks to Bob Fisher, Marie Lacroix, and a workshop on issues in Community Economic Development for suffering through attempts at developing this work and for their respective insights.

car or the patterns of waste production. Similarly, programs such as job readiness attempt to place people in the labour market but do not necessarily raise questions about working conditions or about the pattern of linking jobs to participation in consumer culture. Integration practices support the maintenance of the fundamental power relations of our society and are designed to help people either meet their needs or make gains within existing structures and processes. They assume that the system can expand to accommodate and bring people into either the jobs or the life-styles defined by corporate capitalism. They do not question the limits and competitive nature of the system. Organizing within this approach does not go beyond either the limitation of local, winnable demands or service and development.

In contrast, those working on the opposition side understand local organizing as part of a process of fundamental social change. This can include both organizing opposition to different aspects of society, such as specific policy or forms of oppression and inequality, and creating local alternatives such as cooperatives and services. These practices challenge the basic relations of power and create an alternative political and social culture based on democracy and direct control by citizens of these organizations. Further, the process of reaching these ends is through mobilizing citizens to play an active role. This is a key element, and the one aspect of practice that has been reduced since the 1980s. Power relations can be challenged and shifted only through the collective actions of citizens. Community organizing, to be a force for social change, has to be able to mobilize locally but must act in conjunction with wider alliances that share a politics of opposition.

The differences are not always clear-cut and it is hard to classify actual day-to-day practices. It is for that reason that I have added the middle column—overlapping practices—to the table. In some respects, the actual activities are less important than the processes around them. This means, for example, that specific demands, campaigns, or services at the local level are integral to community organizing and fall within a process of building opposition. The process of organizing is what is important, not just the outcome. This includes raising critical consciousness in those participating in the organizing process about the necessity of social transformation as the means to achieve social justice and democracy. In addition, local work must be connected to broader social movements and coalitions that are part of a struggle for social change. Gutierrez and Lewis (1995), for instance, understand specific activities by feminist organizers at the local level as tied to the broader social movement.

The table illustrates the dimensions of integration/opposition along with the action/development approaches. I have included traditions in order to illustrate each approach.

	INTEGRATION	OVERLAPPING PRACTICES	OPPOSITION
DEVELOPMENT	Service provision and development schemes based on professional leadership and a consensus model. Tradition: Asset/capacity building (e.g., McKnight).	Service provision at the local level.	Building alternatives that create new democratic or non-market economics, new practices that are "pre-figurative." Tradition: Feminist services or green urban development (e.g., collective community gardens).
ACTION	Pluralist pressure group organizing Tradition: Pluralist pressure groups (e.g., Alinsky).	Organizing people in a neighbourhood to pressure for local improvements.	Social movement organizing and critical consciousness, challenging the legitimacy of existing power relations. Tradition: Social movement organizing locally (e.g., anti-globalization activism).

required. Local democracy through participation of citizens is a factor, but the focus is limited to local improvement with an underlying assumption that self-help is a primary element.

Integration/Action is primarily a pressure group approach, which assumes political pluralism in the wider society. The goal of the organizing is to gain local improvements by applying pressure on those with authority to bring about changes. This approach also focusses on the local, although it includes alliances with others with common interests. Some of the organizations operating under this practice have a longer view of building power, but it is within the boundaries of local improvement. Often "radical" or disruptive tactics obscure the more traditional goals that these tactics are used to reach. In both of the Integrative quadrants, there are elements of practice that contribute to wider social change, but this is not their primary focus (this was discussed at the end of Chapter 4). Rather, it is an unintended consequence that comes from people working together for social improvement and beginning to build solidarity and a critical analysis. It is this blurring that creates the overlapping categories on the chart.

Both quadrants under opposition contain practices and organizations that advance wider processes of social change. They go beyond the immediate goals and specific practices shared, at times, with those of an integrative orientation because of a self-conscious commitment to intention and vision. Intention implies an understanding of what the organization is trying to do and naming it. Kovel (2002), in his book on eco-socialism, argues that intentional communities and intentionality can be understood as material forces. He says, "the generation of some kind of collective 'intentions' that can withstand the power of capital's force field will be necessary for creating an eco-socialist society" (p. 194). Naming the essence of our work is the key aspect, although there are risks involved. What will the implications be for the sources of support? Will it upset "partners"? There is a difficult line between pragmatism shaped by the demands of others and an understanding of the goals of social change. There must be an adequate number of people working together who share these directions, rather than a small group of conspirators within the staff of an organization. Community organizations *can* contribute to the building of a

Integration/Development is currently the dominant approach. It includes the community development described in Chapter 4, which is defined by social partnerships, supporting civil society organizations, and consensus-oriented strategies such as asset/capacity-building. Change is understood as an internally defined local process, and solutions to social and economic problems are sought within what already exists in the community, although outside resources may be

wider oppositional culture. In order for that to happen, the analysis and alternative direction has to be articulated in a clear vision.

Vision is naming the long-term objectives of the organizing process and how they connect to the type of society we would like to see. It incorporates the core values of the organization and relates these to its long-term goals and direction, along with defining strategies of how to get there. The vision orients the politics of the organization and helps sustains the direction over time. Gindin (2002) describes vision in the context of the resistance to corporate globalization:

> Social justice demands reviving the determination to dream. It is not just that dreaming is essential for maintaining any resistance, but because today, if we do not think big—as big as the globalizers themselves think—we will not even win small. (p. 2)

This level of vision implies that the community movement has to see itself in fundamental opposition to the basic relations of power and domination in our society and must look toward a future in which all forms of hierarchy and domination are ended. This is a monumental task, and it is only in alliance with others that there is even a remote possibility that it can happen. More importantly, without a vision of what is basic and how this connects to the short term and its related process, it is impossible to get beyond the demands of service or limited campaigns. This does not mean that the vision has to be rigid, but it should act to orient both practice goals and processes. Day-to-day local work requires pragmatic engagement with pressures from funders and working for specific objectives; as a result, long-term goals can be forgotten or ignored. One reason for maintaining and articulating vision is to balance specific short-term demands with long-term values and social change objectives. Differentiating between mandate and vision permits a naming of the long- and short-term aspects of an organization. Specific mandates should be shaped by the wider vision. In other words, it is important that organizations do not restrict their definition of vision to their particular activities. One way of doing this is to emphasize process and alliances.

The Opposition/Action quadrant includes those social action organizations that intentionally work beyond the local. For example, the student left of the 1960s and 1970s was involved in establishing welfare rights and grassroots neighbourhood organizations. These mobilized people, contested policies of government, and demanded social rights for the poor. Similarly, as mentioned earlier, the women's movement put in place new services that recognized needs and redefined social issues from the point of view of women. Many of these organizations continue to exist, and, although they may be less politically engaged nowadays, they are nonetheless present in social struggles.

Social movements, by definition, have a short life. They rise into prominence and then decline. Organizations founded by movement activists provide continuity despite the transformations they go through, such as service development and the replacement of activists by professionals whose practice is to represent those they serve rather than to mobilize them. The initial values and visions do not entirely disappear. As new movements arise or campaigns are launched, community-based organizations play a role in supporting and nourishing them and offer a place from which to mobilize and carry out political education. The IWC is an organization of the Opposition/Action type. Its vision goes beyond specific campaigns such as labour code reforms and rights agenda. It has informal links with anti-globalization activists, participates in a variety of ways with them in demonstrations and other activities, and mobilizes for common actions. It also has connections to international bodies concerned about issues facing migrant workers. Seeing itself as part of an international struggle against exploitation of migrant and other workers, its programs of education aim to draw together immediate problems with a deeper analysis of the wider political and economic context. Many of those interviewed in Chapter 5 see their engagement in a similar way; that is, they combine basic social transformation with specific practices.

Opposition/Development couples services and/or development to the process of social change to create alternatives to the present system as either places free from hierarchies or as models of a different type of society. The organizations with this orientation are democratic and participate in a wider culture of opposition. For example, service organizations that grew out of social movements maintain a commitment to social change work. Two examples illustrate this point. The feminist movement in the 1970s created services such as rape crisis centres and shelters for victims of domestic abuse, but these were contextualized in campaigns for public recognition of these issues. Women mobilized to demand public support for these services. The services themselves were often run by collectives and concentrated not only on providing safe spaces but also on raising the consciousness both of the users of their services and the wider community. Similarly, community clinics, democratically controlled by residents and employees, combined health services with education and popular mobilization on a variety of issues. The Pointe St. Charles Community Clinic continues to employ community organizers who mobilize and educate the public on many different social issues.

There is another tradition that falls within this quadrant. Economic alternatives, in which ownership is collective rather than individual, remove production of goods and service from the market and prioritize need rather than profit as the reason for production. The creation of "green alternatives," such as Eco-Initiatives, is part of this orientation. Morrison's (1995) vision of "ecological democracy" requires the growth of democratic and community-based alternatives. These encompass both human services and other activities. He argues that these associations are "the basic venue for moving power away from state and corporate bureaucracies" (p. 139). The creation of alternatives has to move beyond local work to federated structures that build an "associative democracy" that acts to transfer power from government and market to community. Similarly, Kovel (2002) sees local associations as:

> prefigurative praxes that are to overcome capital in an
> ecosocialist way are at once remote and exactly at
> hand. They are remote insofar as the entire regime of
> capital stands in the way of their realization, and they
> are at hand insofar as the movement toward the future
> exists embedded in every point of social organism
> where a need arises. (p. 217)

Perhaps Kovel overstates the case, but the tradition of creating social alternatives to either the state or capital is a long one, rooted particularly in anarchist traditions. Such organizations play several roles, including demonstrating that people without managers can create forms of local production and services.

Both action and development organizations committed to social change have an impact on the daily lives of citizens, thus encouraging their participation in social change activities. These processes have the potential of helping community organizations move beyond their specific goals and day-to-day activities to create a culture of opposition. As I discussed earlier, community organizations, particularly those founded since the 1960s, grew out of a tradition of direct and/or participatory democracy, creating places in which citizens can have a role in shaping their own lives and local community. As power in our society becomes increasingly remote, activities that are controlled by citizens become more important; open discussion and debate lead to participation in decision-making processes and give people a voice on wider issues. This reduces the passivity generated by a consumer society in which the only real decision people are asked to make is which brand-named product meets their manipulated desires and wants. Real politics is neither about consumerism nor electoral choices every four or five years but about active participation in society where citizens can represent their own interests and create alternatives. Community organizations offer this opportunity.

Community and popular education are important tools in building leadership and local power. Lotz (1997) traces the history of education, community development, and organizing practice as far back as the emergence of university extension departments in 1914 in Alberta. The most developed and long-lasting of these efforts was the "Antigonish movement," pioneered in the 1920s in Nova Scotia by Fathers Jimmy Tompkins and Michael Coady. Responding to the poverty of local fishing and mining communities, they educated workers for action, building new institutions such as credit unions and cooperatives to improve social and economic conditions. According to Lotz (1997):

By the end of 1931, 173 study clubs had been established, most of them in rural Scottish Catholic parishes... By 1939, the movement had established 342 credit unions and 162 other forms of cooperative organizations. The Antigonish approach was summarized in four imperatives: Listen! Study! Discuss! Act! (p. 21)

Education within community organizations can be formal sessions or informal learning situations. In either case, people develop an analysis of interest and power and come to understand the political and social stake they have in the larger society. The lessons can be local and related to organizational self-interest, but underlying these are issues of power, how it operates and how to challenge it. The process demystifies the notion that the political system operates for all of us and helps people learn how to make demands that promote their rights and specific interests. Brandt (2002) describes it as follows:

> Popular education ... aims to unveil, analyze and transform power relations, based on class, race/ethnicity, gender, sexuality, age, religion, or any social dimension of oppression. It promotes democratic practice through teaching/learning processes that are collective, critical, systematic, participatory, and creative. Motivated by principles of equality and justice, it integrates research, learning, and organizing for social change. (p. 68)

It is important that local issues and actions provide opportunities both for making specific changes in such a way that the people involved gain a sense of power through collective action and for connecting to wider movements and deepening a critical analysis of how power is structured and how it operates.

Many community organizations have been effective in building local power and having influence at that level. This is both a strength and an opportunity, but it has its limits. Community organizations participate in local "tables," or groups of organizations, based on

neighbourhoods and/or sectors sharing a common interest. As a result, some degree of local power can be mobilized. There are two weaknesses, however. First, often the main purpose of these "tables" is to negotiate support for the organizations from the government; organizational self-interest shapes the way that they "do business." Second, since the vision of these bodies is limited, either because of locality or sectoral interests, it is difficult for them to go beyond these concerns and engage in broad political and social struggles. However, even with these limits, these bodies have been significant in their participation in campaigns and wider social mobilizations, such as the World March of Women in 2000, discussed earlier. Social movements in general need to see these community-based organizations, even moderate ones, as potential allies who can be brought into action under certain conditions.

Community organizations carry progressive values into practice. Despite all the pressures on them to collapse into some kind of politically innocuous service entity, many have managed to use the resources from the state and/or private foundations to contribute to ongoing political education and mobilization for citizens to struggle for social and economic justice. It is not easy to balance the demands of those funding these organizations with the traditions of social change and wider activism. The three groups briefly presented in this chapter illustrate the financial consequences of promoting social change and community alternatives in terms that are not compromised. Mobilization of citizens for action, education, and agitation, within the democratic process, is the most important work of these organizations. Those that create economic and social alternatives embody progressive values; however, they do not create a new society within the shell of capitalism but do provide a meeting place and a small alternative economy. We need to mobilize for action, but we also need alternatives so we can live our values. As Michael Albert (2002) states:

> We chose issues to better the lot of suffering constituencies and to simultaneously increase prospects for more gains in the future. Short term, we raise social costs until elites begin to implement our demands or

people, it's because they learned what to do with their anger. They learned how to begin to change things. They learned how to turn their anger outward and make it creative…. Our growing up angry was not unusual. Revolutionaries are not adventurers. They come out of ordinary lives and want to make a revolution to change ordinary lives. (p. 4)

Community organizing for social change begins with this impulse. Learning what to do with our anger and outrage, bringing it to local struggles, broadening and extending it, and keeping it to fuel our drive for social justice: this is the challenge.

end policies that we oppose. Longer term, we accumulate support and develop movement infrastructure and alternative institutions, while working toward transforming society's defining relations. (p. x)

Building opposition is thus two-pronged. One dimension is action that transcends the local; the other builds democratic alternatives. Both provide opportunities for political education and contribute to a culture of opposition. Most of the leadership of the community movement from the late 1970s has had a socialist vision of some kind and has understood the limits of capitalism. In our present period, we are taught to believe that "There Is No Alternative" (TINA). We have to rethink some of the older doctrines, but we must name the problem—global capitalism—and renew our vision of the type of future we want and how we see getting there. This is the starting point for renewal.

This book has looked backwards at the contradictory traditions of community organizing and has looked ahead to what might be the future with a renewed commitment to fundamental social change. In acknowledging all the pressures to move practice towards integration, we cannot lose sight of why many of us got into the field. We wanted to do more than "do good," which will always be inadequate in a world that has given more and more power and wealth to the few and impoverishes the many. Doing good maintains these relations and allows social inequalities, social problems, and environmental destruction to grow.

Anger is an appropriate response to injustice; we tend to forget our anger, as the community sector has become more sophisticated and is accepted as an important social actor and as we become "strategic" and "professional." Kathryn Addelson (1991) speaks of her own experience and that of others:

I grew up angry…. Angry because my people, my neighbors, my family were defeated by a sense of powerlessness…. [Consider the] lives of people who grew up angry. If these people are different from other

221

Studying Public Policy*

RICHARD SIMEON   *Queen's University*

In the last few years, the study of policy and policy-making has become one of the most fashionable branches of the discipline. It has spawned new university courses, an Institute for Public Policy Research, and several new journals, including *Policy Sciences*, *The Public Interest*, and most recently, *Canadian Public Policy*. The impetus to focus on policy, on what governments actually do and why, comes from a great many sources. Partly it may be a reaction against the so-called behavioural revolution which seemed often to lead us away from a concern with the stuff of politics. Partly it stems from a growing desire to be in some sense more "relevant" and to apply whatever knowledge we have to contemporary societal problems. Partly it stems from the desires of government themselves to be more systematic in their consideration and assessment of alternative programs.[1] Policy research has also been given urgency by increasing pessimism about the ability of governments to cope in an era of "demand overload" and "the fiscal crisis of the state."[2]

Despite this recent preoccupation with what, after all, is one of the oldest concerns of political science, we have not really advanced very far in increasing understanding of how government policies and actions are to be explained or understood. There is a proliferation of isolated studies, and of different methods and approaches, but precious little in the way of explanation. Indeed, we are not even sure of what it is we want to explain, of what our dependent variables should be. This paper hopes to provide an assessment and critique of some of the principal developments of recent years, and to suggest some potentially more

*This paper is a revised version of a seminar prepared for the Department of Political Economy, University of Saskatchewan, Saskatoon, in January 1975. I would like to thank the department and its members for giving me the opportunity, and also to thank several of my colleagues at Queen's University, and the University of Essex, for their comments – Dale Poel, Graham Wilson, John Meisel, Simon McInnes, Allan Tupper, Finn Hoven, and David McKay.

[1]For a discussion of recent developments in this direction in the Canadian federal government, see G. Bruce Doern, "The Development of Policy Organizations in the Executive Arena," in Doern and Peter Aucoin, eds., *The Structures of Policy-Making in Canada* (Toronto, 1971), 38–78. See also Gordon Robertson, "The Changing Role of the Privy Council Office," *Canadian Public Administration* 14 (Winter 1971), 487–508; and A.W. Johnson, "The Treasury Board of Canada and the Machinery of Government in the 1970's," *Canadian Journal of Political Science* 4 (September 1971), 346–66. See also several of the contributions to Thomas Hockin, ed., *Apex of Power* (Scarborough, Ont., 1971).

[2]See, among others, Daniel Bell, "The Public Household – On 'Fiscal Sociology' and the Liberal Society," *The Public Interest* 34 (Winter 1974), 29–68; Anthony King, "Overload: Problems of Governing in the 1970's," *Political Studies* XXIII (June–September 1975), 284–96; James O'Connor, *The Fiscal Crisis of the State* (New York, 1973); and Richard Rose, "Overloaded Government," *European Studies Newsletter* V (December 1975), 13–18.

Canadian Journal of Political Science/Revue canadienne de science politique, IX, no. 4 (December/décembre 1976). Printed in Canada/Imprimé au Canada

L'étude des politiques publiques

L'auteur évalue et critique les approches les plus récentes utilisées dans l'étude des politiques publiques et formule un cadre de référence pour la conduite future d'une telle étude. Après avoir démontré les limites inhérentes aux études de cas ainsi qu'aux approches fondées sur la prise de décision, lesquelles sont surtout axées sur des préoccupations propres soit à l'administration publique, soit à l'analyse des politiques (« policy analysis »), il suggère que l'étude des politiques doit tenir compte d'un éventail plus large de facteurs politiques et institutionnels qu'elle ne l'a fait jusqu'à présent, de façon, notamment, à ce que la détermination des politiques (« policy-making ») ne réfère plus simplement au règlement des problèmes (« problem-solving »), mais aussi à la compétition et aux conflits qui les ont engendrés.

Selon l'auteur, l'étude comparative des politiques publiques devrait en premier lieu bien identifier l'étendue de l'action gouvernementale, les moyens dont le gouvernement dispose pour atteindre ses objectifs et la répartition des bénéfices et des coûts résultant de ses activités. Un examen critique des divers modèles utilisés pour expliquer ces trois dimensions lui permet de conclure que l'utilité de chacun des modèles est restreinte à des aspects bien particuliers des politiques publiques, si bien qu'aucun d'entre eux ne permet, à lui seul, d'en fournir une explication adéquate.

fruitful lines of inquiry.[3] Almost every aspect of policy-making in Canada remains shrouded in ignorance if not mystery. The need, therefore, is to develop both theory and information-gathering together; each must inform the other. It is also necessary to rescue the study of policy from two or three holes in which it threatens to become stuck.

First, policy study has become rather closely linked with the study of bureaucracy and public administration. Obviously, bureaucratic agencies are central elements in the policy-making process, and no study of policy could ignore them. But bureaucrats and politicians operate within a broader political framework, defined by such factors as prevailing ideologies, assumptions and values, structures of power and influence, patterns of conflict and division, and so on. They make critical choices, but from a rather limited set of alternatives. Moreover, much of the literature on bureaucracy is concerned with questions such as efficiency and effectiveness, which, while important, do not seem to me to be the central ones. Policy-making must be broader than public administration.

It is even more important to rescue the study of policy from what we might call the technologists, whose main concern has been to develop aids to assist official decision-makers make in some sense "better" decisions. In this view, exemplified by writers like Yehezkiel Dror,[4] policy-making is essentially a technical question,

[3]One embarks on yet another review of the literature and presentation of a framework with some trepidation. Should we not actually get on and do the research, rather than endlessly talk about how to do it? I hope, however, the paper does break some new ground both in its formulation of the problems and in its attention to the Canadian case. Among the better recent assessments of the field are: Austin Ranney, ed., *Political Science and Public Policy* (Chicago, 1969); Richard Rose, "Comparing Public Policy: An Overview," *European Journal of Political Research* 1 (1973), 67–94; Hugh Heclo, "Review Article: Policy Analysis," *British Journal of Political Science* 2 (January 1972), 83–108; Anthony King, "Ideas, Institutions and the Policies of Governments: A Comparative Analysis," Parts I–III, *British Journal of Political Science* 3 (July and October 1973), 291–313 and 409–23.

[4]*Public Policy-Making Re-examined* (San Francisco, 1968). See also Erich Jantsch, "From Forecasting and Planning to Policy Sciences," *Policy Sciences* I (Spring 1970), 31–4, and

a matter of developing more systematic means to canvass alternatives, assess costs and benefits, and implement choices. This literature, which appears to have had considerable influence with government decision-makers themselves, is also prescriptive: it seeks primarily not to *explain* how or why decisions are made, but to *prescribe* more effective ways of doing it. It also tends to focus its study narrowly, suggesting "better" policy – that is, policy which is more rational, consistent, cost-effective, and so on – will follow from reforms of administrative structure and development of new analytical techniques. Randall Ripley distinguishes between policy analysis – "advice on the choosing of alternatives" – and "policy theory" – "the explanation of why certain alternatives are chosen and others are not."[5] If we are to understand politics generally, our study of policy must be firmly rooted in the latter view.

In seeking to move beyond the perspectives of public administration and policy analysis, each of which is useful but limited, we need to link up the study of policy with the more traditional concerns of political science and in particular with the three most vital elements: power, conflict, and ideology. What governments do cannot be fully explained either by focusing only on the actions and perceptions of the "proximate policy-makers,"[6] as Charles Lindblom calls them, or by stressing only the impersonal forces of the environment, such as levels of economic development, urbanization, and affluence, as some of the recent American "determinants" literature suggests. Policy emerges from the play of economic, social, and political forces, as manifested in and through institutions and processes. A danger in the emergence of a specialized subdiscipline of "policy science" is that such broad forces will be ignored or assumed.

Second, policy-making is not, by and large, simply a matter of problem-solving, of taking some common goal and seeking the "best" or most cost effective "solution." It is rather a matter of choice in which resources are limited and in which goals and objectives differ and cannot easily be weighed against each other. Hence policy-making is a matter of conflict. There are very few pure public goods,[7] that is, those which are available equally to all citizens. Most goods distributed by government confer differential benefits – some get more than others; some pay more than others. Much of the debate about them is precisely about these questions.[8] Hence the most important question to ask in the study of policy is Lasswell's political question: who gets what, when, and how?

A third basic assumption about policy flows from this perspective: policy study needs to be comparative across both space and time. We need to look at the broad

---

other articles in the same issue. For a Canadian example, see Economic Council of Canada, Eighth Annual Review, *Design for Decision-Making* (Ottawa, 1971). A good critique is found in G. Bruce Doern, *Political Policy-Making: A Review of the Economic Council's Eighth Annual Review and the Ritchie Report* (Montreal, 1972).

[5]"Review of Ranney and Dror," *American Political Science Review* 63 (1969), 918

[6]*The Policy-Making Process* (Englewood Cliffs, N.J., 1968), 20–1 and chap. 9

[7]For a discussion of varieties of public goods, see Peter O. Steiner, "The Public Sector and the Public Interest," in Robert Havemann and Julius Margolis, eds., *Public Expenditures and Policy Analysis* (Chicago, 1970), 21–58. The classic definition is that of Paul Samuelson, "The Pure Theory of Public Expenditure," *Review of Economics and Statistics* 36 (1954), 387–90.

[8]Herbert Jacob and Michael Lipsky, "Outputs, Structure and Power," *Journal of Politics* xxx (May 1968), 510

evolution of patterns of policy over long periods within countries, provinces, and other units, in the ways they deal with similar problems as a first step towards the primary goal of explaining the differences.

Before considering a broader approach, let us examine some of the general characteristics of the existing policy literature. Most obvious is the striking concentration on case studies, examining either a single decision, or policy in a general area such as pensions, or immigration, or foreign policy. Indeed the most common framework sometimes appears to consist of mandatory theoretical chapters at the beginning and end which bear little relationship to the detailed historical reconstruction of a set of events which takes up the bulk of the book.[9] Such studies can be extremely useful, especially when, as in Canada, we have so little basic information with which to work. They can provide a sense of the rich nuance, detail, and complexity of the real world of policy-making, which those concerned with more abstract model-building would do well to remember. While a single case can never confirm a theory, it is possible to design case studies which may falsify one (though the fact is, there are few if any theories of policy-making well developed enough to be tested). Case studies may also suggest new hypotheses or generalizations which could be applied and tested later in other studies.

In general, it must be said that few of these potential benefits have been realized. Individual case studies tend to be isolated and unique, each looking at different issues, using different methods, and asking different questions. This makes comparison extremely difficult. Their focus has often been on the details of the policy itself, rather than on using the policy to generalize about politics.[10] Cumulative knowledge and theory cannot simply grow automatically by piling case studies on top of each other. Case studies have also a tendency not to focus on the "normal" but on the unique, exotic, or important, so insights gained from them may actually be misleading. Moreover, in focusing on a specific decision or piece of legislation, case studies tend to ignore those issues or alternatives which simply do not come up for debate. It is easy to get submerged in the minutiae of the issue itself, and therefore to miss what might be much broader factors influencing the outcome.

Many of these problems might be quite easily overcome. Programs of coordinated case studies applying similar questions, frameworks, and methods to carefully selected issues of different sorts could yield cumulative results. Conversely, applying several different models to a single case, as Graham Allison did with three models in the Cuban missile crisis,[11] is also useful. Similarly, much is to be gained by very simple comparisons and by the selection of cases which offer particular promise of illuminating wider aspects of policy. One of the most interesting examples is Richard Titmuss's *The Gift Relationship*[12] a comparison of the ways in which the United States and Great Britain deal with the common issue of how to distribute blood for medical purposes: in one case, it is largely a commercial, market-based activity, in the other entirely voluntary. The case

[9]This is true even of the best such studies, for example, Kenneth Bryden, *Old Age Pensions and Policy-Making in Canada* (Montreal, 1974).

[10]For example, Freda Hawkins, *Canada and Immigration: Public Policy and Public Concern* (Montreal, 1972)

[11]*Essence of Decision: Explaining the Cuban Missile Crisis* (Boston, 1971)

[12]London, 1970

allowed Titmuss to explore some of the basic value differences between the two countries and to show how in a fundamental way they helped shape policy.

The second major weakness of the literature is its failure to come to grips with what might be called the problem of the dependent variable. As Lewis Froman suggests, "for reasons which are not hard to analyse, researchers are likely to spend a good deal more time constructing explanations of phenomena than in becoming more sophisticated in the description of the behaviour to be explained."[13] What is it about public policies that we want to explain? What dimensions of policy are of special interest to the political scientist? Until we have a much clearer conception of how to answer these questions, policy studies will inevitably be confused and unproductive. Little of the literature seems to try systematically to link some set of independent explanatory variables with some dependent ones; few deal with substance of content. Instead, we have on the one hand studies which look at a particular institution or process – cabinet, federal-provincial negotiations, the bureaucracy, or interest groups – but which simply *assume* that in some sense they are important variables with an impact on policy. The assumption is seldom tested, and research tends to concentrate on explicating and describing the patterns of interaction within the institution or process.

The literature on Congress in the US suffers especially from this malady, as does that on the so-called presidentialization of the prime minister in Canada.[14] To take another example, Bruce Doern, Peter Aucoin, and others have provided excellent analyses of the recent structural and analytical changes (PPBS, ministries of state, strengthened central coordinating agencies, and the like) within the federal government.[15] But the question remains: even if fully implemented, what difference do these changes make in what gets done, or for whom government serves? On the other hand, we quite often have studies which, as do many of the essays in the recent Doern and Wilson book *Issues in Canadian Public Policy*,[16] examine substantive policies, but do little to ask what forces led to one particular set of outcomes rather than another.

A major exception to this observation is the literature on comparative city and state expenditure patterns in the United States, which does systematically try to link a series of independent variables, both political and non-political.[17] The

[13]"The Categorization of Policy Contents," in Ranney, *Political Science and Public Policy*, 43
[14]Denis Smith, "President and Parliament: The Transformation of Parliamentary Government in Canada," in Orest Kruhlak et al., eds, *The Canadian Political Process* (Toronto, 1970), 367–82
[15]G. Bruce Doern, "The Policy-Making Philosophy of Prime Minister Trudeau and his Advisers," in Thomas Hockin, ed., *Apex of Power* (Scarborough, Ont., 1971); Doern, "The Development of Policy Organizations in the Executive Arena," in Doern and Aucoin, *Structures of Policy-Making*, 39–78; Peter Aucoin and Richard French, *Knowledge, Power and Public Policy*, Science Council of Canada, Background Study No. 31 (Ottawa, 1974)
[16]G. Bruce Doern and V.S. Wilson, eds., *Issues in Canadian Public Policy* (Toronto, 1974).
[17]The literature is cited and assessed in: Gary Tompkins, "A Causal Model of State Welfare Expenditures," *Journal of Politics* 37 (May 1975), 392–416; Stuart Rakoff and Guenther Schaefer, "Politics, Policy and Political Science: Some Theoretical Alternatives," *Politics and Society* I (1970), 51–77; John H. Fenton and Richard Chamberlayne, "The Literature Dealing with the Relationships between Political Processes, Socioeconomic Conditions and Public Policies in the American States," *Polity* I (Spring 1969), 388–404; Thomas R. Dye, *Understanding Public Policy* (Englewood Cliffs, N.J., 1972), chap. 11. For another thorough critique, see Joyce M. Munns, "The Environment, Politics and Policy Literature," *Western Political Quarterly* XXVIII (December 1975), 646–67.

general finding is that broad environmental factors, rather than political characteristics, account for the greatest proportion of the variance, though recent work has tended to reinstate them somewhat. Unfortunately, many of the correlations are low, and the selection of variables is rather arbitrary: many of the more interesting independent factors cannot easily be built in to the models used, and the dependent variables seldom go beyond raw expenditure figures. More important, these studies have not yet been accompanied by a theory which would account for the correlations and indicate the steps by which the environmental differences are translated into policy differences. Some recent work in this vein has made international comparisons of spending on social security: in general, they find only weak correlations with economic factors, and indicate that the time of first introduction of the policies explains the greater part of the variance, suggesting that broad political factors like ideology and values are very important, even if day-to-day variations in political leadership are not.[18]

The characteristics of policy which a political scientist might want to explain are very different from those which other specialists would want to. For example, the description of the outcomes of the Canada Pension plan debate given in *Federal-Provincial Diplomacy*[19] would, whatever its merits for a political scientist, have been more unsatisfactory for an actuary interested in designing pension plans, since what he would consider important, I would not. For empirical investigation, it is of course vital to know what those involved felt to be the important characteristics of the policies in question, but we need to go beyond that to posit theoretically relevant categories, typologies, or classifications of the different dimensions of policy. One problem for political scientists doing policy research is that the information presented in such sources as the *Public Accounts* or *Estimates* is not classified according to such criteria.

A third basic danger for policy studies stems from the pressure to be politically and socially relevant. Apart from the eclectic case study approach, the most important recent approach to policy study is what Hugh Helco calls "programmatic" study.[20] The concern is not to explain existing policies but to prescribe general techniques for deciding on policies, and to recommend which among a variety of alternatives government should choose. Introducing the journal *Policy Sciences*, its editor stated the purpose as "to augment by scientific decision methods and the behavioural sciences, the process that humans use in making judgements and taking decisions."[21] In the same issue, Yehezkiel Dror spoke of the "supradiscipline" which would use "systematic knowledge and structured rationality for the conscious shaping of society."[22]

[18]See Frederic Pryor, *Public Expenditures in Communist and Capitalist Nations* (London, 1968); Henry Aaron, "Social Security: International Comparisons," in Otto Eckstein, ed., *Studies in the Economics of Income Maintenance* (Washington, 1967), 14–38; Felix Paukert, "Social Security and Income Redistribution," *International Labour Review* 98 (November 1968), 425–50; Koji Taira and Peter Kilby, "Differences in Social Security Development in Selected Countries," *International Social Security Review* 22 (1969), 139–53.

[19]Richard Simeon, *Federal-Provincial Diplomacy* (Toronto, 1972)

[20]"Policy Analysis," 97–104. See also the essays in Julius Margolis, ed., *The Analysis of Public Output* (New York, 1970).

[21]E.S. Quade, "Why Policy Sciences?" *Policy Sciences* I (Spring 1970), 1

[22]*Policy Sciences*, 137. See also Malcolm Rowan, "A Conceptual Framework for Government Policy-Making," *Canadian Public Administration* XIII (Autumn 1970), 277–96.

To the extent that there is a dependent variable or criterion for assessing policies it is efficiency or cost effectiveness. This literature is concerned with the development of more effective analytical tools, and the objects of its study tend to be decision-makers in central coordinating agencies. It is attractive because it lends itself to a problem-orientation and to multidisciplinary techniques, and because it suggests political scientists really can be useful to government. As Vernon Van Dyke suggests, an all-out focus on policy and analysis in this sense would take us "fully into the realm of normative problems and social engineering."[23]

Like him, I find the prospect most undesirable. Partly this is because the advocates of the approach mislead themselves about the basic nature of the policy process. It is not simply a rational intellectual process; goals are not simply "given." As a guide to decision-makers, PPBS and systems analysis have proved themselves of limited utility, and this is not simply because the tools are not sufficiently refined. More important, the approach is very narrowly focused; it simply takes for granted existing values, norms, institutions, and patterns of power when it is precisely such broad shapers of policy which need exploration. As Aaron Wildavsky notes, the efficiency criterion assumes the current distribution to be valid so it cannot handle the fact of different people having different preferences. "But the question of whose utility function is to prevail is of prime importance in making public policy."[24]

But most important, these approaches do not help us *explain* policy: that is not their intent. Here the divergence between the decision-maker and the political scientist becomes significant. Obviously policy analysis, in the sense of providing tools and giving assessments of the cost and consequences of different alternatives, is desirable for governments (and citizens – providing they can have access to the analyses). But that objective is quite different from the scholarly one of increasing the understanding of political reality. Concentration on the former is unlikely to advance us very far in the latter. There is something of a danger that the lure of influence for academics, and the desire of the federal government to promote mission-oriented contract research, especially in sensitive policy areas, will lead students to a concentration on technique and relevance which will inhibit the development of a more sophisticated understanding of policy. Students of Greek political thought enjoy fewer temptations to stray from the path of academic virtue. Prescription, moreover, is to a large extent made possible only by explanation: the danger is that we are being asked to run before we can walk, with the resulting possibility of misleading both ourselves and governments. However, without better understanding of the general process and without the attempt to uncover basic assumptions and constraints, "applied" research and concentration on technique become no more than ad hoc response to transient events, and risk degeneration into a more fundamental irrelevance.

Several other problems with the literature may also be mentioned. We have focused too much on the official decision-makers and not enough on the influences

[23]"Process and Policy as Focal Concepts," in Ranney, *Political Science and Public Policy*, 35
[24]"The Political Economy of Growth," in Ranney, *Political Science and Public Policy*, 59. See also his "Cost-Benefit Analysis, Systems Analysis and Program Budgeting," *Public Administration Review* XXVI (1966), 292–310.

which shape the alternatives they consider, the assumptions they make, and the kinds of actions they take. One way to look at this is to suggest that at any given point in time there is a large universe of possible problems or issues to which decision-makers could pay attention and which they could consider important. Similarly, within each issue area there is a wide universe of alternative possible governmental actions. In practice, however, we find that only a small subset of all problems, and a similarly small subset of alternatives, is actually considered, and policy seldom alters greatly from one time to the next. The question, then, is what reduces the agenda to a manageable size, and what principles or forces serve to limit the range of alternatives considered? In this sense what political actors assume, or take for granted, becomes what is most important for explanation.[25] Comparison – across time, units within a nation, and between nations – again provides the tool for exploring some of these dimensions. In addition, given the overwhelming evidence of incrementalism and continuity, a longer time span and emphasis on historical evolution is required.[26]

Given these strictures against much of the existing literature, how should we approach the study of policy? What sorts of models might be useful in providing an over-all understanding of policy and its relationship to the political system? At the outset two caveats should be offered. First, as Richard Bird points out, no one single clear and simple explanation of something as many-faceted and huge as modern government is likely to be possible, at least with our current level of knowledge.[27] Rather than searching for a very high level of abstraction and one or two "crucial" variables, our conception should allow us to group and make sense out of a wide variety of determinants of policy. Second, a framework designed to illuminate broad patterns of policy – that is, the tendencies and effects of large sets of individual decisions – may not be terribly helpful in explaining the particular characteristics of individual decisions, such as why an airport was built in one location rather than another.

In the latter case, the detailed actions and perceptions of the particular decision-makers involved are most crucial; in the former, we see those actions as being limited by the operation of much broader factors. The approach used here assumes that the political machinery and the policy-makers at any point in time work within a framework which greatly restricts the alternatives they consider and the range of innovations they make.[28] This framework, or set of constraints and opportunities, defines a set of problems considered to be important, a set of acceptable solutions or policy responses, a set of procedures and rules by which they will be considered. The framework is made up of various characteristics of the broad social and economic environment, the system of power and influence, the

[25]For a conception of political culture which stresses the assumed or taken for granted character of cultural factors, see David Elkins and Richard Simeon, "A Cause in Search of its Effect, or What Does Political Culture Explain?" unpublished paper, 1975.
[26]Good examples of such an approach are H.V. Nelles, *The Politics of Development* (Toronto, 1974), and Ronald Manzer, "Public Policies in Canada: A Development Perspective," paper presented to the Canadian Political Science Association, Edmonton, June 1975, mimeo.
[27]*The Growth of Public Spending in Canada* (Toronto, 1970), 137
[28]Thus the Canadian Tax Foundation estimates that only 31 per cent of federal expenditure could be seen as "controllable" by Parliament. *The National Finances, 1974–75* (Toronto, 1975), 1–6.

dominant ideas and values in the society, the formal institutional structures. The policy process itself – the interaction of formal and informal actors such as politicians, bureaucrats, pressure groups, and the media bargaining with each other – reflects and is shaped by this broader framework, and by the pattern of problems, precedents, and policies received from the past. But the process also has some independent effect on policy outcomes. This perspective suggests a sort of funnel of causality. At the most general level, and most remote from the particular choice of alternative A or B, is the socioeconomic environment; next come the fundamental political variables, power, culture and ideology, and institutions; finally the most proximate source of decision is the operation of the decision-making process itself. To some extent, the more concerned one is with broad patterns of policy, and with international comparisons, the more one will concentrate on environmental, ideological, and structural variables; the more concerned with day-to-day shifts in policy, the more one will assume those prior factors as given and focus on the decision-makers themselves, though some environmental constraints may enter here too. Much of the literature has tended to focus on one end of the funnel without taking account of the other. Thus work on the environment has tended to ignore the "black box" of the political process, while work on the process has tended to ignore the setting within which it operates.

To provide an effective overview of the policy system, two things are required. First, the characteristics of policy to be explained must be specified. That should be the starting point from which, so to speak, we will work our way back into the political process; how far back will depend largely on what aspects of policy we seek to explain. Second, we must link the factors to each other, trying to delineate both their inter-relationships and their independent contributions to explaining the central dimensions of policy. How, for example, do current elites define and respond to problems shaped by received wisdom and general cultural norms? This perspective is just that, a perspective or framework; it is not a theory, or even a model. It is also imperialistic in the sense that it relates policy to the study of politics generally: indeed, it seeks to bring to bear on the dependent variable, policy, a great many elements of politics which have been brought to bear on other dependent variables, such as "democratic stability."[29]

Patterns of policy

Let us now try to flesh out this perspective by examining the framework in more detail. First, how should we conceptualize the dependent variable? Given a comparative focus, what dimensions of public policy are most important? How do we characterize that which we seek to explain – namely, what governments do, or what L.L. Wade calls "the policy balance."[30] This must be the starting point. But how do we describe the almost infinitely complex policies and programs of a country like Canada? The task is daunting. Single pieces of legislation may run to hundreds of pages; a 1970 summary of environmental legislation in Canada

[29]There is an interesting imbalance in the political science literature generally: increasing sophistication and clarity in the specification and measurement of the independent variables, combined with continued lack of attention to what these high-powered tools are explaining.
[30]"Political Science and Public Policy: A Review Essay," *Policy Sciences* 2 (Summer 1971), 321

took two large volumes.[31] Policy includes the revised statutes of eleven governments, their public accounts, numberless ordinances and regulations, white papers and reports, not to mention the informal and unwritten actions of officials in the field. "Government activities in a modern state defy complete analysis or description," observes *The National Finances*.[32] To fully describe policy in a single issue area is hard; to characterize in detail overall patterns of policy is probably impossible without some theoretical guidelines.

Despite this complexity, it is possible to summarize and simplify, and to abstract from the whole range of government activities some dimensions especially relevant for political scientists. The chief criterion for selecting these dimensions should be what aspects of policy are most relevant to the study of politics. The dimensions should also be relevant to the normative concerns of politics, such as equality and participation. And, they should enable us to be comparative. Finally, we should, at least in principle, be able to measure them.

To describe policy simply as what governments do raises a host of other questions. Virtually every writer in the field feels compelled to offer a definition of policy. That will not be done here, but one or two points about the position of the observer should be made. First is the difficult distinction, made by Ira Sharkansky[33] and others, between "output" and "outcome," which is essentially a distinction between what is done and its consequences for the society. In practice the distinction seems impossible to maintain: description of governmental action – money spent, a bill passed, or whatever – seems pointless without consideration of the meanings attached to it by those who decided, by those affected, or by outside observers. It is perhaps more useful to distinguish between first-order consequences, which are intended or immediately perceived, and second-order consequences, either benign or malign, which are not foreseen. In the categories to follow, two – scope and means – are primarily aspects of output, and one – distribution – refers primarily to the effects of policy.

A related question is whether, to be called "policy," actions of government must be accompanied by a statement of intentions or purpose. Anthony King reserves the term policy for "a consciously chosen course of action (or of inaction) directed towards some end," and uses the term "quasi-policy" to describe situations in which governments may have a wide variety of actions, past and present, within a given policy area, without necessarily having adopted consciously an over-all set of goals.[34] For example, Canadian governments do not have a "policy" on income distribution, but they do many things which affect it; they may have a policy on poverty, but no doubt many activities with consequence for poverty are not included in it. The broader a policy field and the more agencies and levels active in it, the more likely it is to be characterized by "quasi-policy." The Trudeau government, it might be noted, has recently attempted to draw together federal activities in broad fields such as urban affairs, and thus to

[31]CIL Ltd, *A Digest of Environmental Pollution Legislation in Canada* (Ottawa, 1970)
[32]*The National Finances, 1971–72* (Toronto, 1972), 79
[33]"Environment, Policy, Output and Impact," in Sharkansky, ed., *Policy Analysis in Political Science* (Chicago, 1970), 61–79
[34]"On Studying the Impacts of Public Policies: The Role of the Political Scientist," in Matthew Holden and Dennia Dresang, eds, *What Government Does*, Sage Yearbooks in Politics and Public Policy, Vol. 1 (Beverley Hills, 1975), 298–316

turn quasi-policy into policy.[35] As King suggests, the domain of policy study must encompass both: to concentrate only on explicitly stated actions and plans would be to rule out a vast proportion of government activity.

Finally, there is the question as to whether the categories used by students of policy should be the same as those used by decision-makers themselves: is policy what those responsible for it say it is, or what the observer infers? It must be the latter; first, because in many areas it will be impossible to find such statements, and, second, because the decision-makers' categories are unlikely to be related to the theoretical concerns of a particular discipline. For example, the *Estimates* do not classify programs by the extent to which they redistribute across regions, or by whether they meet symbolic or material needs. Thus the order that is to be imposed on the data must come primarily from the observer, though it remains an important empirical question to examine the relation between decision-makers' intentions and actual activity.[36]

For research purposes, we usefully distinguish between three levels of analysis. First are specific *programs*: the Canada Pension Plan, the Canada Assistance Plan, or the wage and price control program. This is the level of most existing policy study. Programs do typically involve statements of intent, desired objectives, and specified tools for reaching them. Here, the researcher accepts the categories and definitions of the policy-makers. Second is policy in particular areas – social, economic, cultural, transportation, etc. Policy areas include both programs explicitly related to them, as well as the other actions of government which affect them. Some areas will be defined by the decision-makers; others will be defined by the researchers' theoretical interests. The notion of policy areas lends itself to comparison. A researcher can select one area, such as the environment, and look at the activities that different countries, provinces, or cities pursue with respect to it, and the reasons behind these activities. Finally, at the level of *patterns* of policy we seek to impose or discern order on, or in, a broad range of activities. Here the categories and questions used owe little to the decision-makers' perspective; they are guided by the over-riding theoretical concerns of the student. Policy will thus be carved up and abstracted in different ways to suit these interests.

In the literature on policy-making we find several suggested definitions of the dependent variable. Policies may be classified according to substantive area – social security, agriculture, environment, defence, etc. – or by client group – farmers, workers, manufacturing industry – or by the level of government responsible.[37] Such classifications are useful for some purposes, but seem to offer little theoretical insight. Another set of categories is provided by students of public administration who are properly concerned primarily with matters of efficiency and effectiveness. Two very influential recent classifications are those of David Braybrooke and Charles Lindblom[38] and Theodore Lowi.[39] For the

[35]See Aucoin and French, *Knowledge, Power and Public Policy*, chap. 1.

[36]See Manzer, "Public Policies in Canada," for an example of such inferences.

[37]See Lewis Froman, "The Categorization of Policy Contents," in Ranney, *Political Science and Public Policy*.

[38]*A Strategy for Decision* (New York, 1963)

[39]Lowi's typology, in various formulations, occurs in several places. See "American Business, Public Policies, Case Studies and Political Theory," *World Politics* XVI (July 1964); and "Decision-Making versus Policy-Making: Towards an Antidote for Technocracy," *Public Administration Review* (May–June 1970), 314–25.

former, the question is whether policy outcomes are incremental, that is, are they only small adjustments from the preceding status quo, or are they non-incremental large steps? There is some ambiguity in Braybrooke and Lindblom because incrementalism seems for them to be both a characteristic and a result of the policy process. Taking incrementalism as the dependent variable, we find, first, that it is not easily operationalized (what is a large or small step? What about a lot of small steps resulting in major change?), and, second, that it is not, in itself, a terribly interesting question. Lowi's categories – distributive, regulatory, redistributive, and constituent – focusing as they do on the balance between individual and collective action and on the degree of coercion, is much more important for students of politics. Lowi also relates his categories to a variety of other elements of the process, including level of conflict, locus of decision, and the like. Unfortunately for our purposes, Lowi himself prefers to use his categories as independent variables which themselves shape subsequent policy processes. Moreover, it is very hard to operationalize his categories, especially to distinguish between distributive and redistributive policies.[40]

Three dimensions of policy are fundamental for political science. First is the *scope* of government policy. What aspects or elements of social and economic life in the society are matters about which governments make decisions? What is the place of government in the society? Second is the question of *means*. Which instruments or techniques do governments typically use in order to assure approval or compliance with their decisions? Here we follow Lowi's emphasis on the essential element of coercion which characterizes governmental decisions,[41] and we may broadly classify policies along a continuum running from voluntary compliance to coercive compliance. Third, and most important, is the *distributive dimension*. "Who gets what?" How are the costs and benefits of government activity distributed among the members of the society? To what extent does government serve as a mechanism for redistribution of income or other benefits? These three dependent variables thus ask: What does government do? How does it do it? And with what effects? On all three dimensions considerable variation across nations is likely. The task of policy research is to describe growth and change in them, and to assess alternative explanations. Let us examine them in a bit more detail.

Scope

The scope of government refers to the range of matters which are subject to public choice and in which governments are involved. We thus distinguish governmental choices – characterized by their authoritativeness[42] – from choices made by free

---

[40]This is because, in an objective sense, virtually all expenditure policies are redistributive: to the extent that one group gets a benefit there is less to give to other groups. However, one group's gain may not be *perceived* as another's loss, especially in a system with a large and expanding pie, with a political style which emphasizes log-rolling, and with a fragmented decision structure, in which taxing and spending decisions are taken separately, and decisions in one area are made without reference to others. For a reformulation of Lowi's categories in this direction, see Robert H. Salisbury, "The Analysis of Public Policy: A Search for Theories and Roles," in Ranney, *Political Science and Public Policy*, 151–75.

[41]Lowi, "Decision-Making versus Policy-Making"

[42]There are several problems with the authoritativeness criterion. Most important is the fact that decisions by some private actors, for example, Imperial Oil, may effectively be just as authoritative as governmental decisions. See Mark Nadel, "The Hidden Dimension of Public

individuals, by the market, or by non-market negotiations between groups. One of the most obvious characteristics of modern society is how much the range of government activity has expanded. It is not simply that governments spend more money, but also that they spend it on more things. More and more subjects become politicized; private has become public. The causes and consequences of this expansion remain obscure. Among the causes which have been identified and remain debated are the imperatives of an industrial, urbanized, technologically advanced society, the needs of monopoly capital or technostructure, the demands of newly enfranchised groups, the impact of crises such as war, and the simple availability of resources.[43] No such large literature has examined the implications of growth, though recent writers such as Daniel Bell and James O'Connor have discussed the "fiscal crisis of the state"[44] stemming from a built-in imbalance between revenue availability and expenditure demands, problems in the growth of bureaucracy, and changes in patterns of conflict resulting from increased politicization. In both America and Europe such questions appear to be increasingly urgent: can governments cope?

There are many ways to assess the growth of government. The simplest is to observe what proportion of the gross national product is spent by government or passes through its hands, or to see what proportion of all employees work for the government. Even within Western capitalist countries, substantial variations exist within a common general trend. For example, between 1967 and 1969, total public expenditure (excluding capital transfers) was 19.4 per cent of GNP in Japan, 31.7 per cent in the United States, 33.6 per cent in Canada, 37 per cent in France, 38 per cent in Britain, and 43.9 per cent in the Netherlands.[45] In the previous fifteen years public spending had been rising half again as fast as GNP.

Public spending, however, captures only some dimensions of governmental scope, first because it tells us little about the actual content of what is done (Sharkansky's "spending-service fallacy"),[46] and, second, because spending is only one form of government involvement. While it may be true that "the budget is the skeleton of the state stripped of all misleading ideologies,"[47] governments also affect group and individual behaviour through symbolic actions, through regulation and proscription in the criminal code, and in the activities of regulatory agencies and the like. Moreover it would be hard to infer many of the most important responsibilities of public authorities through budgetary analysis: the

Policy: Private Governments and the Policy-Making Process," *Journal of Politics* 37 (February 1975), 2–34. On the other hand, governments' ability to command compliance is being increasingly questioned. Thus King points out that government may be becoming "merely one among a number of contenders for wealth, power and influence, the others including large companies, trade unions and their members, foreign companies, foreign governments and international organizations." See "Overload: Problems of Governing in the 1970's," 295. Nevertheless, the term does seem to capture an essential difference between governmental and non-governmental acts, and so will be retained here, although the need to study the public effects of private decisions is not denied.

[43]Bird, *The Growth of Public Spending*, provides the best summary and critique of explanations for the growth of government, especially those provided by economists.

[44]O'Connor, *The Fiscal Crisis of the State*. This is an important and sophisticated Marxist analysis of the state. Bell adopts some central aspects of the thesis, though within an entirely different normative framework, in "The Public Household."

[45]Organization for Economic Cooperation and Development, *Expenditure Trends in OECD Countries* (Paris, 1972), 67

[46]Ira Sharkansky, *Spending in the American States* (Chicago, 1968), 110–11

[47]Rudolf Goldscheid, quoted in Bell, "The Public Household," 30

extent of public ownership, management of the economy, and so on. Similarly, the significance of the federal bilingualism policy is not evident in the budgetary allocations made to it. Thus a variety of more sensitive measures, both of the general activity of governments and of particular policy areas, such as social security, need to be developed. In these areas, too, international variations seem important. For example, Canada appears to have a somewhat more fully developed welfare state and a higher level of public ownership than the US. Canadian governments also seem to have played a somewhat greater role in economic development than those in the US,[48] and to have more explicitly played a "nation-building" role, both economically (the National Policy, the CPR) and culturally (the CBC, bilingualism, etc.).

If we are able effectively to explain such international differences, we will have progressed far towards development of theories of policy formation. Differences in the scope of government and the content of policies should illuminate many other aspects of comparative politics as well. For example, it would be interesting to know the extent to which the economic imperatives (if such they are) of industrialism and postindustrialism lead to a convergence and similarity between nations, or whether national historical, cultural, and institutional differences perpetuate important differences in scope.

Means

The second dimension of the dependent variable is the means by which governments make and enforce policy choices.[49] Several ways of classifying these dimensions might be used. The most important stems from the fact that, as Lowi emphasizes, government decisions are characterized by an element of compulsion: they apply to everyone, and all are, nominally at least, obligated to obey. This is especially true for those policies which, to use Lowi's terminology, are either regulatory, defining permissible or impermissible behaviour, or redistributive, taking benefits from one group and giving them to another. In Lowi's third category of policy outputs, distributions, governments only distribute benefits and are not perceived to be imposing costs. In seeking some goal, governments have in principle a choice of means. They may seek to persuade the recipients through appealing to their sense of citizen duty, as in Finance Minister Turner's unsuccessful efforts to get business and labour to agree on wage and price limitations, or they may seek to induce them to behave in certain ways by offering rewards or incentives, such as with DREE grants. In both cases compliance is sought through primarily voluntary means. On the other hand, government may direct, prohibit, or require people to do things, using not a carrot but a stick and invoking coercive penalties for those who do not comply. Within any country various combinations of these techniques will obviously be used.

A second distinction of means, also used by Lowi, is between public and

[48]See Nelles, *Politics of Development*, for a superb discussion of these activities at the provincial level. Using O'Connors category of "economic development" spending, about a quarter of Canadian federal spending in 1967 was on economic development, compared with only 11 per cent for the US federal government.
[49]Bruce Doern defines the content of policy as "means." See "The Concept of Regulation and Regulatory Reform," in Doern and Wilson, *Issues in Canadian Public Policy*, 12.

private. That is, governments may implement policies through their own governmental agencies, or they may delegate some or all of the implementation to other groups: licensing boards made up of doctors, marketing boards made up of producer's representatives, and so on. The British and Canadian strategy of operating social and medical insurance directly through state agencies contrasts sharply with the more common continental European practice of running such programs through trade unions, employers, and other associations.

Third, we may distinguish between situations in which governments act directly on individuals or groups and those in which it acts indirectly by altering the environment within which individuals make their own decisions. For example, in economic management, governments might want to restrict individual borrowing: they could use direct controls, or try to influence behaviour by manipulating interest rates.

Policy is likely to vary on these three dimensions from issue to issue, from time to time, and across systems. It should be possible to suggest a variety of hypotheses linking these dimensions to various aspects of the political process, especially political culture, levels of conflict, and patterns of dominance and submission.

Distribution

Despite the fact that "who gets what" is at the heart of politics, we have very little information about the distributional impact of government programs. To what extent does government act to promote equality? Virtually all spending programs have a distributional effect, whether or not they are deliberately planned. We need to look at both individual programs and policy fields, and at the over-all impact of government. Yet what is true of the US seems true of Canada also: that "one is impressed by the lack of knowledge or even raw data of program impact including the distribution of program benefits. It is as if these were impolite if not impolitic questions to raise."[50] There are two reasons for this lack of knowledge. First, decision-makers do seem to think of such questions as impolitic: they much prefer to think they are solving problems and finding solutions and that what they do benefits everyone equally. An important part of the politician's task, indeed, is to find policies which are, or can be presented as, satisfying as many groups as possible. Conflict may be much greater if all groups can easily calculate their wins and losses in the political arena. Decision-making is much harder when the game is perceived as a zero-sum situation.

But even more important are the immense technical problems involved in identifying and weighing the costs and benefits for different groups. Despite major problems involved in making assumptions about the incidence of many kinds of tax, it is possible to identify rather clearly the way in which the taxation system allocates the burdens of financing government and alters the income distribution curve, as Joseph Pechman and B.A. Okner show in the recent book *Who Bears the Tax Burden?*[51] But, as Robert Havemann points out, taxes are visible and

[50]James T. Bonnen, "The Absence of Knowledge of Distributional Effects: An Obstacle to Effect Policy Analysis and Decisions," in Havemann and Margolis, *The Economics of Income Maintenance*, 246–70

[51]Washington, 1973. For Canada, see Allan M. Maslove, *The Pattern of Taxation in Canada* (Ottawa, 1972).

painful while benefits of public expenditure are less visible and often intangible.[52] Recent work by economists[53] suggests that it is relatively easy to make these measurements with transfer payments such as welfare or pensions, where the groups benefiting are easily identifiable. Even here, however, the beneficiaries may be seen less as the recipients and more as those elements in the population who benefit from maintaining social peace. Similarly, relatively little problem is posed by pure public goods, since by definition they affect everyone equally. But how does one identify such goods? Even such a classic public good as defence has a distributional impact to the extent that defence contracts or bases provide benefits to particular industries or localities. It gets even more complex if one assumes the benefits from defence spending are proportional to an individual's stake in the community, or if one takes into account that some people are pacifists, for whom spending on arms is a direct "illfare."[54]

Whole classes of government activity become extraordinarily difficult to deal with effectively. What assumptions must one make to assess the benefits of spending on highways or airports? Are DREE grants providing windfall benefits to the companies that receive them, or, through a trickle-down process, to citizens in the communities where they locate, or to the country as a whole by reducing the threat to natural integration of regional grievances? Are manpower training programs benefiting the worker who is trained, or the company that employs him, or both?

These are all problems associated with expenditure programs. But there are equally severe problems with the many government actions which do not involve direct spending or transfers. Thus the whole process of law and regulation, involving rules governing the behaviour of groups in the marketplace, the provisions of licences and the like, confers benefits and alters the competitive advantages of different groups. In addition governments provide symbolic and intangible benefits. Canada's adoption of the maple leaf flag was a clear psychic benefit to some and a psychic deprivation to others. Similarly in programs such as the promotion of bilingualism in the federal public service, the symbolic costs and benefits almost certainly outweigh the monetary ones. Even in a predominantly financial program like welfare, the means by which it is administered may have a major effect on the sense of dignity and well-being of the recipient, and on either the feeling of outrage or of moral satisfaction on the part of the donors.

One wonders, therefore, whether even in principle it is possible to make progress in this area. The answer is a tentative yes, even though the perfect calculus will probably always elude us. Work by economists, such as Dodge, Gillespie, Johnson, and Maital,[55] has made considerable progress in attempting

[52]"Public Expenditures and Policy Analysis: an Overview," in Havemann and Margolis, *Public Expenditures and Policy Analysis* (Chicago, 1970), 1–20
[53]For a very good discussion of some of the necessary assumptions and difficulties in this field, see Morgan Reynolds and Eugene Smolensky, "The Post-fisc Distribution: 1961 and 1970 Compared," *National Tax Journal* XXVII (December 1974), 515–27.
[54]The term is Richard Titmuss's. See his *Social Policy, an Introduction* (London, 1974), 27.
[55]W. Irwin Gillespie, *The Incidence of Taxation and Public Expenditures in the Canadian Economy*, Studies of the Royal Commission on Taxation No. 2 (Ottawa, 1962); James A. Johnson, *The Incidence of Government Revenues and Expenditures*, Study for the Ontario Committee on Taxation (Toronto, ND); David Dodge, "Impact of Tax, Transfer and Spending Policies," *Review of Income and Wealth* 21 (March 1975), 1–52

to assess the over-all fiscal impact of government by calculating the incidence of taxation, and of spending, and then subtracting the difference. They have been forced to make some heroic assumptions, and to leave many programs out of their calculations because the benefits could not be allocated, but in a short time considerable advances have been made. David Dodge, using recent data, suggests the net impact of government *is* progressive, providing large benefits to those families with incomes of less than $4000 a year, declining benefits to those with incomes between $4000 and $13,500, and a rising net tax to those with higher incomes. But, using a different assumption, Shlomo Maital argues that in the US, and to a lesser extent in Canada, the redistribution takes from the middle income groups and gives to those above and below.[56]

In a general review of this literature from several countries, S.M. Miller and Martin Rein conclude that, despite a large increase in governmental transfers in recent years, inequalities of income remain substantially unchanged: it appears that increased redistribution has just kept pace with the increased inequality in original incomes (which may in itself have been promoted by government policies). Government moves to promote equality have been "less than effective, despite the so-called welfare state."[57] Clearly considerable refinement is needed. Studies have been made of individual programs, such as David Springate's on DREE.[58] Similarly Meyer Bucovetskey and Richard Bird have clearly set out the alterations of the federal tax burden (which turn out to be minimal) of the recent Canadian tax reform process.[59]

Unfortunately the difficulties in these analyses are more than technical; they are also normative. For example, Cy Gonick and others argue that the "Vast proportion of public expenditure" subsidizes the business community through the "blue chip socialism" of subsidies, tax concessions, and the like.[60] They also argue that education spending subsidizes business by socializing the costs of training manpower, and that welfare spending subsidizes the failure of the private market. However, spending on social programs such as pensions, welfare, unemployment insurance, and the like is most commonly seen to be "progressive," representing redistribution to the less well off segments of society and "compensation" to the victims of the failure of the economic system. The extension of such programs is similarly seen to represent to some degree the increased political power of workers. But for a Marxist analyst of the state, like James O'Connor, such spending grows primarily from the needs of monopoly capitalists, stemming, in part, from their desire to socialize many of the costs of production and, in part, from a desire to ensure social peace and harmony. "Thus the fundamental effect

[56]"Is Redistributive Taxation a Myth?" Discussion Paper No. 122, Institute for Economic Research, Queen's University, 1973
[57]"Can Income Redistribution Work?" *Social Policy* 6 (May–June 1975), 3–18, esp. p. 3
[58]"Regional Development Incentive Grants in Canada," DBA Thesis, Harvard University, 1972
[59]"Tax Reform in Canada: A Progress Report," *National Tax Journal* XXV (March 1972), 15–41
[60]Cy Gonick, "Sociology and the Economics of Growthmanship," in Laurier Lapierre, ed., *Essays on the Left* (Toronto, 1971), 139. See also Ian Adams et al., *The Real Poverty Report* (Edmonton, 1971); and Dimitri Roussopulos, *The Political Economy of the State* (Montreal, 1973). For a lively discussion of "socialism for the rich," see David Lewis, *Louder Voices: The Corporate Welfare Bums* (Toronto, 1972); see also Trevor Lloyd, "State Capitalism and Socialism: The Problem of Government Handouts" in Lapierre, *Essays on the Left*, 161–73.

of social security is to expand productivity, production and profits. Seen in this way, social insurance is not primarily insurance for the workers but a kind of insurance for capitalists and corporations."[61] "Welfare" and "warfare" expenditures, he adds, are thus not at root contradictory, but are rather different expressions of the same needs. Thus as Bertram Gross suggests, the "recipients" of welfare may not be the real "beneficiaries."[62] Other Marxists, especially Miliband, Poulantzas, and Gough,[63] explain the welfare state more as the necessary concession which must be made to ensure continued dominance for the ruling class. It may be impossible to judge between such opposed interpretations of the same phenomena, derived as they are from such divergent ideological premises. However, examination of the circumstances under which such programs were initially developed, of the political forces arguing for and against them, and of the justifications by their proponents can help.

In many ways it is the *perceptions* of benefits and costs which are important; therefore we need to pursue some other avenues of inquiry. For example, case studies should examine the perceptions of winning and losing, or of mutual gain, of the participants in the decision process and of those directly affected by it. Similarly, large scale surveys can elicit the perceptions of voters. Much would be gained by increased focus on policy-related questions in survey research, exploring such areas as who the voters see government as serving, the degree of their knowledge of policy, and their evaluations of the packages of services and programs available to them.[64] Some work relating voter opinions to the agenda and decisions of government is available, but much more needs to be done. How they are perceived is of course the only way of assessing the distribution of symbolic or non-material benefits.

Given the complexity of measuring the tangible benefits and costs (taxes, subsidies, transfers, and the like), the perception of benefits and costs remains vital, since it is the basis of action. Such perception in fact is one of the most important of the many uncertainties facing political actors. It is important therefore to examine what concepts of fairness they employ, what categories of beneficiaries they have in mind, and what rules of thumb they follow in assessing distribution. Where possible we may compare the objective distribution with the perceived one. Over the longer term, the work of historians may lead us to perceive patterns in broad variations in national policies over a long period, such as shifts from a stress on nation-building and economic growth to the welfare state or regional disparities.

In Canada we need to focus especially on redistribution as it relates to the primary cleavages in the social structure – that is, the pattern of benefits and costs as they affect economic classes, regions, ethnic groups, and industrial sectors. Again, at present, there are few data classified in these ways. Indeed T.N. Brewis

[61]*The Fiscal Crisis of the State*, 138

[62]"Review" of Frances Fox-Piven and Richard Cloward, *Regulating the Poor: The Functions of Social Welfare*, which appeared in *Social Policy* 3 (May 1972), 57

[63]Ralph Miliband, *The State in Capitalist Society* (London, 1969); Nicos Poulantzas, *Political Power and Social Classes* (London, 1973); and Ian Gough, "State Expenditure in Advanced Capitalism," *New Left Review* 92 (July–August 1975), 53–92

[64]Some aspects of citizen perceptions are found in *To Know and Be Known*, Report of the Task Force on Government Information (Ottawa, 1969).

observes that it is even impossible at the moment to quantify net transfers from Ottawa to the provinces, despite our preoccupation with regional disparities.[65]

Fundamentally this emphasis on distribution links up with some of the basic questions of democratic theory. In whose interests does government work? Does it, as Marx and Marxists like Ralph Miliband[66] suggest, operate to maximize the interests of the economically dominant? Or of some middle majority? Or of the working class? Does it, as the pluralists suggest, reinforce the status quo by giving all groups a hearing and distributing benefits according to the resources they can bring to bear, or is it rather an instrument through which equality is promoted or the balance between interests altered? The distributive question also confronts us with the question of social conflict, since it assumes that most of the time all cannot benefit equally, and that policy-making is competition over scarce resources. Finally it poses the fundamental question: What is the role of the state in advanced industrial society? The distinction between scope and distribution reminds us that the development of the "positive state" is not necessarily the same as the development of the egalitarian state.

Explanations

In order to understand variations along these dimensions, five general approaches can be identified.[67] I will look in turn at policy as a consequence of the *environment*, of the distribution of *power*, of prevailing *ideas*, of *institutional* frameworks, and of the *process* of decision-making. Each seems to have some capacity to explain patterns of policy, but none alone provides a full understanding. In part, they are competing approaches; for example, one might have an environmental versus an ideological explanation. However, they are more usefully seen as complementary: each makes some contribution, and policy emerges from multiple causes. But, for the dimensions of policy outlined, the most powerful models appear to be the power-resources and cultural-ideological ones. Moreover, the utility of each approach varies depending on the aspect of policy one wants to explain: aspects of the process are more powerful in explaining small, detailed variations in policy; ideology and the environment explain broader variations. The approaches are not mutually exclusive, indeed the interactions between them are important objects for study. Together they encompass most of the policy literature; some also suggest ways material not so commonly focused on understanding policy can be incorporated. Here I will sketch only some general characteristics of each approach.

ENVIRONMENT

First, patterns of policy may be explained by reference to certain characteristics of the environment of politics. In the most general sense, these refer to such broad characteristics as demography, geography, and levels of urbanization,

[65]T.N. Brewis, *Regional Economic Policies in Canada* (Toronto, 1969), 85. For one attempt at such a calculation, see Hartley Lewis, "Statistics on the Impact of National Fiscal and Monetary Policies," *B.C. Studies*, 13 (September 1972), 43–54.
[66]*The State in Capitalist Society*
[67]These categories bear considerable resemblance to those suggested by Anthony King in "Ideas, Institutions and Policies of Government," op. cit.

wealth, industrialization, and the like. The work of Dye, Hofferbert, and others in the US suggested that it is such environmental factors, and not any characteristics of the political process, which best explain variations in the patterns of spending of American states – politicians, parties, the extent of maldistribution of votes in the electoral system, and the like have only marginal effects.[68] D.J. Falcone and Michael Whittington come to similar conclusions in their examination of trends in Canadian federal government activity,[69] though other studies find political factors outweighing environmental ones in explaining Canadian interprovincial variations – in contrast to findings for the US and Mexico.[70] Some more recent American work, such as that of Brian Frye and Richard Winters,[71] who looked at the extent of redistribution in state government policies, also suggests that the "political variables" are indeed more important than Dye's work suggests. Some international comparative analyses of spending on social security find that variations within developed countries are only weakly related to socioeconomic indicators, and are more strongly associated with an historical factor – the time at which such policies were first introduced[72] – and with such "political" factors as degree of centralization.

Thus this literature remains somewhat confused and tentative, and little has been done to trace out the mechanisms through which the environmental factors actually bring about certain outcomes. Nevertheless the setting, geographic, demographic, technological, and so on, is clearly an important starting point for policy. It both defines a set of problems which need to be dealt with and places limits on the resources – material, technological, and intellectual – available for dealing with them. Thus the growth in government everywhere in the West seems to be clearly related to the imperatives generated by population and economic growth and the like, and there are broad similarities in the role of government in all these societies.[73] However, the designation of certain issues or problems as important is not simply a matter of objective conditions. And once a problem *has* become defined as important, study of the environment alone cannot tell us just how the issue will be perceived, or what policy responses will be made to it. Thus, urbanization generates the need to move people around, it does not tell us how the costs will be distributed. Environmental changes may benefit some groups more than others, or they can generate social conflict, but the changes themselves do not tell us which groups' interests will be most prominent in the policy responses. Thus environmental variables alone have only limited explana-

[68]See note 17.

[69]"Output Change in Canada: A Preliminary Attempt to Open the Black Box," paper presented to the Canadian Political Science Association, Montreal 1972, mimeo

[70]James Bennett Hogan, "Social Structure and Public Policy," *Comparative Politics* 4 (July 1972), 477–509. See also Dale Poel, "Canadian Provincial and American State Policy," paper presented to the Canadian Political Science Association, Montreal 1972, mimeo.

[71]Brian Frye and Richard Winters, "The Politics of Redistribution," *American Political Science Review* 64 (June 1970), 508–22

[72]See note 18. For the most thorough recent study of this problem, see Harold Wilensky, *The Welfare State and Equality* (Berkeley, 1975).

[73]An alternative view of the environment stresses not so much the technological and other imperatives of such processes as urbanization, but also the specific character of the dominant economic system, such as Galbraith's "technostructure." This is an example of the interdependence of the various factors, but it seems more reasonable to deal with the role of technocrats, capitalists, and others under the heading of power.

tory value. They probably explain more about the variation in the *scope* of government than they do about either the means selected or the distribution of benefits involved. To the extent they do shape policy, it is as they interact with cultural and ideological predispositions, with the distribution of political resources among social groups, and the like.

For comparative analysis, the environment serves as a valuable starting point. Given two or more societies with similar environmental characteristics (say an energy shortage, or a certain percentage of the population below the poverty line), we can ask how and why they vary in their response to them. In some policy areas, perhaps those such as fiscal and monetary policy, where the level of interdependence among nations is high, where a mode of analysis such as Keynesian economics has become internationally accepted, and where economic and social structures are similar, policy variations may indeed be small. In other areas, such as cultural policy, they are likely to be greater. Even among countries which share broad socioeconomic characteristics such as industrialization, there remain quite large differences in such things as government's share of per capita income, proportion of GNP spent on social security, levels of government ownership, and the like. It seems unlikely that such large variations are to be explained simply by environmental differences.

A final aspect of the environment is especially important for students of policy in Canada. The interdependence of societies means that policies, especially economic policies, have very great spillover effects. Thus, American policies with respect to matters like inflation crucially affect Canadian well-being and pose problems for Canadian policy-makers. Similarly, Canadian policy-makers are greatly constrained in what they can do with respect to taxation, and fiscal or monetary policy. The limits of these constraints have not often been tested, and they may indeed be partly imaginary. Nevertheless it seems impossible to fully explain Canadian policy in many areas without reference to our dependency on the US.[74] Another sense in which the US presence is important is the extent to which the Canadian political agenda is set by whatever is on the American agenda at the time, and the extent to which major policy innovations in the US, like President Johnson's War on Poverty, are imported into Canada. Similar phenomena of course exist in the interdependencies among provinces, and between them and the federal government.

POWER

The second model suggests that we explain what governments do by reference to the distribution of interests in the society and the resources available to these interests. Most simply, the pattern of policy will reflect the distribution of power and influence, given certain patterns of division and cleavage. This is at once the most plausible and most complex of the perspectives. We would expect policy outcomes, especially the distributional dimensions, to be a function of the number of interests involved, the degree of disagreement or conflict among them, and the relative means of influence which each is able to bring to bear in the policy

[74]There is a growing literature in this area. For a variety of approaches, see Andrew Axline, et al., *Continental Community* (Toronto, 1974), and Ian Lumsden, ed., *Close the 49th Parallel etc.* (Toronto, 1970).

process. But grave problems arise in the conceptualization and measurement of power itself, and in describing the structure of power in society. The debate between the Millsian elitists, the neo-Marxist class analysts, and the pluralists shows no sign of abating. Nor does the methodological debate between those who, like Dahl, argue that power can only be attributed when its exercise is visible in concrete situations of conflict, and those, like Bachrach and Baratz,[75] for whom non-decisions and the exercise of power through anticipated reactions and limiting the political agenda is crucial. Nevertheless, the elitists and pluralists agree that power does provide the key to understanding policy. They disagree about the real nature of that structure. For the pluralists, policy distributes benefits widely, and is usually a compromise among interests, because political resources are distributed widely; for the elitists, policy benefits the few because only the few exercise influence successfully. Note that each of these models includes both a statement about the dependent variable (benefits are widely shared or are narrowly concentrated) and about the independent variable (power is fragmented, power is centralized). A third model might separate participation in decisions from sharing of the benefits: thus the "Red Tory" image suggests that individual citizens participate little, but that the elites generating policy seek to serve the interests of the followers. The self-interestedness of elites should not be assumed. We obviously cannot resolve these questions here, but I do not think that their difficulty should lead us to abandon the influence focus altogether. One strategy for dealing with the problems is again to focus on the end product, on the distribution of burdens and benefits among social groups. One cannot automatically infer that because group A received benefits this was entirely due to A's successful exercise of influence. But if we take the distribution as a starting point, we can work back into the political process to examine such things as the role group A played, the attitudes that other groups had towards group A, the pattern of alliances that evolved, and so on. One problem with a great deal of the power literature has been that it assumes a relationship between power and outcomes, without actually demonstrating it or even describing the outcomes in very much detail.

We might also consider whether certain particularly illuminating case studies might be undertaken. For example, a major study of the Canadian tax reform process which began with the appointment of the Carter Commission in 1961 would be especially valuable for two reasons.[76] First, it was clearly an issue in which every citizen in the society had a stake and would therefore presumably have an incentive to mobilize whatever resources he possessed. "Few things so clearly reveal the naked play of vested interests in any country as do attempts to change an existing fiscal structure."[77] Second, it appears possible for economists

[75]Robert A. Dahl, "A Critique of the Ruling Elite Model," *American Political Science Review* 52 (June 1958), 463–9; and Peter Bachrach and Morton Baratz, *Power and Poverty* (New York, 1970), chaps. 1–2. See also Raymond Wolfinger, "Non-Decisions and the Study of Local Politics," and Frederick Frey, "Comment," *American Political Science Review* 65 (October 1971), 1063–80 and 1081–1101.

[76]See Bucovetsky and Bird, "Tax Reform in Canada"; and Bucovetsky, "The Mining Industry and the Great Tax Reform Debate," in A. Paul Pross, ed., *Pressure Group Behaviour in Canadian Politics* (Toronto, 1975), 87–114.

[77]Richard M. Bird, "The Tax Kaleidoscope: Perspectives on Tax Reform in Canada," *Canadian Tax Journal* XVIII (Sept.–Oct. 1970), 444.

to measure rather precisely the impact of the tax burden. In the Canadian tax reform process we had: T_1, the preexisting tax system, distributing costs in certain ways; a political process occurring within a royal commission, leading to the proposal T_2, which would have altered the distribution of the burden; another political process, including public debate, pressure on the government, and so on, leading to T_3, the White Paper, which again altered the distribution; another political process including parliamentary committee hearings and Edgar Benson's exercise in participatory democracy, culminating finally in T_4, the legislation. A research project which, on the one hand, concentrated on measuring the shifts in tax burdens for a large variety of social and economic groups at each point and, on the other hand, closely investigated the political process in between each point would seem to offer considerable promise of directly relating process to outcome in a way which would likely cast considerable light on the real patterns of influence in the country. It would also be relatively easy to extend the analysis to experiences with tax reform in other countries.

Despite the difficulties, power seems obviously related to all three dimensions of policy I have outlined. In the capitalist societies, at least, the expansion of the scope of government seems to have coincided with the accession of previously excluded groups to a share of political power, though some writers argue that this expansion has also been turned to the benefit of the already powerful; for example, Galbraith's notion of socialism for the rich and free enterprise for the poor, or Theodore Lowi's notion that expansion of the role of government was accompanied, in the US, by parcelling out the responsibility to private groups.[78] Kenneth Bryden's recent study of pension legislation in Canada shows how social reform can become domesticated, so that current pension policies provide little in the way of redistribution among income classes.[79] Similarly, the means by which policy is carried out is related to the level of conflict and to the distribution of power: the more widely influence is distributed, as in the pluralist model, the more voluntaristic the means; the more intense the conflict, the less the likelihood of compromise, and the more chance of coercion.

IDEAS

The third approach focuses on cultural and ideological factors: policy is a function of the dominant ideas, values, theories, and beliefs in the society.[80] Fundamentally, these factors may be seen as providing the basic assumptions and framework within which policy is considered. By culture here we mean simply such basic orientations to the political system as the definition of the relevant community to which obligation is felt; optimism or pessimism regarding man's ability to change his world; orientations to political activity; orientations towards conflict, and the like. By ideology, we mean more explicit, detailed, and politically focused ideas, which explain the political world, provide a framework for interpreting particular events, and offer a recommendation and prescriptions for future action. For the analysis of public policy, three dimensions seem particularly important.

First, we can distinguish between procedural and substantive ideas. Procedural

[78]*The End of Liberalism* (New York, 1969)
[79]*Old Age Pensions*
[80]Ibid., 11

norms or values suggest rules of the game or methods which are considered legitimate. They include such things as the decision-rules to be employed (majority rule, proportionality, unanimity), perceptions of the situation as 0-sum or not, views about what tactics are permissible, views about who the legitimate participants in the policy process are and about how much secrecy is permitted, and the like.[81] Very important here, I think, is the extent to which the participants in the political process are basically self-regarding or public-regarding in their approach to politics. Such factors appear to be to a large extent (but not completely) independent of individual issues, or levels of conflict, and thus seem to have an independent effect on how the policy process operates, and to influence especially the means.

Perhaps the most fully developed recent statement of a procedural hypothesis is Lowi's discussion of the "public philosophy" of interest group liberalism, which he suggests can account both for the procedures of American policy-making and for some of its distributive characteristics, such as its continual reinforcement of the status quo.[82] Work by George and others on the "operational code" and by Putnam on elite attitudes is also important in this vein.[83] Hugh Heclo provides an interesting contrast between the procedural styles of Swedish and British policy-making which had some important consequences for policy results: "in general, Swedish discussions of social policies have begun from an assumption that the primary requisite for policy decision is more information, clarification and analysis among the interested parties. British discussion has generally begun from the assumption of divergent interests resolvable only through partisan conflict, and certainly not through joint committee work."[84] In the Canadian case a variety of procedural analyses of this type have been made, as in the emphasis on Canadian deference to elites, lack of entrepreneurial talent, and relatively greater Canadian collectivism identified by writers like Lipset, Porter, Presthus, and others. We need more detailed studies of the procedural values of political elites. Some valuable insights are found, for example, in Presthus's study of Canadian interest groups and Meisel's analysis of Liberal "hubris."[85]

Substantive values relate to what governments *should* do; what general goals should be pursued. The most obvious aspect here is of course the left–right dimension, which is closely related to scope and distribution. More generally, substantive values relate to such things as the emphasis on economic growth. Other

[81] For an interesting analysis of the interplay between culture and the policy process, see Thomas Anton, "Policy-Making and Political Culture in Sweden," *Scandinavian Political Studies* 4 (1969), 88–102.

[82] "The Public Philosophy: Interest Group Liberalism," *American Political Science Review* 61 (March 1967), 5–24

[83] Alexander George, "The Operational Code: A Neglected Approach to the Study of Political Leaders and Decision-Making," *International Studies Quarterly* 13 (June 1969), 190–222; Robert Putnam, "Studying Elite Political Culture: The Case of Ideology," *American Political Science Review* 65 (1971) 651–81, and "The Political Attitudes of Senior Civil Servants in Western Europe," *British Journal of Political Science* 3 (July 1973), 257–90; and Thomas Anton et al., "Bureaucrats in Politics: A Profile of the Swedish Administrative Elite," *Canadian Public Administration* 16 (Winter 1973), 627–51.

[84] *Modern Social Politics in Britain and Sweden* (New Haven, 1974), 313–14

[85] Robert Presthus, *Elite Accommodation in Canadian Politics* (Toronto, 1973), chs. 2, 11; John Meisel, "Howe, Hubris and 1972," in his *Working Papers in Canadian Politics* (3rd ed., Montreal, 1974)

aspects of substantive ideology are also important, especially in the Canadian situation; the most important ones have to do with the definition of the Canadian nation and views about French–English relations, regional disparities, and the relative roles of federal and provincial governments.

It is unlikely that particular policies are very often simply deduced from some explicit ideological framework (though Trudeau's policies in the area of bilingualism come close to a clear implementation of ideas enunciated previously), but ideas do seem to provide a general framework within which discussion of particular options takes place. Thus the development of the welfare state was not simply a result of a changed environment, or of the accession to power of the workers, it was also a product of changes in ideas about what the role of the state should be, what its obligations to citizens are, and so on. Anthony King makes a good case for what he calls "ideas" as being the fundamental causes of the relatively small scope of government in the United States as compared with other industrialized countries, and of its relatively poorly developed welfare system.[86]

More narrowly, it is useful to examine what might be called the prevailing theories held by decision-makers about the causes of problems and how to deal with them. J.M. Keynes observes that "the ideas of economists and political philosophers are more powerful than is commonly understood. Indeed the world is ruled by little else. Practical men, who believe themselves to be exempt from any intellectual influences, are usually the slaves of some defunct economist." Keynes's own influence bears him out: "one cause above all others" accounts for the success of full employment after the Second World War – the publication in 1936 of the *General Theory*.[87] Ron Manzer's study of developmental sequences of policy in Canada similarly stresses the importance of theories of poverty and crime and punishment, and the ways in which theories shaped policy in those areas.[88] These ideas or theories stem not only from generalized ideologies, but also from contemporary knowledge in social sciences, learning from the experience of other countries, and the like.

The second distinction is between elite and mass values. What role do citizens play – are they subjects, participants, spectators, or rebels? Are the elites relatively constrained or relatively free and autonomous? Are citizens willing to defer to political authority, or do they demand a voice? Similarly what about elite orientations: how do they view their role? Much of the conflict in recent years surrounding the demand for greater governmental responsiveness and greater participation is related to changing views about the citizen's role, on one hand, and an inability or unwillingness of governmental institutions to respond on the other. In understanding the making of individual policies, elite orientations are probably most important factors. Several suggestions are found in the Canadian literature, for example the view of Canadian politicians as brokers, or as irrationally preoccupied with problems of national unity, or as cooperative elites in the consociational democracy model holding the country together by overarching cooperation while keeping the masses quiescent. None of these observations is particularly well founded, but much room for research is available.

[86]"Ideas, Institutions and the Policies of Governments"
[87]Michael Stewart, *Keynes and After* (2nd ed., Harmondsworth, Eng., 1972), 13. The quote from Keynes is on p. 25.
[88]"Public Policies in Canada"

Third, we need to look at the dimension of ideological homogeneity and heterogeneity. Ideology in general may play two roles: it may serve to support and legitimize the existing status quo – the existing institutions, procedures, power structures, and patterns of policy. Or it may play a role of opposition, attempting to mobilize people to challenge the existing order or the existing patterns of policy. The policy process and policy outcomes are likely to be very different in societies where one ideology is dominant (indeed such societies may be seen, as some Americans see themselves, as "non-ideological") than they are in situations of ideological diversity and conflict. In both cases, ideology is very closely linked both to patterns of power, either challenging or legitimizing them, and to the institutional structure, which may be seen to embody or support the existing ideological order. In this sense, ideas, like power, need to be related to the groups whose interests they promote or defend.

Like King, I lean strongly towards "ideas" and differences in dominant ideas from country to country as the basis for explaining policy differences, though I would place more stress on the link between ideas and the interests and influence of different groups. Ideas seem to be the essential both to the substance and to the means by which policy is made. They are especially useful, I think, in understanding broad policy shifts over long periods of time, such as the development of the welfare state,[89] and in understanding the more gross differences in the patterns of policy in different countries. They are less useful the more rigid the environmental constraints. Ideas do not provide complete explanations. They tend to be general and thus to account for broad orientations rather than the specific details of policy; in this sense they are especially important in providing the assumptions which define the problems and limit the range of policy alternatives considered at any point.

It might be objected that the stress on ideas implies an unrealistic view of the policy process, seeing it as explicitly goal-orientated, in which some group of decision-makers with clear ideological purposes simply promotes policies that conform to its ideology. A contrasting view sees the policy process as much more chaotic and incoherent, with policy the result of the clash of many interests in which no central thread is discernible. This viewpoint also stresses the importance of unanticipated consequences, the possibility of people agreeing on policy even though they disagree on final ends, and so on.[90] This is indeed the case: policies are the result of long accumulations of small decisions; decision-makers, especially in non-crisis situations, seldom do self-consciously select a single purpose; policy is the result of a complex bargaining process. But that process does go on within a framework of assumptions, norms, and values concerning both the procedure and the substance of policies, and from a long-term and comparative perspective it is this framework that is most important.

INSTITUTIONS

The fourth approach concentrates on the policy consequences of the institutional structure – the formal rules and regulations – of the political system. The way in which government is organized, the degree of centralization or decentralization,

[89]For a statement of this view, see Richard Titmuss, *Social Policy: An Introduction*, 22.
[90]See the work of Lindblom, and Braybrooke and Lindblom cited above; and Judith Sklar, "Decisionism," in Carl Friedrich, ed., *Nomos VII: Rational Decision* (New York, 1967), 3–17.

the way authority is shared, the formal mechanisms for registering decisions are all involved here. Thus, for example, A.H. Birch argues that it is the "complications of federalism" which account for the rather late development of the welfare state in Canada.[91] Or E.E. Schattschneider, R. MacGregor Burns, and a host of others argue that certain features of American political institutions so fragment authority that innovation is systematically prevented and immobilism results. Similarly, many have argued impressionistically that somehow cabinet systems are able to move more decisively and effectively than systems with the separation of powers. Or, to use another example, N.H. Lithwick argues that the present structure of urban government in Canada is inherently incapable of dealing with contemporary problems.[92]

Now to sort out the independent effect of institutional factors is extremely difficult. Institutions are obviously the result of broader political factors: Canada has federalism *because* regional and linguistic divisions are strong; the United States has the separation of powers at least in part because James Madison and others wanted to limit the scope of government and control the power of the masses. Similarly, in the long run, if political pressures are sufficiently strong, institutional hurdles can be cleared and institutions changed. But in the short run, institutions do place constraints on decision-makers and help shape outcomes. They do so in primarily a negative sense, by making some solutions harder, rather than by suggesting positive alternatives. It does not seem unreasonable to suggest that the greater the number of veto points, or the greater the emphasis on gaining the consent of all, the fewer innovations there will be, and the more limited will be the scope of the government.

There is considerable debate about the effect of institutional factors. Anthony King points out that in the US it is not so much that radical proposals were vetoed because of institutional fragmentation, but that they were never seriously proposed.[93] On the other hand, governments exercizing very centralized constitutional powers may, because of their own internal divisions, or the pressures on them, act extremely cautiously. Similarly, J. Roland Pennock finds none of the differences in agricultural policy in Britain and the United States that might have been predicted from differences in institutional structure.[94] On the other hand, in his comparison of American, Canadian, and Swedish air pollution policy, Lennart Lundqvist concludes that "structures do indeed matter. ... Although it is equally clear that other factors influence policy choices, political structures have considerably more impact on the choice of alternatives than one would have expected, given the similarity of the problems and the similarity of (possible) available solutions."[95] Arnold Heidenheimer, examining social policy in the US and Western Europe, argues that it is the interaction of interest groups and institutions which best explain differences.[96]

[91]*Federalism, Finance and Social Legislation* (Oxford, 1955), 204
[92]*Urban Canada: Problems and Prospects* (Ottawa, 1970)
[93]"Ideas, Institutions and Policies," 416
[94]"Responsible Government, Separated Powers and Special Interests: Agricultural Subsidies in Britain and America," *American Political Science Review* LVI (September 1962), 621–33
[95]"Do Political Structures Matter in Environmental Politics?" *Canadian Public Administration* 17 (Spring 1974), 139
[96]"The Politics of Public Education, Health and Welfare in the USA and Western Europe," *British Journal of Political Science* 3 (July 1973), 315–40

Institutional factors may also influence the means: the more veto points there are, the more consensual and voluntaristic the means, and the more policies are likely to be distributive rather than redistributive. Finally, institutions may have implications for distribution, for who gets what. We may see institutions in this sense as conferring formal authority, as requiring that certain formal steps be taken before policy is enacted, and giving certain authorities the right to make those decisions. To the extent that these authorities are linked to certain interests and groups within the societies these actors are likely to exert more influence. Thus in Canada, federalism does have some fairly clear policy consequences. It tends to structure our thinking about policy problems, so that we see them in regional terms. It gives special weight to certain interests which are regionally based, and disadvantages to some others which are nationally distributed.[97] Because of the process of federal–provincial negotiation on the Canada Pension Plan which federalism engendered, it seemed clear that certain elements in pension policy were given great weight; others, which would have been more prominent had the institutional framework been different, were neglected.

The institutional factors are so bound up with the other approaches that it seems impossible to weigh their over-all impact on policy. The most fruitful approach will probably be to conduct comparative studies of similar issues across units with clear institutional variations. We should also remember that institutions themselves have no particular policy content; their effects lie in the way in which they interact with other social forces, and in the way they give advantages to some interests and disadvantages to others. The way institutions structure political competition and therefore policy debate can also be examined in the sense that they may provide incentives to politicians to pursue some kinds of strategies as opposed to others, as Alan Cairns suggests is the case for political parties in the Canadian electoral system.[98]

In a longer-run perspective, institutional arrangements may themselves be seen as policies, which, by building in to the decision process the need to consult particular groups and follow particular procedures, increase the likelihood of some kinds of decisions and reduces that of others. For example, a legal requirement that public hearings be held before a development project can go ahead increases the bargaining resources of local residents and environmentalists. The establishment of new Departments and agencies reflects not only the growth in the scope of government, but also the recognition of the importance of newly mobilized groups and interests, which can then use these new institutions to promote favourable policies. Change in governing structures may thus be seen in part as a process of institutionalizing interests. Hence institutions are both dependent variables, reflecting earlier decisions, and independent factors, conditioning the future play of political forces.

PROCESS

Closely associated with institutions, and in a way almost indistinguishable from them, is a focus on the process of decision-making itself. The vast bulk of the

[97]See Richard Simeon, "Regionalism and Canadian Political Institutions," *Queen's Quarterly* 82 (Winter 1975), 499–511.
[98]"The Electoral System and the Party System in Canada," in Orest Kruhlak et al., eds., *The Canadian Political Process* (Toronto, 1970), 139–64

policy literature, of course, is primarily concerned with this level, in describing the ways in which the proximate policy-makers – bureaucrats, politicians, interest group leaders – interact with each other in the making of policy. Much of this literature takes the form of the rather sterile debate between the "disjointed incrementalists," the "rationalists," and the "mixed scanning" advocates, a debate marked by a confusion about whether these models are actually descriptive or prescriptive.[99]

We need to look at process in this sense in two ways. First, it is these decision-makers who actually make the formal decisions and carry them out. It is *through them* that the broader political forces operate. Their agenda and behaviour reflect the pressures of the environment, the play of political influences surrounding policy disputes, the norms, assumptions, and values found in the culture and the ideology, and the opportunities and constraints imposed by the institutions. The causal arrows do not jump straight from environment to legislation; power and influences are exercised and brought to bear on particular decision-makers; and assumptions, norms, and values must be made concrete. Up to this point, the models we have sketched have been rather static; they are sets of variables which the process sets in motion. This perspective has important implications for a research strategy. Power, ideology, and the other factors can all be studied in the abstract; indeed, they usually are. The problem has been to bring them to bear in explaining policies. In part I have suggested we do that through examining the *outcomes* themselves: Whose interests have been served? What values are implicit? What means have been used? Examining the *process* can show how these results came about. Thus comparative case studies can illuminate many of the broader aspects the earlier approaches implied. We can interview the participants to find out not only what happened when, but also to probe deeper. How did the problem come to be defined in this way? Why were alternatives *a*, *b*, *and c* considered, but not *d* and *e*? Which groups was it important to listen to, and why? And so on. In exploring the actions, assumptions, perceptions, and strategies of participants, we should begin to see more broadly how these wider features of the political system impinge on the policy process. Through comparison we are able to highlight what may be the most important facts: those which are simply taken for granted by the participants themselves. Process, then, becomes the bridge on which we work forward from what we know about institutions, ideology, power, etc., to policy outcomes; and on which we work backwards from variations in policy outcomes to seek explanations.

Process is important in another sense; that is, as an independent contribution to policy outcomes. The proximate policy-makers may have their own interests, such as the bureaucratic need for maintenance and expansion, and their own ties to clientele groups. Similarly, writers like March and Simon, and Braybrooke and Lindblom, have stressed certain characteristics of the situation facing the decision-makers themselves: complexity, uncertainty, a limited capacity for analysis, and the like. They have suggested some of the strategies, such as incrementalism and satisficing, by which decision-makers can simplify their decision processes and which do have consequences for outcomes.

[99]For a good discussion of this debate, see Peter Aucoin, "Theory and Research in the Study of Policy-Making," in Doern and Aucoin, *The Structures of Policy-Making in Canada*, 10.38.

Related to a process approach but also closely linked to the power and institutional dimensions – is the work of "public choice" theorists. This "new political economy," undertaken primarily by economists, seeks to build deductive models of individual behaviour and collective decision from a simple set of assumptions, the most important being the assumption of self-interest. Thus, politicians are vote-maximizers, and bureaucrats are motivated to increase the size of their agencies. Given constraints such as information and transaction costs, predictions about behaviour and outcome are deduced. In addition, much of this literature is normative, asking what justifies replacement of individual or market choice mechanisms with public or governmental choices. The parsimony and logic of many formulations are persuasive, indeed beguiling. They provide important insights and may be a useful baseline against which to observe real world activities. The abstract and general character of this mode of analysis, however, renders it of somewhat limited value in exploration of substantive policy. Moreover, many of the assumptions about motives, structural constraints, and the like take for granted factors which I have argued must be investigated. For example, we may accept the self-interest motivation, but what an actor will define as his self-interest is not evident. Politicians may seek to maximize votes and bureaucrats the size of their budgets; what they will have to advocate to succeed in these goals depends heavily on the distribution of political resources, the dominance of certain ideas and the like.[100]

There are a multitude of frameworks available for the study of policy process.[101] Many suggest a temporal or functional sequence ranging from placing an issue on the agenda, to formal decision, to implementation, appraisal, and determination. Most such frameworks are simply a way of organizing information. Two process approaches which do fairly clearly relate the character of the process to the character of the outcome are those of Allison in *Essence of Decision* and Lindblom in *The Intelligence of Democracy*.[102]

Lindblom emphasizes both an intellectual process, incrementalism, and a political bargaining process, partisan mutual adjustment. In his model, decision-makers do not attempt to consider all alternatives or to ask the grand questions; they take the existing situation as given and seek to make only marginal improvements. Individual decision-makers do not try to take into account each other's point of view; rather, each acts selfishly. But bargaining resources are widely distributed and the actors engage in mutual adjustment. The result for Lindblom – but not for Lowi who by and large accepts Lindblom's description of what goes on – is policy outcomes in which the largest number of interests are likely to have got at least some of what they wanted, in which there is considerable compromise, in which policy changes in only small steps, and so on.

[100]There is a large and diverse literature in this field. Some important examples are: Albert Breton, *The Economic Theory of Representative Government* (London, 1974); James M. Buchanan and Gordon Tullock, *The Calculus of Consent* (Ann Arbor, Mich., 1962); Mancur Olson, *The Logic of Collective Action* (Cambridge, Mass., 1965); Anthony Downs, *An Economic Theory of Democracy* (New York, 1957); Robert Bish, *The Public Economy of Metropolitan Areas* (Chicago, 1971). For a good summary of the literature and an application to the study of Canadian and Australian Federalism, see M.H. Sproule-Jones, *Public Choice and Federalism in Australia and Canada* (Canberra, 1975).
[101]For example, Richard Rose, "Comparing Public Policy"
[102]Lindblom, *The Intelligence of Democracy* (New York, 1965)

Allison, after generally rejecting the view that policy can be seen as the rational, clear decision of a single actor such as the president, postulates two alternative models. One is similar to Lindblom's model: policy is the result of bargaining among the bureaucratic agencies and leaders involved. The other stresses the imperatives of bureaucratic organization – the need to simplify, the failure to learn from the environment, the inertia, and the commitments to standard operating procedures. One might also explore how much bureaucratic expansionism is now a central force in the growth of government itself. The results again are limited flexibility and incremental change.

These two models do generally describe the day-to-day operation of the policy process. And they are likely to have certain independent consequences of their own, such as marginal change and reinforcement of the status quo. Certainly to explore minor changes in particular policies we probably would not need to go much further than the immediate process. But these are only very partial models. They deal with the routine and the stable, rather than with change or crisis. More important, they take far too much for granted. Why one set of bureaucratic structures, and not another? Why one set of alternatives being debated and not a narrower or broader one? In fact, Lindblom for example, *assumes* a decentralized institutional structure much like the American, a general consensus, both procedural and substantive, on the basic characteristics of the system, a shared commitment to the rules of the game, and limited levels of conflict. But what is the process like when these characteristics do not prevail?

In a way much of this boils down to the question of what is the role of the politician and bureaucrat in the policy process. For some of the environmentalists, the role is minimal: the black box of politics does not make such difference. The process writers place considerably more emphasis on the political role, though their results suggest that it is limited too, since policy at any time t_2 is best predicted by seeing what it was at time t_1. The approach developed here, by emphasizing the framework of the environment, ideas, power, and institutions within which the process operates may suggest in one sense that the process and its participants are unimportant. But in another, broader, sense the argument is that the process is crucial. For it is the focus, the impact point, of all the other variables. The environmentalists tend to downplay the political variables altogether; the bureaucratic process writers, on the other hand, study a rather narrow set of political forces. The approach outlined here seeks to define policy-making as political, but in a much wider sense.

A brief illustration will demonstrate the sorts of hypotheses which might be derived from each of these approaches. Let us take anti-poverty policies, and, for the sake of argument, simply assert that they have failed to achieve social justice for the poor. How might each approach try to explain why?

The environmental approach might suggest such factors as the lack of the necessary resources to fully close the poverty gap; the possibility that to do so would lead to levels of taxation which could not be achieved given Canada's dependence on foreign investment; the simple lack of information about *how* to eliminate poverty even if the resources or the will were there. None of these alone seems very persuasive.

A power approach might take a variety of forms. A more elitist approach would assert that policy benefits a small dominant group, which has little interest in alleviating poverty except for a desire to avoid social unrest, and which, moreover, operates an economic system which inevitably generates poverty. A more majoritarian power explanation would assert that the poor are a minority, and that it is not a small elite but the non-poor majority which would object to bearing the necessary burdens. Both would agree that the poor themselves lack most of the political resources to make their needs effectively heard.

An ideological approach would stress the dominance of a complex of ideas concerning the need for self-reliance, the moral worthlessness of the poor, a preference for the market system, weakness of a sense of community obligation, the prevalence of concern for economic growth over concern for equity, and so on. Similarly, it might argue that the procedural norms of the system freeze out the poor from participation because they cannot speak the appropriate language and do not understand the rules of the game.

An institutional approach would, like Birch, stress the "complications of federalism," including federal–provincial conflict, and the imbalance between revenues and the division of constitutional responsibility for social policy, and the like. It might also stress the problems of bureaucratic fragmentation within levels of government and the resultant inconsistencies in policy and failure to coordinate.

Finally, a process approach would look at the ways various official and unofficial policy-makers interacted in the considerations of anti-poverty policies. In doing so, it would draw on the other approaches: on power, by looking at who the participants are, what interests they represent, what resources they possess; on ideas, by looking at both the procedural and substantive values of the participants; on institutions, by examining the constraints and opportunities they present, and by assessing the ways certain assumptions, precedents, standard operating procedures, and the like become entrenched within certain departments and agencies. The process focus would also stress the strategies and tactics of participants as influenced by the other factors, and would look at the relationship between policy-making in the policy field with that in other fields.

Most of the above assertions are, at least to some degree, testable even within the context of a single country like Canada. More progress would be possible using comparison. No one approach seems fully persuasive: shapers of social policy are likely to be complex. Nevertheless use of this framework – combined of course with a much fuller description and assessment of anti-poverty policies themselves – does promise both to encompass most of the factors adduced to study policy in the past and to compare their utility more systematically than before. It also suggests that while specialization inevitably means individual students will mine particular parts of the field, they must both be more aware of the existence of the other potential foci and explicitly relate the fruits of their work to the contents of policy itself.

I have tried to present a very general framework for the study of policy, together with a few tentative hypotheses which might be explored. In a way it is an argument for the role or place that studies of policy should have in political science and it is a response to the apolitical, atheoretical, non-cumulative, and non-comparative characteristics of much of the recent work in the area. The framework here is most unhelpful in one way: it presents not a theory, but a way of looking at policy; it does not simplify study, but instead makes it more complex. I hope it has isolated the issues, has suggested a guide to the important questions, especially those concerning what is to be explained, and has provided some criteria for selecting and presenting information.

More generally, several suggestions for how we should conduct policy research arise. First, we need much better descriptions of what governments actually do, what the allocation of values and costs is. At the moment we have too many independent variables chasing too few and too vague dependent ones. Second, as political scientists, our concern at the moment should be primarily with describing and explaining, rather than recommending techniques and solutions to policy problems. Third, case studies can be a very valuable tool: but they must be comparative, the cases must be carefully selected, and they should be used to penetrate the political process in order then to ask some of the broader questions. At the same time case studies are not enough. We need longitudinal studies of the evolution of policy over long periods, and we need to take studies of culture, voting, and the like and try to formulate hypotheses by which they might be related to policy.

The task for policy research outlined here is a vast one. At every level we are faced not only with a lack of data, but also with difficult theoretical, methodological, and even ideological problems. Some attempts to provide an over-all view, however tentative, and to summarise what is already known will be extremely valuable. But it is not intended that everyone should try to answer all these questions. Specialization is inevitable, but the perspective outlined here will have served its purpose if it has sketched a general outline of the whole forest, and indicated on which clumps of trees it is most important to concentrate. Similarly, specialists will make their greatest contributions if they can keep in mind that it is the forest we ultimately want to understand, and that policy studies will advance to the extent that clear and explicit links between dependent and independent variables are established.

SICK AND TIRED

The Compromised Health of Social Assistance Recipients and the Working Poor in Ontario

Produced by the Community Social Planning Council of Toronto, the University of Toronto's Social Assistance in the New Economy Project and the Wellesley Institute

February 2009

Sick and Tired: The Compromised Health of Social Assistance Recipients and the Working Poor in Ontario

February 2009

ISBN: 978-1-894199-18-6

Produced by the Community Social Planning Council of Toronto (CSPC-T), University of Toronto's Social Assistance in the New Economy Project (SANE) and the Wellesley Institute.

RESEARCH PARTNERS

Wellesley Institute, University of Toronto's Social Assistance in the New Economy Project and the Community Social Planning Council of Toronto

RESEARCH TEAM

Ernie Lightman, Principal Investigator, University of Toronto's Social Assistance in the New Economy Project
Andrew Mitchell, Coordinator, University of Toronto's Social Assistance in the New Economy Project
Beth Wilson, Senior Researcher, Community Social Planning Council of Toronto

REPORT AUTHOR

Beth Wilson, CSPC-T

RESEARCH SUPPORT

Jim Dunn, Centre for Research on Inner City Health
Raluca Fletcher, CSPC-T
Bob Gardner, Wellesley Institute
Esther Guttman, CSPC-T
Dean Herd, SANE
Dianne Patychuk
Michael Shapcott, Wellesley Institute
Zachary Tucker-Abramson, CSPC-T

CSPC-T RESEARCH ADVISORY COMMITTEE

Tam Goossen, Chair
Mario Calla
Celia Denov, ex-officio
Rick Eagan, project advisory committee liaison
Luin Goldring
Mazher Jaffery
John Myles
Rhonda Roffey
Cheryl Teelucksingh
Armine Yalnizyan

REPORT DESIGN

Christopher Wulff, CSPC-T

FUNDING SUPPORT

This project was made possible through the financial support of:

WELLESLEY INSTITUTE
a decade of advancing urban health

United Way
Toronto

TORONTO

Social Sciences and Humanities
Research Council of Canada

Acknowledgements

I would like to extend my heartfelt thanks to Ernie Lightman and Andy Mitchell for the wonderful support and thoughtful direction that they provided throughout this project. It has been a priviledge and my pleasure to work with Ernie and Andy – both outstanding researchers, dedicated advocates and keen observers of the political landscape.

Special thanks to Michael Shapcott for his careful review and thoughtful comments on draft reports, continued support and enthusiasm for this project, and his and the Wellesley Institute's ongoing commitment to put research into action for social change.

I would like to extend my appreciation to Bob Gardner, Dianne Patychuk, Dean Herd and Jim Dunn for their helpful advice and assistance with this project. Many thanks to Rick Eagan, CSPC-T research advisory committee member and project advisory liaison for his active engagement and grounded perspective. I would also like to thank CSPC-T research advisory committee members Luin Goldring, Tam Goossen, Rhonda Roffey and Cheryl Teelucksingh who provided important feedback contributing to the development of this report.

Many thanks go to Raluca Fletcher, Esther Guttman and Zak Tucker-Abrahmson for their thorough research assistance.

I would like to acknowledge the vital financial contributions of our project funders, the Wellesley Institute and Social Sciences and Humanities Research Council of Canada, and CSPC-T's core funders, City of Toronto and United Way Toronto.

Many of the 1.3 million Ontarians living in poverty are sick and tired of being sick and tired. This project builds on a strong base of compelling research demonstrating the critical need to invest in the social determinants of health. It's in the interest of individual health, and the fiscal health of our health care system and the economy. It is my hope that this work will help propel our governments forward to take real action on poverty, bad jobs and poor health.

Beth Wilson, *Report Author*

About the partners

Community Social Planning Council of Toronto (CSPC-T) is a non-profit community organization committed to building a civic society in which diversity, equity, social and economic justice, interdependence and active civic participation are central. CSPC-T works with diverse communities, engages in community-based research and conducts policy analysis with an aim of improving the quality of life of all Toronto residents.
www.socialplanningtoronto.org

The **Social Assistance in the New Economy** (SANE) research initiative is a multi-year, multi-disciplinary inquiry into the changing nature of social assistance in Ontario and its relation to precarious employment in a globalizing economy. Funded primarily by the Social Sciences and Humanities Research Council (SSHRC) through four major grants, the research program comprises a number of complementary research projects which are investigating: the welfare and post-welfare experiences of social assistance recipients as well as the labour market experiences of those precariously employed. Our methodologies include primary data collection through qualitative in-depth interviews through to secondary analysis of large data sets such as the SLID and CCHS. Aside from publishing extensively in the academic literature, SANE has advised various non-profit community-based agencies and governments on policies towards income support for those with low incomes.
www.oise.utoronto.ca/fsw/exponent/fsw/fswsupport/sane/

The **Wellesley Institute** is a Toronto-based non-profit and non-partisan research and policy institute. Our focus is on developing research and community-based policy solutions to the problems of urban health and health disparities. We identify and advance practical and achievable policy alternatives and solutions to pressing issues of urban health; fund research on the social determinants of health and health disparities, focusing on the relationships between health and housing, poverty and income distribution, social exclusion and other social and economic inequalities; support community engagement and capacity building; work in numerous collaborations and partnerships locally, nationally and internationally, to support social and policy change to address the impact of the social determinants of health.
www.wellesleyinstitute.com

Table of Contents

Sick and Tired: The Compromised Health of Social Assistance Recipients and the Working Poor in Ontario

"Inequity in the conditions of daily lives is shaped by deeper social structures and processes; the inequity is systematic, produced by policies that tolerate or actually enforce unfair distribution of and access to power, wealth, and other necessary social resources."

- World Health Organization, 2008

Introduction

In August 2008, the World Health Organization released a groundbreaking study on the social determinants of health – the political, social and economic forces that shape people's health and people's lives. Closing the Gap in a Generation documents health inequities between and within countries revealing the central role of public policy on individual health. Drawing from a broad base of research, this renowned team of scholars, policy makers and former heads of state and health ministries calls all governments to action on the social determinants of health.

They offer concrete proposals and real world examples that can close the health gap within a generation – from action to ensure fair and decent employment, access to safe and affordable housing, and the provision of quality education and child care to the promotion of gender and racial equity, inclusive social and political decision-making and adequate social protections to ensure healthy living.

As one of the signatory countries to the World Health Organization's Commission on Social Determinants of Health, Canada has made a commitment to advance the social determinants of health domestically and internationally. In December 2008, the Ontario provincial government introduced a poverty reduction strategy to reduce child poverty by 25% in 5 years – a landmark commitment in the history of Ontario (Government of Ontario, 2008). The provincial plan is an important vehicle for reducing poverty, stimulating the economy, and taking action on the social determinants of health.

Many individuals and groups have offered moral and ethical arguments for the need to act on poverty as it relates to ill health. Research also supports the economic benefit

of reducing poverty. In a recent study on the economic costs of poverty in Ontario, researchers pegged poverty-induced costs related to provincial health care at $2.9 billion (Laurie, 2008). Real investments to address poverty in Ontario are critical to supporting individual health and safeguarding the fiscal well-being of our health care system and our economy.

In this report, we focus on the health of social assistance recipients and the working poor in Ontario – two groups that should be at the centre of Ontario's poverty reduction plan. We first present results on the health and health care use of these low income Ontarians, and we then offer a series of recommendations to strengthen the provincial government's poverty reduction strategy, to address the disproportionate burden of poor health experienced by low income Ontarians, and to promote health equity within Ontario.

Sick and Tired is the companion piece to *Poverty is Making Us Sick: A Comprehensive Survey of Income and Health in Canada.* In our first report, we examined the health and health care use of the Canadian population by household income quintile. Income quintiles divide the population into five equal groups starting with the bottom 20% of the population with the lowest household incomes, followed by the next 20% and so on, up to the top 20% with the highest household incomes. This report documented dramatic health inequities among income groups across a broad range of chronic conditions and health measures, as well as different patterns of health care use according to income. Not only did the rich have better health outcomes than the poor, health status improved at each successive step up the income ladder. Using multivariate analyses, we found that an increase of $1,000 in household income for the lowest income Canadians was associated with substantial decreases in rates of many chronic conditions.

Building on our first report, *Sick and Tired* focuses on health equity issues in Ontario. In this document, we focus in particular on recipients of social assistance and on the working poor. Our findings are broadly in line with those of the earlier study, though the differences among groups are often more pronounced in the present report.

Method

This analysis is based on Ontario data from the most recent Canadian Community Health Survey (CCHS) conducted in 2005. Statistics Canada's CCHS is the most comprehensive survey of the health and health care use of Canadians. Health outcome and health care use information for the Ontario population aged 18-64 years was utilized in this analysis. A total of 24,464 Ontario respondents were included. Standard methods were used to weight the data in order to represent the overall population.

We compared the incidence of specific chronic conditions, health-related measures and health care use, adjusted for age, for three groups:

· **Working Poor:** respondents whose main source of household income is from wages, salaries or self-employment and whose household income is at or below the Low Income Measure (LIM)

· **Social Assistance Recipients:** respondents whose main source of household income is from provincial or municipal social assistance or welfare and whose household income is at or below the LIM; this group includes both Ontario Works (OW) and Ontario Disability Support Program (ODSP) recipients

· **Non-Poor:** respondents whose household income is above the LIM

Statistics Canada's LIM was used to categorize respondents as low income or not. The LIM is a widely used measure of low income. LIMs are set at 50% of the median household income for Canada and take into account family size.

The CCHS does not distinguish between OW and ODSP income sources. For this reason, the social assistance group includes both OW and ODSP recipients.

Multivariate analyses were conducted to better understand the multiple factors associated with ill health. These analyses included the following variables: age, gender, racialized status (referred to by Statistics Canada as visible minority), Aboriginal status, educational attainment, participation and activity limitation (used as a proxy for disability), physical activity level, daily smoker status, employment status, adjusted household income, and social assistance receipt (as main source of household income). These analyses allowed us to consider the question: when multiple factors associated with ill health are taken into account, are household income and/or social assistance receipt still significant predictors of ill health? As well, multivariate analyses allowed us to look at the association between social assistance receipt and ill health when disability status (among other factors) is taken into account (i.e. held constant).

A detailed description of the methodology is available online at www.socialplanningtoronto.org.

Context

Some important changes have occurred since 2005 when the survey was conducted. Rising unemployment and full-time job losses have hit Ontario workers hard (Statistics Canada, 2009, January 9). Ontario manufacturers have shed a staggering one in ten jobs between 2003 and 2007, with further declines into 2008 (Ontario Federation of Labour, 2007; Statistics Canada, 2009, January 9). Early effects of this historical economic crisis are likely to have pushed more people into poverty, further compromising individual health – and it's far from over.

On a positive note, Ontario's minimum wage rate was increased by $1.30 per hour between 2005 and 2008 (Ontario Ministry of Labour, n.d.). While welcome, these recent increases have only helped to make up for lost ground from a rate freeze that extended from 1995 and 2003 under the previous provincial government. At $8.75 per hour, the current rate offers minimum wage earners just about the same purchasing power as their counterparts had in 1995. Today's minimum wage remains a poverty wage, and as such, a health hazard to these low wage workers.

Beginning in 2003 and continuing since 2005, the provincial government introduced periodic 2-3% increases to social assistance rates (National Council of Welfare, 2006; National Council of Welfare, 2008). Prior to these rate increases, social assistance recipients endured a 21.6% cut in 1995 followed by an 8-year rate freeze under the previous government. While a step in the right direction, the current government's inflation-matching increases have done little to fundamentally change the position of social assistance recipients. In 2007, their incomes remained at 33% to 61% of Statistics Canada's Low Income Cut-Off. Research suggests that these modest increases have contributed little to improving the quality of life or health outcomes for social assistance recipients in Ontario (Lightman et al., 2008a, 2008b, 2005a, 2005b).

Today's global economic crisis, coupled with the continued disadvantage of low income Ontarians, offers no reason to imagine that the health prospects of low income working-age Ontarians have improved since our survey data was collected in 2005. In fact, forecasts for a continued steep downturn through 2009 suggest even tougher economic times ahead for growing numbers of Ontarians, and greater risks to individual health.

Results

Table 1 shows the characteristics of the poverty status groups included in this analysis. Poverty status groups vary substantially on many characteristics. The poor groups have disproportionately larger numbers of women, Aboriginal people, members of racialized groups, and immigrants.

Women comprise nearly two-thirds of the social assistance group compared to 55% of the working poor and just about half of the non-poor group. Nine percent of the social assistance group is Aboriginal compared to just 3% of the working poor and 2% of the non-poor group. Almost half of the working poor are members of racialized groups compared to 40% of the social assistance group and just 20% of the non-poor group. Over one-half of the working poor group are immigrants compared to just over one-third of the social assistance group and 28% of the non-poor group.

The social assistance recipient (40 years) and non-poor (41 years) groups have higher mean ages than the working poor group (37 years).

The social assistance group includes disproportionate numbers of single people (32%) and lone parent families (31%). In contrast, single people make up 17% of the working poor and 13% of the non-poor, and lone parent families comprise 13% of the working poor and just 6% of the non-poor. Households with children make up a full 60% of the working poor compared to 45% of social assistance recipients and 43% of the non-poor.

At 84%, the non-poor rate for post-secondary graduate attainment is twice that of the social assistance group (42%). Almost 7 in 10 of the working poor completed post-secondary studies. In contrast, the social assistance group (29%) has 10 times the rate of not completing high school compared to the non-poor group (2.7%). At 6.1%, the working poor group had more than two times the rate of not completing high school compared to the non-poor.

More than four out of five of the non-poor have current jobs compared to nearly three-quarters of the working poor and just 14% of the social assistance group. All of the working poor and almost all of the non-poor reported household income from wages, salaries or self-employment. Although considerably lower than the working poor and non-poor, still more than one-quarter of the social assistance group reported some household income from wages, salaries or self-employment.

Median household incomes varied considerably with the non-poor reporting $80,000, compared to just $21,000 for the working poor and a meagre $13,000 for social assistance recipient households.

Table 1. Characteristics of poverty status groups (percent unless otherwise noted)

	Non-poor (unweighted n=22,127)	Working poor (unweighted n=1,612)	Social assistance (unweighted n=725)
Gender			
Male	51.5	44.6	38.5
Female	48.5	55.4	61.5
Age			
Mean age	40.6	36.6	40.1
18-24	12.6	22.5	15.5
25-34	20.9	21.3	17.3
35-44	27.0	27.9	28.8
45-54	23.4	18.8	21.4
55-64	16.1	9.4	16.9
Ethnoracial/cultural group			
Aboriginal person	1.5	2.6	8.9
Member of racialized group	20.4	47.8	39.5
Immigrant status			
Immigrant (born outside of Canada)	28.1	53.3	36.6
Household composition			
Single person	12.6	16.5	31.6
Couple with child/children	51.9	52.0	21.0
Lone parent with child/children	5.7	12.8	31.2
Couple without children	21.8	8.6	10.7
Other family composition	8.1	10.1	5.6
Households with children	43.2	60.0	45.1
Educational attainment			
Less than secondary school	2.7	6.1	29.0
Secondary school graduate	8.9	15.4	17.7
Some post-secondary	4.7	9.4	11.6
Post-secondary graduate	83.8	69.1	41.8
Employment status, income and income source			
Has current job	83.3	74.4[1]	13.8
Has household income for 12-month period preceding interview from wages, salaries or self employment	96.7	100.0	27.6
Median household income for 12-month period preceding interview	$80,000	$21,000	$13,000

Health and Health-Related Measures

In almost every instance, the social assistance group had dramatically higher rates of health problems and chronic conditions across a broad range of measures compared to the working poor and the non-poor groups. Strong statistically significant differences were found between the social assistance group and the other two groups.

The working poor had significantly worse health than the non-poor on several measures. Unexpectedly, the non-poor were found to have higher rates on some health outcomes compared to the working poor. This latter finding was largely a product of the 'healthy immigrant effect', a phenomenon discussed below in the Implications section.

This section focuses on selected major findings from the analyses. Full results are provided in the Appendix.

Self-rated health - Respondents were asked to rate their health as excellent, very good, good, fair or poor. Self-rated health is a valid and reliable measure, strongly correlated with objective measures of health including physicians' ratings (see Shields & Shooshtari, 2001 for review).

On average, Ontarians rate their health highly. However these ratings differ significantly between poverty status groups. As shown in figure 1 (shown below), the social assistance group had significantly higher rates of poor or fair health compared to the working poor and non-poor groups – more than 3 to 5 times higher. The working poor had significantly higher rates than the non-poor group as well.

Disability - Respondents were asked about participation and activity limitations that affected their daily lives at work, school, home and in other settings. The social assistance group had significantly higher rates of participation and activity limitations – 3.5 to 4 times higher than that of the other two groups.

Respondents reported the number of days during the two-week period preceding their interview that they spent all or most of the day in bed because of illness or injury. Again the social assistance group had significantly higher rates at 2.8 days compared to .8 days for the other two groups.

Stress - The social assistance group had significantly higher rates of high stress compared to the other two groups. Over one-third of the social assistance group reported feeling quite a bit or extremely stressful most days compared to around one-quarter of respondents from the other two groups.

Suicide[2] - Particularly disturbing results emerged in analyses pertaining to suicide. As shown in figure 2 (on the following page), the social assistance group had significantly higher rates of considering suicide and attempting suicide than the other two groups. In the 12-month period preceding their interview, one in ten respondents from the social assistance group considered suicide and 2% attempted suicide – rates that are 10 times higher than the non-poor group.

The working poor also had significantly higher rates of considering and attempting suicide than the non-poor group. The working poor group was twice as likely to attempt suicide in the 12-month period preceding their interview compared to the non-poor group.

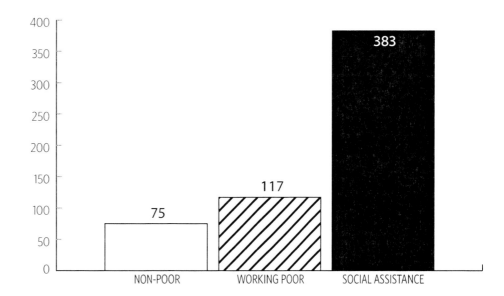

FIGURE 1

**'Poor' or 'Fair'
Self-Reported Health**
Age-Adjusted Rates per Thousand
Population by Poverty Status

Ontario, Population 18-64, 2005

FIGURE 2

**Considered and
Attempted Suicide**

Age-Adjusted Rates per Thousand
Population by Poverty Status

Ontario, Population 18-64, 2005

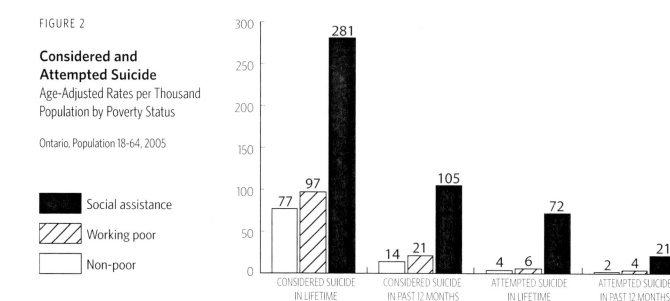

Chronic conditions - Respondents were asked whether a medical practitioner had diagnosed them with various chronic conditions. The presence of at least one chronic condition is quite common among working-age Ontarians. However rates vary widely by poverty status.

The social assistance group had significantly higher rates of chronic conditions, multiple conditions and total number of conditions compared to the other two groups. A total of 85% of social assistance recipients had a chronic condition compared to 69% of the non-poor and 63% of the working poor. The non-poor had significantly higher rates of having at least one chronic condition compared to the working poor. However, the working poor had significantly higher rates of multiple chronic conditions compared to the non-poor.

Diabetes - As shown in figure 3 below, social assistance recipients had a significantly higher rate of diabetes compared to the other two groups. With more than one in ten individuals affected, the diabetes rate was 2.1 to 3.6 times higher in the social assistance group compared to the other two groups. The working poor also had significantly higher rates compared to the non-poor – 1.7 times higher.

Heart disease - Social assistance recipients had significantly higher rates of heart disease compared to the other two groups. At 8%, the rate was more than 2 to 3 times higher among social assistance recipients compared to the other two groups. The working poor also had significantly higher rates at more than 1.3 times that of the non-poor group.

FIGURE 3

Diabetes

Age-Adjusted Rates per Thousand
Population by Poverty Status

Ontario, Population 18-64, 2005

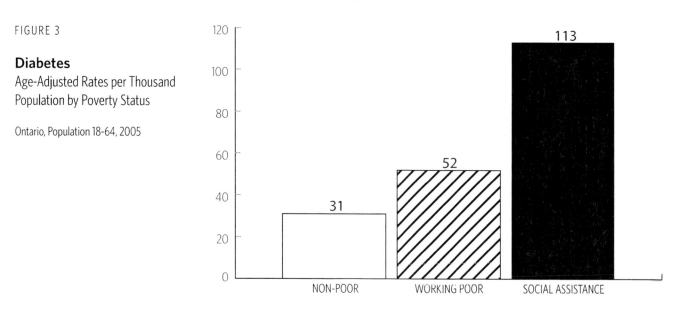

FIGURE 4

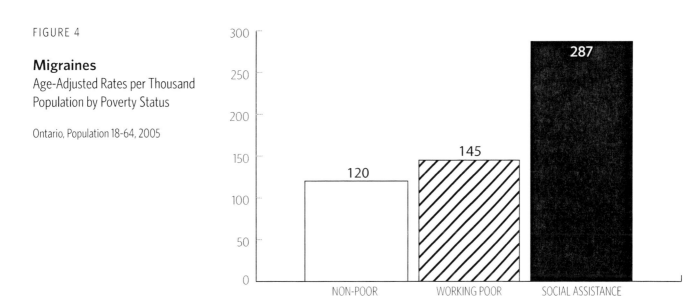

Migraines
Age-Adjusted Rates per Thousand
Population by Poverty Status

Ontario, Population 18-64, 2005

Migraines - As shown in figure 4 above, the social assistance group had significantly higher rates of migraines at nearly double to over 2.3 times the rates of the other two groups. The working poor group also had significantly higher rates than the non-poor group.

Chronic bronchitis - Again the social assistance group had significantly higher rates of chronic bronchitis at 2.8 and 4.6 times that of the other two groups. Rates were significantly higher among the working poor compared to the non-poor as well.

Asthma - At 16%, the asthma rate among social assistance recipients was double that of the other two groups.

Arthritis and rheumatism - Figure 5 below shows the elevated rates of arthritis and rheumatism among social assistance recipients compared to the other two groups. The social assistance group had rates more than double that of the working poor and non-poor.

Mood disorders - As shown in figure 6 (on the following page), the social assistance group had significantly higher rates of mood disorders at nearly four times that of the other two groups.

Health Care Service Use

The social assistance and working poor groups were significantly more likely to report not having a doctor (13-15%) compared to the non-poor group (10%).

Despite being less likely to have a regular medical doctor, social assistance recipients reported significantly more consultations with all medical professionals, general

FIGURE 5

Arthritis or Rheumatism
Age-Adjusted Rates per Thousand
Population by Poverty Status

Ontario, Population 18-64, 2005

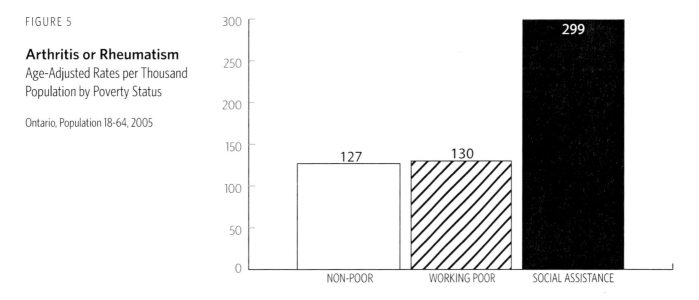

FIGURE 6

Mood Disorder

Age-Adjusted Rates per Thousand
Population by Poverty Status

Ontario, Population 18-64, 2005

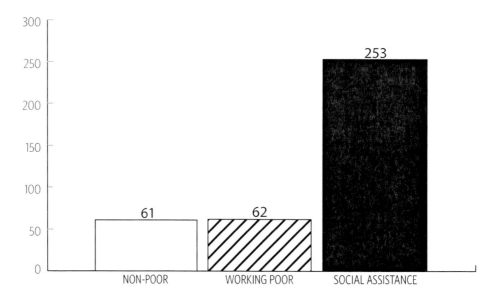

practitioners, specialists, and other medical practitioners compared to the non-poor and working poor groups.

The non-poor group had significantly more consultations with all medical practitioners, specialists, and other medical practitioners compared to the working poor group. In contrast, the working poor group had significantly more consultations with general practitioners than the non-poor group.

Figure 7 below shows the differences in consultations with medical practitioners among poverty status groups.

The social assistance group had a significantly higher number of nights spent in a hospital, nursing home or convalescent home compared to the other two groups.

Preventative Health Care Service Use

In general, the working poor and social assistance groups were less likely to have accessed various preventative health measures than the non-poor group. In some cases, the working poor group had lower rates than the social assistance group.

Most working-age Ontarians have had an eye exam and visited a dentist in the past. However important differences emerged for poverty status groups.

The working poor were significantly more likely to report never having an eye exam compared to the non-poor

FIGURE 7

**Consultations with
Medical Practitioners**
Age-Adjusted
Totals per Thousand Population
by Poverty Status

Ontario, Population 18-64, 2005

■ Social assistance

▨ Working poor

□ Non-poor

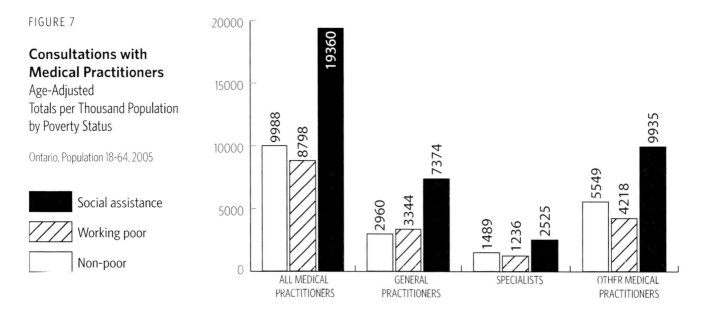

group. The non-poor group was significantly more likely to report having a recent eye exam compared to the poor groups.

The working poor group was significantly more likely to report never having visited a dentist compared to the other two groups. Again, the non-poor group was significantly more likely to report having a recent visit to a dentist compared to the poor groups.

With regard to women's health, the working poor and social assistance groups were significantly more likely to report never having had a breast exam, a mammogram among women 40-64 years of age, or a pap smear test compared to the non-poor group.

Among 40-64 year olds, the working poor group was significantly more likely to report never having had a colorectal cancer screening test compared to the non-poor and social assistance groups.

Unmet Health Care Needs

Social assistance recipients reported significantly higher rates of unmet health care needs compared to the other two groups. Over one-quarter reported unmet health care needs compared to 13-15% of the working poor and non-poor groups.

Respondents from the poor groups were significantly more likely to report cost (20-22%) as a reason for not receiving care compared to the non-poor group (9%). Poor respondents (4-7%) were also significantly more likely to report transportation problems compared to non-poor respondents (1%).

Access to Health Insurance

Strong significant differences were found among poverty status groups on access to health insurance. About four out of five respondents from the non-poor and social assistance groups had health insurance for prescription medications compared to just over two out of five respondents from the working poor group. Similarly, about 70% of respondents from the non-poor and social assistance groups had insurance for eyeglasses and contact lenses compared to 29% of the working poor group.

A different pattern emerged for dental care coverage and hospital charges. Non-poor respondents (78%) had the highest rate of dental care coverage, followed by the social assistance group (66%) and then the working poor

group (39%)[3]. Significant differences were found between all three groups. Almost three out of four non-poor respondents have insurance to cover hospital charges compared to 24-28% of the social assistance and working poor groups.

Food Insecurity

The rate of household food insecurity among social assistance recipients was 15 times higher than that of the non-poor group, and almost 3 times higher than the working poor group. Almost half of all respondents from the social assistance group were in food insecure households compared to 17% of the working poor and 3% of the non-poor. These differences were highly significant.

Chronic Conditions: Examining Multiple Factors

We conducted a series of multivariate analyses to test for associations between household income and ill health, and social assistance receipt and ill health, when other factors related to ill health are taken into account (see Table F in the Appendix). These control variables included: age, gender, racialized status, Aboriginal status, educational attainment, participation and activity limitation (a proxy for disability status), physical activity level, daily smoker status and employment status.

After taking into account all of these factors, household income and/or social assistance receipt continued to be significantly associated with 6 out of 8 chronic condition categories, and 15 out of 21 specific chronic conditions.

It is important to stress that these associations are statistically significant after taking into account (i.e. holding constant) the effects of demographic, educational, employment, health behaviour factors and disability status.

Implications

Social Assistance and Sickness

Results of this study paint a grim picture of the health of social assistance recipients in Ontario. Social assistance recipients have significantly higher rates of poor health and chronic conditions on 38 of 39 health measures compared to the non-poor, and 37 of 39 health measures compared to the working poor. Their rates on conditions such as diabetes, heart disease, chronic bronchitis, arthritis and rheumatism, mood disorders and anxiety disorders are 2.4 to 4.6 times higher than that of the non-poor. Not surprisingly, over one-third report high stress levels. Forty percent of the social assistance group often experience participation and activity limitations that interfere with their everyday lives.

Perhaps most distressing, over one-quarter of social assistance recipients considered suicide in their lifetime and one in ten in the 12-month period preceding their interview. The social assistance group reported attempting suicide at rates that were 5 to 18 times higher than the non-poor and working poor groups.

Multivariate analyses resulted in powerful findings linking household income and social assistance receipt to a broad range of chronic conditions, even when other factors, including disability status and health behaviour factors such as smoking and physical activity, were taken into account.

The median annual household income for this highly stressed, health compromised and vulnerable group was a mere $13,000.

While data from this study cannot directly address the causal relationship between income and health, researchers that have explored this question have found that while poor health affects income by diminishing a person's ability to engage in paid employment, the strongest causal influence shows low income leading to poor health (Phipps, 2003). Regardless of whether individuals initially experience falling incomes as a result of ill health or declining health as a result of low income, the fact remains that poverty further compromises health and undermines a person's ability to cope with chronic health problems and to get well.

An Illness Producing System

Our analysis raises important questions about Ontario's social assistance system – a system that leaves the most health compromised group of working-age people in the province to subsist on meagre income assistance. In fact, rates are so low that almost half of all recipients live in food insecure households.

Ontario's social assistance system includes two main programs: Ontario Works (OW) and the Ontario Disability Support Program (ODSP). OW is intended as the short-term income assistance program of last resort, providing financial and employment assistance to recipients. ODSP

provides longer-term income and employment assistance to Ontarians with disabilities.

OW and ODSP rates are abysmally low. In 2005 when our data was collected, estimated annual incomes[4] for OW recipients were $7,007 for a single person, $14,451 for a lone parent with one child and $19,302 for a couple with two children (National Council of Welfare, 2006). A person with a disability receiving ODSP had an estimated annual income of $12,057. These incomes were between 34% and 58% of the poverty line[5], with single OW recipients at the lowest level.

Comparing Ontario inflation-adjusted social assistance incomes between 1986 and 2005, the National Council of Welfare (2006) found the lowest incomes for three out of four family types occurred in 2005. The lowest social assistance income for a couple with two children occurred in 2003. By 2005, the annual income for this family type had increased by $75, about $6 more per month.

While the provincial government has made modest 2-3% periodic increases to social assistance rates in recent years, these rates remain troublingly low (National Council of Welfare, 2006; National Council of Welfare, 2008). Social assistance income statistics for 2007 reveal further declines for a single employable person and a person with a disability, when inflation is taken into account (National Council of Welfare, 2008). Since 2005, families with children fared better with an increase in social assistance incomes of 9.1% for a lone parent with one child and 4.7% for a couple with two children. However, estimated annual social assistance incomes remained at 33% to 61% of the poverty line in 2007, with single individuals receiving OW continuing to be the worst off. Inflation-matching increases alone have not changed the woeful inadequacy of Ontario's social assistance rates.

While disability assistance rates are well below the poverty line, ODSP provides higher levels of income assistance to recipients compared to OW. With their increased burden of compromised health and corresponding health care expenses, access to ODSP is vital to people with disabilities in financial need. We found very high rates of chronic conditions and ill health among social assistance recipients in general. While it was not possible to distinguish between OW and ODSP recipients in the dataset, these alarming rates, coupled with very low incomes, raise questions about the extent to which people with disabilities are gaining access to ODSP.

Several studies have documented the considerable barriers that Ontarians with disabilities face in accessing ODSP (Centre for Addiction and Mental Health, 2003; Income Security Advocacy Centre, 2003; ODSP Action Coalition, 2008; Social Planning Council of Ottawa, 2001; Street Health, 2006). While some improvements have been made since the program's inception in 1998 (Ombudsman Ontario, 2006), advocates continue to raise serious concerns about access to ODSP. Lack of access leaves people with disabilities either with no income or struggling to survive on OW (Ombudsman Ontario, 2006).

Social assistance recipients in Ontario live in grinding poverty. For the large numbers struggling with ill health, poverty further undermines their ability to cope with health problems and to improve their health. In addition, social assistance recipients have the extra burden of dealing with Ontario's social assistance system – a complex and punitive bureaucracy that promotes stress, anxiety, depression and self-blame (Community Social Planning Council of Toronto & Family Service Association of Toronto, 2004; Herd et al., 2005; Herd & Mitchell, 2002; Lightman et al., 2003a; Lightman et al., 2003b). As well, social assistance recipients are confronted with societal judgment and social exclusion associated with being 'on welfare' (Power, 2005; Reid & Tom, 2006; Swanson, 2001). Rather than a source of support in hard times, the system and the societal baggage associated with it further undermine the health of social assistance recipients.

Poor Health and The Working Poor

The health of the working poor is a more complicated story. The working poor have higher rates of diabetes, heart disease, chronic bronchitis, migraines, multiple chemical sensitivities and learning disabilities compared to the non-poor group. They have lower self-reported health and mental health, a higher rate of household food insecurity and are more likely to report multiple chronic conditions compared to the non-poor group.

Compared to the non-poor, the working poor were more likely to consider suicide in their lifetime and in the 12-month period preceding their interview. They were twice as likely as the non-poor group to attempt suicide in the year prior to their interview.

While the working poor group had higher rates on a number of health problems, they did not differ from the non-poor group in the average number of days spent in bed due to illness or injury. This is likely related to working conditions in the precarious labour market that generally provide low wages with no benefits. While the working poor may need time to recover, and their health may be further compromised by continuing to work through illness and injury, taking time off may be a luxury that they simply cannot afford. In contrast, the non-poor group was more likely to enjoy both higher wages that would allow them to take time off, and benefits such as sick days and long-term disability plans that prevent or reduce losses of wages related to illness and injury.

The Working Poor and the Healthy Immigrant Effect

While the working poor have compromised health outcomes on a number of measures, the whole story of their health is more complex. The non-poor, compared to the working poor, were more likely to report having at least one chronic condition, and had higher rates of endocrine and metabolic conditions, circulatory system conditions, musculoskeletal conditions, miscellaneous conditions, allergies other than food allergies, high blood pressure, urinary incontinence, bowel disorder and other chronic conditions.

These differences can be explained, in large part, by a phenomenon called the "healthy immigrant effect". National data strongly support the existence of the healthy immigrant effect, whereby immigrants and particularly newcomers to Canada enjoy better health, including lower rates of chronic conditions, than their Canadian-born counterparts overall (Newbold, 2006; Ng et al., 2005). Researchers have found that this health benefit diminishes over time until immigrant health levels begin to approximate that of their Canadian-born counterparts, and is particularly evident among non-European immigrants.

Researchers have explored this issue in some depth. They point to the impact of immigration policies that exclude immigrants with 'medically inadmissible' conditions as a reason for newcomers' superior health relative to their Canadian-born peers and barriers to health care services that result in lower rates of medical diagnoses (Newbold, 2006). The declining health of immigrant groups over time has been attributed to the impact of disproportionate rates of poverty, poor working conditions and the lack of recognition of internationally-acquired credentials.

In our sample, over half of the working poor are immigrants compared to 28% of the non-poor group. Despite their income levels, it is not surprising to find better than expected health outcomes for the working poor as a result of the healthy immigrant effect. We conducted additional analyses showing that immigrants in the working poor group had been living in Canada an average of 12 years compared to 22 years in the non-poor group. This data further suggested that the healthy immigrant effect was at work.

Additional analyses revealed that the healthy immigrant effect was a significant factor in explaining the contrary results between the working poor and non-poor groups. We conducted separate analyses for the Canadian-born and immigrant populations in Ontario for the ten health outcomes where the non-poor group had higher rates than the working poor group.[6]

In analyses of the Canadian-born population controlling for age, the results either reversed themselves, where the working poor had higher rates of ill health than the non-poor or no differences were found between groups.

In analyses of the immigrant population controlling for age and length of residency in Canada, we found either no significant differences between the working poor and non-poor groups, or a significant but diminished difference between groups where the non-poor continued to have higher rates for some health problems compared to the working poor group. After taking into account age and length of residency in Canada, the non-poor immigrant group had significantly higher rates of the following chronic conditions/categories compared to the working poor immigrant group: having at least one chronic condition, musculoskeletal conditions, miscellaneous conditions, allergies other than food allergies, high blood pressure and bowel disorder. Differences in experiences with the health care system may also explain some of these findings. Additional research is needed to further unpack these results.

Low Wages, Precarious Work and Compromised Health

Labour markets in industrialized countries like Canada have undergone major restructuring over the past 30 years, resulting in an expansion of precarious employment. In Canada, 37% of jobs are part-time, temporary or self-employed positions (Community-University Research Alliance on Precarious Employment, 2005). In 2005, 22.5% of Canadians, aged 25-64 years, working full-year full-week had an annual income of less than $30,000, up from 21.1% in 2000 (Statistics Canada, 2008). Among women,

aged 25-64 years, working full-year full-week, 23.5% had an annual income below $30,000 compared to 21.7% of men. Almost one-quarter of all jobs in Ontario pay less than $10 an hour (Workers' Action Centre, 2007a). Studies show that women, immigrants, and workers of colour are over-represented in the ranks of Ontario's working poor (Campaign 2000, Citizens for Public Justice & Workers' Action Centre, 2006).

The working poor in our study had a median annual income of $21,000 and low rates of insurance coverage for dental, vision, prescription drug and hospital expenses. Nearly half were members of racialized groups. More than half were immigrants, and more than half were women.

The working poor group is likely employed in low wage and precarious positions. These jobs typically include short-term, temporary and contract work with low pay and few, if any, benefits. Part-time employment is also a feature of precarious work. While some workers may desire part-time employment, many part-time workers seek and require full-time jobs to make ends meet. Workers in the precarious labour market may also juggle multiple jobs, are vulnerable to exploitive employers and generally lack access to collective representation.

In Toronto, the Workers' Action Centre (2007b) has documented widespread employment standards' violations, the complete exclusion of many workers from employment standards' protections, and a lack of enforcement of standards for workers who are covered by the provincial Employment Standards Act (an issue that the Province is beginning to address through its poverty reduction strategy). This research links poor working conditions from precarious employment to increased stress resulting in poor physical and mental health.

Due to restructuring of the Employment Insurance (EI) system (formerly Unemployment Insurance) in the mid-1990s, many workers with precarious employment are now ineligible for federal Employment Insurance (EI) benefits when laid off. This is particularly pronounced in Ontario, compared to the rest of Canada, and in the big urban centres such as Toronto. Drastic changes to the program rendered many workers with short-term and/or part-time positions – particularly women – ineligible due to inadequate insurable hours (Canadian Labour Congress, 1999). When short-term jobs end, these workers must scramble for other employment or turn to the social assistance system with its considerably lower benefit levels.

Lack of an adequate minimum wage has long been an issue for low wage workers in Ontario. The former Conservative provincial government froze the minimum wage at $6.85 per hour during both of its terms in office from 1995 to 2003 (Ontario Ministry of Labour, 2003). While the Liberal provincial government elected in 2003 began making modest annual increases to the minimum wage, these increases have not been sufficient to pull minimum wage earners out of poverty.

In recent years, workers, community groups and labour organizations mounted a vigorous campaign calling on the provincial government to raise the minimum wage to $10 per hour immediately. The provincial government responded by slating annual increases to bring the minimum wage up to $10.25 per hour in 2010 (Ontario Ministry of Labour, n.d.). Despite these advances, the current rate at $8.75 per hour still leaves minimum wage workers in poverty. Economists from the Canadian Centre for Policy Alternatives peg a living wage for Toronto at $16.60, nearly double the current rate (Mackenzie & Stanford, 2008).

Low wage and precarious employment contributes to the compromised health of the working poor. Lack of access to EI benefits puts short-term contract workers further at risk by leaving them to the inadequacies of the social assistance system when their employment ends. On a bright note, recent provincial actions promise to improve the position of some vulnerable workers in Ontario. In response to workers' advocacy efforts, the Ontario provincial government recently adopted legislation to extend protections for temp agency workers, arguably some of the most vulnerable workers in the province (Ontario Ministry of Labour, 2008). This legislation represents a first step toward improving protections for temporary workers in Ontario.

Health Care Inequities

Not surprisingly, the social assistance group with its much higher rates of chronic conditions and poor health reported significantly more consultations with medical practitioners of all kinds. These results are also expected given the requirements of ODSP applicants and recipients to provide detailed documentation from medical doctors to access and maintain benefits. Despite their frequent consultations with various medical professionals, the social assistance group was less likely to have a regular medical doctor compared to the non-poor group. While the working poor group reported more visits to general practitioners compared to the non-poor group, they were also less likely to have a regular medical doctor compared to the non-poor group.

In a 25-year review of health care utilization in Canada, Curtis and MacMinn (2008) report some parallel findings. This study showed that people in Canada with lower socioeconomic status (SES) were less likely to visit a physician compared to other residents. This inequity appears to be growing more prevalent over time. However, these researchers also found that once initial contact was made with a physician, residents with lower SES consulted with physicians more frequently than others. Similarly, we found both poor groups had more consultations with general practitioners compared to the non-poor group but were less likely to have a regular medical doctor.

Similar to our results with the working poor, these researchers found people in Canada with lower SES were less likely to see a specialist. Once initial contact was made with a specialist, these researchers found that income was no longer a factor in the number of specialist consultations between groups. While the working poor in our study had fewer consultations with specialists than the non-poor group, social assistance recipients had more consultations with specialists compared to the non-poor and working poor groups. This latter finding demonstrates that important differences exist within the lower SES group.

In addition, our data showed lower rates of preventative health care utilization among poor groups compared to the non-poor group. Rates were especially troubling regarding women's preventative health care where substantial numbers of women in the poor groups had never had a pap smear test, breast exam or mammogram for those over 40 years of age.

As well, the working poor were much less likely to have insurance to cover additional health services compared to the non-poor group. Social assistance recipients reported lower rates for dental care and hospital expense coverage compared to the non-poor. Although social assistance recipients had higher rates for dental coverage than the working poor, their government-provided coverage is limited to emergency services only.

In Ontario, delisting of some health care services has forced Ontarians without insurance to pay for additional services out of pocket (Browne, n.d.). Data from our study suggest that poor Ontarians are forgoing some health services due to cost. We found higher rates of unmet health care need among the poor groups compared to the non-poor group, and cost cited as a factor for one in five poor respondents with unmet health care needs.

Our data and related studies reveal troubling inequities regarding health care service utilization (Curtis & MacMinn, 2008; Steele et al., 2002; Street Health, 2007). With regard to physicians and specialists, Curtis and MacMinn (2008) found that the largest inequities exist at the point of first contact. Their work documents a growing gap in the amount of health care received between the rich and the poor, Canadian-born and immigrant populations, and residents with lower levels of education compared to more highly educated residents. These trends have important implications for Ontario's working poor and social assistance recipients.

Curtis and MacMinn offer some recommendations to address Canada's growing health care inequities. They suggest an increased focus on language and cultural issues with regard to health care service provision, improved access to pharmaceuticals for residents who are unable to pay, increased access to physicians in poor areas, training of more physicians from diverse communities, public education, including development of multilingual materials, to promote use of preventative health care services, and development of clinical guidelines for physicians regarding appropriate referrals to specialists. These authors point out that improved access to primary care including medications may lessen the burden on emergency services and hospitals.

Human Costs, Health Care Costs

The increased burden of compromised health among social assistance recipients and the working poor undermines the quality of life of poor Ontarians and results in increased costs to the health care system. In a study of the impact of chronic conditions, Schultz and Kopec (2003) found moderate to severe quality of life impacts for people with Alzheimer's disease, urinary incontinence, effects of a stroke, arthritis and rheumatism, bowel disorders, chronic bronchitis and emphysema, back problems, epilepsy, heart disease and cataracts. Several of these conditions were more common among the poor groups in our study, particularly for social assistance recipients.

Individuals living with health problems and in poverty face difficult challenges. As supported by our research and others, they may lack the funds to pay for a nutritious diet which is critical to good health (Sieppert et al., 2004). The stress of living in poverty, unable to pay the bills and cover basic needs, including health-related needs, further exacerbates ill health. People living with ill health and in poverty are also disadvantaged by the lack of affordable housing and problems of substandard housing in Ontario. For social assistance recipients, the ongoing surveillance, and arbitrary and punitive nature of the system contributes to poor health (Community Social Planning Council of Toronto & Family Service Association of Toronto, 2004; Herd et al., 2005; Lightman et al., 2003a; 2003b; Baker Collins, 2005).

Both social assistance recipients and the working poor are engaged in systems that reduce their sense of control over their lives – whether as a result of interactions with the social assistance system or within precarious labour markets where workers have little control over their work environments. The loss of personal control, characteristic of social assistance systems and precarious work environments, has important implications for individual health.

Poverty also affects people's relationships and connections to community. It can limit a person's ability to participate in the broader community which may already be hindered by illness, contributing to social isolation which further undermines health. Material deprivation can erode relationships among family members (Hamelin et al., 2002). Worried parents sacrifice their own material needs to provide for their children in an attempt to spare them from the impact of poverty. For families living in poverty, a parent or family member's illness adds additional strain to an already difficult situation.

In addition to the human costs, poverty also contributes to added financial costs to the health care system. Our study found longer in-patient stays for social assistance recipients compared to the working poor and non-poor groups. In Canada, total acute care inpatient costs were $17,046.6 million for 2004-05, representing over 37% of overall public health expenditures (Canadian Institute for Health Information, 2008a). Diseases of the respiratory and circulatory systems – conditions disproportionately present among the social assistance group and in some cases, the working poor group – account for 28.8% of all acute care inpatient costs. In a recent study on the economic costs of poverty in Ontario, researchers pegged poverty-induced costs related to provincial health care at $2.9 billion (Laurie, 2008).

The human and financial costs associated with poverty and ill health are considerable. Whether on moral or economic grounds, the need for bold action is clear.

Recommendations

We offer the following recommendations to support the reduction of poverty in Ontario, to address the increased burden of ill health faced by poor people in Ontario, and to promote equitable access to health services in Ontario. These recommendations are based on the results of this study and supported by related research.

Improving the Provincial Poverty Reduction Strategy

Recommendation 1

The Province's poverty reduction strategy includes a plan to review social assistance with an aim of "removing barriers and increasing opportunities". The proposed review is focused on improving rules to better facilitate movement of people from social assistance to work. Re-evaluating complex and contradictory social assistance rules is an important undertaking, however the strategy does not acknowledge one of the fundamental problems with social assistance – inadequate benefit levels that leave people living in deep poverty that compromises individual health and undermines the ability of people to move from social assistance to work. In addition to reviewing social assistance rules, we recommend that:

The provincial government establish an independent panel to set Ontario Works and Ontario Disability Support Program rates, through an evidence-based process, to reflect the actual cost of living in Ontario communities. The basic needs and shelter portions of social assistance should reflect the actual costs of meeting basic needs, including health-related needs, and maintaining decent housing. Rates should take into account regional differences in the cost of living. The Canada Mortgage and Housing Corporation rental housing survey and local nutritious food basket measures can assist in this regard. Once established, rates should be fully indexed to inflation.

Recommendation 2

As a signatory country on the United Nations International Covenant on Economic, Social and Cultural Rights and the Rome Declaration on World Food Security, Canada has recognized the human right to food and has committed to take action domestically and abroad. However our data show that half of all social assistance recipients and

17% of the working poor live in food insecure households. In March 2008, a total of 314,258 Ontarians received food from a food bank (Ontario Association of Food Banks, 2008). Between September 2007 and September 2008, food banks in Ontario reported an average increase of 13% in the number of people receiving food. Social assistance recipients, the working poor and people with disabilities rank high among food bank recipients. Access to a nutritious diet is vital to individual health. It is unacceptable that there are Ontarians going hungry because of poverty, that mothers are sacrificing meals to feed their children, and that residents are filling up on water and rationing bread slices to make it through the month (Community Social Planning Council of Toronto & Family Service Association of Toronto, 2004; Daily Bread Food Bank, 2008; Human Resources and Social Development Canada, 1999; Smilek et al., 2000). Therefore, we recommend that:

The federal and provincial government take immediate action to bring Canada into compliance with its commitment to the human right to food under various international treaties. Local nutritious food basket measures assess the cost of a nutritious diet in specific communities. These are useful tools to guide government action on the right to food.

Recommendation 3

Social assistance recipients in our study had much higher rates of ill health, chronic conditions and activity limitations compared to others, and reported very low household incomes. These findings raise questions about Ontarians with disabilities and their access to ODSP. Related literature and advocate accounts reveal considerable barriers to ODSP for people with disabilities (Centre for Addiction and Mental Health, 2003; Income Security Advocacy Centre, 2003; Lightman et al., in press; ODSP Action Coalition, 2008; Social Planning Council of Ottawa, 2001; Street Health, 2006). Access to ODSP is vital to the health of Ontarians with disabilities in financial need. Therefore, we recommend that:

The provincial government undertake a review of ODSP, including a broad-based community consultation, to identify barriers to access and implement changes to ensure that people with disabilities in financial need have timely access to this essential program.

Recommendation 4

Low wage work and poor working conditions in the precarious labour market impact on the health of the working poor. Recent provincial action to introduce protections for temp agency workers is an important first step in improving the working conditions and by extension, health and well-being of Ontario workers. The provincial government's commitment to increase funding for employment standards' enforcement is also a promising move. Following from these steps, we recommend that:

The provincial government report transparently on its efforts to protect temp agency workers and enforce employment standards. We also recommend that the provincial government update labour standards' legislation to protect the rights of workers engaged in other forms of precarious employment. These workers include those deemed self-employed by employers seeking to offload employee-related responsibilities and expenses. Finally, we recommend that the provincial government set minimum wage rates to ensure that no full-time, full-year worker in Ontario lives in poverty.

Recommendation 5

The Province's poverty reduction strategy sets a goal of reducing child poverty by 25% in 5 years. While an important and laudable goal, the strategy sets no target for reducing adult poverty. In particular, adults without children are not a focus of the plan. According to data from our study, over half of social assistance recipient households and 40% of working poor households do not include children. Therefore, we recommend that:

The provincial government expand its existing target to reduce poverty by 25% in 5 years for *all* Ontarians. In addition to recognizing the full face of poverty in Ontario, an inclusive goal will also reflect the fact that poor children live in poor families and that child poverty cannot be addressed without a simultaneous focus on family and adult poverty.

Taking Action on the Federal Level

Recommendation 6

Countries such as the United Kingdom and Ireland have adopted national poverty reduction strategies. In Canada, provincial governments in Ontario, Quebec and Newfoundland and Labrador have taken the lead in developing their own plans. Ontario's poverty reduction strategy recognizes the role of the federal government in reducing poverty. In the last federal election, all major political parties with the notable exception of the Conservative Party made a commitment to introduce a federal poverty reduction strategy. Poverty reduction is critical to promoting the health of Ontarians and Canadians alike. Therefore, we recommend that:

The federal government introduce a national poverty reduction strategy with concrete targets and timelines, and that it monitor and provide regular public updates on the progress of this plan.

Recommendation 7

Dramatic reforms to the Unemployment Insurance system (now named Employment Insurance) have left the majority of unemployed workers in Ontario and across Canada without access to the benefits that they pay for. Women, youth, immigrants and big city dwellers were most affected by program reforms, showing the lowest rates of access to EI (Black & Shillington, 2005; Canadian Labour Congress, 1999; Townson & Hayes, 2007). Lack of access to EI benefits leaves unemployed workers to the health-compromising inadequacies of provincial social assistance. Rather than the income assistance program of last resort, Ontario Works has become the only option for tens of thousands of unemployed workers in Ontario. It is simply a matter of fairness that workers during periods of job loss, and particularly during these tough economic times, should have access to the benefits that they pay for. Therefore, we recommend that:

The federal government restore Employment Insurance as a universal social program by expanding the eligibility criteria to address the needs of workers in the precarious labour force, ensuring equal access to benefits regardless of residence, improving benefit levels and increasing coverage periods. Rather than divert EI contributions to cover federal deficits and pay down debt, as has been government practice for the last decade, these funds should be used for their intended purpose, to support unemployed workers.

Improving Health Care Access, Promoting Health Equity

Recommendation 8

Our data and related studies reveal troubling inequities regarding health care service access and utilization. Social assistance recipients and the working poor in our study had higher rates of unmet health care needs compared to the non-poor group. One in five people from the poor groups with unmet health care needs cited cost as a factor in his/her inability to get needed care. Individuals from poor groups were less likely to have a regular medical doctor and had lower rates of various preventative health care services. The working poor also had lower rates of insurance coverage for vision, dental, prescription medication and hospital care compared to the non-poor group, and in most cases, social assistance recipients. In related studies, researchers have documented a growing gap in the amount of health care received between the rich and the poor, Canadian-born and immigrant populations, and residents with lower levels of education compared to more highly educated residents, and more out of pocket health care expenses related to the delisting of health services in Ontario (Browne, n.d.; Curtis & MacMinn, 2008).

These inequities were present and growing during prosperous economic times. In light of the current economic crisis, they are likely to widen and affect increasing numbers of people caught in the downturn. Therefore, we recommend that:

The provincial government take action to ensure equitable access to health care services irrespective of income and poverty status, and reduce the ability to pay as a factor in accessing health care in Ontario. Expansion of and increased funding to community health centres (which focus on the health needs of marginalized communities), expansion of dental, vision, prescription drug and hospital care coverage, and expansion of the Ontario Trillium Drug Plan are key areas for action. Language interpreter services and health ambassadors (non-professionals within communities that can provide information and referrals) are critical supports to promote preventative health care and deliver culturally-appropriate health services.

Improving Research Tools, Focusing on Equity-Seeking Groups

Recommendation 9

To better understand the health and health care use of Canadians receiving income from different types of social assistance programs, we recommend that:

Statistics Canada revise future versions of the Canadian Community Health Survey to allow for the collection of income data that distinguishes between general social assistance (short-term assistance) programs and disability support programs (long-term) in each province.

Recommendation 10

The focus of this research has been primarily on the connections between ill health and different forms of poverty status. We have included analyses examining factors such as gender, ethnoracial status, Aboriginal identity, immigration status and disability status. However additional work is needed to examine the specific health outcomes of particular groups. As well, this study is limited to a province-wide analysis for Ontario and does not incorporate other geographic levels including urban, rural and neighbourhood-level analysis. Therefore, we recommend that:

Additional research be conducted to better understand the effects of income inequality, poverty, social assistance and labour market conditions on the health and health care use of women, racialized groups, Aboriginal people, immigrants and people with disabilities. We also recommend that analyses be conducted to better understand how place of residence, such as neighbourhood or region, may relate to poor health.

References and Related Literature

Baker Collins, S. (2005). An understanding of poverty from those who are poor. Action Research, 3(1): 9-31.

Black, J. & Shillington, R. (2005). Ontarians can no longer count on Employment Insurance to provide temporary income between jobs. Toronto, Ontario: MISWAA.

Browne, P.L. (n.d.). Public pain, private gain: The privatization of health care in Ontario. Ottawa, Ontario: Canadian Centre for Policy Alternatives.

Campaign 2000, Citizens for Public Justice & Workers' Action Centre (2006). Working, yet poor in Ontario. Toronto, Ontario.

Canadian Institute for Health Information (2008a). The cost of acute care hospital stays by medical condition in Canada, 2004-2005. Ottawa, Ontario.

Canadian Institute for Health Information (2008b). Reducing gaps in health: A focus on socio-economic status in urban Canada. Ottawa, Ontario.

Canadian Labour Congress (1999). Left out in the cold: The end of UI for Canadian workers. Ottawa, Ontario.

Centre for Addiction and Mental Health (2003). Barriers to ODSP: Experiences of people with mental health and addictions. Toronto, Ontario.

Community Social Planning Council of Toronto & Family Service Association of Toronto (2004). Community voices: Young parents in Toronto speak out about work, community services and family life. Toronto, Ontario.

Community-University Research Alliance on Precarious Employment (2005). Ten ways of seeing precarious employment. Toronto, Ontario: Toronto Training Board.

Curtis, L.J. & MacMinn, W.J. (2008). Health care utilization in Canada: Twenty-five years of evidence. Canadian Public Policy, 34(1): 65-87.

Daily Bread Food Bank (2008). Who's hungry: 2008 profile of hunger in the GTA. Toronto, Ontario.

Galabuzi, G.E. (2001). Canada's creeping economic apartheid: The economic segregation and economic marginalisation of racialised groups. Toronto, Ontario: CSJ Foundation for Research and Education.

Government of Ontario (2008). Breaking the cycle: Ontario's poverty reduction strategy. Toronto, Ontario.

Hamelin, A.M., Beaudry, M. & Habicht, J.P. (2002). Characterization of household food insecurity in Quebec: Food and feelings. Social Science & Medicine, 54(1): 119-132.

Herd, D. & Mitchell, A. (2002). Discouraged, diverted and disentitled: Ontario Works new service delivery model. Toronto, Ontario: Community Social Planning Council of Toronto.

Herd, D., Mitchell, A. & Lightman, E. (2005). Rituals of degredation: Administration as policy in the Ontario Works program. Journal of Social Policy and Administration, 39(1): 65-79.

Human Resources and Social Development Canada (1999). Coping with child hunger: Mothers do without. Ottawa, Ontario.

Income Security Advocacy Centre (2003). Denial by design ... The Ontario Disability Support Program. Toronto, Ontario.

Laurie, N. (2008). The cost of poverty: An analysis of the economic cost of poverty in Ontario. Toronto, Ontario: Ontario Association of Food Banks.

Lightman, E., Herd, D. & Mitchell, A. (2008a). Percarious lives: Health, hunger and welfare in Toronto. Journal of Policy Practice, 7(4): 242-259.

Lightman, E., Mitchell, A. & Herd, D. (2008b). Globalization, precarious work and the food bank. Journal of Sociology and Social Welfare, XXXV(2): 9-28.

Lightman, Mitchell, A. & Herd, D. (2005a). One year on: Tracking the experiences of current and former welfare recipients in Toronto. Journal of Poverty: Innovations on Social, Political and Economic Inequalities, 9(4): 5-26.

Lightman, E., Mitchell, A. & Herd, D. (2005b). Welfare to what? After Ontario Works in Toronto. International Social Security Review, 58(4): 95-106.

Lightman, E., Mitchell, A. & Herd, D. (2003a). Struggling to survive: Ontario Works recipients talk about life on welfare. Toronto, Ontario: Social Assistance in the New Economy Project.

Lightman, E., Mitchell, A. & Herd, D. (2003b). Suspicion and surveillance: Navigating welfare's bureaucratic maze. Toronto, Ontario: Social Assistance in the New Economy Project.

Lightman, E., Mitchell, A. & Wilson, B. (2008). Poverty is making us sick: A comprehensive survey of income and health in Canada. Toronto, Ontario.

Lightman, E., Vick, A., Herd, D. & Mitchell, A. (in press). Not disabled enough: Episodic disabilities and the Ontario Disability Support Program. Disability Studies Quarterly.

Mackenzie, H. & Stanford, J. (2008). A living wage for Toronto. Ottawa, Ontario: Canadian Centre for Policy Alternatives.

METRAC & WACT (2008). No cherries grow on our trees. Toronto, Ontario.

National Council of Welfare (2006). Welfare incomes 2005. Ottawa, Ontario.

National Council of Welfare (2008). Welfare incomes, 2006 and 2007. Ottawa, Ontario.

Newbold, K.B. (2006). Chronic conditions and the healthy immigrant effect: Evidence from Canadian immigrants. Journal of Ethnic and Migration Studies, 32(5): 765-784.

Ng, E., Wilkins, R., Gendron, F. & Berthelot, J.M. (2005). The changing health of immigrants. Canadian Social Trends. Statistics Canada Catalogue No. 11-008.

ODSP Action Coaliton (2008). Accessibility survey – Canvassing the views of ODSP recipients. Toronto, Ontario.

Ombudsman Ontario (2006). Losing the waiting game. Ombudsman report. Toronto, Ontario.

Ontario Association of Food Banks (2008). Ontario hunger report 2008: The leading edge of the storm. Toronto, Ontario.

Ontario Federation of Labour (2007). Provincial election 2007: Manufacturing job loss. Toronto, Ontario.

Ontario Ministry of Labour (n.d.). Minimum wage. www.labour.gov.on.ca/english/es/guide/guide_4.html

Ontario Ministry of Labour (2003). Ontario's minimum wage increase. www.labour.gov.on.ca/english/news/2003/03-65f.html

Ontario Ministry of Labour (2008). Fairness for temporary help agency employees. Backgrounder. www.labour.gov.on.ca/english/news/2008/08-119b.html

Ornstein, M. (2006). Ethno-racial groups in Toronto, 1971-2001: A demographic and socio-economic profile. Toronto, Ontario: York University, Institute for Social Research.

Phipps, S. (2003). The impact of poverty on health: A scan of research literature. Ottawa, Ontario: Canadian Population Health Initiative and Canadian Institute for Health Information.

Power, E. (2005). The unfreedom of being other: Canadian lone mothers' experiences of poverty and 'life on the cheque'. Sociology, 39(4): 643-660.

Reid, C. & Tom, A. (2006). Poor women's discourses of legitimacy, poverty, and health. Gender & Society, 20(3): 402-421.

Schultz, S.E. & Kopec, J.A. (2003). Impact of chronic conditions. Health Reports, 14(4): 41-53.

Shields, M. and Shooshtari, S. (2001). Determinants of self-perceived health. Health Reports, 13(1): 35-52.

Sieppert, J., Linde, J.T. & Rutherford, G. (2004). Poverty as a determinant of health: Capturing the voices of low-income Calgarians. Canadian Review of Social Policy, 53: 122-139.

Smilek, S.M., Bidgood, B.A., Parent, M. & Thompson, J. (2000). When the fridge is bare: Challenges to food security in Waterloo Region. Waterloo, Ontario: The Food Bank of Waterloo Region.

Social Planning Council of Ottawa (2001). The experience of people with disabilities in Ottawa and the Ontario Disability Support Program. Ottawa, Ontario.

Statistics Canada (2009, January 9). Labour force information. Ottawa, Ontario.

Statistics Canada (2008). Income table. Catalogue no. 97-563-XCB2006026. Ottawa.

Steele, L.S., Lemieux-Charles, L., Clark, J.P. & Glazier, R.H. (2002). The impact of policy changes on the health of recent immigrants and refugees in the inner city: A qualitative study of service providers' perspectives. Canadian Journal of Public Health, 93(2): 118-122.

Street Health (2006). Failing the homeless: Barriers in the Ontario Disability Support Program for homeless people with disabilities. Toronto, Ontario.

Street Health (2007). The street health report 2007. Toronto, Ontario.

Swanson, J. (2001). Poor-bashing: The politics of exclusion. Toronto, Ontario: Between the Lines.

Toronto Public Health (2008). The unequal city: Income and health inequalities in Toronto. Toronto, Ontario

Townson, M. & Hayes, K. (2007). Women and the Employment Insurance program. Toronto, Ontario: Canadian Council for Policy Alternatives.

Workers' Action Centre (2007a). Poverty is on the rise in Ontario and low wages are a big reason why. Toronto, Ontario.

Workers' Action Centre (2007b). Working on the edge. Toronto, Ontario.

World Health Organization (2008). Closing the gap in a generation: Health equity through action on the social determinants of health. Geneva, Switzerland.

Endnotes

1. 74.4% of the working poor respondents reported having a job at the time of their interview. Why don't all of the working poor have current jobs if they are the 'working poor'? The working poor group is comprised of respondents who reported that the main source of their household income over the 12-month period preceding the interview came from salaries, wages or self-employment, and reported household incomes below the Low Income Measure. Respondents may have gotten most of their income from work in the past 12 months but were not working at the time of their interview. It is also possible that other members of the household were working, contributing to the main source of household income, but the respondent did not have a current job.

2. Due to a flaw in the CCHS questionnaire, lifetime attempted suicide rates included in this report are likely lower than in actual fact. Respondents who had considered suicide in their lifetime but not in the 12-month period preceding the interview were not asked about lifetime suicide attempts.

3. Social assistance recipients have limited dental coverage for emergency services only.

4. National Council of Welfare provides estimated annual welfare incomes for four family types. These incomes include basic social assistance, additional benefits, federal child benefits, provincial/territorial child benefits, federal GST credit and provincial/territorial tax credits, where applicable.

5. While Canada has no official poverty line, Statistics Canada's Low Income Cut-Off is commonly used to assess low income in Canada. Note that the working poor and social assistance groups utilized in our study are constructed using Statistics Canada's Low Income Measure (LIM) which is another widely used instrument. For further details, please see the extended method section available at www.socialplanningtoronto.org

6. We used the GEN MOD procedure in SAS to conduct these analyses. The sample was split into two groups: Canadian-born and immigrant. In the analyses with the Canadian-born group, age and poverty status were included in the model predicting various chronic conditions. In the analyses with the immigrant group, age, poverty status and length of time residing in Canada were included in the model. Results are described in the text (p<.05 was used to assess statistical significance).

Sick and Tired: The Compromised Health of Social Assistance Recipients and the Working Poor in Ontario | **27**

281